TRANSNATIONAL NATION

TRANSNATIONAL NATION

*United States History in Global Perspective
Since 1789*

IAN TYRRELL

First published 2007 by
PALGRAVE MACMILLAN
Houndmills, Basingstoke, Hampshire RG21 6XS and
175 Fifth Avenue, New York, N.Y. 10010
Companies and representatives throughout the world

PALGRAVE MACMILLAN is the global academic imprint of the Palgrave
Macmillan division of St. Martin's Press, LLC and of Palgrave Macmillan Ltd.
Macmillan® is a registered trademark in the United States, United Kingdom
and other countries. Palgrave is a registered trademark in the European
Union and other countries.

ISBN-13: 978–1–4039–9367–0 hardback
ISBN-10: 1–4039–9367–x hardback
ISBN-13: 978–1–4039–9368–7 paperback
ISBN-10: 1–4039–9368–8 paperback

This book is printed on paper suitable for recycling and made from fully
managed and sustained forest sources. Logging, pulping and manufacturing
processes are expected to conform to the environmental regulations of the
country of origin.

A catalogue record for this book is available from the British Library.

A catalog record for this book is available from the Library of Congress.

Printed and bound in Great Britain by
CPI Antony Rowe, Chippenham and Eastbourne

To the La Pietra Gang

Contents

Preface

This book provides a brief overview of US history since 1789 from a transnational perspective. It brings together specialized work accumulating over the past 15–20 years on this topic as well as general American historiography essential to contextualize such a subject. Such a book can in no way be definitive. It is an exploratory essay, and I hope others will follow in these footsteps. I suggest a framework for interpreting American history afresh, explore new interpretations of particular episodes and identify gaps in the literature that need filling. The foundations of the American nation-state's transnational relations, I argue, were forged fundamentally in the nineteenth and early twentieth centuries, and hence considerable space is given to these developments. Since the 1920s the United States has been caught in contradictions created by those inherited traditions, and the roots of the contemporary tension over the nation's global position can be found in earlier periods. Deeper historical perspective for assessing change and continuity remains vital.

The vastness of the subject makes extensive documentation a challenge, to say the least, but footnotes will lead readers to appropriate and accessible sources. For the same reason I have generally refrained from quoting from the primary sources that have often informed my views – views that have been reached in a career of 30-odd years considering aspects of American history transnationally.

The book could not have been written without the contributions of literally hundreds of fine historians of the United States upon whose scholarship the conclusions rest. The footnotes only hint at the richness of the work available. I have benefited from advice from many people, but space restrictions preclude naming all of them in detail. I must especially thank the 'La Pietra gang' from the Conferences on Internationalizing American History, Florence, 1997–2000, to whom the book is dedicated. In addition, without the inspiration of Thomas Bender, David Thelen and others in Florence, Paris, New York, Cambridge, Amsterdam and many places across North America, this book could not have been

written. Jay Sexton (Oxford University) graciously and perceptively read
Chapter 2. Mary Dudziak helped with the final four chapters despite being
in the middle of a trans-continental move. Emeritus Professor Michael
Pearson (University of New South Wales) generously cast his eye over the
whole text from the perspective of Asian and world history. Fellow Amer-
icanists in Australia – especially Shane White, Frances Clarke and Stephen
Robertson – commented helpfully on parts of the book. My colleague Peter
Schrijvers reviewed the final three chapters and made many shrewd sugges-
tions on international relations. To my family, gratitude is due, as always,
and to my Australian Research Council assistant Tina Donaghy I owe
much for her conscientiousness in following up leads. ARC funding also
allowed Marie McKenzie to proofread and check sources, which she did
diligently. Former Palgrave Macmillan commissioning editor Terka Acton
encouraged this project, and her colleagues Sonya Barker and Beverley
Tarquini have helped the book through to publication.

Introduction

Some say the United States was born free but it was also born deeply connected – to the world, its peoples, its traditions and has been wrestling with the consequences ever since. In the course of re-examining the manifold and intricate links of American history beyond the nation's borders, this book necessarily questions common conceptions that Americans have held regarding their history. Stated baldly, policymakers, publics, some textbooks and even a good many professional historians – when they generalize – have depicted the progressive shaping of a nation in which key developments occurred from the American Revolution to the early twentieth century. For much of this period, the nation grew along a trajectory determined primarily by domestic forces and debates, whether over republican institutions, democracy, slavery, economic growth or frontier expansion. Yes, the nation did draw upon European culture in obvious ways but internal influences shaped the fundamentals of the American Republic. After securing its independence and fending off European interference in the early republican era, the nation moved from a nineteenth-century focus on continental economic and political development through to greater integration with the world community from the mid-twentieth century. With a strong internal market and assimilation of immigrant groups, the nation had consolidated in the period before 1914 intellectually and socially, albeit unevenly, into a complex American identity. Neither international relations nor cross-national influences were dominant features and Americans had 'free security' until, depending on one's point of view, either the First World War or 1941. Even then, the United States continued to be distinct in its people's self-conception.[1]

To be sure, people 'within' the nation interacted with others elsewhere and disagreed, sometimes violently, among themselves. Class, race and gender provided sources of division as did sectional conflict. But the nation's borders remained sacrosanct. Once in the nation, incorporated areas came to be viewed conventionally in relatively unproblematic ways as if they were always destined to be American. Thus places previously part of Mexico were often treated from annexation in 1848 with their earlier Mexican history as a romantic prelude. The later history of those places close by from which the territories had been separated became suddenly 'foreign' – part of international relations, and a source of immigrants rather than part of a wider regional story.

This depiction of historiography is obviously over-simplified. American-centred accounts have been questioned in professional historiography, and empirical studies have unsettled the general narrative. Multicultural diversity within the nation has been thoroughly recognized. Immigration histories and intellectual histories have long recognized cross-national connections, particularly with Europe. Foreign policy studies have moved beyond diplomacy to consider not simply economic expansion but cultural relations as well. Borderland influences have been explored and new Hispanic American histories developed. Even textbooks have been affected deeply by a transnational turn.[2] These have now begun to add sidebars on linkages to the world but the United States and 'the wider world' are still the fundamental categories and the additions are often tokenistic. Rather, it is necessary to synthesize newer research to produce a different kind of American history that does not simply 'add on' international influences, explore US 'foreign relations' or chart the nation's role in 'the wider world'. This book argues that transnational links were too far reaching to allow us merely to tinker around the edges of any generally accepted sketch. A new American history must instead be envisaged, and this book attempts an outline of how that history might look. Though new synthetic studies of American transnational relationships are beginning to appear, there is as yet no overview setting out the relationships of state, society, globalization, and transnational political, social and cultural actors.[3]

There are two main themes in the work that follows. One is to emphasize that the boundaries between American and foreign developments were culturally, economically and socially porous in the nineteenth century; a profound connectedness to world history was aided by the relative weakness of the American state, by the pressures of other empires, by economic and social modernization in the wider world and by domestic forces of economic and political change which drew in and reworked foreign influences. The second major theme is the development of a distinctive 'empire' – if that is the correct term for such an economically and politically powerful force – out of these experiences of connectedness.

The book places the United States within broad movements of world history such as the development of the nation-state, the movement of peoples, imperialism, economic growth and the struggle for equality. It does not aim to show that the history of the United States is the same as that of other countries. Differences as well as similarities must be recognized, and this book provides a comparative perspective on many key topics of American history. The list has a familiar ring because these topics are so important for understanding the shaping of American history.

But the perspective is new – the transnational relationships between the United States and comparable countries.

What is transnational history? It is the movement of peoples, ideas, technologies and institutions across national boundaries. It concerns the period since the emergence of nation-states as important phenomena in world history. This can be dated technically from the Treaty of Westphalia in 1648, which set out the international law of relations between sovereign states. In the American case, however, there was no nation as such until 1776. Though some historians have argued that a nation in waiting had developed before then, the arguments are not convincing. Until the time of the American Revolution, the thirteen colonies that became the United States were not clearly distinguished as a cohesive unit from other places in British North America. The revolution and its aftermath forged a nation. For this reason, technically a national history of the United States begins from 1776 to 1789, by the end of which period the federal republic had come into being. That is not to deny the importance of transnational imperial history and colonial relations among British, French and Spanish colonies before 1776 and their impact on the future United States.[4]

Transnational history does not mean that the nation is unimportant. In many ways, the nation-state has determined who we humans are and what we do. Thus, for example, though transnational environmental issues have become increasingly important and national boundaries do not correspond with physiographical regions, much environmental policy is rooted in the nation because the nation remains sovereign. Though multiple, our identities have also been primarily national ones since the late nineteenth century, shaped by national symbols and institutions. The transnational identities of humans are less tangible though not insignificant.

While this book does not contest the currently reigning primacy of the nation as a legal and political fact, I do argue that the 'national' must not be assumed; other influences on people than the nation must be recognized, because the relative strength of the interactions of people, ideas and institutions across and within nation-states changes over time. The nation is not the only historical 'actor'. Cross-national institutions such as non-governmental organizations (NGOs) and supranational bodies, for example the League of Nations and United Nations, have had influences, and economic and intellectual currents breach boundaries too. Material circumstances such as climate and demographic change also constitute constraints upon nations, and many other such influences were shared with the world's peoples even though these affected different peoples in different ways.

But this study goes further. It argues that the nation itself is produced transnationally; that is, the regional and global context of security, economic competition and demographic change means that the boundaries of the nation have had to be made. They do not exist in isolation. National identities have been defined against other identities, including the transnational phenomena that impinge upon the nation as it is constructed. As Catherine Hall argues, 'We can understand the nation only by defining what is not part of it, for identity depends on the outside, on the marking both of its positive presence and content and of its negative and excluded parts.'[5]

The geographic focus of this transnational history is multilayered, including regional and global dimensions. First, there are regional contexts. The best known of these is the Atlantic world. A great deal is being done on Atlantic history. Originally with an Anglo-American focus, such work went back to Frank Thistlethwaite's *The Anglo-American Connection in the Early Nineteenth Century*, published in 1959, and to a long tradition of colonial studies before that.[6] Anglo-American history is, however, only a part of the story of Atlantic connections, which historians have increasingly argued must encompass Africa and the whole of the Americas. Moreover, as Gary Okihiro has argued, 'The Atlantic world, however inclusive, still centers Europe and the expansion of its peoples and their deeds upon indigenous Africa and the Americas wherein whites act upon nonwhites.'[7]

While many American transnational connections in the nineteenth century appear to have been Atlantic centred, that is not so true for the twentieth, nor is it true of all nineteenth-century links. Historians have only just begun to integrate the Pacific into American history as a whole. The common assumption has been to focus on immigrants moving from Europe – they and their descendents often moved west, where, it is assumed, they became truly American in contact with a radically different environment. The movement of peoples and goods east across the Pacific from Asia confounds this idea. The United States took substantial immigration from China from the 1850s, and East and Southeast Asia had already been an important source of American trade since the 1790s. The frontier was not a one-way east to west process of Americanization but a multilateral experience with an uneven cultural transmission and assimilation.

This new American history must have more than a regional vision. It must also tackle the global dimensions of the transnational. One of the nation's most notable characteristics from the beginning of the republic has been the way it developed networks of cultural, political and economic relations covering the world. It must be remembered that the United States was principally a maritime nation through to the Civil War. The nation's foreign trade was vital to economic development and virtually all this cargo was necessarily carried by ship. This gave the United States not merely an Atlantic outlook but a global vision, as the United States was, from the 1790s onwards, trading in all oceans and with a wide variety of the world's peoples. This commerce spread from Massachusetts and its famous trading and whaling centres all the way to the South Pacific. The publications of America's first great fictional writer Herman Melville registered this wide cultural vision in *Typee* and *Moby Dick*.[8]

Melville's protagonists started their journeys in the ports of Massachusetts, hardy seafaring communities as much as Puritan strongholds. This New England heritage of seafaring commerce and Puritanism turns our attention back to the Atlantic but the tentacles of trade and culture spread more broadly. Judging from rough trade averages, the Atlantic focus can explain perhaps as much as 70 per cent of American connections with the rest of the world in the nineteenth century and less than 50 per cent in the twentieth century. Laudable though it is, a purely Atlantic approach to transnational history leaves a good deal unexplained. As in all fields of history we must look for more encompassing frameworks. The multilateral framework encouraged by the Pacific connection adds a new dimension to the more common focus on the Atlantic, enabling us to broaden our vision towards the global. The nation's global reach pre-dated the beginnings of American formal empire in the 1890s, but after 1898 strategic as well as economic reasons made Americans more aware of the global significance of their economic and cultural expansion. The United States now had a two-ocean navy, facing west as well as east as a global power. The two world wars realized the potential.

While maritime connections are a large part of this story, continental relations of Americans to Canadians, and to the countries of Central and South America, especially Mexico, must be recognized too. In earlier decades some historians did begin to write a continental history of the United States. Some such as Herbert Eugene Bolton advocated a hemispheric analysis of 'Greater America'.[9] While these approaches became less fashionable from the 1950s, they are now being revived in borderland studies. Yet they represent more familiar moves in historiography than the one I am advocating here.[10] It is the global rather than any one purely regional framework that best encompasses Americans' transnational contacts and aspirations because the driving forces were those of larger systemic change. These can be compared with different phases of the processes known as 'globalization', bearing in mind that these processes were (and are) highly contested, controversial and inseparable from the dreams and ambitions of social classes and individuals.[11]

In contemporary discourse, historians speak of noticeable transformations in the world since the 1970s that they call 'new globalization'. Since that time, the integration of the world's economy and cultures has accelerated. The agents of this change have been international capital, governments seeking freer trade, supranational organizations promoting greater degrees of economic integration or environmental governance worldwide and the proliferating NGO sector such as Médecins sans Frontières and Amnesty International. The means of integration have been satellite communications, ubiquitous jet transport, optic fibre cables and the development of the Internet. The evidence of global integration can be found in patterns of renewed migration, the diffusion of terrorism, trade disputes and environmental degradation and regulation as well as new flows of capital, the downsizing of the state and financial deregulation. Market forces have not come out of thin air, however. Change came from reform within government and business favourable to the opening of internal economies to globalization. The period since the 1970s has also seen the ending of the Cold War, an outcome that was in part a product of new globalization, and yet a circumstance in which American dominance was soon challenged as new economic and political influences emerged from East Asia.

All this is true, but the adjective 'new' is advisedly added. The world has been globalizing at least since Columbus arrived in the Americas in 1492. Ferdinand Magellan's Spanish expedition circumnavigated the world in 1519–22, and Europeans soon brought their diseases to the Americas and the Pacific. Arguably the first 'world war' was that fought between France and Britain in the 1750s, when the military forces of these nations clashed in India, the north American colonies, the Atlantic Ocean and Europe. Historians have also argued that there were 'archaic' globalizations. Medieval European civilization was not hermetically sealed but interacted extensively with Islam, and Islam itself had extensive trading and cultural networks, for example, across the Indian Ocean linking Africa and Asia.[12]

Yet the tentacles of the global market economy stand out as the feature marking increased cultural and economic integration in the nineteenth century. Marx and Engels announced the globalized economy of world capitalism in the 1848 *Communist Manifesto*: 'The bourgeoisie has through its exploitation of the world market given a cosmopolitan character to production and consumption in every country'. The result was the creation of a new world order of the 'universal interdependence of nations' that came in 'place of the old local and national seclusion and self-sufficiency'.[13] The negative side of globalization Marx and Engels did not fail to point out. 'Established national industries' had been 'destroyed or [were] daily being destroyed'. These were not merely inexorable economic processes but rather the results of political manoeuvres and class interests within and across states. The way that the new imperial powers after 1870 took control of large parts of Africa and the Pacific world was an extension of these globalizing influences, though the development of imperialism clearly had cultural and religious as well as economic and political dimensions.

Globalization is not an even process as a focus on class relations indicates, nor was it as inexorable or sudden as the accounts of Marx and Engels suggested. The tendency towards global markets and cultural interpenetration has typically produced new syncretic cultures and new forms of diversity as Arjun Appadurai has argued.[14] Localism (like nationalism) was globally produced. The United States' own culture evidenced this production of cultural nationalism even while it became in due course a culture to be incorporated selectively or resisted elsewhere. Not only was globalization the subject of overt resistance but also it could be deflected or adapted. Arguably the tendency towards global homogenization was reversed in the 1930s and 1940s when rampant nationalism and economic autarchy prevailed in Europe and the world was plunged into economic crisis and global conflict. Arguably too, there was more globalization at least in a trade sense in the nineteenth century than later.[15]

In this process of the uneven growth of globally focused influences and institutions, the United States' contradictory role has been both to promote and to retard globalization. At the heart of globalization since the 1970s have been American ideas and institutions through the promotion of neoliberalism in government, trade liberalization and flows of capital, and through the dissemination of American popular culture. But paradoxically, the United States has also been an obstacle to globalization. This process has been a rough ride because the nation has for many decades been pulled by tensions between forces such as capital flows promoting integration and the intellectual traditions and institutional structures making American integration difficult. These opposing tendencies were centred on ideological notions of American difference and nationalism, and on practical institutions focused on the state structure. Such political forces have ensured that action by the nation-state to promote global citizenship must run the gauntlet of a myriad of obstacles from opposition to immigrants, to the demands that US foreign policy be unilateralist through to trade protectionism.

Globalization has led, some would say, to the development of an American Empire in the twentieth century. Certainly the growing power of the United States as a distinctive form of hegemony cannot be denied. That power is located in the globalization process and American conceptions of the wider world in which borders have been permeable. But empire conventionally understood is only one of the ways in which the United States has connected with regional and world history, and far from central to the ways in which American citizens conceived their identity. The integration of the United States as the centre of a new global empire has also been contradictory and unstable.

Granted globalization's importance in these ways, its processes provide simply one, albeit important, transnational context. Given the uneven nature of globalization it would be wrong to focus entirely on this process. Rather, this book treats the multifarious transnational connections of the United States, and its simple aim is to show these exchanges through American history. This book also argues that two key forces drove the expansion of the United States. One was the economics of a dynamic trading and commercial nation. The other was a set of cultural imperatives. Because the United States drew from the rest of the world for its immigrant population, the transmission of culture was as inevitable as it was profound. Other cultural influences superficially seem more 'home grown' and insular: American evangelical religion and the sense of national exceptionalism (the idea that the United States is radically different from – and, in the more common formulations, superior to – other countries as a unique civilization outside the historically determined path of human societies).[16] Yet these moral and ideological forces were also intrinsic to a transnational outlook. They mixed in a potent brew encouraging the United States to look outward to provide moral leadership while at the same time marking the nation off from other nations.

Though the United States was connected transnationally, these links were not one-way but reciprocal. People, ideas, institutions and capital moved back and forth. This interchange was most obvious in the area of immigration but it can be shown for many aspects of culture and economy. Despite reciprocity, the connection was unequal. At first the United States tended to draw heavily, especially for people, skills, labour, capital and ideas from other countries, particularly but not exclusively from Europe, and the nation's relatively weak state structure, open immigration and economic policies in the nineteenth century encouraged rapid flows. The United States became a major debtor nation, though the balance of forces changed over time. From drawing on the world for labour, capital and culture to supplying the world economically and culturally, the nation's balance sheet eventually tipped in favour of outward flows. This change was complete by the time the United States fought in the First World War, but reciprocity was never lost.

Within these connections, the relationship between state and civil society changed. With the drastic decline of immigration from 1924, the impact of two world wars, the Cold War and the growth of a strong domestic economy, the American people became, I shall argue, more insular than in the nineteenth century. This narrowing of horizons occurred at the very time when world events forced the government into greater political and military involvement abroad. The nation-state grew in power and mediated the transnational links of individuals and groups. This occurred through immigration controls, quarantine, passports, nation-state programmes of patriotism and the creation of new cultural symbols of national identity. The nation-state thus had its own trajectory of growth. Within this trajectory were different phases.[17] While a transnational history of the United States might include the era of British mercantile imperialism, this book does not treat the colonial background to the American nation. The emphasis here is on periods since the formal emergence of the federal state. I first briefly chart the growth of the newly independent federal republic within the context of European war and revolution, then focus on its developing regional and global relations to the end of Reconstruction, a period that encompasses also an expanding continental girth. This stage was marked by settler capitalism, powered by international economics and migration flows of great importance. The second period is the consolidation of a stronger nation-state from the 1880s to the 1920s within the context of new imperial rivalries, which drew the United States more deeply into world affairs. Here, modern American nationalism was forged against external threats, and the nation's muscle flexing was reinforced by the national wealth and power accumulated through exploitation of abundant resources. The second stage can be conveniently terminated with the passage of the highly restrictive Immigration Act of 1924. Next came the projection outward, backed by the stronger nation-state through which transnational influences could be mediated, of American political, cultural and economic products upon the world from the 1920s to the 1970s. This third stage was marked by the growing global dominance of American mass production known as Fordism and its consumer derivatives. The fourth and final stage involves the era of new globalization since the 1970s in which the power of nation-states has been compromised afresh by the rise of economic deregulation, freer trade, mass migration from the developing world and the enhanced mobility of capital. Within these stages the nation's transnational connections developed. To the period when the United States attempted to forge its own federal republic out of the turmoil of war and revolution, we must now turn.

1

Born in the Struggles of Empires: The American Republic in War and Revolution, 1789–1815

On October 8, 1789, Thomas Jefferson, American Minister Plenipotentiary to France, set sail from the grim port of Le Havre bound, via Cowes in the Isle of Wight, for the United States, thus ending 4 years of diplomatic service at a time of revolutionary change in France. Jefferson left his household in Paris, apparently intending to return, but fate intervened. On disembarking in Virginia in late November, Jefferson learned of President George Washington's offer of the position of Secretary of State. This honour he received initially with 'great regret'. Parrying the request, he ultimately responded favourably in late December to a second entreaty.[1] By handling the matter in this way, Jefferson displayed a certain reluctance to abandon the pleasant and intellectually attractive life he had led in Paris.

Jefferson had enjoyed his years abroad since 1785. His days were taken up with the affairs of a busy ambassador. He conducted consular services and diplomatic correspondence, observed industries and commerce across Europe, sought opportunities for American trade, kept an eye out for useful inventions and explored possible plant importations into America. The intriguing political situation engaged him too. He witnessed the early events of the French Revolution as they unfolded. His letters in 1789 and his autobiographical essay tell the story of that momentous final year of his stay, and the first of the French Revolution: on May 5, 1789, he attends the opening of the Estates-General at Versailles. On June 3 he urges, as a result of conversations with the Marquis de Lafayette, that the King should come forward with a Charter of Rights, the aim being to 'avoid the ill which seems to threaten'.[2] On July 13, he witnesses milling crowds around his carriage, the same menacing people that regathered the following day to storm the Bastille. In August, Lafayette and other moderate leaders meet at Jefferson's house to discuss formation of a constitution.

Far from the provincial world of American politics and before the revolutionary turmoil erupted, he embraced the cultural life of Europe's greatest capital too. He travelled widely across France, visited the Low Countries, England, the Rhineland and Italy. He sunned himself upon the Canal du Midi in Languedoc with 'cloudless skies above, limpid waters below', and travelled to Vienne and Nimes to admire the relics of Roman occupation. In affairs of the heart, the enchanting Englishwoman, Maria Cosway, turned his head. But ultimately he rejected her, perhaps because of the alternative attraction of his slave, Sally Hemmings. Or was it the fact that Maria Cosway was a married woman? We will never know for sure. We do know, however, that for Jefferson home as well as heart and head competed. He loved France, but he loved his Virginia more. In some ways Jefferson, a Francophile, was also critical of many aspects of the society he observed. Like Jean-Jacques Rousseau, he expressed horror at the foppish French court and scowled at the coquettish French aristocratic women – they were not good republicans, not exemplars of womanly virtues of domesticity.[3]

Jefferson's own account of his leaving, written in 1821, shows how he chose to remember the revolutionary changes in his life; he was turning his back on Europe. As the small packet ship ploughed through the swell of the English Channel, France disappeared behind him. He left a country in the midst of a tumult in which he could only be a commentator. Soon, in Virginia, he would have new roles that meant turning from observer to actor, from Europe to America. Crossing the blue–grey ocean symbolized that shift. Despite his recollections to the contrary, he must have wondered if he would ever see his friends again; he must have anticipated the pull of American politics as the new republic started on its course as a federal state under the leadership of its first President.

France as an intellectual field of influence was not so easily discarded. Jefferson's letters teem with the events and consequences of the European revolutions; they display his affection for French friends and correspondents. Jefferson understood that the United States could not escape the global impacts of the French Revolution any more than France could the effects of its American forerunner. He thoroughly recognized global interconnectedness. The French Revolution was 'a wondrous instance of great events from small causes', he wrote. 'So inscrutable' was 'the arrangement of causes & consequences' that a two-penny duty on tea in one small part of the world 'changed the condition of all of it's [sic] inhabitants'. It was like the flapping wings of butterflies thousands of miles away. This was the 'Age of the Democratic Revolutions', as historian R. R. Palmer put it. The world was experiencing, Jefferson foretold, only 'the first chapter' of the history of that upheaval – the appeal of the rights of man would spread globally. He laboured over the recollections of his time in France because of 'the interest which the whole world must take in this revolution'.[4]

The early American Republic, not just Jefferson's own career, was forged in the context of the French Revolution and the Napoleonic Wars from 1789 to 1815. The influences were reciprocal. The United States' independence and its revolutionary catchcry that 'all men' were created equal had been infectious, and influenced the changing intellectual climate underlying the coming of the French Revolution. The American Revolution also affected the international movement against slavery as reformers in Britain responded to the loss of their colonies by seeking 'moral capital' in the rise of humanitarianism and reform of the British Empire.[5] But the United States could not avoid feedback from this turmoil. Quakers and other humanitarians sought to overcome the contradiction of slavery in a nation supposedly devoted to equality, and emancipated the relatively small numbers of slaves in the Northern states by individual and state action in the 30 or so years after the revolution. Yet even though Jefferson railed against slavery, he and other Southerners did little concretely to weaken its hold, largely because the economic costs of emancipation for the slave-dependent South were so high.[6]

The entire period from the 1750s to 1815 was an era in which the nascent republic had indisputable links to transnational processes, chiefly through global warfare. Nation-states were in formation, but the forces of nationalism and democracy were duplicated across two hemispheres. Americans had to shape their own sense of national identity in a complex triangulation with both France and Britain. By the end of the decade of the 1790s, the republic's leaders had gained a stronger sense of national difference despite their internal conflicts, but this new national identity was produced transnationally as American leaders navigated the perilous European conflicts.[7] The relationship with France had many a positive aspect in this early period that encouraged affiliation with this point of the triangle because the two great republics were born in the same moment of revolution. The United States had signed a Treaty of Alliance in 1778 that bound the new republic to that nation 'forever'.[8] The debt of French help in the revolutionary war remained an emotional tug, but historical affection soon clashed with the necessities of circumstance that the larger struggle for European supremacy produced. When Edmond Genêt (the French Minister to the United States) tried in 1793 to recruit Americans to fight in the European conflict sparked by the French Revolution, Jefferson as well as his Anglophile rival Alexander Hamilton cautioned George Washington to stay neutral.

Nevertheless, the American relationship with Europe was a source of deep internal division in the 1790s. As the rivalries of the Federalist and Democratic-Republican factions coalesced into the first American political parties, these depicted their opponents as on the wrong side of the great ideological contest. Federalists led by Hamilton and John Adams tended to be pro-British while the new Democratic-Republicans aligned with Jefferson and James Madison sympathized with the ideals if not the detailed practice of the French Revolution. American politics in the 1790s was essentially fought out around these international interests – not in terms of foreign policy alone, but as touchstones of different ideological, cultural and political objectives.[9]

The United States was torn between intellectual affinity to the French Republic and the resurgence of commercial and cultural ties to the former mother country. Despite the political earthquake of 1776, US trade depended on Britain. Federalists favoured British financial connections while many Americans recoiled at the violence of the French Revolution and its attacks on organized religion. American evangelical religion grew in a similar reaction to that in Britain as a form of conservative inoculation against the virus of republican extremism. New England clergyman like Timothy Dwight preached evangelical domesticity as an antidote to revolution. Women would become the foundation of this conservative republican strategy. Republican motherhood rather than equal rights would be the favoured approach to the woman question among these American preachers and their congregations. Women should, through moral instruction of their young, provide the virtuous citizens required by a republic that could not depend upon force for the achievement of consensus and the maintenance of social stability. Dwight denounced Mary Wollstonecraft, the British author of *Vindication of the Rights of Woman,* as 'a strumpet' for her impertinent, immoral and politically dangerous doctrines of female equality.[10] Evangelicals across the North established colleges called ladies seminaries to ensure that, while women should receive an education, it should be geared towards piety, purity and the cultivation of genteel arts and literature, not political participation as full citizens.

Simultaneously, the US government improved relations with Britain in 1795 through the Jay Treaty, settling maritime disputes and the boundary with Britain's Canadian possessions. Enhanced transatlantic trade with the former mother country beckoned, but at the price of offending pro-French Republicans. The United States soon found itself defending its commercial interests against French naval interference. Attempts to negotiate a settlement of these differences produced further controversy. As a result of the XYZ affair of 1798 in which French officials tried to bribe American envoys, relations soured even more. The United States was now virtually in an undeclared war with France, and the crisis spurred creation of a Department of the Navy in 1798–99. Federalists pushed through the Alien and Sedition Acts in 1798 to crack down upon dissent and prevent naturalization of subversives. The leading publicists of the Jeffersonian party included European refugees, and they were among the foreigners targeted in the acts. Though a new treaty with France settled outstanding differences in 1800, the alliance of 1778 was formally abrogated and wariness concerning the French Revolution survived. George Washington's attack on 'insidious' foreign influences in his famous farewell address in 1797 reflected the meddling of the French and Democratic-Republicans in attempting to thwart the diplomatic initiatives of the Federalist regime. He established a tradition of non-interference in European affairs, but the reality of Europe's influence upon American strategic and economic interests could not be conjured away.

A reaction against the extremism of the French Revolution was also tied to its implications for the future of American slavery. No event of the 1790s abroad resounded more emphatically in the United States than the Haitian Revolution. In response to the French catchcries of liberty, equality and fraternity, slaves in the French colony of St Domingue rose in bloody revolt against their white and mulatto masters in 1791. The spectacle of whites being slaughtered by blacks brought to the fore the Southern planters' worst nightmare. Not only did the island's slaves kill whites; they also displayed capacity for organized rebellion and military action, thus threatening the growing American belief in the racial inferiority of blacks, especially when the Haitian rebels finally won their independence in 1804. Even abolitionists, aware of the volatility of the situation refrained in the most part from endorsing the right of rebellion: 'The entire antislavery movement was being debilitated'.[11] Jefferson worried that a trade treaty of 1799 might inadvertently allow black Haitian seamen to bring their revolutionary views into American ports, thereby infecting Southern slaves with the idea of freedom.[12]

The impact of the Haitian Revolution on the United States was demographic as well as ideological. Where wars and revolutions occur, a refugee problem is almost certain to follow. So it was in the late twentieth century, and also in the early nineteenth, when the Haitian upheaval promoted the American nation's 'first immigration crisis'.[13] Over 15,000 whites, mulattos and free blacks escaped with their slaves into the Southern states, especially Virginia. Others went to Spanish Louisiana (and many eventually became US citizens after 1803). The sudden influx heightened racial anxieties over emancipation and the colour line. The presence of free blacks was an inspiration to the enslaved, as was the Haitian path to revolution itself. The Gabriel Prosser plot of 1800 in which Virginian slaves conspired against their masters was stimulated by the Haitian example, which provided a 'metaphorical tool' to inspire resistance.[14]

Indirectly the French Revolution had impacts on the western hemisphere by throwing European society into such turmoil that the colonial rulers of mainland Latin America could no longer contain the dissent of local elites. Under the diversion of the Napoleonic Wars, all of South and Central America's Spanish and Portuguese possessions gained their independence in the decade or so after 1807. Mexico, the United States' most important neighbour over the next 100 years, threw off Spanish rule in 1821. Both Latin America and the United States shared a common heritage in this respect: they gained political leverage from the preoccupations of Europeans with events elsewhere. The new Latin American nations diverged from the patterns of North American growth thereafter, but in the 1790s to 1810s, they did not seem completely different in potential. Latin American revolutionary general, Simón Bolívar, matched the exploits of George Washington.

European diversions enabled the United States to acquire the Louisiana Purchase, and so begin the process of pulling away from its Latin American rivals as a potential world power. The American takeover of this vast tract of territory, encompassing the whole of the Mississippi Basin to the west of the river, is often thought of as an act of 'internal' expansion that turned the country towards continental fulfilment. It all seems so inevitable from a national perspective. The United States may have been in Jefferson's view 'destined' to spread its 'empire of liberty' westward but success depended on European contingencies. The territorial acquisition was neither possible nor necessary without the Napoleonic Wars. France had regained Louisiana in 1800–01, after losing it in the settlement of the Seven Years War in 1763. The French Emperor found himself master of the western Mississippi Valley, yet needed money for his military campaigns in Europe and the Middle East. More than finance was at stake, however. Napoleon was determined not to have the territory fall into the control of his mortal (British) enemy and viewed the expansion of the American Republic as a move in a larger game. As E. W. Lyon noted, Napoleon felt 'he would so strengthen America that she would become in time a worthy rival of Great Britain'.[15] Thus did the Napoleonic Wars condition American territorial expansion. That development was not inevitable. Rather than the result of clever American diplomacy alone, European foreign policies and military imperatives facilitated the transfer.

Americans had their own objectives, to be sure. Jefferson was interested in the West and its environment partly out of scientific curiosity. In 1803, he sent out the Lewis and Clark expedition to explore the upper Mississippi Valley and the Pacific Northwest, but American attitudes were shaped not so much by the allure of the West as by the exigencies of European trade and politics. How could the future farmers of the Mississippi get their grain to markets? Lewis and Clark were asked to report on the likelihood of developing an efficient line of communication to the Pacific that would link the United States to potential markets in East Asia, and channel the fur trade of the Pacific Northeast into the Mississippi Valley. Of more immediate concern, Jefferson wanted the port of New Orleans and its hinterland for American commerce. 'I would not give one inch of the waters of the Mississippi to any nation', he remarked.[16] Reflecting his fears of the impact of the Napoleonic Wars on the issue of American naval and commercial security, Jefferson preferred Spanish control to that of the stronger French.

The other serious concern was security of the homeland – the safeguarding of the nation against further foreign meddling. Jefferson wished to create a space for alternative expansion that would not in future duplicate the conflicts of the Atlantic market economy; this strategy rested on the yeoman farmer dream recreated in the spaces of the west. Territorial acquisition would enable the United States to avoid the Malthusian trap of Europe – the pressures of European population growth that must inevitably affect American security and social stability. Jefferson saw that the laws of Thomas Malthus on population did not apply to the United States within the foreseeable future, so long as there was an area of land in which to expand.[17]

This site of expansion required more than land pure and simple, however. It required the removal of any opportunity for European nations to interfere in the taking of territory from American Indians. Jefferson was particularly worried about alliances between foreign powers and the surviving tribes. A 'central concern' of Jefferson's Indian policy, as set forth in his first presidential message to Congress, was 'to prevent the encircling British, Spanish, and French from subverting the all-too-corruptible savages and inciting them to war against the frontiers of the United States'. Jefferson noted to Governor William Henry Harrison on February 27, 1803 that the renewed French presence was 'already felt like a light breeze by the Indians'. Under 'the hope of their protection they will immediately stiffen against cessions of land to us'.[18]

The Louisiana Purchase was one prong in Jefferson's policy for the Valley. A related one was the removal of the Indian threat in existing territory as a prelude to further US expansion. Prior to the acquisition of the French territory, Jefferson wanted to complete the removal of Indians from east of the Mississippi in order 'to be prepared against the occupation of Louisiana by a powerful and enterprising people'.[19] Removal would simultaneously allay fears of European–Indian alliances, and create a homogeneous population loyal to the American Republic. This empire of liberty had no place for other racial groups. Jefferson could not tolerate in the expansion of American population any 'blot or mixture'[20]; he was advocating an ethnic homeland – based on a two-edged policy of assimilation and/or driving the Indians out. Historical anthropologist Anthony F. C. Wallace describes Jefferson's civilizing program as a form of 'cultural genocide', but the strategy of removal by sale or force could also be called 'ethnic cleansing'.[21] 'The empire of liberty', John Murrin observes, was 'for whites only'.[22] Any other group, especially the Indians in view of their long history of skilful military alliances with foreign powers, would always be a potential fifth column within the United States or a meddlesome force adjacent to it.

In the *Federalist Papers* Jefferson's ally James Madison had, in 1787–88, faced arguments first raised by Enlightenment thinkers such as Montesquieu that popular government was incompatible with an extensive territory. In a clever addition to political theory, Madison responded that the geography of federalism would actually enhance vital political checks and balances by rendering the republic more regionally complex.[23] In power as President from 1801, Jefferson conceded that geographical expansion might indeed accentuate centrifugal tendencies, but argued that it would not matter if the Louisiana Purchase eventually spawned separate nations to the west because these would be members of the same family of liberty. Even if not united, the 'future inhabitants of [both] the Atlantic and Missipi [*sic*] States' would 'be our sons'.[24] Fears of regional fragmentation could be countered by stressing the duplication of self-determination *within* a federal system. Jefferson's dream of national loyalty buttressed by liberty depended on the rapid admittance of new territories to self-government within the Union. Behind the deeply felt belief in the superiority of this form of government was the need for national security. As Peter Onuf puts it, 'political self-determination on the periphery of Jefferson's empire would cement western loyalties, preempting separatist alliances with America's enemies'.[25]

Jefferson skilfully exploited the divisions within the European presence to consolidate the new American possessions. His refusal to supply support for the French army in Haiti from 1802 to 1804 'was probably', states John Murrin, 'a necessary precondition for Haitian independence', but his 'primary motive' was to negate Napoleon's influence. By 1806, the tables had turned. Jefferson was willing to place severe sanctions on Haiti in return for French assistance in acquiring Spanish West Florida. Here Jefferson used one European power against another.[26] But Jeffersonians did not rely wholly upon diplomacy. They exploited local conditions in which disgruntled American settlers seized Baton Rouge in 1810 and proclaimed West Florida as part of the American Republic.[27] Viewed from the perspective of day-to-day diplomatic and military correspondence, such independent local action was a chaotic and uncertain process. Nevertheless, it served functionally as an adjunct to 'national policy, a way to expand the national borders of the United States into Spanish territory without waging an actual war'.[28]

Despite the long-term importance of the Louisiana Purchase, attention should not be focused too heavily upon North American geo-politics. For the United States, the Atlantic remained the major source of interest, where the seamen of many nations as well as pirates operated in the eighteenth century. That plebeian mingling created inevitable transnational exchanges in which the culture of seafaring people spread around the port cites of the Caribbean, North America and Europe. On the ships of the Atlantic trade, people of many different ethnic and racial groups mixed freely and switched national allegiances.[29] If this intra-oceanic community influenced American culture, American economic and strategic interests also pointed across the Atlantic, not towards the western American states. It is significant that the first American military deployment abroad was in the Mediterranean, where the US Navy fought against the Barbary pirates' interference with commerce. The American Marines' famous song did not contain the phrase 'To the Shores of Tripoli' for nothing, because US forces had seen action along the coast of North Africa from 1801 to 1805, when Jefferson ordered an end to monetary tributes exacted by the region's rulers against commercial shipping. So important was the region thought to be that successive administrations kept a Mediterranean naval squadron on patrol. Not until the 1830s, when the French takeover of Algeria extended European sovereignty in North Africa did the American military deployment diminish.[30]

These 'small wars' loomed large at the time in American culture, but larger still was the renewed threat of war with either Britain or France. In a letter of July 1803 to French friend Pierre Cabanis, Jefferson noted: 'Our distance enables us' to pursue peace, while France was 'again at war'. But the president recognized interdependency when he added the hope that the United States should 'be *permitted* to run the race of peace'. Here he conceded the continuing threat, as American policy was not entirely a matter of its own making, but depended upon the role of Great Britain as its titanic struggle with the French resumed.[31] The American nation could easily be drawn into this conflict. And so it was. The Embargo of 1807 against trade with the European belligerents in response to the threats to American commerce posed by the British Navy showed that despite the gain of Louisiana, the realities of American policy still led east. The War of 1812 was part of the last play in the great struggle for world supremacy between Napoleon and the British Empire. The United States was drawn into this conflict principally in reaction over impressment of American sailors by the British, and in defence of maritime rights for neutrals. President Madison put this argument strongly in his declaration of war against Britain in 1812.

Control of North America was also at stake in the friction; western representatives supporting the administration wanted to conquer Canada. Why? Because they craved security against Indian attacks and a possible British invasion? Or for a sordid land grab? Evidence for the latter motive before the war began is inconclusive, but American settlers and their representatives believed that the British had intrigued with Indian tribes to strengthen the prospect of an Indian confederacy on the American North-west border. These Indians alone stood in the way of further land acquisitions by American settlers, and Indian restiveness was mounting. Across the old Northwest from Ohio to Wisconsin, Tecumseh, the Shawnee Prophet had nurtured a messianic religion aimed at the overthrow of European civilization through a revitalized Indian nation. He had already clashed with the Americans at the Battle of Tippecanoe (1811), where forces under William Henry Harrison were victorious. Independent existence and survival for the Indians now depended even more on alignment with the British. The irreconcilable conflict between Indian desires to remain on their land and the pressures of western expansion led the Northwestern tribes to fight with the British after the War of 1812 was declared.

When Tecumseh was killed at the Battle of the Thames on October 5, 1813, however, the Indian confederacy fell apart.

Badly bruised though the United States was in the military conflict with Britain, the war confirmed American independence and ended Indian power in the old Northwest. Typically, the peace treaty that followed has been marked as the beginning of a long period of inward looking by Americans. Yet the conflict exposed American vulnerability. The invading British had burned the city of Washington and Americans suffered more casualties than their opponents. The war had not been won, though it had not been lost either. Also exposed was continued internal disunity with the Federalists opposing the war at their Hartford Convention in 1814. Their inability to influence the outcome contributed to their decline as their dissent was associated with treason. Most important, the war enhanced Americans' concern about their armed forces and the nation's security.

Despite the internal dissension, the period of the embargo and the War of 1812 helped solidify the economic and military lineaments of national power. These years saw the early development of American manufacturing industry in the Northeast. The conflicts with Europe encouraged import substitution and served as a de facto tariff. Soon after the war the Jeffersonian Republicans abandoned ideological opposition to a national bank and charted the Second Bank of the United States as an agent of economic development in 1816. The war not only spurred the creation of manufacturing industry and the growth of finance but also increased defence spending – the army remained bigger after the war than before, and expenditure on national roads grew as a way of improving national security.

Jefferson could never be free of Europe, intellectually or politically, and neither, at least for political and military affairs, could James Madison during his presidency from 1809 to 1817, or Madison's successor James Monroe. He proclaimed the Monroe Doctrine, warning European powers against interference in hemispheric affairs, but the War of 1812 left a legacy of anxiety over the nation's borders and its defence. Andrew Jackson in the 1830s and Zachary Taylor, president from 1849 to 1850, were among the veterans of the war who subsequently emphasized a strong American defence as the key to American security. They had learned their lesson in the decades of revolution and military service. Though Americans could turn after 1815 to the task of internal nation building, their leaders would always have to consider, as Monroe did, that the American security position depended on a Pax Britannica. Domestic debates came by the 1830s to dominate politics, yet these debates sprang nonetheless from political, social and economic changes that were transatlantic in scope. The spread of democracy, the inception of social reform, and the market revolution that characterized the era from the 1810s to the 1850s were not American phenomena alone. The fates of Americans remained intertwined with the wider world. The key to those changes was the economy.

2

Commerce Pervades the World: Economic Connections and Disconnections

We are accustomed to think of the nineteenth-century United States as a nation that in economic matters did not need the rest of the world. The abundant frontier provided the resources that Americans demanded, and the home market supplied by a growing population created economies of scale for the growth of business. This interpretation is backed by statistics on trade. Whereas some European countries 'commonly relied upon exports' to dispose of 20–30 per cent of their domestic output, US exports remained mainly between '6 and 7 per cent of GNP and slowly declined over time'. Relatively speaking, one authority puts it, 'the U.S. depended far less on [external] trade' than did European countries.[1] Yet it would be wrong to conclude from these figures that the US economy was unconnected globally.

First, within the United States certain industries depended more heavily on foreign trade than others did. Their earning power had multiplier effects on the economy, and these industries frequently possessed, because of the structure of representation in Congress, great political power. Debates over foreign trade were therefore extensive and intense. Far beyond trade's total value to the economy, the political economy of the United States was structured around the impact and implications of foreign economic connections. Roughly a fifth of agricultural production went into foreign markets. This foreign pull was particularly strong for cotton, which comprised about 50 per cent of American exports by value in the 1850s. In turn, as established long ago by Douglass North, the staple export of cotton fuelled a good deal of antebellum inter-regional economic growth, at least until 1840.[2] Cotton for the American economy was in the early nineteenth century what oil was to the Arab states of the Persian Gulf of the late twentieth century.

Second, American involvement in foreign trade was important in another way not immediately apparent. The United States in the second half of the nineteenth century 'occupied a share of world trade disproportionately large' when compared to its population. The nation produced about 16 per cent of the world's exported primary products from 1880 to 1900 and 8–9 per cent of all manufactured exports. It also imported about 9 per cent of primary product imports generated in global trade. All this was well above the US population, which stood at 4.7 per cent of the world total in 1900.[3] The import and export ratios to GNP quoted above refer to the period from 1869. For the antebellum years, the involvement in world trade is likely to have been even higher, given the importance of cotton within the world economy. Particularly from 1789 to 1860, the United States was fundamentally a trading nation, well integrated into the world economy centred at that time on the Atlantic trade.[4]

Yet weighing the relative importance of 'external' and 'domestic' trade will not advance the debate much. It is unwise to separate 'international' and 'internal' forces. To do so would be a conceptual flaw – because the 'internal' sector was part of a wider transnational network that reached deeply into the American economy. The agencies of this network were the investment houses, banks and other aspects of finance, but equally vital was a developing cross-national transport and communications network centred on the telegraph cable system, railroads and steamships. The US economy tapped into this increasingly global system.

Though the United States was less in need of an external market than were some European countries, the nation sucked in the labour and capital that at times remained underemployed in Europe and so changed the demography and economic development of that continent. The same was true in different ways for regions outside Europe. When the United States instituted tariffs against cheap cotton textiles in 1816, for instance, it damaged the textile industry of India more than that of Britain, because the former produced cheap goods that the United States had been buying. In this and many other ways, the United States affected other countries and was affected by them. The insularity of the nation's economy relative to Western Europe does not mean that the United States failed to affect the rest of the world. Indeed its sometimes-insular behaviour in tariff matters had severe international repercussions. The US economy's global connections also had positive effects on the social well-being and economic development of other places. When American farmers exported grain, these food supplies not only damaged European grain farmers, but also thereby freed up the economies of Europe, enabling greater specialization of agriculture and manufacturing and supplying sustenance for urban factory workers. The abolition of the restrictive Corn Laws in Britain in the 1840s was predicated on the notion that cheap American foodstuffs could be imported, and that more labour and land in Britain could therefore be converted to urban and industrial uses. The United States thereby helped to avert the possible Malthusian implications of high population growth in Europe.[5]

The Atlantic provided the major focus of the economic interconnection in the years from 1790 to 1900 in shipping, finance and capital investment, and to a lesser extent in labour supply and trade. Together, finance and transport improvements had already effectively created by the 1830s one market that was transatlantic. Three-quarters of American exports went to Europe and 60 per cent of imports at mid-century came in return. Europe supplied the nation's major trading partners throughout the nineteenth century, yet things were changing. The percentage of American exports going to Europe dropped only slightly by 1900, but imports from outside Europe rose to one-half of the total at the turn of the twentieth century and to 70 per cent by 1920. The United States was becoming dependent on diverse international sources for its raw materials and exotic goods. By 1920, Europe was no longer so central to American commercial connections.[6]

Even for the first half of the nineteenth century, the global rather than Atlantic nature of these economic relationships must be recognized. As one gushy newspaper editorial put it, 'Young America . . . pours its energies through all the channels of commerce in all quarters of the globe'.[7] Antebellum American commerce responded to this globalizing process by thinking globally on a commercial level. In 1857, Freeman Hunt, editor of *Hunt's Merchant's Magazine* in New York City, could proclaim, 'Commerce now pervades the world'.[8] Boston merchant and peripatetic traveller George Francis Train wrote of Southeast Asia that Salem sea captains 'know foreign markets, understand supply and demand, and the art of treating with the natives, and carry in their heads the whole history of these islands, and the ports where you can exchange, or buy and sell'.[9] Freed at the end of the American Revolution from British mercantilist policies that required trade to be via Britain in British vessels, they sought direct trading opportunities, including the Mediterranean region,[10] the South Pacific and South and East Asia. American imports from Asia were 8.3 per cent of the American total in 1860, with spices from the Dutch East Indies, tea and silk from China and whaling products from the South Pacific, all important commodities in American trade. The patterns of trade were complicated and multilateral, spanning the hemispheres across the Orient to the Mediterranean and the Americas as shown by enterprising Salem and Philadelphia merchants. They scoured the ports of the Ottoman Empire and the Western Mediterranean for opium to sell to China and in return took many products back to the United States. Since the Chinese did not want large quantities of American goods, Yankee merchants also joined the Latin American silver trade with China, taking specie to pay for imports of Chinese tea, porcelain, silk and nankeen cloth, and other items from the Orient. From 1795 to 1831, hundred of American ships visited the coast of the then independent Muslim sultanate of Atjeh (Aceh) to trade in pepper, sandalwood and opium. The Salem, Massachusetts market, set the world price for pepper for several decades.[11]

These complicated transnational networks themselves are not the only story. Along with global integration went attempts to assert national distinctiveness amid growing global competition. Americans conceived of and responded to these pressures by striving to create national economic independence, because they wanted to maintain political and social independence. Thus there was tension between the economic imperatives of global integration, and national political debates and economic agendas – such as the enhancement of national security through a strong industrial and financial base. American integration into global markets was therefore uneven. The contradictions were shown when Americans raged against banks and other instruments of international finance and in the way that they raised protective tariffs.

These 'national' aspects of the economic connection were mediated by the role of the state. The position of the United States was akin to that of many developing countries post-Second World War wishing to pull themselves up by the bootstraps in the development race – but the young republic did not have the vehicle of a strong ideology of state intervention to create investment. States rights and republican traditions worked against any such course of action, though one must not discount the role of the state entirely. Capital was mobilized with state aid, but usually in the form of land grants and monopoly charter grants to private enterprise, mostly supplied by individual state rather than federal legislatures. From the late 1820s, the federal government was reluctant to get directly involved in economic growth, though the provision of land grants to corporations to promote railroad development in the 1860s provided perhaps the single most important federal government assistance to the development of the American economy.

The web of international finance influencing the United States reached back into the eighteenth century, but colonial communications were relatively slow and the colonial economy lacked the complexity of a modern industrialized state. Moreover, British policy had mediated colonial relations. After 1776, the United States forged its own global connections. Spurred by improved marketing opportunities, American farmers spread their international commerce as part of the 'market revolution'. There is debate over when this 'revolution' began and how rapid or extensive the transformation was.[12] Certainly farmers exported in the eighteenth century; colonial Pennsylvania was a major source of grain supplies for Europe, as South Carolina was for rice sent to the Mediterranean and Virginia for the European tobacco industry. Colonial and early republican farmers were commercially oriented in part, yet transport in the backcountry was poor. For example, as late as 1818, the cost of wagoning corn about 140 miles in Pennsylvania equalled its total market value in Philadelphia. But the world was changing rapidly.

The period 1789–1815 stimulated the development of a more economically diverse and yet integrated economy and connected western American
farmers to the world. As Britain industrialized and consolidated its position as the dominant world power with the defeat of Napoleon, it loomed
as a model for America. The need to develop industry was recognized,
because the British dumped, after the Napoleonic Wars, cheap industrial
goods upon the American market, thus threatening household production and other small industries. The United States could not avoid being
involved in the global pressures of European economic change. Jefferson's
attempts at autarchy had, during the Embargo after 1807, showed that
non-involvement in European commerce simply hurt the US economy,
which depended upon foreign trade more heavily than it later would.

The international framework of American economic development was a
compelling influence. The industrial revolution in Britain spurred demand
for raw materials, particularly cotton. In the period 1820–60 the United
States snared by far the largest stake in the cotton market, producing
74 per cent of the world's supply delivered to the four leading manufacturing countries abroad.[13] Without the engine that was the English
industrial revolution centred on cotton textiles and railroads, US economic
growth would have been slower. Export staples powered the economy in
the early stages of national economic development. Northerners benefited
from Southern cotton exports via shipping, banking and finance, and
expansion of the fledgling cotton textile industry in New England. Westerners supplied food to the South, though this was not a significant factor
in the growth of the Midwest after 1840.[14]

A communications revolution was also occurring globally. We think
of riverboats romantically as a Southern phenomenon; similarly, railroads evoke the drama of the American west. Yet by the 1830s, canals
crossed Europe as well as the Northern United States; steamboats plied the
Danube and the Ganges as well as the Mississippi to carry trade.[15] Though
Samuel Morse cabled the results of the Baltimore Democratic Convention in 1844 to an expectant Washington in a pioneering communication,
Europeans also took up the technology with alacrity. Underwater cabling
crossed the English Channel in 1851. An Anglo-American consortium of
entrepreneurs led on the American side by Cyrus Field laid an experi-
mental cable across the Atlantic in 1858, but Field was not able to get a
transatlantic cable that worked properly until 1866, and then it was the
British ship the *Great Eastern* that completed the exercise. By that time,
cables had reached the Eastern Mediterranean from London and went on
to Singapore by 1870. The North American cable network also spread
rapidly, bringing San Francisco into almost instant communication with
New York by 1861, while the transcontinental railroad was completed
8 years later in 1869. Clearly the development of American railroads was
part of a broader movement of steam technology into India, Australia and

across Europe. The world was being joined by iron and steel networks, in which rail worked in tandem with cable. The latter helped keep the railroads to timetable by providing scheduling information across continents, and that was not all. In the world of the gold standard, exchange rate stability depended on knowledge of the available gold ready for shipping to provide hard currency backing for trade movements. Cable facilitated this essential process.[16] The impact of advances in international communications was financial in this way, but it was emotional too. *The Times* of London proclaimed the beginning of a new Anglo-American union to replace the old political links of the first British Empire: 'The Atlantic is dried up, and we become in reality as well as in wish one country. The Atlantic Telegraph has half undone the Declaration of 1776 and has gone far to make us once again, in spite of ourselves, one people.'[17] Poet Walt Whitman also took note of the effects of this girding of the globe, but with a different emphasis upon American achievement. His 'The Moral Effect of the Cable' emphasized the Anglo-Saxon triumphal march now led by the Yankee contingent: 'It is the union of the great Anglo-Saxon race, henceforth forever to be a unit, that makes the States throb with tumultuous emotion and thrills every breast with admiration and triumph.'[18]

The Pax Britannica and its gunboat diplomacy ultimately guaranteed the financial and communications framework but the gold standard provided the pillar on which international commerce could rest. Gold gradually became, especially from the 1830s, the dominant system for all major economic transactions – and remained so until the Great Depression of 1929. This was so, even though the United States did not fully adhere to the Gold Standard in the mid-nineteenth century in its internal finance policies, especially during the Civil War period. The Gold Standard relied on a fixed rate of exchange against sterling. Adjustments within the international economy made desirable in response to national economic problems were quickly translated globally through contraction and expansion of credit. 'Because of fixed gold prices and the possibility of gold shipments, nineteenth-century merchants enjoyed an element of stability in their calculations', notes J. T. R. Hughes. Having a system of specie payments (physical transfers of gold and silver) meant that American state and local banks' freedom to move was circumscribed by international conditions.[19]

This system did not bring economic stability, however. Business cycles of the nineteenth century, with all of their potential to ruin as well as reward nations and individuals, gradually became integrated on a global level. Increased foreign investment and trade locked the American economy into the booms and busts of the global scene. As historian Richard Ellis has noted, 'the American economy became' not less but 'more sensitive to the vicissitudes of the international marketplace'. Domestic growth 'did not make the United States economically independent from Europe, as many had hoped'.[20] Starting with the 1819–22 Depression, Americans experienced these fluctuations in profoundly unsettling ways. Financial panics in 1837 and 1857, and the Depression years of 1839–43, 1873–77 and after 1893 were linked to currency fluctuations, stock and specie speculation and trade difficulties. These recessions were not closely synchronized at first, and local circumstances varied. The banking panic of 1857 is generally regarded as the one when the crises became truly global. British bankers blamed Americans as American financial houses in London were the first to fail. The world had become interdependent.[21]

A key case for the analysis of the interplay of 'external' and 'internal' factors in the growth of the American economy is the panic of 1837 that followed Jackson's 'war' on the Bank of the United States, the political implications of which will be discussed further below. Historians have argued over whether Jackson's highly politicized handling of the bank brought on the depression that followed. Peter Temin contended in a celebrated economic analysis that the stereotype of Jackson's bank policy as maladroit was incorrect. It was not the internal events of the Bank War that brought about the subsequent depression but external circumstances, including the Bank of England's tightening of credit, which affected a heavily trading economy.[22] Emphasizing federal land sales and the 'soaring property values of the 1830s boom', revisionists have challenged Temin's analysis. As Richard Sylla argues, frontier states embarked on an orgy of borrowing for 'internal' (infrastructure) improvements, 'in anticipation of future bank and property tax revenues that would service the state debts'. Investment banks became 'heavily involved' in marketing 'state securities on both sides of the Atlantic', and when in 1839 they met financial trouble, the liquidity problem spread. Banks could no longer 'meet their obligations to borrowing states'. State internal improvements stopped, thus affecting land development and its values. With property values collapsing, runs on the banks took place, and a number of states in the South and Midwest defaulted.[23] This revisionist argument does not negate the most obvious point, however. The transnational *interaction* of land sales, canal speculation and international borrowing contributed to the depression of 1839–43. The internal and the external economy cannot be neatly separated.

International influences were translated into domestic circumstances in several ways. The most notable foreign contribution was capital. Throughout the nineteenth century the United States was a debtor nation. Foreign borrowings allowed Americans to run a larger current account deficit than otherwise possible. Thomas Baring of the famous finance house, Barings of London, called the United States 'a country of limited capital and abundant enterprise',[24] and his firm did all it could to take advantage of this situation by brokering loans, especially to governments and state-chartered companies. Foreign investment and loans lowered American interest rates and provided the capital to encourage innovation, particularly the substitution of machinery for scarce labour. The total foreign indebtedness of the United States rose from the 1820s figure of 85 million to 297 million by 1839,[25] and to 1.5 billion by 1869. By 1900, foreign investment had reached 3.4 billion dollars. Cheap and ample overseas capital fuelled the United States' powerful economic growth.[26]

This would all seem axiomatic, yet economic historians have disputed foreign capital's significance. Revisionists argue that the role of foreign capital was smaller, later and less effective than previously thought. Railways, for example, relied little on the United Kingdom for capital prior to 1872; so too mining, where in the 1860–80 period Britons invested only £5.6 million. Some historians such as D. C. M. Platt have strained at de-emphasizing the role of foreign capital, but economists on whom Platt drew for data were more sanguine. As Raymond W. Goldsmith – one of those authorities – stated, 'If the United States had been limited to domestic saving, the growth of national wealth would certainly have been slower until near the end of the nineteenth century'.[27] Foreign investment was critical in certain periods and in industries that underpinned economic growth. Transport was a key sector in which foreign funding was vital before 1860, not through the well-known case of the railroads whose expansion came later, but the canals. These had contributed to a remarkable economic boom in the 1830s that was almost unthinkable without the provision of foreign capital. Canal building began after the American Revolution, but North Central states such as New York and Pennsylvania, and Ohio and other Midwestern states entered in the 1820s and 1830s on a binge of canal construction. Railroads did not supersede waterways in economic significance until after the Civil War. Canals provided cheap transport when connected to the river system and the Great Lakes; the most important example was the Erie Canal linking Buffalo and New York from 1825. The building of canals and associated improvements in rivers and harbours, like railroads later, determined the fate of cities and would-be cities, which is why political turmoil occurred over the financing of infrastructure, as shown in the considerable amount of time spent debating internal improvements in Congress and the state legislatures. The Erie Canal helped cement New York's role, via the Hudson River link, as the United States' largest commercial centre and demographic powerhouse. The original issues of stock in the Erie went to New Yorkers but large-scale foreign investors flocked in after 1822. They had by 1829 purchased half the canal's debt.[28] In the frantic boom of the 1830s across the Northern and central states, more than a third of the total invested in canal construction came from foreign banking houses.[29]

Direct investment in which foreigners owned enterprises outright was not common anywhere in the antebellum economy, including the case of canals. Investment occurred principally through loans to the states and to state-chartered joint stock companies, which then financed these projects. More than the dollar amounts of investments were at stake in this process of canal boosting. British investment played an important role in stimulating a sense of boundless opportunity and facilitating risk taking. Bond issues were encouraged by the well-advertised 'eagerness' of the London financiers 'to purchase state bonds'. [30] All this was checked in the 1840s slump and badly burned British investors did not return to this segment of the market.

Though canal construction moved away from foreign investment in its second phase during the 1850s, railways went in the opposite direction, starting with local capital but from the 1850s beginning to use foreign money. [31] Again, state grants provided early incentives to railroads. Of the 172 million dollar state debt in 1838, 42.9 million was allocated to railroads, and of the state debts, half was held in Europe. [32] True, the British contribution to US railroads was not more than 10 per cent before the Civil War rising to a peak 16.5 per cent immediately after the war. [33] Yet as Platt himself concedes, 'Any simple deduction from these figures is likely to mislead, since even small amounts of foreign financial assistance might have had a disproportionately large effect.' The really big foreign investments in railroads came in the 1880s onwards. Dorothy Adler argues that the 1880s was the first decade in which the British dominated, when 'American railroad securities gained substantial popularity in London'. [34] This investment was 'indispensable', for example, to the inception of such ambitious plans as James J. Hill's to build the great Northern transcontinental line later traversed by the Empire Builder from Seattle to Minneapolis, [35] and allowed expansion and renewal of track capacity of many lines across the country. By 1914, over half the total foreign investment was in railways, but this was private, not public debt, in sharp contrast to the antebellum years. [36] True, the federal government had incurred its own substantial national debt – during the Civil War – when British financiers shied away from funding expenditures needed for the military effort, and the flow of private capital was disrupted. However, British purchase of treasury bonds to cover the federal government's indebtedness resumed after the war's end, the national debt was steadily reduced over the rest of the century, and private capital poured in. [37]

More important than direct investment, securities or loans was the role of the credit system. British money substantially aided the United States by supplying the short-term credit market that oiled the machinery of exporting and importing. In the 1860s, London financiers underwrote one-quarter of all US exports and the percentage was undoubtedly larger earlier on. [38] British banks lent money to American importers and exporters and Americans abroad joined in the financing of the cotton and other transatlantic trade. One example at mid-century was George Peabody, a silver-haired Massachusetts-born merchant and financier who grew wealthy in Baltimore by 1830 but then lived predominantly in England from 1837. He helped bankroll American canals and railroads by supplying British capital, as well as financing the import trade. Peabody held famous Fourth of July meetings in London, and became a noted philanthropist on both sides of the Atlantic. When Congress failed to provide funds for the Crystal Palace trade exhibition of 1851, he gave $15,000 for the display of American products and inventions.[39] Though he died in 1869, Peabody's legacy continued through the role of Anglo-American financiers of even greater clout in later decades. The J. P. Morgan dynasty began in a London partnership with Peabody in the 1850s.

Through canals and later the railroad boom, foreign investment stimulated economic development. Improved transport infrastructure had multiplier effects on employment and the beginnings of urbanization. Thus Rochester on the Erie Canal developed from a sleepy village into a prosperous middle class and industrializing city in the 1820s and 1830s. Yet the opening of wider international markets was equally important. When we speak of the market revolution in the United States in the first 60 years of the nineteenth century, we must understand that the market was global. The nascent but booming city of Chicago in the 1850s was linked to New York and European consumers through the Great Lakes and the Erie Canal – this in turn aided the farmers of the Midwest who could now sell their wheat, pork and corn abroad. It could be said that in this area, all (rail)roads led to Chicago, and from there to the world. With the increased patronage of the Great Lakes and its connecting locks and canals to the Hudson River, the Midwest became aligned more closely with the North instead of provisioning the South's plantations after 1840.

The international economic impact came also through immigration, most obviously via provision of much needed labour. Irish and other immigrant workers reduced the price of labour and so helped to fuel economic growth. From the 1840s, a cheap Irish workforce flowed into the United States. Irish women supplied the factory employees for the Lowell Mills by the 1850s, men the hard labour for the New York wharves and street cleaning, and the canals and railroad across the Northeast also utilized foreign labour in their construction phase. The Irish were legendary on the antebellum canal projects, even though foreigners could not supply all the labour. The prominence of the Irish in gangs of workers drinking and indulging in rowdy behaviour on the Sabbath disturbed the small villages and farmers along the Erie and other canal routes in the 1820s and 1830s. Canal business also sucked up seasonal labour from locals including farmers who did supplementary construction work in bad times. Altogether some 30,000 toiled on these projects in the 1830s (about 1 in 20 non-farm workers in 1840). Apart from factory work, canal labour was the largest group of quasi-proletarian workers in the country in the 1830s. By the 1860s, immigrant labour served similar infrastructure projects across the American west, where new migrant groups became significant. The period 1864–69 saw the Union Pacific Railroad build westward with Irish labourers working feverishly to finish the transcontinental line, yet Chinese workers vitally assisted construction eastward from Sacramento.[40]

Immigrants not only brought labour, they also carried with them invisible assets. A hidden contribution in the 1830s was money. Platt estimates on the basis of Leland Jenks's work[41] that Britons brought an average of perhaps 15 British pounds per head in that decade. This translated to about 45 million dollars. These immigrants thus may have added an extra sum equivalent to about one-quarter of the total import of foreign capital in the 1830s boom.[42] Immigrants also introduced fresh human capital in the form of skills and technological expertise. The canal companies imported know-how as much as foreign money. They got managers, contractors and ideas from Britain and Canada. One of the better-known early imports was the mind of Benjamin Latrobe, who worked on the Susquehanna and Delaware canal projects after being recruited from Britain in 1796. Later he became famous for his architectural work in Washington, DC, designing the Capitol building and other public projects.

An important aspect of the broader immigration pattern was technology transfer. Immigrants introduced, for example, brewery technology in the 1840s. The Germans' pioneering of the lager beer industry changed drinkers' tastes and began the shift of American drinking away from whiskey. After the 1860s, beer consumption boomed and the chief beneficiaries were German-born or descended brewers. Many of the largest American breweries had German names, for example Anheuser-Busch of St Louis and the Pabst Brewing Company. The latter can be dated from the immigration of the Best family from Mettenheim, Germany to Milwaukee in 1844. Jacob Best essentially relocated his existing German brewery and sold his first lager beers in Milwaukee by 1845. Another German, Frederick Pabst joined the profitable firm in 1864 and assiduously marketed beer under the Pabst label. Besides giving his name to the reorganized firm, Pabst sought from Germany the best-trained chemists and brewers to work at the Milwaukee plant.[43]

Other ethnic groups were equally highly prized for the know-how that their traditions provided. Cornish tin miners dominated that industry, as did English potters theirs; Britons' contribution to the dissemination of blast furnace technology and coal mining was also considerable.[44] Later in the nineteenth century, highly prized Italian stonecutters would fashion churches and fancy private residences, supplying a traditional skill that was scarce in North America. In contrast, the contribution of English immigrants to textiles and steel had certain more innovative features. The relative abundance of English machine makers among immigrants meant ample labour to build new machinery – machinery that could provide the basis for the machine tools industry for which the United States became famous.

The role of immigrants in this process of technological transfer in the textile industry was most noticeable in the early industrialization of New

England. According to the leading authority, David Jeremy, immigrant know-how was 'indispensable' in the earliest stages. The Society for Establishing Useful Manufactures recruited artisans in Britain in the 1790s such as Samuel Slater, who introduced commercially viable Arkwright water frame technology and established the Slater Mills system in Rhode Island. British laws prohibiting the export of technology were ineffective largely because the technology was 'embodied in the artisan'.[45] Those who conveyed the new technologies from Britain to America in that period were, admittedly, a small minority of immigrants. The vast majority were not helpful in the same way; they were ordinary workers with few usable skills. Many, such as the handloom weavers working in Philadelphia in the 1830s were actually refugees from new technology.[46] Most of the carriers of useful know-how were more mature immigrants compared to the mass of young males possessing preindustrial skills.

After the War of 1812, other techniques supplemented or overtook the role of direct artisan immigration as a way of stimulating the American textile industry. Industrial espionage of a sort became common and played an important role in technology transfer. In acquiring knowledge about power loom weaving for the cotton textile industry, 'American visitors to Britain largely displaced the immigrant artisans'.[47] Ostensibly in Britain for health reasons in 1810–11, Francis Cabot Lowell (one of the Boston capitalists behind the soon-to-be famous Lowell Mills) inspected Glasgow factories in 1811 and visited Manchester to secure 'all possible information' on cotton manufacturing 'with a view to the introduction of the improved manufacture in the United States'.[48] He obtained a drawing of Radcliffe and Johnson's patent dressing frame and learned enough to convince himself that textile manufacturing could succeed in North America. Because of the limitations of artisans as carriers of technology and the difficulties of spying upon foreign firms, international exhibitions and manufacturers' conferences superseded these techniques by mid-century but, by this time, New Englanders were also exporting the new technology of the Lowell Mills into Britain.[49]

'Americans were not merely imitators', notes Jeremy. The textile mills' first experiments copied the English but the Boston business classes introduced mechanical, organizational and labour innovations that disquieted English manufactures as early as 1826. Lowell became a model town, visited, for instance, by Charles Dickens in 1842. The great English novelist and social commentator drew the contrast with the dark English mills of Manchester: 'between the Good and Evil, the living light and deepest shadow'. Replete with its carefully supervised dormitories for factory girls, its rigid time, leisure and work patterns, and the relative cleanliness of its semi-rural surroundings, the model New England mill attracted wide international attention. Yet it was not a totally unique experience for foreign travellers to see a well-ordered mill that promised technological

Utopia. Travellers compared Lowell with New Lanark in Scotland as a progressive factory environment.[50]

It would be false to focus too heavily on the importation of skills in the wider immigration experience. The vast majority of imported labourers had outdated, traditional competences or little skill. Yet this very lack of skill among the bulk of newcomers had its own indirect effects on technological change, encouraging use of 'more labor-saving technology'.[51] Factory owners could bypass production bottlenecks, which had benefited native-born artisans proud of their liberties and work privileges, by employing unskilled immigrant factory workers using machines. This was increasingly the case in the Massachusetts boot and shoe industry by the 1850s.[52]

Other factors than immigration and investment aided economic development too. Demographic growth was well above world standards. The nation surged from 2 per cent of the world's people in 1850 to 5.7 per cent by 1920. The growth came partly from immigrants (23 and 31 per cent of the total increase from 1840 to 1860 in each decade respectively), but immigrants did not provide the only demographic powerhouse. This population boom came from a high birth rate until the 1850s, produced by the fact that a relatively large proportion of the female population was in childbearing years. Such fecundity was, however, common in rural society in Europe as well as the United States. It was the surplus European rural population that, as in the case of the Irish in the 1840s, walked off or were pushed off the land by landlords and ended up in European factories and London or New York slums. There they added to the proportion of the population in the child-producing age group and so reinforced the demographic balance that was favourable towards higher rates of growth. Since immigrants were younger than the average citizen, the result was to emphasize the 'youth' of the population, with an average age still as low as 19 in 1860 compared to over 30 in the late twentieth century. Whatever the sources of population growth, demographic change greatly stimulated home demand and spurred the innovations of mass production. The population increase never dropped below 33 per cent per decade in the first 60 years of the nineteenth century and, after the Civil War, the absolute gains remained impressive. The population total went from 31 million in 1860 to 76 million by 1900 and to 105 million by 1920, though decadal growth had dropped to 20 per cent by 1900.[53]

Population alone was not enough to overcome international competition and strengthen American independence from Europe. Political intervention was necessary. Key 'protective measures' enhanced American autonomy and security. One theme concerned political animosity towards banks and focused on international finance. A negative and sometime paranoid response to globalization pressures stemmed from the impact within American politics of the dependence or perceived dependence on foreign credit. In the eighteenth century, Southern tobacco planters had demonstrated great animosity over their indebtedness to Scottish lenders. Now, the anger spread more widely, both geographically and socially. Middling and lower social groups among city artisans, and free farmers in the western states indebted to the foreign banks, complained loudly and looked for scapegoats. Credit was vital to farmers; it allowed them to buy seed, machinery, fertilizer and casual labour, and thus kept them afloat. Their borrowing came in the form of promissory notes with local banks redeemed ultimately against gold. The Second Bank of the United States, chartered by Congress in 1816 and opened in 1817, served as the ultimate lender. In turn, the BUS, as it became known, was partly owned by foreigners, chiefly English investors. The Bank also bore a superficial resemblance to the Bank of England in its structures and monopoly position within the banking systems of the respective countries. Moreover, the BUS's directors such as Nicholas Biddle were popularly viewed as Anglophiles.[54]

Farmers and businesses held these Anglophile directors responsible for the periodic downturns in the economy, starting in 1819. Yet little chance would the farmers have had of overturning the bank's financial control without the support of state banks resentful of BUS power and desirous of cheaper credit for land speculation. Political motives also contributed to the discontent. When the bank's political allies in Congress tried to engineer a recharter prior to the 1832 Presidential election, the ploy backfired. President Jackson detected the work of his political enemy Daniel Webster and opposed the measure. He made the bank a key issue in the 1832 election, denouncing it as a monopoly oppressive of the people – a bastion of special privilege hostile to republican values. However, in his veto message Jackson spent an inordinate amount of time attacking the bank's foreign connections – inordinate, that is, unless we regard transnational connections in banking and finance as a vital force within the antebellum political economy. Foreigners owned nearly a quarter of the stock, with government and private individuals in the United States holding the rest. Jackson's grandstanding to public xenophobia and anti-English feeling in the so-called 'Bank War' was successful. The veto message was hugely popular, the bank's federal recharter was defeated and Jackson decisively won re-election.

Jackson was able to highlight fears of distant economic control of the country by emphasizing the issue of foreignness. The bank issue showed how pressures of globalization stimulated American nationalism and spurred a search for self-sufficiency. Jackson was greatly motived by fears derived from his experience as a youth during the war for American independence. His rhetoric in the Bank War – to preserve American autonomy against the threat posed by a foreign-owned bank in the event of military hostilities – coincided with the views of American security he derived from the American Revolution.[55] To defend the republic's integrity, foreign financial influence over the government had to be eliminated. Though the Bank did not have a majority of foreign stockholders, he played for political purposes upon public fears of a tendency towards such a state of affairs.

Despite Jackson's bluster, the anti-banking impulse did not actually shield the United States against foreign influences. By destroying effective federal banking regulation in the 1830s, the easy money campaigns ironically opened the economy to even greater influence from foreign capital. In the immediate aftermath, Nicholas Biddle turned the Bank of the United States, now chartered within the state of Pennsylvania, into an investment bank recruiting British capital, thus further inciting the hothouse economy of the late 1830s. By setting Biddle loose to act in this way, and releasing the state-chartered banks from any central regulatory discipline, the veto of the Bank's federal recharter partly backfired. Whether this be political misjudgement or not, the American economy was denied effective federal bank supervision. The National Banking Act of 1864 made a modicum of changes to banking law but it did not create a federal reserve system. Laissez-faire policies prevented effective defences to protect the American people against the fluctuations that integration within the international economy could produce. As a result, anti-banking rhetoric continued to merge in the absence of strong state institutions with anti-foreign feeling and fears of distant financial forces.

This concern with remote economic power surged back unabated much later in the century. But its reincarnation focused not on centralized banking, which Jackson had eliminated. Rather, later political struggles over malevolent economic forces centred on the international monetary system regulating the exchange value of the currency and specie payments. The attack on the gold standard from the 1870s reflected the desire of farmers for an inflationary currency based on the use of cheaper silver rather than expensive gold as the specie backing. This, the so-called 'Free Silver' crusade, became merged in the minds of popular writers with protests against the machinations of Jewish financiers in Europe and New York. As historian Richard Hofstadter stated, 'It was not enough to say that a conspiracy of the money power against the common people was going on. . . . It was not enough to say that it stemmed from Wall Street. It was international: it stemmed from Lombard Street.' The anti-gold standard campaigns led all the way to London. The cheap money platform spearheaded by the People's Party of the 1890s pursued this anti-Eastern states and anti-foreign stance. Free Silver advocate Ignatius Donnelly asserted in the 1892 presidential election: 'A vast conspiracy against mankind has been organized on two continents, and it is rapidly taking possession of the world.'[56] This time, however, xenophobia was not politically triumphant as the Republican Party skilfully countered with protectionist policies to compensate for the impact of international market forces, and after the depression of 1893–96 prosperity returned under President McKinley.

The inflow of foreign investments was also the subject of criticism, particularly where land acquisition and attendant policies were concerned. But attitudes towards foreign capital were, Mira Wilkins observes, characterized by 'persistent ambivalence' and division of opinion because investments spurred economic growth from which many people benefited.[57] The anti-foreign rhetoric on the gold standard also revealed ambivalence, as it had been deployed, ironically, by farmers who were exporters, thus revealing the deep contradictions between international integration and national self-assertion. Poor agricultural prices could be blamed upon the vagaries of distant, unseen forces, yet the effect of introducing a free silver policy would have been to support exporters and those in the transport industries. Such people would have benefited from a depreciating currency not tied to the gold standard.[58] The farmers of the American West dependent upon exports for their profit margins at a time of drought and high railroad rates were keenly aware of their connection, courtesy of banks and currency, to world markets. They were pursuing policies that would give them greater competitiveness against other countries not on the gold standard. The same logic drove many of them to support contradictory policies of state aid in the area of tariffs. Here the role of the American state was vital. But first, the prior commitment of state assistance to manufacturing must be considered.

The state did not always play such a negative role as in the issues of banking and money supply. The federal government extended an encouraging hand in the development of manufacturing. Again national security drove the process, with government officials seeking cheap and reliable firearms for the nation's military defence. From this source came key innovations within American manufacturing in the nineteenth century: the 'American System' began in the development of small arms factories holding government contracts.[59] Lacking skilled craftsmen, and aware that rifles would have to be used on the frontier without access to skilled repairers, the US government wanted machine-made weapons using interchangeable parts that could be easily fixed, discarded and replaced. Borrowing from French examples, the quest began with a contract by inventor Eli Whitney during the War of 1812, but the American System of manufacture matured slowly. By the 1840s, the armouries at Springfield and Harpers Ferry had pioneered a system in which hand finishing of weapons would not be required. They developed gauges to check the measurements used in the manufacture of parts and introduced 'sequential operation of special-purpose machines'.[60] From this example was derived the pattern for inexpensive production of many industrial goods.

In addition to its use in firearms manufacture, entrepreneurs applied the American System to popular consumer items, for example Waltham watches in the 1840s and the Singer sewing machine in the 1860s.[61] When displayed at the great international exhibitions as early as the 1850s, simple American products such as revolvers astounded Europeans. They were inexpensive, mass-produced and had the advantage of standardized replaceable parts. They quickly made American exports very competitive internationally. Though the system was usually associated with consumer goods, capital goods such as the locomotive engines made by the Baldwin Manufacturing Company were also produced using the American System by the 1860s. With superior production techniques, Baldwin locomotives achieved significant inroads into British Empire and Latin American markets by the late nineteenth century. Its manufacturer had become a Boeing Corporation of its time.[62]

The federal government aided industrialization in other ways than the stimulus given to the American system of manufacture. One of the conditions facilitating the large, increasingly well-integrated internal market in the nineteenth century was the encouragement of tariff protection. The first Secretary of the Treasury, Alexander Hamilton, had established the principle of tariffs at the founding of the American Republic for revenue reasons. At first, tariffs benefited mainly Northeastern industry, and Southerners tended to opposed them. Thus the years of Democratic ascendency from the late 1820s to the Civil War were with some exceptions marked by tariff reductions. However, special political interests such as the Pennsylvania iron industry were able to extract high tariffs from Democrats as well as from Whig legislators.[63]

The Civil War ushered in a period lasting until the 1930s when high tariffs generally prevailed. These were mostly the years of the so-called 'Republican Ascendency' in federal politics. The chief alternative source of federal revenue was land sales – a diminishing possibility as the best arable land had already been taken up by the time of the Civil War. After 1865, tariffs generated about half of government revenues. Though tariffs were closely identified with 'infant' manufacturing industries seeking to get started within shielded domestic markets, sectional interests in agriculture also assiduously sought protection for many commodities such as hemp, wool, rice and sugar in the early nineteenth century and even broader agricultural as well as industrial subsidies in the late nineteenth century. The Republican administration after 1897 introduced tariffs on such items as wool and hides for regional political reasons to placate western ranchers and farmers even though few people benefited directly. (The party was thought to be hostile to the west because of its opposition to the monetary policy of free silver.) Tariff policy on wool, for example, stymied trade, hurt the export industries of Australasia and also made shoes, other leather products and woollen goods more expensive in the United States. In the period 1860–1930, tariff protection remained tied to politics and specifically to the special interests that regional diversity and federalism allowed to flourish. As economist Douglas Irwin has noted, 'the institutional structure of Congressional decision-making was biased in favor of protection-seeking interests, thus resulting in relatively high tariffs'.[64]

Tariffs were often ineffective from a macro-economic standpoint, to be sure. Modern economists emphasize their marginal impact on growth, particularly in the longer term. Yet protection boosted specific industries, distorted the domestic economy, influenced the timing of development and caused international friction. Tariffs aided the growth of a home market in conjunction with the rapid expansion of population and transport improvements; reliance on this domestic market only made sense because it was large and expanding. It should be noted, however, that Americans were not alone in seeking higher tariffs. The Germans, among other European nations, did so too, and European tariffs in the 1890s were at least an excuse for, if not a possible cause of, the high American tariffs of that decade. Tariff politics, like so much else, was not a uniquely American game.

The impressive home market backed by protective tariffs and vigorous population growth encouraged a certain economic insularity from the middle decades of the nineteenth century. After the Civil War, the nation relied heavily on domestic consumers for two decades, with a lower rate of exports per capita than the six leading European countries. However, by the 1880s, attention was turning once more to the importance of exports with the rate of growth in key areas of the American economy such as railroads slowing. Export orders were particularly valuable for providing economies of scale and profits at the marginal cost of production, and for tiding over fluctuations in local markets. Thus the Baldwin Locomotive Company used foreign orders to counter slumps in demand within the United States in the 1880s and 1890s.[65] This concern over excess industrial capacity and the limits of post-Civil War domestic growth underlay the demands of American manufacturers as well as farmers for a more aggressive policy towards prizing open foreign markets in the two decades after 1895.

At the same time, growth in the internal market had created obstacles to an 'open door' foreign economic policy. The effects of the post-1865 inward turning were shown in the maritime industry. From a nation which had thrived on maritime trade and carried most exports in the nation's own vessels in the early antebellum period, the trade became dominated by overseas carriers. Post-Civil War American investment did not go into ocean shipping. Tonnage registered for foreign trade declined steeply to its lowest point by 1898, with only 8.2 per cent of international cargo in American vessels. By contrast, American vessels had carried nine-tenths of the nation's foreign commerce in 1800. Though many conditions contributed to this changed state of affairs, such as restrictive labour laws intended to promote a trainee naval force of American nationals, the most important was the 'greater profits' in industrial and western development that domestic capital could find.[66] Ironically, this insular attitude towards fostering American shipping actually meant that the United States was even more deeply connected to the global economy. Because the country remained heavily involved in international trade in agriculture, desirous of exporting more manufactured goods and was in need of certain imported raw materials, the absence of an American merchant marine made Americans ever more reliant on the ships of other nations. Paying for foreign shipping added to the negative balance of payments as well. When war broke out in Europe in 1914, American dependence proved to be a strategic and diplomatic problem as well as a commercial one. The United States could not find sufficient ships to carry wheat and other vital supplies to Britain after 1915, let alone troops after 1917.[67] Government action during the war began to change this situation, but insular and contradictory attitudes towards international trade exhibited in the neglect of shipping capacity continued to plague the American economy in the 1920s.

All this lay in the future, however. The effect of the government's encouragement of industry, the growth of the home market and the demographic surge together had pushed the United States towards greater connection with the world economy by the necessities of disposing of its ever-increasing productivity. At the same time, powerful forces favouring parochial trade policies inhibited total integration with that economy. The result was that the United States exported more, but had less interest in importing, except where raw materials or luxury goods could not be obtained within the nation's boundaries. Small wonder that by the 1880s the nation no longer had a balance of trade deficit, even though its balance of payments remained in the red because of foreign debt servicing and the reliance on foreign shipping. Europe also dominated the finance and insurance underwriting that facilitated external trade, and capital continued to flow in because the United States still borrowed heavily to fund its further westward expansion, especially for railroads.

On the eve of the First World War, the United States remained the world's largest foreign debtor,[68] but it also became increasingly connected to the world economy by investing abroad by the later decades of the nineteenth century. Yankee investments headed for geographically proximate Mexico and other central American states after the Civil War,[69] then became significant in South America before the First World War, in resources such as timber, cattle ranching, railroads and mining.[70] At the time of the Boer War Britain drew (temporarily and partially) on American sources to help finance that conflict, but the transatlantic movement remained mostly the other way until 1915. Then the promise of the Boer War example was fulfilled. War loans to the British coupled with US economic growth supplying the allies allowed the American Republic to move from a debtor to a creditor status. The nation was, by 1918, ready to assume world financial pre-eminence. It now had the material dominance to back its aspirations to establish a new world order.

3

The Beacon of Improvement: Political and Social Reform

Ideas travel just as money and trade can cross frontiers. In the last chapter we discovered how closely the United States was linked internationally in the first half of the nineteenth century through economics. The improved communications that channelled commerce also brought ideas, immigrants and visitors. One of the best remembered visitors was Alexis de Tocqueville, who toured North America in 1831, from New York City as far north as Quebec and as far south as New Orleans, filling many notebooks on the politics and social structure of the antebellum republic. His grand theme was the radical experiment of American democracy and its implications for Europe. Political democracy should not, de Tocqueville understood, be construed narrowly. Rather, it was rooted in voluntary associations and social reform. This makes it appropriate to link reform movements and political democracy as elements in transnational exchanges aimed at improving society. Despite indigenous impulses within American reform movements, there was a transatlantic pattern of reform in the first 60 years of the nineteenth century. Not only were European impacts upon the development of reform important, but equally influential were American efforts to export reform ideas, institutions and movements to Britain and continental Europe. American reform activity, however, was never entirely limited to North Atlantic circuits of trade. Reform aspirations became for Americans increasingly global.

For a country that in the twentieth century denounced radicals, the new republic itself had a radical past. The post-1815 era was one in which foreigners placed the United States in democracy's vanguard. In some quarters commentators viewed the nation and its people as a potentially subversive influence, aiding and abetting radicalism abroad. European travellers journeyed west across the ocean to view the face of the future. For many it was a beacon for moral improvement. Among these were the justly famous Tocqueville and his fellow French aristocrat Gustave de Beaumont. Together they found the United States to be an egalitarian society in which the rich were formerly poor, their fortunes were not retained over generations to produce a quasi-aristocratic class and where the 'middling sort' dominated. These judgements were not strongly rooted in the social history of the period if we look at the statistics of wealth, social mobility and the like. Like most travellers, Tocqueville's purely tourist comments sometimes tended towards the superficial, and informers fed him a good deal of overly optimistic information. But on the subject of political and civil society his arguments had a sound empirical foundation. By 1830, more than three-quarters of the American states had achieved 'universal' (white) manhood suffrage.[1]

No country in Europe had gone this far. France had its radical experiment with republicanism in the French Revolution, but this gave way to dictatorship and then the restoration of the Bourbon monarchy. The liberal revolution of 1830 had failed, but its existence did suggest the spread of the liberal currents that mirrored the timing of Jacksonian democracy's rise. Britain achieved a middle-class franchise in 1832 by a law giving the vote to 800,000 property holders. The extension of voting was part of a larger reform movement that included factory acts, the abolition of slavery in the West Indies (1833) and elimination of the Test Act, which discriminated against Dissenters, Catholics and Jews by requiring office holders to be Anglicans. The latter measure passed in 1828, near the beginnings of Daniel O'Connell's campaign for Irish emancipation that came with his election to the British parliament in 1830. More or less coinciding with these events was the rise of 'Jacksonian Democracy', with former military hero Andrew Jackson's rise to power as President of the United States in 1829. Political reform seemed to be in the transatlantic air.[2]

The British and French achievements in the franchise were obviously less impressive than the American, and came later – but it must be remembered that one-fifth of the potential American male electorate was automatically excluded as slaves. The United States had a racial democracy, forged with strong caste lines. Nowhere had women won the right to vote any more than in Europe, and in fact the demand for women's suffrage had hardly appeared, though it was in the United States where this agitation began in the 1850s, after the famous Seneca Falls Woman's Rights Convention of 1848. This convention drew self-consciously on the Declaration of Independence and showed its roots in American republicanism. Still, attention focused until after the Civil War on the extension of women's educational, property and legal rights. From there, woman's rights agitation, originally associated with Mary Wollstonecraft, spread back to Britain.[3]

British intellectual journals and newspapers debated the role of American democracy. William Cobbett, the unorthodox English commentator, cheered on Jacksonian Democracy from a distance, seconding Jackson's attack on monopolies and republishing political economist William M. Gouge's work on the subject under the title *The Curse of Paper-Money and Banking*.[4] According to George Lillibridge, Europeans of democratic inkling looked westward. Radicals such as the London Workingman's Association identified an American 'beacon of freedom' with their own struggles.[5] But too much attention has been paid to Radical opinion. Historian of ideas Paul Crook has noted the complexity, variability and ambivalence of British views, and presents a more realistic picture of American influence on Britain. Radical, Tory and Whig opinions diverged, and people found in their reception of American ideas largely what they wanted to find.[6]

Spurred by the London Workingman's Association's pioneering work, the Chartist Movement demanded from their government not only American-style universal suffrage and payment of members of Parliament, but also other claims of radical democracy not yet attained in the United States, such as equal electoral districts. They espoused social reform to ameliorate the economic conditions of the working class, including land reform. Their thinking influenced the National Reform Association of the late 1840s in the United States in its quest for a safety valve of government-provided 'free land' on the frontier for the less well to do.[7] Indeed, some 500 Chartist leaders migrated to the republic to escape either political persecution or economic gloom, where they were briefly prominent in reform and the labour movement, but with their numbers dwarfed by the huge influx of economic immigrants, their distinctive identity was lost. They found political conditions on the other side of the Atlantic different, and the opportunities for land reform greater, with legislators more sympathetic, and undeveloped land available, whereas most was spoken for in Britain.[8]

As the Chartist influence indicates, political and ideological struggles within British politics could be reworked on the American side of the Atlantic. The Whig party that emerged as the Democratic party's opponent in the mid-1830s drew upon the anti-court rhetoric of the British Whig tradition to combat what its leaders claimed to be the dictatorial tendencies of 'King' Andrew Jackson and a 'mob' democracy. The American Whigs, Daniel Walker Howe notes, found attractive Britain's 'mixed' parliamentary system that functioned between 1832 and 1868 on the basis of an aristocratic and middle-class sharing of power: 'This balance provided a model of progress synthesized with stability.'[9] American conservatives like Calvin Colton felt 'affinity' for British Whigs. Colton in fact lived in Britain for 4 years, and wrote extensive accounts of his residence abroad, becoming an important transatlantic conduit of information on the United States – like English-born American radio broadcaster Alistair Cooke in the twentieth century, but in reverse for the 1830s. Colton also became a staunch defender of the American Protestant Episcopal Church derived from the Church of England, an indication of his Anglophilia.[10]

Whigdom was a minority tradition, however, and did not indicate dissent from the profound republicanism of antebellum political thought and practice. This tradition Americans wanted to export, just as the Soviet

Union did with Communism in the twentieth century. Most Americans were simply content with preaching the superiority of American institutions, yet others wanted to go further. The vehicle was the filibuster – a term that came into common usage in 1850–51, but which can be given to earlier ventures by individuals or groups invading foreign countries in the name of liberty.[11] When Canadians rose in rebellion against oligarchic power in 1837, Americans believing strongly in republican institutions resolved to help them. Ideologically driven sympathizers supplied arms to rebels, and 88 'patriot' men from the borderlands of New York invaded Canada in 1838, only to suffer ignominious defeat. Those captured were sent to distant Van Dieman's Land to cool their heels as political prisoners. Though functionally they were exporting American democracy to Canada, from the patriots' point of view these hotheads espoused regional identities grounded in transnational republican convictions.[12]

Such filibustering was not centrally orchestrated. In fact, it created huge diplomatic problems for the American government. As Robert May shows, filibusters 'seriously disrupted' foreign relations and business interests abroad, and may even have 'retarded America's territorial expansion' by discrediting the entire process.[13] By the 1850s, individualistic filibusters became both more common and more controversial. They were now more closely tied to wacky commercial expansionist schemes and pro-slavery intrigues in the Caribbean, like the exploits of the reckless William Walker who invaded and proclaimed himself President of Nicaragua in 1855 in the name of democracy, then became mired in sleazy land deals and local opposition. In an era in which slavery was becoming more negatively regarded, filibustering had ceased to be an expression of high-minded republican ideology.

More commonly Americans sought to sympathize from a distance with other peoples' struggles to be free. As early as 1831, Americans held demonstrations to express their solidarity with the Polish people oppressed by the Russian Tsar and denied independence. To a packed Boston public meeting, eminent clergyman Lyman Beecher 'fervently and eloquently invoked the Divine Blessing on the cause of the Poles, and of civil and religious freedom generally – praying that the rod of the oppressor might be broken, and the oppressed of all nations be emancipated'. The *Essex Register* referred to these remarks as 'patriotic and truly Republican sentiments'.[14]

American sympathies swelled with each wave of failed European revolution. The most intense period of activity surrounded the attempted liberal uprisings of 1848 in central Europe put down with the power of Prussia and the Russian and Austro-Hungarian empires. The United States gave refuge to the defeated revolutionaries of 1848; the Italian patriot Giuseppe Garibaldi spent several years in the early 1850s living in New York. Though he did not receive an official government welcome because he was regarded as too radical,[15] Garibaldi had support in the Italian community on Staten Island. About 3000 refugees from the failed 1848 revolution in Italy lived in New York,[16] among whom he found a fertile field to raise money for political causes in his homeland. After time in Central America Garibaldi did precisely that, helping to bring about the unification of Italy. German refugees came to the United States after 1848 too; these included Carl Schurz, later to be a prominent supporter of Abraham Lincoln. That other 1848 agitator, Karl Marx moved to London, but some of his German socialist followers such as Friedrich Sorge made it to New York where they joined a Communist Club in 1857 and became affiliated with the Communist International in 1869–70.[17]

Hungarian patriot Louis Kossuth received a much more impressive reception than any other rebels in the European revolutions of 1848 did, because he was able to exploit growing anxieties about the expansionist intentions of the Russian Empire in East Asia. Kossuth had failed to establish a Hungarian nation-state in a liberal revolution against Austrian oppression backed by Russia, fled to America and became just the second foreign leader to address Congress (revolutionary war figure, the Marquis de Lafayette of France, was the first). The Hungarian hero toured the United States seeking help for his cause and applauding federal republicanism as a model for Europe. Despite their sympathies, Americans flinched from providing the quixotic and unrealistic Kossuth with actual financial or military aid as a violation of neutrality. (This circumspection was doubly wise, as Kossuth was himself intolerant of ethnic dissent among the Hungarians he had hoped to lead.) Moreover, American desires to export liberal revolution to Europe sat uneasily with Southerners, who feared that Northern agitators were seeking parallels for the demand that freedom be given to Southern slaves.[18] The United States was to remain in political terms aloof from the conflicts of Europe – though Kossuth warned them that this would soon be impossible, given Russian expansionism.

These goings-on were part of the ferment of an ultranationalist movement known as Young America. In historian Paola Gemme's words, this 'radical fringe of the Democratic Party ... enjoyed a brief period of political preeminence around the 1852 presidential campaign'.[19] The concept can be traced back to 1845 and explicitly drew upon the nationalist revivals in Europe, which went under names such as Young Ireland and Young Italy. Young America adherents were not, however, all of a piece. Under that name there flourished pro-slavery Southwesterners for whom expansionism provided a solution to the problem of slave profitability, but Northern idealists for whom republicanism and democracy would produce liberal progress also embraced the idea in the late 1840s. Poet of democracy Walt Whitman expected a 'holy millennium of liberty'.[20] Behind both pro-slavery and pro-republican tendances lay the demands of expectant entrepreneurs seeking to use the self-assertive nationalism to achieve economic expansion in the Atlantic world through markets for American agriculture and industry.[21]

Radical republicanism meant more than the right to vote. It included a moral and millenarian dimension, one that was embraced by many of the evangelical clergy of the time. Foreign observers repeatedly noted the point. The political history of democracy could not be divorced from the context of social and moral reform. Textbook writers traditionally treat this period as an 'era' or 'ferment' of reform. In part, they take their cue from France's most famous tourist of the time. Tocqueville believed that American democracy's strength lay in the voluntaristic institutions of civil society, and in the underlying moral values of the people. In fact among the chief examples he drew was the moral reform movement known as temperance.[22] British evangelicals and moral reformers were similarly drawn to the American example because religious freedom and denominational competition seemed to have reinvigorated the Protestant churches and spurred revivals.[23]

This transatlantic link in reform movements is well known; yet, American reform was part of wider multilateral circuits of information exchange. The United States was not the sole model attracting the attention of Europeans; the reception of American reform models was complicated. Typically American influence was mediated through local institutions and other non-American channels. Moreover, the United States drew upon foreign sources for inspiration in the first place. Both the United States and the Europeans were, in this 'ferment of reform', part of larger shifts in the global economy and society towards forms of liberal contractual humanitarianism and self-control.[24] Whether we accept that slavery came under attack as an attempt to distinguish legitimate 'free' labour exploitation from other forms of politico-economic coercion or not, self-styled enlightened reformers inveighed against a whole host of practices deemed irrational.

The literature on reform has particularly focused on the Anglo-American connection. That the most intense exchanges occurred along this route is hardly surprising, given the trade patterns. Not only did the transatlantic highway of commerce carry reformers as moral cargo to Britain. While on that highway the moralist passengers proselytized. Aboard the steamship *Great Western* on route to Britain in 1838, temperance reformer Edward C. Delevan got 57 passengers to petition against serving liquor at the ship's dining tables.[25] Once across the Atlantic, American influence spread to many places. Returning immigrants carried some of the American penchant for moral reform, as with Danes and Swedes who brought temperance home in the 1830s and 1840s. And influence on the United States also came from a broader range than the Anglo-American reform connection would suggest. The Frenchman, Charles Fourier planned kibbutz-like communitarian colonies that would abolish sexual inequality and essentially replace the traditional bourgeois family structure. Through these examples, society could in theory be reformed from the bottom up. Americans took on these ideals through the work of New York journalist

Albert Brisbane, who studied in Paris with Fourier and adopted his principle of 'Association' in 1840. Best known in adapting these ideas was the Brook Farm Colony in Massachusetts (1844), but a variety of communitarian settlements in the United States drew upon Fourier and his fellow Frenchman St Simon, and erected what historian Arthur Bestor called 'Patent Office Models of the Good Society' for the rapidly expanding frontier settlements.[26]

The reciprocal and multilateral nature of social reform is shown most clearly in the case of penitentiaries. In the 1820s several American states developed innovative programmes aimed at cleaning up the mess of the prisons. They were based on management of prisoners through solitary confinement and separation of offenders in elaborate and geometrical schemes of architecture such as the 'radial' system, whose advocates promised reformation by isolating inmates from corrupting prison and societal influences. The Eastern Penitentiary designed by British-born and educated John Haviland in Philadelphia was one key model. Europeans studied this example and the Auburn New York system, reporting back favourably to home governments. Continental visitors included not only the pair of Tocqueville and Beaumont, but also observers from Britain, Germany, Belgium and Russia.[27]

The American prisons were part of a broader Euro-American penal reform shift from harsh punishment to more rational concepts of prisoner management. These ideas had origins in eighteenth-century Enlightenment and English Quaker thought, the work of humanitarian campaigner John Howard, and Jeremy Bentham's utilitarian *Panopticon*, published in 1795. Howard's English designs for reformatory prisons were well known in the 1810s. The scheme for physical and geometrically designed separation of inmates in the 'Lunatic Asylum' plan, published in London in 1814 when Haviland was studying architecture in that city, 'clearly indicated' that the radial plan 'was almost fully developed at that time'. It made the 'inspiration' for Haviland's prison designs 'quite obvious', states a biography of the reformer.[28] Subsequent treatment of the insane followed a similar course of transatlantic influence: the example of the English Quaker, Samuel Tuke, provided in his description of his Retreat in Yorkshire 'a text for the establishment of a Quaker retreat' near Philadelphia as well as asylums in Massachusetts and New York.[29]

Not only did Britain provide personnel and designs for the new American prisons that later generations assumed were purely internal responses to American conditions but the reciprocal influence was broader still. Alexander Maconochie's reform of the Norfolk Island convict colony prison in the South Pacific around a graded system of rehabilitation in the 1840s found its way, via adoption in Irish prisons in the 1850s to the Elmira, New York, reformatory created by legislation in 1869 and opened in 1876.[30] Prison reform was rooted in the development of strong institutions, and rational social reform. It was conservative in its attempts to fashion through the asylum model a model of stability in a changing social order. It was also transnational in character.

Where the American prison model was influential, that impact was internationally mediated through its complicated reception in Europe. The radial plan, though 'originally developed in English and Continental prisons, was not widely recognized or accepted for large-scale prisons until it had first been transplanted to America by Haviland and then reintro- duced to European reformers'. This move came courtesy of observers sent to the United States by European governments. The English model prison, Pentonville, built in emulation of Haviland's Trenton, New Jersey, penit- entiary became the world's most copied penal institution of the era. After official visits 'by Dr Nicolaus Julius to America and Frederick William IV to Pentonville', the Prussian government built a new model prison 'in the Moabit district of Berlin in 1844 on the Pentonville design'.[31]

Not all the secular, rational reform of this era was focused on creating coercive institutions. A strong strain of secular reform appeared in the 1820s that drew upon the promise of the American Revolution and older traditions of transatlantic radicalism. English factory owner, phil- anthropist and radical reformer Robert Owen's New Harmony colony in Indiana in the 1820s stressed the perfectibility of man in a frontier environment. Like most such colonies, it wilted, but Owenites such as Owen's son Robert Dale Owen helped to reform the marriage laws of Indiana, making them progressive by nineteenth-century standards in their relatively permissive approach to divorce. Early rationalistic women's rights ideas, articulated by Frances Wright, herself a member of New Harmony in the 1820s, belonged to this same tradition. Her work drew upon the Englishwoman Mary Wollstonecraft's defence of the rights of women during the French Revolution, and centred on the anti-clerical 'free thought' movement.[32] This equalitarian strain of radicalism continued in diminished form in the 1830s, but was increasingly challenged by a second and more powerful phase of reform. This was the development of a millenarian religious and moral reform movement.

One of the strongest European–American connections linking reli- gion and reform developed in the temperance movement. Once again, commerce proved an important stimulus. As early as 1829, Massachusetts ship captains had introduced the American Temperance Society pledge of abstinence from hard liquor to the port of Liverpool, and temperance soci- eties quickly formed. From almost the beginning of the society in 1826, its leaders sought to reform the entire world. American sea-going commerce and missionaries proved vital conduits for the spread of temperance tracts to China, India and the East Indies by 1835. The reform models were intended to provide a shining example, but temperance reformers did not rely solely on the serendipity of sympathetic ship captains. They also sent across the busy Atlantic trade route their own 'agents'. The earliest, Rev. Nathaniel Hewitt, toured France and Britain in 1831, helping to organize the British and Foreign Temperance Society and distributing pamphlets warning potential immigrants of the dangers of drinking in America.[33] The aim was to inoculate the United States against contamination by foreign social problems by changing European drinking habits at their source. In the employ of the American Temperance Society, Philadelphia's Rev. Robert Baird visited Sweden in 1836 and 1840, and had temperance pamphlets translated. With Swede Peter Wieselgren, and George Scott, a Scottish clergyman active in early Methodist missions to Scandinavia, he aided the founding of the Swedish Temperance Society.[34]

The American stimulus combined with discontent born of indigenous social roots as poor artisans hit by the industrial revolution sought paths to self-improvement. The result was the innovation of teetotalism in Lancashire in 1833; the very term 'teetotal' – T for total abstinence – was first used in England to describe a new pledge in which the signer foreswore beer and wine as well as spirits. This radicalization of the temperance movement from moderate reform to the desire to perfect society through total abstinence found a fertile field in the United States, where doctrines of religious perfectionism surged increasingly to the fore as the result of the work of evangelist Charles G. Finney. The American Temperance Union was formed in 1837 and adopted a teetotal pledge. European influence did not stop there, however. Irish Capuchin priest Father Theobald Mathew converted many thousands in Ireland to a Catholic total abstinence movement through his charismatic style in the 1840s. When Mathew toured the United States in 1849–51 he ministered from Boston to New Orleans before a reputed 600,000 Irish, many of whom were part of his movement in Ireland and had already come across the ocean with their Father Mathew medallions and temperance pledges. Mathew stirred up controversy within American reform circles because he refused to condemn slavery, as such a course would prevent him from holding meetings in the South. Nonetheless, Mathew's input was greatly solicited by American temperance reformers who had turned to prohibition. They viewed drunken Irish and other Catholics as the major obstacles to their campaign, and so sought to make their newest enthusiasm – the legal prohibition of the alcohol trade – into a transnational campaign to combat immigrant alcohol use at its source in Europe. Once the American temperance movement had embraced prohibition in the passage of the Maine Law in 1851, the concept was exported, first to New Brunswick, then Britain where the United Kingdom Alliance adopted the strategy upon its formation in 1853.[35]

This is not to say that the moral reform movements were identical in outcome on both sides of the ocean. The institutional pressures differed. Prohibition did not succeed in Britain, where the temperance movement was handicapped by the power of both the aristocracy and the drink trade, as well as by the tepid and divided response to teetotalism and prohibition within the state church, the Church of England.[36] Teetotalism remained a movement of Protestant dissenters against the establishment, whereas in the United States in the 1840s and 1850s the temperance movement had come close to being the establishment. The strength of perfectionist doctrines on the American side also aided the reform movement and coloured campaigns that were superficially identical. Even with the radical secular reformers, trans-oceanic influences were applied with subtle differences. Whereas Fourier rooted his 'social science' in Enlightenment rationalism and his European disciples professed a vague harmony between Fourierism and religion, says Carl Guarneri, 'American Associationists drew deeply from their Christian heritage'.[37] They developed a Christian millennialist strain within their socialistic doctrines.

One key characteristic of American reform, therefore, was its strongly evangelical character and millenarian drive. This was best expressed in the thought of prominent Protestant clergyman Lyman Beecher and his daughter, Catherine, author of *A Treatise on Domestic Economy* (1841), who became famous as an expert dispensing advice to women on how to make their homes work better.[38] Her approach was heavily moral. She shared a widespread belief that the United States was part of a providential plan to prepare for the coming of Christ. Both she and Lyman Beecher stressed the moral uniqueness of the American people: 'The democratic institutions of this Country are in reality no other than the principles of Christianity carried into operation', stated the daughter. The American Republic was the means by which the Messiah of the nations would reform the earth and establish his earthly kingdom.

The millenarian and messianic fervour of American evangelicals in extending the benevolent empire of the Lord within the United States is well known. Beecher's *Plea for the West* (1830) implied that, by reformers Christianizing and domesticating the new frontier areas, the godly struggle would be won *within* the nation. Sunday Schools and Tract and Bible societies led the charge – backed by temperance and other moral reform groups. Less understood is that the American evangelicals saw their work as an indivisible global struggle against Satan. Distinguished American clergy including Beecher visited Britain in 1846 to start a worldwide Evangelical Alliance, but they were cut off from active involvement by the insistence of the British, under the impact of abolitionist William Lloyd Garrison's argument that a global evangelical push must contain an anti-slavery clause. An American auxiliary to the Alliance was not established until 1867 – after slavery had been abolished.[39]

This controversy over the Alliance points to the key importance of slavery as a problem fracturing the Anglo-American reform crusades. The internecine feuds over tactics in the United States between the radical Garrisonians, who favoured a broad coalition of emancipatory causes, moral reform and religious perfectionism, and narrower abolitionists led by the Tappan brothers were projected onto the European stage. It was at the World's Anti-Slavery Convention in London in 1840 that women's right to speak in public – supported by the Garrisonian faction – injected rancour into the proceedings, and women were excluded as official delegates.[40] This schism within the anti-slavery movement led rejected women such as Elizabeth Cady Stanton to return to the United States determined to advance the cause of woman's rights. Yet the radical model of emancipation had antecedents in British work by Elizabeth Heyrick's *Immediate, Not Gradual Emancipation*, published in England in 1824 and later reprinted in the *Genius of Universal Emancipation*.[41] The shift in abolitionist tactics was part of a shared Atlantic sensibility concerning the nature of moral reform and the conceptualization of particular social problems as sins.

Controversies over the rights and wrongs of slavery embroiled the British movement's leaders and agitators when they visited the United States, though Britain itself had, along with France, its own experience in the abolition of slavery in the West Indies. Britain had beaten the United States to legislate emancipation of its own slaves in 1833 (completed in 1838), which is why American abolitionists sought to exploit this great evangelical reform achievement tactically.[42] From Britain, abolitionists could press the embarrassing point. The mother country was more advanced on race and abolition than its former colony that had revolted in 1776 in the name of liberty.

Further evidence for this proposition came from the violent antiabolitionist reaction in the United States, which exposed the limits of toleration in democratic practice. Many Americans objected to visitors' judgements on slavery. When George Thompson toured in 1834–35 he was denounced as a foreign emissary and almost literally stoned out of the country. Thompson's 'harsh and denunciatory' style of stump oratory and his partial affinity with Garrison's radicalism contributed to the backlash. In the 1840s this fiery response was diluted somewhat. Abolitionism had become a broader concern and turned to politics. Anti-abolitionist mobs became less common. Besides, other British anti-slavery visitors such as Quaker Joseph Sturge (in 1841) presented a more moderate face of abolitionism and created less friction.[43]

At the same time, American abolitionists frequently toured Europe to drum up moral and financial support. Thrice Garrison visited Britain, in 1833, 1840 and 1846, each time stirring controversy. He viewed antislavery as part of the indivisible chain of global human progress. So indivisible in fact that he yearned for a 'universal language' – a forerunner of Esperanto to enable free communication across the globe on a variety of democratic crusades. He championed Irish emancipation as much as freedom for slaves and sympathized with the fledging English liberal agitation against the British acquisition of an empire in India. Especially did the example of Irish emancipation stimulate him. Garrison used Daniel O'Connell's idea of a repeal of the Irish political union with Britain to argue for 'No Union with Slaveholders'.[44]

'World's' reform conventions were among the platforms that Garrison and other abolitionists used. The gathering held in London in 1840 was not the last occasion on which American abolitionists traipsed to Britain for such meetings. Garrison came with Henry C. Wright and Frederick Douglass to attend the rancorous World's Temperance Convention in 1846 and the Evangelical Alliance meetings at which the issue of slavery was so divisive. The most famous visitor was Frederick Douglass, who as a slave escapee from the South had better reason than most to seek foreign climes. When Douglass crossed the Atlantic in 1845, the Cunard Line segregated him[45] and American passengers threatened to throw him overboard.[46] Foreign residence in Britain from 1845 to 1847 changed Douglass, giving him 'a critical perspective'.[47] Being treated as equal made him acutely conscious of racism at home and any form of paternalism abroad. Even abolitionists were known to harbour hierarchical views of race and class and, under the impact of the British experience, Douglass tired of Garrison's supervisory role. While Douglass found Britons freer of the grosser forms of racial oppression in a way that emphasized for him the racial hierarchies of his own caste society, he knew that racism of a different sort permeated British culture. To maximize his value to the movement, it was necessary to appeal to white Britons' fascination for the exotic Other. He had to play up his negritude by keeping his hair as woolly as possible.[48]

In Britain, Douglass joined a church dispute that raged on both sides of the Atlantic. The Rev. Thomas Chalmers, a Scottish clergyman, had in 1843 raised money from slaveholders in America to aid the poor of Glasgow. A gift by South Carolinian Presbyterians enraged abolitionists within the Scottish churches, who enlisted Douglass' aid.[49] He conducted a highly divisive campaign to send the money back, and the controversy hounded Chalmers to his grave within 2 years. After lecturing in Europe, and obtaining official freedom with the aid of British donors who paid his former owner his market value, Douglass received donations from British friends that in 1847 enabled him to return to the United States to start a newspaper, the *North Star*. This paper included foreign anti-slavery material in its columns. In the succeeding decade, British and American reformers continued to cooperate against slavery; the movement for 'free produce' boycotts of slave-generated goods – which Garrison opposed after initially flirting with it – became centred in Britain because the British textile industry drew upon Southern cotton and so sustained the entire slave economy. British cotton textile mills even began to look further afield for cotton from India and Egypt, but in 1860, American cotton was still indispensable and a war over slavery bound to hurt British industry.[50]

This economic strength of the South in an Atlantic trading system partly explains the 'divided hearts' of the British public on the subject of slavery during the early stages of the American Civil War. Opinion was further complicated by the Republican Congress's Morrill Tariff of 1862 against industrial goods (which hurt Britain especially), and the absence of a clear ethical position against slavery from the Lincoln administration. Yet large numbers of Britons from the middle and working classes sympathized with the Union government. In their protest meetings, the articulate elements of the working class remained by and large on the side of the North; this opinion helped to prevent the British government from giving the Confederacy official recognition.[51] This outcome can be partly attributed to the 30-year transatlantic agitation that had gone before. The transnational links of the abolitionists in the long run sensitized Britons to the continued evils of slavery, and so kept large sections of public opinion generally favourable to the Union.

We began with Tocqueville, and this chapter ends with him too. Both he and Beaumont saw the divisiveness of slavery, though neither was a radical abolitionist. Shocked at the harshness of the racial hierarchy decreed on the basis of a single drop of African blood, Beaumont planned a now-forgotten novel, *Marie; Or, Slavery in the United States*, exploring the tragic flaw of race in American society.[52] Historians have neglected Beaumont's work, and literary critics have winced at its impossible plot and turgid prose. But this defect is no good reason to neglect the negative judgements upon American society concerning race delivered by Beaumont, or to dwell instead upon how Tocqueville majestically explored the ingenious lineaments of American democratic achievements. For Tocqueville too, the American version of the democratic model compromised 'the permanence of republican forms in the New World'.[53] This was one reason for his focus in the second volume of *Democracy in America* on the theoretical and general workings of a civil society; he cautioned that the United States did not provide the only version of a democratic system. The efficacy of the American example remained contingent upon resolution of the racial problem, a gigantic question mark. He saw slavery's evils as the result of history, not American exceptionalism. He set the issue in comparative perspective, with race conflict and hierarchy shared across European cultures to varying degrees. Indeed, Tocqueville expressed, in terms similar to Abraham Lincoln, distaste for the physical features of the African-American as 'hideous'.[54] American distinctiveness lay only in the historical grounding of racial oppression in the very institutions of civil society that held the nation together. Tocqueville understood that the United States was a racialized democracy; that equality between the races would not be accepted, that the Anglo-Saxon race would almost certainly remain dominant and yet that slavery could not survive. Either slave revolt or emancipation would end the institution, but not bring racial egalitarianism. He even predicted a bloody civil war, though not as it turned out between North and South, but between whites and blacks as the latter struggled for their freedom. Tocqueville could not, any more than Lincoln, see a way forward to racial equality. Race would be the problem that would not go away.

4

People in Motion: Nineteenth-Century Migration Experiences

Americans normally conceive of migration as a one-way process. Immigrants entered Castle Garden (and later Ellis Island) in New York from Europe to begin the painful and inevitable process of losing their culture and assimilating. Though the melting pot concept existed even before the term was popularized in 1908, the resistance of immigrants to rapid assimilation has proven undeniable. Nowadays other metaphors prevail, designed to represent the diverse origins and interwoven cultures of Americans. Historians tend to see the United States as a salad bowl, a quilt or a continuing conversation over national identity. The new multiculturalism recognizes important transnational influences in the making of immigration, but to a large degree the nation's internal social history is still treated as distinct from migration considered as an economic and cultural system. The legal frameworks of immigration created national boundaries, but until 1924, there were few controls over immigration and none except for those against Asian people were effective before the First World War. For this reason alone the transnational aspects of migration stand out, not only as a diverse process, but also as a reciprocal and multilateral one. Topics such as internal geographical and social mobility are also difficult to separate from migration's ebbs and flows. It is preferable to think, therefore, of immigration as part of a larger system of 'movement' made possible by global changes in communications and market dislocation.[1]

It is a cliché to call the United States a nation of immigrants. With this glib phrase goes a connotation of exceptional status that is not entirely warranted. All new human settlement involves the mingling of peoples and cultures, and even when comparing migration only in the modern period since the age of the democratic and industrial revolutions, the American case is not unique. From 1820 to 1924, the United States was linked to a global system centred partly upon the export of Europe's surplus population – to North and South America and Australasia – to lands where disease and warfare reduced, eliminated or subjugated the indigenous peoples. Why only 'partly'? Because this immigration also involved substantial movements of population from China and India to other countries in the Pacific, and towards the end of the nineteenth-century Koreans, Japanese and Mexicans joined in too. For Americans, Chinese immigrants were the most significant Asian group, but Chinese no more than others made a beeline for the United States. They went to the west coast of *both* North and South America from the 1850s, following the gold rushes to Australia and New Zealand and contract labour routes to Hawaii and Peru. Intracontinental movement must also be included. The focus on trans-oceanic travel distorts the total international migration picture. In the American case these movements included from French Canada to New England factory towns after the Civil War, and Mexican and other Latin American migration from the 1890s into the American southwest. Though the Chinese and Japanese immigration was much smaller than the European in the US case, these 'contra' flows were of great regional importance, and influenced the development of immigration policy.

Only about half of the world's trans-oceanic migration in the years 1846–1940 went to the Americas – both North and South; if cross-national land migration is included, the contribution of the Americas drops to around one-third of the global total.[2] While there has been a tendency among migration scholars to treat Pacific and Atlantic patterns of migration as incommensurable, the ebbs and flows within the world economy tell a different story. Similar push and pull factors applied, though mediated by different border control policies. State intervention from the 1880s led this Asian immigration in the case of the United States and other Anglo-settler societies around the Pacific basin to be increasingly shut off. This 'great white wall' of restrictive policy presaged the more extensive immigration restrictions of the 1920s. The Immigration Act of 1924 ended the relatively open American participation in international migration patterns. But the 1930s depression and the Second World War soon meant that all international migration patterns were severely disrupted.

Best known and most significant for the American case were transatlantic migration flows but many European migrants chose Canada, Brazil or Argentina. It was not the United States but Argentina that had the largest proportion of foreign-born residents in the nineteenth century – and was therefore more entitled to be called a 'nation of immigrants'. For some migrant groups thought to be especially drawn to the US, for example Italians, the fact remains that other destinations were more popular in the first two-thirds of the nineteenth century. Italian migrants preferred South America, with only 9 per cent going to the United States before 1870. Until the end of the Risorgimento, most people leaving Italy went elsewhere in Europe or to South America, where over half of Italians abroad lived.[3]

That said, the United States still had certain advantage of location in the trans-oceanic migration so far as most Europeans were concerned. The voyage across the Atlantic was relatively short at about 3–4 weeks by sail at mid-century; it was much cheaper, quicker and less hazardous than the 3-month trip to Australia and New Zealand or even the voyage to South America or Southern Africa. This, more than the special, 'abundant' opportunities offered in the United States, explains the fact that the nation garnered 65 per cent of European migration to the Americas over the whole of the nineteenth century.

The class implications of this flow were considerable. A poorer class of immigrant tended to go to North America – people who became day labourers, farmers and factory workers. They included the cast-offs of the English industrial revolution, including the skilled tradesmen no longer wanted in the world of mechanization as well as poorer agricultural labourers and farmers driven from the rapidly consolidating commercial estates of Britain. In addition, tin, coal and other miners brought their special skills and were among the many groups from the British Isles contributing to the development of a working class in the Northern states before the Civil War. From Britain, the better off tended, if they emigrated, to consider New Zealand or Australia. Yet with the important exceptions of convicts and the very well to do, colonial immigration authorities in Australia had to provide cash incentives to encourage enough people to migrate, and in the interests of empire they concentrated their efforts on Britain and Ireland.[4] For these reasons, among the settler societies spawned by the British, the United States had more culturally diverse sources of immigrants, with Germans, Scandinavians and Irish joining the English and Scottish. This special pattern of greater US diversity was not to be maintained in the twentieth century as increasing numbers of Mediterranean, and eventually Asian immigrants made the settlement societies of Australia and Canada as well as the United States ever more complex multicultural destinations.

When looking at immigration it is important to consider the different experiences of gender as much as race. In the first half of the nineteenth century, immigration tended to be of family groups, particularly for emigrants from the British Isles.[5] Though drunken Irish male canal workers disrupted quiet American hamlets in the 1820s as the market and transportation revolutions spread, the caricature is undeserved for Irish newcomers as a whole. Irish men and women came in approximately equal numbers from the 1840s because the potato famine drove them both out. Irish women offered a major source of domestic labour, often with English-speaking skills, and could also take the place of New England's native-born factory girls as these moved up the social scale in the 1850s. In contrast, gender experience in Mediterranean families was contained within larger kinship networks that stretched back to the home countries. Thus Italians and Greeks were much more likely to migrate as single (male) workers and seek to return to their kin or to bring their families to join them later in America. Because of their highly patriarchal family structures back home, these groups tended to restrict wives and daughters who did come to the United States to the home, and provided the American economy with extra 'putting out' labour in the garment industry – working on machines finishing apparel in their own homes. An extreme case of highly specialized immigration by gender was that of the Chinese who came to the United States after 1850 as mostly poor men from village society. Later, Chinese entrepreneurs imported single Chinese women – the daughters of destitute peasants – to provide both brides and, much more commonly, prostitutes for this class of manual workers.[6]

Demographers talk of push and pull factors in migration history, though a more organic metaphor of breathing in and out would be equally appropriate to such systemic phenomena. There was, Brinley Thomas showed, an Atlantic economy and the flows across that ocean responded to the booms in the American economy and its recessions.[7] To that Atlantic perspective must be added our increasing knowledge of the globalization of the world economy and its effects. The boom times of 1845–57 after the depression of the late 1830s proved the first major spurt. The discovery of gold in California helped power the fundamentals of manufacturing and transportation growth after 1849. Immigration peaked to the United States in 1854 at about the same time that gold's discovery in Australia saw the colony of Victoria's population surge. The city of Melbourne rivalled San Francisco as a boomtown within the emerging global migration system that matched the global economy. Immigrants flocked to the gold fields of California in 1849, including a good many from Australia; the latter returned after the great discoveries in Victoria, along with gold-seeking Americans and immigrants from Europe and China in the mid-1850s.

Migration to the American west, whether internal or from overseas, had a strong economic motive of striking it rich, but economic improvement was fundamental to European immigration to the East coast too. Despite the common image of the Ellis Island intake as oppressed peoples struggling to breathe free, the stimulus to emigration everywhere was overwhelmingly economic – the search for a better life or, not uncommonly, for the means to make life better back in the home country. The transatlantic economic revolution of industrialization, transportation and communications meant greater knowledge of available jobs and land in North America – knowledge that demographers say drew immigrants across the Atlantic. Immigrants were also driven out of their home countries by a variety of factors. Certain groups sought escape from political or religious oppression. Jews fleeing from the anti-Semitic pogroms of the Russian Empire in the 1880s and 1890s best fitted the category of religious persecution. Though Germans entering the United States in the decade after the revolution of 1848 included some who qualify as political refugees, within the vast stream of German migration relatively few came for this reason. Like the poor farmers of most of Northeastern Europe, the imbalance between population and land induced them to leave as the birth rate rose. Landlords seeking to take advantage of the industrial revolution in Europe introduced more efficient land management and began to dispossess tenant farmers. The extreme case was that of the Irish, with some 1 million leaving in the wake of land enclosure and the famine of 1845–48. In all, over 5 million immigrants entered the United States from 1820 to 1860, and 32 million by 1924.

US migration has been typically conceived of in terms of first and second waves. This is a Eurocentric and Atlantic-centred notion. As is well known, a shift in the composition of European migrants occurred from the 1880s, when the pace of capitalist market change spread to southern and eastern Europe, but the global pattern complicated these neat sequences. If first-wave European immigrants had begun by the 1860s to be assimilated, Asian immigration is more difficult to fit into this two-wave model. With China also drawn more into a world economy in which the need for labour mobility was becoming apparent, the 1850s to 1870s – during the first wave – saw substantial Chinese migration to the west coast of the United States. These Asian immigrants moved East instead of West, going as far as the Massachusetts town of North Adams where a shoe factory owner imported them as strike-breakers, though more commonly they spread to such states as Oregon, Washington and Nevada and introduced multilateral patterns to immigration. Congress largely eliminated Chinese immigration as a political and cultural issue through the Chinese Exclusion Act of 1882 because, while the act specifically excluded 'labourers' only, the category was very broadly interpreted. But the Asian labour threat persisted in the form of the Japanese until 1908 when that in turn was restricted. At the same time, Mexican and other Hispanic immigrants began to move north of the border. Truly the old model of a unidirectional flow across the Atlantic will not work any better than first and second-wave theory.

The contrast between geographically restless, mobile Americans and a static, sedentary European population cannot be maintained either. The United States became known in the nineteenth century as a nation of movers. Small islands of what Peter Knights and Stephan Thernstrom called the persisting group – the prosperous residents who formed the backbone of communities – stood proud and highly visible amid a seething tide of migrating manual workers, farmers and assorted people on the make.[8] High rates of geographical mobility applied not only in frontier districts, but also in Eastern cities, where migrants swelled the ranks of the transient. But how unique was this highly fluid social structure? Comparative cross-national studies measuring geographical mobility are few and far between[9]; most work focuses on social mobility rather than questions of geographical motion or class. In the case of William Sewell's study of mobility in Marseilles, a substantial proportion of residents in that booming port city were peasants migrating from the hinterland. Over two-thirds of those entering the marriage registers in Marseilles' population by 1870 were born elsewhere compared to one-third of the city's population in 1820. Granted that this case may overstate the argument somewhat, the shift is still impressive. As in the United States, there was a great deal of internal mobility from city to city and country to city, and in Marseilles immigrants were the upwardly mobile, enterprising and creative elements in the culture, and more likely to get white-collar jobs than class-conscious artisans.[10] Europe, not just the United States, was in motion.[11] By the 1880s, Germany, for instance, had about half of its population residing elsewhere than their places of birth. Early nineteenth-century Germans were more likely to migrate to southeastern and eastern Europe than to the US, and later in the century Germany hosted many Poles and other foreign workers as its factory system expanded. The migration movement to the United States did not start (or end) with the trip across the Atlantic. German immigrants to the United States were part of a shift from rural to urban environments; many went to Bremen or Hamburg and stayed there; others used these ports as way stations.[12] Similarly, large numbers of Irish fleeing enclosure went to Glasgow, Liverpool, London and the industrializing towns of the north of England. Many remained there while others then migrated to Canada or the United States. Many who went to Canada used Montreal as an entrance port and ended up in the United States eventually. What was true of economic migrants was also true of political dissenters. European countries provided the initial destination and residence for most of the early political refugees from the failed 1848 liberal revolutions.[13]

The circulation of peoples did not finish at the ports of New York, Philadelphia and Boston. The Irish tended to remain in the eastern cities, but they did circulate among these places; the poorer class became a transient proletariat. Also transient were the canal labourers who could find themselves as far afield as the American South, working like navvies among a population of planters and slaves because the slaves were too valuable to risk losing in such dangerous jobs. Immigrants went west on contract in labour gangs to build the railroads, and the Chinese joined this epic phase of transcontinental construction eastward.[14] Norwegians and other Scandinavian peoples more commonly sought farmland, particularly in the Midwest, while Germans often took an in-between position helping to build the new cities of the west of the antebellum years such as Cincinnati and Chicago. There they persisted and prospered.

Movement is, however, different from social mobility. Sewell drew a contrast between the levels of social mobility in France and the United States, and argued for greater inherited class-consciousness in holding back upward mobility in the French case.[15] Rates of property acquisition and occupational mobility on the American frontier were higher than back east and in Europe. Yet studies projecting concepts of social mobility in this way tend to reproduce American exceptionalism by focusing on too narrow a range of questions. Historians and social scientists tend to assume that immigrants to the United States followed individual social mobility, whereas most had family and community in mind. In so far as mobility was achieved, it reflected family cohesion as a labour and reproductive system as much as anything else.[16] In any case, many immigrants did not go west. Either they could not afford to, or were discouraged, as in the case of the Irish, by previous experience on the land. For them social mobility needed to occur within the industrial economy.

Higher wages for unskilled, relative to Europe, with smaller margins for skill, attracted poorer immigrants to the United States, but wealth distribution was unequal, as in Europe, according to Edward Pessen. After the Civil War numerous skilled jobs opened up within the expanding industrial economy while the same industrial development simultaneously squeezed out artisans with preindustrial skills. For those lucky enough to mount the ladder to success, *inter*generational change from blue to white-collar work was the norm rather than ascent within a single generation (*intra*generational mobility). Rags to riches gains were rare. Stephan Thernstrom's classic study of Newburyport showed that the best most Irish people could do was to attain small property holdings. But it helped to start with some material resources.[17] Modern cross-national sociological studies of social stratification indicate that the chances of the poor rising out of their situation today are in fact less in the United States than in Nordic Europe and Germany, but the image of a classless society in which mobility is possible continues as an important part of American self-perceptions.[18] The 'self-made man' myth has survived the assaults of historians and it definitely had some purchase in nineteenth-century American society, despite the existence of class structures. Both American and European commentators tended to depict the United States as a land of great opportunity, and this attracted immigrants. Letters home and migrants returning with stories of material wealth and evidence of success reinforced this sense of exceptionalism as did patterns of geographical mobility. The 'persisters' – often the respectable middle-class people of native-born origin – exaggerated by their very presence the sense of upward social mobility; those who moved, many immigrants from Europe among their number, did not stay long enough anywhere to measure their rates of ascent or decline.[19] These people included those who would not or could not assimilate – ever-potential recruits for the return army to the countries of origin or on to some other destination, such as Canada or Mexico.

Assimilation put a brake on this transnational process, but assimilation was uneven and by no means inexorable. British-born immigrants blended in best. The ability to speak English and – except for most of the Irish – their Protestantism provided an important ticket to smoother integration. Other groups took much longer to assimilate precisely because they spoke foreign languages, but also because they chose to migrate in groups and stayed that way; Swedes and Norwegians who came from rural backgrounds often established their own settlements in the American Midwest in the antebellum period, as Finns did later, and within these communities spoke their own languages and kept their own cultures. Though the Homestead Act of 1862 provided powerful incentive for migrants becoming American, as free land grants could only be allocated to citizens, many immigrants remained foreign nationals. Among the enterprising Swedes, for example, a majority waited 20 years to apply for citizenship.[20] With the rise of industrial America and the closing of the frontier the incentive to assimilate and take out American nationality actually declined post-1880. In 1908–14, only 57 per cent of all adult foreign-born males were citizens and the figure was 'sharply' lower among industrial workers.[21]

Immigrants in cities as well as the country built their distinctive institutions such as clubs and churches and introduced their own religious and cultural festivals. Catholic Irish sent remittances back to relatives and contributed at great cost to the building of cathedrals and churches when more rational market-oriented action would require them to seek personal financial mobility. The Irish preferred to buy houses rather than put money into the next generation's educational improvement. They reproduced a form of peasant tenure in America; property mobility, however, did not secure upward social mobility and the Irish progressed up the social ladder slowly, partly as a result. Through the formation of ethnic churches as quasi-national institutions, new immigrant groups after 1880 such as Poles, Lithuanians and Slavs became more attached to membership of a (foreign) national community than in their homelands, a process that caused considerable conflict within the Catholic Church and between ethnic groups. In Europe they remained pre-eminently members of families and villages.[22]

Within the transplanted communities, mental migration was out of kilter with the physical. Some migrants were in America but not really of it. This was not a new phenomenon in the nineteenth century. A prime example was the Mennonites. Mennonites were Anabaptists, products of the sixteenth-century Protestant Reformation. Many came to the future United States in the eighteenth century in response to persecution, but others had gone to Russia where they were in turn driven out in the 1870s. They also eventually headed for the United States and Canada, though some migrated from the Anglophone farmlands of the North American west to Mexico to escape persecution during the First World War. These repeated population shifts came about because the Mennonites' prime allegiance was to their religious group and not to the nation-state. They remained pacifists. Some had left Prussia and Russia to avoid military service and those in America eschewed the military during the Civil War and the First World War – thus bringing the wrath of surrounding

communities down upon them. Mennonites had their own specific tele-
ology and eschatology. Though this tradition of separation from the
nation-state began to change by the 1920s, their mental world was forged
in a separate history. They had their own set of heroes and religious
martyrs, just as the Jewish and Irish diasporas did in different but comparable ways. Mennonites, able to succeed to some degree economically in
rural society because they were industrious farmer stock, retained their
transnational identities for generations.[23]

The extreme example of lack of assimilation was repatriation. Studies
of migration have typically neglected this subject, but nineteenth-century
observers did not. Charles Dickens discovered a hundred returnees in
1842 in steerage aboard his ship out of New York. Some had stayed
3 months, others just a few days; many were destitute and 'living on
food donated by others on board'.[24] In the 1860s and 1870s unwanted
Chinese on the American west coast began to leave, often driven out by
prejudice. After 1880, waves of repatriation accompanied every economic
downturn. For Sweden, often thought to be a source of respectable middle-
class migrants who integrated relatively well, the repatriation average
was around 18 per cent, though the figure stood at 23.5 per cent in the
economically depressed years of the 1890s.[25] But return was particularly
common in the case of Balkan peoples and Mediterranean immigrants.
Returnees brought stories of American material wealth, as well as new
fashions and work practices. Greek-American repatriates were distinctive
in their home villages; they had changed and they changed their home
communities. However, the intercultural causes and effects were subtler
than commonly understood. The returnees had not been made indelibly
American; their reception in their homelands emphasized stereotypes of
foreignness. Returning migrants exploited this exotic status and reinforced
misconceptions of them as having become Americanized.[26]

Naturally the rates of repatriation varied over time, between groups and
by original motive for migration. Returnees in the first half of the nineteenth century constituted no more than 10 per cent of the in-flow. The less
regular and more taxing forms of ship transportation made return more
difficult, especially for the poor, a position which changed after the Civil
War.[27] Generally speaking, the improvement and cheapening of cross-
Atlantic transportation allowed the flow of labour post-1870 to include
a substantial element of the 'birds of passage' – people working during
the summer or for a few years in the United States before returning to
their villages, perhaps richer. Italian stonecutters could build the mansions
of the elite in New York in June and rejoin their families in December
when outdoor labour in the colder North American climate slowed. From
1880 to 1914 about 35 per cent of all immigrants to the United States
went home, though many subsequently migrated again. The other major
variable was political or economic oppression. Only 5 per cent of Jews
repatriated, a reflection of the anti-Semitic behaviour of the Russian

and Austro-Hungarian governments. Nor did the Irish go back permanently. Their traumatic experiences of the famine meant they did not want to return. By contrast, for the period from the 1880s to 1914, up to 89 per cent of some Balkan peoples and 46 per cent of Greeks went home.[28] Studies of the Swedish immigrants who left show that these tended to be single, able-bodied men with lower skill levels who had stayed for relatively short periods. Literacy and marriage to an American were important indicators of a decision to remain permanently in the US. It was the footloose, the young single men in motion who were more likely to repatriate. For them, return was 'a stage in a transatlantic labor migration'.[29]

This phase of repatriation ended in 1914. In fact, the First World War changed many of the patterns discussed in this chapter. War stemmed the flow of return migration from 1915 to 1919 just as it did for the general outward flow of migrants from Europe to North America. As a consequence of the European war and the prosperity it brought to American industry, factories had to find new sources of cheap muscle. They drew upon African-American workers from the cotton fields, and Mexican-Americans. These new patterns were part of the ever-flexible and diverse international flow of human capital. In the case of Southern blacks, this was an 'internal' migration to Northern cities that demonstrates just how much movement within the United States was connected to transnational migration cycles.

Meanwhile, forces within the host society reinforced ethnic identities. Lack of assimilation was aided by prejudice, discrimination and political 'nativism', in which native-born identities were constructed and the immigrants denounced because of their strange habits. Prejudice focused particularly on immigrants' drinking liquor, not observing the Sabbath and practicing Roman Catholicism. The potential transnational conflict of allegiance involved in the latter – to Rome and Washington respectively – was important. Native-born Protestants saw the Catholic Church and its schools as a threat to the stability of the republic, as what held Americans together was their civic identity, not place of origin or ancient cultural traditions. They drew, however, not upon self-invented American identity in this reaction, but the heritage of anti-Catholicism of their English and Protestant-Irish ancestors. Anti-popery was hardly a uniquely American urge, but now it was joined by fear of the sheer numbers of arrivals to prompt construction of a national identity around Protestantism. Native-born Americans saw the schools as the inculcators of this sense of nation – a nation founded on Protestant ideas of personal liberty, and this religious tradition made the Catholic Church's forays into education a grave threat. In the 1840s and 1850s, the nativist Know Nothing movement sought ineffectively to restrict the entry of immigrants and, more important, their ability to vote in American elections, and wished to erect permanent barriers against this transnational influence. But because the need for labour was too intense, American attitudes remained contradictory. The work of immigrants was needed, but the cultures that they brought with them were not wanted.[30]

Race proved to be a more potent way of erecting barriers to define American identity than religion. Irish immigrants illustrated this process. Though mainly Roman Catholic, they quickly identified themselves with American republicanism and the hegemony of the white race. From the point of view of native-born Americans in the 1840s to 1860s, the Catholic Irish were on a lower rung of the social chain, but they were essentially competitors against free African-Americans for day labour and wished to distinguish themselves by their colour and their political activity as members of a higher social caste. They resented the call to fight for the slaves' freedom in the Civil War. The Draft Riots of 1863 in New York in which Irish gangs participated revealed the depth of feeling.[31] Yet whiteness had to be defined against not only the obvious target of African-Americans, but also the west coast Chinese. By the 1870s Irish-Americans figured strongly in California's working class, and under the leadership of Denis Kearney of San Francisco spearheaded racist opposition to Chinese threatening their jobs.[32] The process was similar to the Irish identification with labourism, trade unions and nationalism in which the Chinese were eventually excluded from Australia. To Americans, the Chinese seemed alien because of cultural and racial characteristics. Opium smoking, wearing of traditional Chinese dress and a tendency to live in ethnic enclaves made them visible targets. Hence opposition was extreme and spread well beyond the working class as moralists deplored the possible impact of Chinese habits upon their middle-class families, but other immigrants also worried the latter group. Founded in 1887, the American Protective Association sought to control the flood of Southern European immigration, a flow that included for the first time massive numbers of allegedly distinctive racial types such as Slavs and Jews. In the Social Darwinist theories of the time, these were inferior people whose racial and intellectual characteristics were probed by fledgling sociologists such as Edward Ross and crackpot race theorists.[33] Not unmindful of the continuing possible threat from Chinese, Japanese and other non-white emigration, the APA began to push for stronger entrance controls. Against this trend, American employers' economic needs created conflicting object-ives that needed to be resolved. It was the political and intellectual repres-entatives of business that lobbied most vigorously for tolerance towards immigrants in the pages of staid elite periodicals like the *North American Review*. If immigrants were to come, it was hoped that they would assimilate and stay. But many did not stay, in part precisely because of the discrimination.

The impact upon Europe of the entire pattern of emigration and return was considerable but ambiguous in its effects. A loss of about 60 million people from 1820 to 1920 lowered Europe's population growth rates – these were much less than those of receiving countries, and in fact were a third of the American figure. The shifting balance helped the United States achieve economic predominance within the world economy before the First World War. Exported peoples tended to be younger, more agile workers and those who were more innovative represented an important loss of human capital to Europe, and later China, Japan and Latin America. The poorest elements of Swedish society, for instance, did not emigrate in the mid-nineteenth century, but a slightly higher 'aspiring' class. On the other hand, the sending countries lost surplus population in rural industries that were in need of rationalizing precisely because the United States was flooding the markets of Europe with cheaper agricultural produce. (The movement of rural people to the United States was in this sense similar to that of New England farmers forced to move to Northeastern cities to escape the competition of higher-yield western American agriculture after 1840.) If Europe's population could not stand still, those who remained did benefit in other ways from regular remittances to poor rural communities, as happened with Greeks and Italians. Moreover, returnees brought home money to their villages and produced cultural change in their home societies such as the introduction of American-style shopping and retailing methods to Hungary.[34] By the time of the First World War, nearly 1 in 20 Italians had lived for some period in the United States and up to a quarter of all males in parts of Norway had done likewise. When a US Immigration Commission toured Europe in 1907, its members observed that considerable numbers spoke English and had 'a distinct affection for the United States'.[35] The impact of the American demographic attraction was less, however, on China (and Japan), as China's population was larger than Europe's and as Asian immigration to the United States was a much smaller part of the cross-national migration of Chinese people.

Relatively few American-born joined the outflow of peoples in this era of transnational movement, a fact shared with citizens of that other great republic, France, as well as the kindred white 'settler' societies of the British Empire. Like the latter, the United States was mainly a receiver of immigrants, not a giver. Those American-born that did move east to enrich European society were businessmen and members of the cultural elite. Though Second Empire Paris of Louis Napoleon's era in the 1860s was popular, Anglophile attitudes were often manifest in the phenomenon of transatlantic brides who married into the European aristocracy, as did the mother of Sir Winston Churchill, the socialite Jenny Jerome, in 1874.[36] Similarly, some social reformers such as members of the Quaker Robert Pearsall Smith/Hannah Whitall Smith family ended up in Britain and married into the upper middle classes. (One daughter married – unhappily – philosopher Bertrand Russell.) Their Quaker connections were effectively trans-oceanic anyway. At the opposite end of the social scale, the escaped slaves who went to Canada constituted another counter-movement.[37] This was migration by quasi-political refugees, as was the earlier movement of Revolutionary-era Loyalists. A different and later example was that of plains state farmers who headed north across the 49th parallel to the prairie provinces after 1896 in response to the political defeat of the Populist Party and agrarian protests against high railroad rates. When offered cheap or free land in the Canadian west by governments, more than a million departed. But many of these farmers were reportedly unnaturalized European immigrants; land and economic prosperity combined to keep most American-born at home. [38]

Finally, there were the coerced migrants. Here again the comparative perspective is important. Whereas the British West Indies after abolition of its own slavery in the 1830s witnessed increased reliance on indentured workers from Asia, who became a major feature of labour systems not only in the Caribbean but also in the Pacific islands, in the US cheap, free labour prevailed post-1865. Why was indentured labour not sought? In part there were exceptions where this system was indeed used. For instance, incoming Chinese girl prostitutes could be classed as coerced, as could Chinese and Japanese entering Hawaii, as the latter were imported to work as gang labour on sugar plantations. But the major form of coerced labour had been the slave. The abolition of American slavery in 1865 and the availability of a peon-like workforce after Reconstruction meant that for large areas of the economy's agricultural production, indentured labour was simply not needed. But by the same token, the emergence of very restricted forms of freedom in the American South through sharecropping and tenant farming depended on the absence of labour shortages in the North. Immigrants from Europe had plugged that gap. What appeared to be a unique American racial caste system following the demise of Reconstruction was dependent upon the vagaries of the international labour supply. The South's racial institutions were, like everything else, globally 'connected'. That topic, rooted in the unwilling immigrants of slavery, will be treated separately.

5

Unwilling Immigrants and Diaspora Dreams

The experience of slavery was one of the most obvious ways linking the United States to the rest of the world in the era of the new American Republic. Slavery supplied the labour force driving the cotton production that fuelled the British textile industry, the world's leading manufacturing industry in the world's leading industrial economy. The slaves, numbering 1 million in 1810 and reaching nearly 4 million by the eve of the Civil War, were all either imported from Africa or, far more commonly, descended from Africans. Brought by European traders not only from West Africa, but also from Angola and as far afield as Madagascar, the 'unwilling immigrants' of eighteenth-century slavery were part of a much larger European trade of some 10–11 million slaves captured and shipped across the Atlantic from the time of Columbus. In turn, these transatlantic cargoes represented one, albeit large, segment of a global slave market that spread as far east as the Dutch East Indies and involved African and Arab traders as well as Europeans.[1]

Traditional accounts emphasize the internal history of American slavery once the period of the external trade had ended, but enduring transnational influences must not be neglected. These will be the focus of this chapter. Even conventional topics such as slave religion, rebellion, resistance and family – upon which so much exciting work has been done – will be (briefly) discussed in the context of a diaspora, in which the distinctive mental map of African-American experience continued to mark the behaviour and aspirations of slaves. The places of slave attachment were both local, in the land they worked, and elsewhere in the invisible bonds that drew them to figurative and actual lands of freedom – in the United States and beyond.

One result of the American Revolution had been the tacit decision made in the constitutional settlement in 1787–88 to sanction continued slave importation for another 20 years. The United States did outlaw American participation in the African slave trade from 1808 and Britain acted in tandem by banning its own nationals' involvement, but the failure to prohibit earlier allowed a substantial further inflow of Africans. Historian Philip Curtin modified early estimates to come up with a figure of 92,000 slaves for the 20 years from the constitutional convention of 1787, but this may be too low. Allan Kulikoff has put the total trade from 1782 to 1810 in South Carolina, Georgia and the Gulf Coast at 113,000, while another estimate credits South Carolina alone with nearly 50,000 imports after it resumed the trade in 1803.[2] However large, such imports were intended to aid expansion of the cotton industry, which had begun to prosper in the 1790s, just after the time when the abolition of slavery was first being seriously canvassed. The last human cargoes from Africa and the Caribbean extended the transnational cultural influence of the African diaspora in the United States well into the antebellum period as many of these slaves would still be alive 20–40 years later. This contributed to what historian Ira Berlin calls a 'reafricanizing' of the lower Mississippi and the Carolina low country after 1786; from one-tenth of slaves in 1790, the African-born rose to 20 per cent in 1810 and Africanisms such as plaited hair were reincorporated into the Creole population.[3] Though the Haitian Revolution after 1791 led to cessation of trade in slaves with the Caribbean due to fear of importing revolutionaries, connections with and knowledge of the African diaspora in the region had been perpetuated. The experience of Haiti, especially, was to form a vital background to efforts to undermine slavery.

Creolization rather than importation was, however, American slave society's long-term trajectory. Some 600,000 Africans had been imported into what became the United States by 1808. Unknown numbers of Caribbean and African-born slaves, possibly up to 50,000 by some estimates, may have entered illegally after that time, but the American slave population became predominantly American-born. From a purely physical standpoint, slaves had thrived in North America and, though constituting only 6 per cent of bondsmen brought by Europeans into the New World, the African-American population of the United States constituted about 36 per cent of all people of African descent in the Americas by 1825. Clearly, the slave population survived – and reproduced – better in North America. Whether this was due to a more benign form of slavery is doubtful, and the better survival rate should not be attributed to more intentionally benevolent masters. Rather, tobacco growing did not require the exhausting physical labour needed on Caribbean sugar plantations. The impressive reproduction of the population was also due to the more favourable sex ratio in which tobacco planters purchased, where possible, female Africans and African-Americans in higher proportions than in the Caribbean and Brazil and, sensing the benefits for their industry of an almost 'free' increase in their human capital, encouraged procreation. Family life was thus made more likely, though not necessarily more stable in the United States than in, say, Jamaica or Cuba. Families formed and

African-American society had creolized before the 1750s in the Tidewater of Virginia and Maryland, whereas slaves continued in the case of Brazil and the Caribbean in the early nineteenth century to die early from harsh labour conditions in the sugar industry and be replaced with new African infusions. The North American counter case of early nineteenth-century Louisiana's sugar parishes, where this natural-born demographic increase did not occur, reinforces the argument.[4]

The debate over African survivals within the United States, initiated through the pioneering work of Melville Herskovitz, is unlikely ever to be conclusive. Granted, in areas most exposed to imports and higher concentrations of African slaves such as colonial South Carolina and Louisiana, speech dialect, dances and music contained African rhythms and expressions. Customs such as voodoo survived in those same districts, though not to the extent in Haiti. The artefacts of slave society did contain numerous traces of African influence as well. Sea Island South Carolina basket weaving was similar to that in West Africa, while Louisiana drums and slave-built cottages strongly resembled patterns in the motherland. But the 'survivals' that can be documented do not add up to a general pattern. The African population gradually became Americanized, but the experience and mental 'map' of their place in the world was subtly different. Their culture was a fusion – an actively forged African-American experience, a fact which actually made it more, not less, transnational as it was neither 'American' nor 'African'. Moreover, the descendents of numerous African kinship groups and nations, though initially making their own distinctive contributions, had blended through the process of enslavement to produce a truly intercultural mixture.

When the American Colonization Society was formed late in 1816 to encourage planters to send freed slaves back to Africa, this effort met with suspicion among the small African-American elites in the free states of the North where slaves had been either emancipated after the American Revolution or set upon a path to final manumission. The Colonization Society project seemed tinged deeply with racism – an attempt to purge American society of a racially distinctive and potentially dangerous element by siphoning off the more articulate slaves and ex-slaves and sending them to a continent whose culture now seemed foreign. It turned out that most of them did not want to go. Most of these sent in the early days were actually free blacks, a fact that underlined crypto-racist motivations within the project. However, they could draw for inspiration and examples of the possibilities for colonization from the exploits of Afro-Indian trader and Quaker, Paul Cuffee, who had taken a small number of African-Americans to settle in Sierra Leone in 1816.[5]

The Colonization Society was able to establish a beachhead on the coast of West Africa with the settlement at Monrovia, Liberia late in 1821, and several other small settlements under de facto US tutelage were soon made in the same vicinity. This colonization idea was not unique to American slavery. The move mimicked the British abolitionist effort to establish a haven for freed slaves, begun with the shipping to the colony of Freetown (later Sierra Leone) after 1787 of free British blacks and escaped African-American slaves from the American Revolution. Some 1200 that had sided with the British cause and had been living in Nova Scotia ended up in Sierra Leone.[6]

Among African-Americans freed in the Northern states after the revolution, some began to look for new homes outside the United States as early as the 1810s, but early efforts concentrated on establishing African-American emigration to the West Indies or Central America. This interest was often centred on the independent state of Haiti, which proved an inspiration to black people. It was not until the Colonization Society's settlements became united and independent as the Republic of Liberia in 1847 that interest in Africa began to increase. The British and French governments recognized the new nation, though the United States did not, due to opposition from the Southern states. Black abolitionist Henry Highland Garnett announced 2 years later that he no longer held Liberia to be a mere plaything of the Colonization Society and predicted a bright future for the economic development of West Africa. Interest was further stimulated by news of European explorers opening up the formerly 'dark' continent and by missionaries' accounts of their work. Englishwoman Charlotte Tucker's *Abbeokuta; or, Sunrise within the Tropics: An Outline of the Origin and Progress of the Yoruba Mission* appeared in 1853, followed by white American missionary Thomas Jefferson Bowen's *Central Africa*, published in 1857. Also appearing in 1857 was David Livingstone's influential *Missionary Travels and Researches in South Africa*. Clearly black abolitionists' interest in Africa was part of a larger transatlantic intellectual discovery, centred on the proto-imperial penetration of that continent by missionaries and explorers.[7]

Several North American emigration conventions beginning with a meeting in Toronto in 1851 aimed to foster emigration, but at first these still focused concrete discussion on the western hemisphere.[8] Canada and Haiti remained the main targets. The leaders of the incipient movement made serious plans for the Caribbean, but after 1857 some began to advocate the African alternative, in response to the intellectual stimulus of the literature on West Africa appearing in the previous few years. This led to a pioneering exploratory mission to West Africa in 1859–60 by Martin Delany, a free black from Pittsburgh, joined by Robert Campbell of Philadelphia. The two duly reported the possibilities in glowing terms. Their visit aimed to dispel concerns about the unhealthy climate of Africa and to try to stimulate African economic development as part of the anti-slavery free produce campaign discussed in Chapter 3. The idea was to wean the European economies from their reliance on American cotton. Why should not Africans be able to produce cotton better and cheaper in West Africa? They would have access to cheaper land, would be closer to

European markets and could avoid the nasty potential for slave revolts or ever-possible political instability that existed between the Northern and Southern American states. Delany stressed black pride, autonomy and the need of an economic base for racial advancement. Though he had been involved earlier in the idea of a West Indian destination for ex-slaves, Delany essentially argued for a form of black nationalism centred on the revival of Africa. This was to be a recurrent theme in African-American life. This movement would be led by and for blacks rather than, as with the American Colonization Society, one based on white paternalism.[9]

Did African-Americans want to leave? Certainly the United States was not for them a hospitable place. The extension of Jacksonian democracy, as de Tocqueville observed, was of no comfort to blacks. A caste system existed in the Northern states, in which racism hardened by the 1840s. Blacks could vote without discrimination in only five (New England) states and in a sixth, New York, faced a stiff racially specific property qualification, whereas poor white voting was rarely restricted in the nation.[10] Even some schools in relatively pro-abolitionist New England and other places in the Northeast became segregated by the 1850s. African-Americans could not feel included in this democracy. Northern racism as much as the evils of slavery provided encouragement for the development of black nationalism and engendered transnational allegiances.

Only a small minority of blacks chose to work actively for emigration, however. Measurable support remained limited though difficult to estimate because opinion on the issue was fluid and responsive to changes in American and international conditions. Within the black elite of free, Northern anti-slavery reformers, opinion in the 1850s was divided. Frederick Douglass and Delany became bitter enemies, with the former regarding the issue as a distraction from the aims and possibilities of freedom within the United States.[11] Moreover, it is doubtful whether Delany's schemes were common knowledge within the larger slave community. But the failure of African-Americans to leave the country should not be read as positive endorsement of the United States or as an absence of any emotional or intellectual affinity to an African motherland.

Free emigration was a phenomenon of the entire African diaspora and reflected the complex circulation of opinion within this transnational community. In some societies such as Brazil free blacks seem to have migrated to Africa more routinely than did Americans. The fragmentary history of such migration patterns has led some to conclude that links between African and the United States were weak because the demography of the creolized US population reduced memory of and interest in Africa. Carl Degler argues that migration of Brazilian ex-slaves to Africa reflected the fact that the Brazilian slave trade existed longer and hence economic and other ties with Africa were stronger.[12] This matter needs more attention from scholars and would be a useful subject for comparative treatment. However, it is not clear what implication we should draw from this connection. The Brazilian population contained much more racial intermixture and a more substantial free black element – able to move easily and achieve the higher economic and legal status when free that allowed the possibility of long-distance migration. Opportunities for economic advance were greater for free blacks; hence the chance to engage in foreign trade may have been greater. Brazil, moreover, was closer to Africa, a fact that facilitated trade. In any case, the main point is not about how many blacks went back to Africa but whether African-Americans were part of a transatlantic diaspora in which the mental as well as the material world included both the Caribbean and Africa. American blacks' African heritage was, above all, a field of inspiration. The location of and possibilities for migration changed with circumstances in the United States and opportunities to leave. American blacks would continue to cultivate a transnational sense of 'Africanness' as a cultural mark of distinction, regardless of whether they migrated.

Practical concerns such as family ties, climate and the fear of tropical diseases stood in the way of any emigration, not ideological opposition or attachment to the United States. Delany and Campbell spent much time explaining to readers of their reports how tropical fevers could be overcome. And justly so, because blacks settling in West Africa died as easily as did white counterparts. Moreover, colonization schemes encountered well-documented local opposition. Even though it never became an official American colony, Liberia had been founded and secured only through the protection of the American navy. The indigenous continued to resist incursions. Other concerns centred on the relative powerlessness of African-Americans to make their own decisions on whether to repatriate as most remained slaves. Leaving the South, let alone the United States, was a difficult act in which only the lucky and the exceptional succeeded.

For most slaves, memory of Africa remained more important than movement to that continent – as part of family lore, customs and legends and perhaps rumours too. In this sense, Africa was always an undercurrent in America as an intellectual interest and ancestral presence. Martin Delany, though always a free black, may provide an indication. According to David W. Blight, Delany 'grew up knowing his African ancestry; one of his grandfathers was a Mandingan prince and the other a Golah village chieftain'.[13] But for slaves remaining in the South the realities of white physical surveillance and numerical superiority (slaves were in most areas around one-fifth to one-third of the total population) made flight, let alone rebellion, difficult. Day-to-day resistance was common in the shape of subverting planter authority and economic priorities, but rebellions on the scale of Brazilian or Caribbean experience were few. African-American slaves could try to escape, but few succeeded. An estimated 50,000 bondsmen are thought to have fled permanently in the period 1810–60, though many more temporarily absconded. Some personal and physical attributes made flight easier. The young, singles and males dominated the profile of those who sought to leave permanently. Even then they could be pursued north, especially after the passage of the Fugitive Slave Law in 1850. Many 'escaped' slaves did not head north but hung about their plantations seeking loved ones. The great majority of able-bodied slaves capable of absconding did not leave at all; they stayed instead on their owners' plantations. They did this not because they loved their masters, but because they loved their families. The slave family as a multigenerational, extended family was an enduring institution despite the fact that slaves could be and often were sold in ways highly disruptive of kin networks. Family bound the slaves to slavery so long as the institution remained intact.[14]

Those that escaped lost an important haven after the Americans took Spanish East Florida in 1819–21. Some escapees, however, still resided among the Seminole Indians and fought the US forces as late as the 1840s, while others escaped to Mexico, which had abolished slavery. But Canada was the major haven with at least 20,000, mostly former slaves, fleeing there to settle, many of them around the town of Chatham, Ontario. Among their number was the abolitionist Harriet Tubman, whose 1850s efforts in the 'underground railroad' shepherding other blacks to Canada and freedom attained legendary status. These refugees became sources of African emigrationist sentiment, urging the remaining free black majority to join them in rejecting the republic as the land of the unfree. Emigrationist advocate Rev. James T. Holly called on fellow African-Americans to 'swarm in a ceaseless tide' to Canada and 'hang like an ominous black cloud over this guilty nation'.[15]

Emigration draws attention to the Black Atlantic concept.[16] Leaving America was not influenced solely by internal debates, nor simply undertaken directly from the United States to Africa. A transnational circuit of contacts and influences comprised Africa, African-Americans, the Caribbean, British abolitionists and Canadians. The efforts to get back to Africa were aided especially by British anti-slavery sources. Delany raised money for his schemes from an African Aid Society that he formed in London in 1860, and his fellow traveller Campbell was originally from the British West Indies. The Back-to-Africa movement was never purely an American creation but the work of the larger diaspora. The idea of a Black Atlantic broadens our vision, but too much focus should not be put on Anglophone connections to the exclusion of the non-Anglo-Caribbean and Latin America. The persistent interest in black Haiti should not be forgotten, especially. Emigration there was based on the idea that settlement of African-Americans in the western hemisphere would provide a more aggressive challenge to North American domination of the new world and would, by proximity to the United States, encourage slave rebellion and further emigration. Certain Haitian settlements were begun, though like the ones in Liberia, only a few thousand blacks were drawn to them.[17]

The outbreak of the American Civil War in 1861 initially stimulated emigration plans. Soon the North became a magnet for escaped slaves who could potentially emigrate along with free blacks. A major effort to colonize Haiti through a Haitian Bureau of Emigration began, with white abolitionists as well as blacks taking part. The profile of Africa was simultaneously raised because with Southern opposition now removed, the US Government recognized Liberia as an independent nation. Yet when President Lincoln called on free black leaders in Washington in 1862 to establish colonies in Panama and Haiti,[18] few joined up. With the announcement of the proclamation of slave emancipation as a war measure on January 1, 1863, interest in emigration waned substantially. Delany had already returned from Britain in 1861 and after 1862 threw his efforts into the war; he eventually gained command of a black regiment. Blacks were now fighting for their freedom in America. Slaves fleeing from plantations likewise showed little interest in going to Africa after 1863, preferring to work for the defeat of the South by joining the Union Army – 186,000 African-Americans joined in all. Upon the end of the conflict in 1865, black veterans and ex-slaves increasingly argued that they should gain the rights to the land that they had worked for nothing for generations. These lands in the South were now their place. Herein lay the cry for 40 acres and a mule for every African-American family. The attitude was based on expectations for the post-slavery period. Black abolitionists, too, did not in this euphoric period of early Reconstruction focus on emigration. Delany and those like him were no longer committed to an exodus.

For all their bitterness towards the racial hierarchies of the United States, the emigrationists were not only ambivalent about leaving. When they went abroad, they carried American values with them. They were aware that they differed from Africans and Haitians. As English speakers and products of a largely creolized African-American culture in which evangelical religion was a vital source of strength, they often sought to Christianize, reform and modernize the places to which they went. This made adjustment to the new lands difficult and many migrants returned to the United States for this reason, not only from Africa but also in the case of Haiti, where Catholicism and African religious accretions such as voodoo distanced the population from black Protestants. The emigrationists were not simply ideologues searching for a new nation. They were 'in-between' figures, negotiating between cultures, both American and African-American. They were truly transnational.[19]

The return of emigrants as well as the shifting targets of their explorations raises the question whether the fluctuations in black opinion merely constituted a tactic in the struggle to obtain American rights. The black abolitionists were pragmatists and sought to maximize opportunities for their race anywhere and everywhere. When after the Civil War black freedom proved to be so circumscribed, new attempts at colonization began. In reaction against the horrors of the Ku Klux Klan and the fail-ures of Reconstruction policy, blacks in the South began to emigrate once more, but with a novel twist. The first focus of emigration was now within the United States. Called the 'exodusters', discontented ex-slaves moved as whole communities to Kansas to take up free land under the 1862 Homestead Act.[20]

Distant lands abroad and at home functioned similarly as places of exodus for an oppressed people seeking a collective earthy salvation; emig-rationists drew this imagery from the Bible and the deliverance of the people of Israel out of Egyptian slavery into the land of Canaan. Their aspirations and dreams mirrored also the slave songs in which African-Americans celebrated the biblical stories of Moses' escape – Heaven, Kansas, Africa, Haiti and Canada all could serve as points of exodus into a promised land. Though the Kansas settlement was a gruelling and disappointing experience for the colonists, this was not to be the last time that blacks sought a new homeland. The American North would in fact become, after the 1890s, the major destination of black emigrants as the South's cotton agriculture stagnated under the combined weight of bad agricultural prices, and share-cropping and tenant farming that replaced slavery, as well as the impact of the cotton boll weevil insect. But the Back-to-Africa movement with Africa as the ancestral homeland of an African-American race remained part of the cultural inheritance too. In the 1870s, 'Liberia fever' grew, particularly among the poor and dispossessed. Well-to-do blacks and those politicians dependent on black votes were more likely to stay and fight. There is little doubt that, as Nell Painter states, in parts of the Deep South 'Liberia fever and Kansas fever flourished in the same fields' with similar organizational character-istics.[21] With the defeat of Radical Reconstruction and the dashing of hopes of economic prosperity for blacks on the western frontier, interest in African grew stronger once more. In the 1890s, Bishop Henry Turner argued that a Back-to-Africa movement was the only way to solve the economic plight of poor disfranchised and landless African-Americans in the post-Reconstruction period.[22] As faith in equality's promise in America faded, African-American identity and self-improvement would be linked again in the 1920s to the search for a new homeland inspired by exodus rhetoric. Black nationalism would be reborn in the context of European imperialism.[23]

6

Racial and Ethnic Frontiers

Case one: Frances Slocum, captured by Delaware Indians in the Wyoming Valley of Pennsylvania in 1778, was adopted by an Indian family and named for their own recently dead daughter. She vanished without trace from white society. Frances' natural mother grieved the loss throughout her life and charged surviving children on her deathbed in 1807 to find their sister and bring her home. The brothers pursued her on and off, but unbeknown to them, Slocum had married into a Miami Indian tribe in 1794. After many false leads, the family made contact in 1837. But at the tearful reunion at Slocum's village in Indiana, the long-lost sister would not agree to return to white society. Despite the impending doom of the Miami in the area, she chose to stay with her people. 'They cannot live out of the forest', her mixed race daughter stated of her family.[1] To historian Charles Sellers, cases of Indian captivity where the victims chose to remain in Indian society suggested that, for some poor whites and mixed race people on the frontier, Indian society could be an attractive place because it lay outside the vicissitudes of the market economy. Certainly Indian society could fascinate whites as well as repel them.[2] Indian–white relations were at the time of the early Republic more complex than a simple binary opposition.

Case two: On November 3, 1813, at the site of a terrible massacre of a 'Red Stick' Creek village during the War of 1812, Andrew Jackson's marauding troops discovered an Indian babe lying with its dead mother. Perhaps because he had been an orphan himself but also because Jackson's relations with Indians had a strongly paternalistic streak he adopted the male child, called Lyncoya. The vicious slaughter that preceded the act was now matched by individual generosity. The child could assimilate to white society and provide a model for his people of civilization's advantages. Back to Nashville and Jackson's grand residence Lyncoya went. He had the opportunities of an education in white society and was treated like the natural son that Jackson never had.[3] Yet there can be little doubt that he was made aware of his Indianness; the Indian presence on the frontier and Jackson's military and political exploits made sure of that. Lyncoya could not adjust to Euro-American ways. He remained an unhappy in-between person, dying in 1828 of pneumonia. Perhaps he felt the two-edged nature of Jackson's paternalism.[4]

Such stories reveal major themes in American transnational history: assimilation, the rejection of assimilation and the tangled and often tragic intercultural relations between European and indigenous peoples on the North American continent. These cases concern Native-American tribes, but the frontier was also a borderland inhabited by other European peoples. In national myth and much historical writing, the frontier is seen as internal to American history. That was not the case with earlier historians such as Frederick Jackson Turner, who understood the American West as a place where international diplomacy and economic exchange occurred. Eighteenth-century studies now tend to accept that the British colonies were parts of larger empires in which zones of contact based on the fur trade and political alliances were intrinsic. Not so for our understanding of the nineteenth century. Yet the frontier remained transnational until at least the Civil War. In the first place, frontier relations involved several independent nations, notably Mexico and Britain. Further, it concerned Indian peoples who regarded themselves as independent, though the United States increasingly refused to agree. Borderlands involved political relations of diplomacy and military relations of war. For the purposes of this study, however, cultural influences across frontier boundaries are the most important. Sexual contact was an important conduit for and site of transnational activity and power relations.[5] Through practices including both sex and prohibitions on sexual relationships, Americans forged their identity. This identity incorporated but at the same time suppressed evidence of cross-cultural exchange.

Related to this theme is inter-racial mixture. Miscegenation was, according to many accounts, practiced less in the American case than that of Spain or France. Culturally tolerant attitudes among French and Spanish Catholics compared to the more exclusivist English Protestants was perhaps one factor. Another was demography. Because English Puritans tended in colonial times to migrate in families, there was no pressing sexual rationalization for consorting with Indians or African-Americans. The sex ratio in Anglo society was relatively equal. In contrast, Portuguese, French and Spanish did not send out women in equal proportion. European men found themselves in situations where they were vastly outnumbered and they succumbed to the temptations. Mestizo societies resulted and more complex, less polarized attitudes towards diverse gradations of colour developed in tandem.[6]

Most of the literature on miscegenation for the United States deals with contact between the dominant white society and African-American slaves and freedman. Indeed, the term 'miscegenation' was not coined until 1863, precisely when racial contact upon the freeing of the slaves became an issue. This is not to deny sexual/racial anxieties prior to the Civil War, but the less biologically derived term, racial 'amalgamation', applied. Studies of the demography of the plantation South suggest that black–white sexual contact may well have been exaggerated by the lurid accounts of abolitionists. The latter described that section as one vast brothel in which the power of planters was supreme and sexual availability triumphed. This hyperbole aside, the races did indeed mix and the mixture was sometimes complex. In New Orleans, the law recognized complex racial gradations of mulattos, quadroons and octoroons. This was an instance of the variable status of the free black population in the South and part of the inheritance of pre-existing legal and practical arrangements within Spanish and French culture. Blood still determined status and economic possibilities, however, and, as the sectional conflict grew, states imposed tougher restrictions on free African-Americans to separate the races more efficiently.[7] In American society generally, the one-drop theory accompanied the rise of racism and condemned the offspring of inter-racial unions to the lowly and undifferentiated status of non-white. These white–black sexual relations by the early nineteenth century were, apart from the legacies of other European colonial powers and relations between imported African slaves and Euro-Americans, not strictly transnational but intercultural. The relationship with American Indians was a different story.

Boundary lines between whites and Native Americans were certainly there. Laws against miscegenation sometimes included the indigenous. Hysteria reigned whenever Indians captured young white women and children, as the case of Frances Slocum hints. These events typically involved fear of savagery overwhelming civilization represented in the childbearing and rearing capacity of women to reproduce English stock. The Indian captivity narrative constituted an important genre of sensationalist writing blending fact and fiction and expressing these racially related horrors. Whites could simply not understand why white women would opt for 'savagery'.

For all these anxieties, the realities of Indian–white relations on the frontier had much more flexibility than with slaves. Inter-racial unions on the frontier in the late eighteenth century were hardly unknown; facilitation of trade and lack of access to white women were the two major factors inducing such sexual contact. Fur traders and trappers led lonely lives on the frontier, lives that brought them into close contact with Indian tribes. The intercultural connections of the people of the Great Lakes region in the eighteenth century were profound. The French who searched for furs in the upper Mississippi Valley cohabited and intermarried with Indians as part of trade, just as they did across Canada. The Méti people of mixed race with their own separate culture resulted from this racial contact. Thus when the United States took the Louisiana Purchase in 1803 the nation inherited a territory with some mestizo people who continued to intermarry with each other and to a lesser extent with Indians. But English-born people in the same circumstances could also join the intercultural mixture. Regarding the Great Lakes region, Patrick Jung claims, 'There is a persistent myth in history that British men did not marry as frequently with the Indians as the French Canadians [did], but this was only because their numbers were smaller. Those English and Scottish men who went into the Great Lakes region generally practiced the same marriage customs as their French-Canadian counterparts.'[8] Similarly in the Southeast there were close relations between traders, trappers and Indians. Many Cherokee were the product of such unions. Sequoyah, the inventor of the Cherokee alphabet, was one who had a white father.[9]

Such events do not suggest comparability with black–white relations. There were clear differences in the way that African-Americans and Indians were treated. Miscegenation laws regarding Indians were not strictly enforced even where they existed. Race was not a rigid category, but was, as Patrick Wolfe explains, socially constructed.[10] Even blacks and whites did mix sexually, especially through illicit unions of which Thomas Jefferson's with his slave, Sally Hemmings, is the most celebrated example.[11] Black women, however, could only be covert concubines with planters in Anglo-American society; openly consorting with or marrying them was condemned.

With Indians the situation was entirely different. In fact, a figure like Jefferson could publicly canvass the issue of blending the Indian population with whites as part of cultural assimilation of the indigenous. Indians were a product of the American environment and could hardly be viewed in the same negative light that Jefferson regarded African-Americans. Otherwise the degenerative effects of savage nature on whites might need to be conceded. Jefferson disparaged Frenchman Count Bouffon's remarks on this subject. As is well known, in his *Notes on Virginia* (1784) the future president speculated that African-Americans might well be racially inferior. In contrast, the Red Man was a figure of some respect in the same text. 'They astonish you with strokes of the most sublime oratory; such as prove their reason. But never yet could I find that a black had uttered a thought above the level of plain narration.'[12] Indians were capable of military alliances and political intrigue. They were known to be formidable foes; they were free whereas slaves had surrendered their liberty. Because they were a threat to republican stability, Indians must, however, be assimilated through breeding to the point of practical genetic extinction. This logic underlay Jeffersonian and early republican policy. The policy was ruthless to a Machiavellian intensity, but it was not conventionally racist. That would require categorizing American Indians as biologically unequal.[13] As the pre-eminent Indian fighter and architect of the harsh Indian policy of the 1830s, Andrew Jackson himself could show callous disregard of Indians and yet humanitarian affection for them so long as they thoroughly mimicked the white population. The case of Lyncoya demonstrated this fact.

Assimilation was not the opposite of removal and extermination, but a tactic aimed at achieving the same result of a homogeneous civilization based on small farms and possessive individualism. Apart from his more vigorous advocacy and his partisan siding with the states, Jackson's initiatives seem remarkably congruent with Jeffersonian policy. But the power relations behind the rhetoric had changed since the eighteenth century. This change led gradually to a reconstruction of racial identities to ones in which whites and Indians were separate. Euro-American interest in intermarriage was connected to the fur trade and as that declined in the early nineteenth century so too did intermixture. Attempts at regulating interracial marriages in the interests of white society broadly corresponded with politico-economic change. Territorial expansion took two stages: first, a trading economy of the seventeenth and eighteenth centuries in which intermixture was tolerated, and in some cases encouraged, and second an agricultural economy of the nineteenth century in which white domination and exclusion was the aim. Assimilationist policies came to the fore as a way of ensuring access to land, but complemented by the idea of removing Indians entirely if they did not adopt white ways. Says Patrick Wolfe with great analytical clarity: 'a shift of this magnitude – that is, from a trade-centered to a land-centered form of colonialism – would involve a shift in miscegenation discourse. Thus it is significant that, on the advent of settler colonization proper, miscegenation no longer underwrites the cross-cultural political alliances.'[14] The result was a hardening of racialist attitudes.

Indians responded to the growing white presence in varying ways. One strategy was resistance. Creeks, Shawnee and many others had fought against the Americans since colonial times, but Indians increasingly developed syncretic religious strategies to survive. The Shawnee prophet Tecumseh's revitalization movement in the Northwest from 1809 to 1813 blended white religious and Indian traditional beliefs under the control of the Indian shaman. The movement split the Creeks between those favouring peaceful coexistence and warriors know as Red Sticks who resisted assimilation, fought Indian collaborators and attacked whites. Defeat came for both Creek and Shawnee in the War of 1812, though sporadic revolts among other Indian groups continued down to the Black Hawk War of 1832. The ceding of vast tracts of land followed each time an Indian tribe resisted and the pattern gradually convinced other Midwestern tribes of the necessity for submission. With the removal of the British influence, the ability to fight when allied to a European power no longer existed.

Despite wars and losses of territory through treaties, whites and Indians continued in the Southeastern states to live in close proximity until the 1820s when the pressure grew for new land suitable for cotton production using upland cotton seed. Assimilation was no longer acceptable, except where Indians became effectively 'white' in property terms. That spurred a policy of removing Indians from their remaining Southeastern lands and exchanging these for space in the Indian Territory west of the Mississippi, though the local Indians there were not consulted and the lands available vastly different.[15]

The case of the Cherokee is most famous, though similar outcomes were achieved for other Southern tribes that adapted to western expansion, such as the Choctaw. In some ways the Cherokee were models of assimilation. Embracing Christianity and its accoutrements of Western civilization, they shifted from mixed farming on the long rotation system and hunting and gathering to settled European-styles of agriculture. Producing cotton after 1800, they even began trading in and using black slaves, something that might have marked them as part of the putative 'civilization' of the white South. They also built schools with the help of Protestant missionaries and established a written alphabet and newspaper. But tribal leaders saw adaptation to Western ways as part of a process of national revitalization, not capitulation. In 1808 they had established a Cherokee National Council and in 1827 a written constitution. This growing cultural confidence conflicted with the desires of Georgia farmers to exploit Indian lands. The conflict worsened in the late 1820s when gold was discovered within the Cherokee territory and gold-seekers poured into the area.

At precisely this point, the economic demand for land intersected with a political and jurisdictional theme crossing 'national' boundaries. That was the legal character of the relations between Indian tribes and whites, which were irreducibly transnational from the Native-American viewpoint. The tribes regarded themselves as nations, a practice partly reflected and encouraged in the treaty making provision, as Indians could not under the constitution cede lands except through treaties and were 'the objects of foreign policy'.[16] Even within the boundaries of the United States as recognized by European powers, some tribes claimed national status. This created an anomalous legal situation. As early as the 1820s Chief Justice John Marshall spoke of Indians as 'subjects' and 'conquered inhabitants', and he also reflected the ambivalence of assimilationist rhetoric and policy by stating that Indians could be 'safely governed as a distinct people'.[17] The US Supreme Court in the case of Cherokee Nation v. the State of Georgia (1831) rejected the contention that the Cherokees were completely independent. As Marshall put it in his judgement, 'They may, more correctly be denominated domestic-dependent nations. They occupy a territory to which we assert a title independent of their will, which must take effect in point of possession when their right of possession ceases. Meanwhile, they are in a state of pupillage. Their relation to the United States resembles that of a ward to his guardian.'

The political position of the Cherokee, as of other so-called 'civilized' tribes of the South, might seem akin to that of the Baltic states in the era of the Soviet Union, in that they were small, fledging or would-be 'nation-states' incorporated within a vast territorial empire. But the United

States did not allow the concept of multiethnic empire to survive, let alone prosper. Rather, the power of the state was nakedly employed to remove the challenge that the Cherokee posed to the states of the South and hence to the federal union. As President from 1829, Jackson sided with Georgia in its land grab and forced tribes to yield to his will. Though in Worcester v. Georgia (1832) the Supreme Court struck down a Georgia law preventing pro-Indian Christian missionaries from entering Indian land, Jackson refused to enforce the ruling. Instead he pressed ahead with the coercive Treaty of New Echota, which provided for removal (1835). Because tribal leaders split over whether to sign, the forced expulsion of recalcitrant Cherokees then took place to land west of the Mississippi. The ceded land would be divided up for sale. Acquisition of this valuable land underwrote removals and removal then increased the social and racial distance between whites and Indians.

The growing separation between these peoples was not limited to frontier settlers with functional economic reasons for wanting removal. The trend could also be seen in areas well away from the colonization process. The issue surfaced in the case of Protestant missionaries sent to the Cherokee by the American Board of Commissioners for Foreign Missions. These showered Christian love upon the Indians and defended them against the states and violent white elements. It was one of these missionaries, the Rev. Samuel Worcester, who challenged the operation of Georgia's laws in the Cherokee country on behalf of the Indians. Ministering to these people was God's will, but benevolence turned to consternation when Cherokee men looked towards white Christian women among the missionary families for brides. In 1824 a young Cherokee student Elias Boudinot (Buck Watie) studied at the foreign mission school in Cornwall, Connecticut, and fell in love with a white woman, Harriet Gold, to whom he proposed. The would-be couple faced the full fury of a hardening racial sentiment. Gold's family and the wider community tried, though without success, to stop the wedding. Figures of the bridal couple were burnt in effigy. As a result, the mission school was closed. Sympathetic to the spiritual, political and economic plight of Indians though they might be, the missionaries and their supporters in New England revealed the trend of racial sentiments in white society. The Connecticut community denounced such marriages as a way of making white women the 'squaws' of 'tawny' Indians.[18] In the West, too, one author argues, the many 'Anglo-Americans from the eastern seaboard' who 'spilled into the Great Lakes region during the 1830s and 1840s ... held very negative ideas toward racial miscegenation and mixed marriages. The Méti were increasingly labelled either "white" if they had only a little Indian blood' or typecast as 'Indian' where 'they had a large amount of it. Not surprisingly, many Méti joined their kin among the Indians rather than assimilating into Anglo-American society.'[19]

These practices had not yet hardened into scientifically precise racial sentiments, but rather were still based on the dichotomy of Indian savagery versus white civilization. By the mid-nineteenth century racial attitudes congealed decisively in the case of blacks and this later rubbed off on Indian–white relations, especially after the emergence of the doctrine that weaker races were unable to cope in the struggle for the survival of the fittest. Marshall had treated Indians as dependent nations in the 1830s, but American law through the Supreme Court ended treaty negotiations after 1870 and discarded the domestic-dependent nations terminology entirely. Indian–white relations could no longer be regarded even remotely as transnational. From this time on, the federal government could frankly treat Native Americans as wards of the nation and policies focused on moving the remaining 'wild' Indians onto reservations. Intellectual changes and popular culture reinforced the shift. By the 1880s, most white Americans regarded the indigenous as the 'vanishing Red Man', a theme reinforced by Social Darwinism, and Indians could be treated humorously in sideshows and circuses rather than feared, as shown in Buffalo Bill's Wild West Show. In response to the pressures on Indian society after the Civil War, well-meaning reformers sought with renewed intensity to domesticate the remaining Indians through the Mohonk Conference, which advocated abandonment of tribal property as the key to civilization and prosperity. The General Allotment Act (the Dawes Severalty Act) was the result in 1887, with each Indian head of household entitled to 160 acres. From the sale of land surplus to the agricultural requirements of the remnant (formerly hunter-gatherer) tribes, the Native Americans of the West lost roughly two-thirds of their remaining ancestral territory.[20]

The racial mix on the frontier was further complicated by the United States' westward collision with Mexico. In the 1820s, American cotton farmers and their slaves poured into Mexican Texas. Though drawn there by land grants from the Mexican government, they soon became dissatisfied with the attempts of the central government to enforce its policies – including torturous Mexican attempts to stop the imports of slaves into their supposedly free-labour nation. The revolt against the Mexican government that led to the formation of the Lone Star Republic in 1836 proved a short-lived phase. Pro-slavery forces within the United States allied with interests in Texas to produce a political drive for annexation – consummated in 1845. Meanwhile the Democratic Party under Jackson's protégé James K. Polk won the 1844 Presidential election on a platform of continental expansion underpinned by ideas of Manifest Destiny.[21]

The precise term 'Manifest Destiny' was first enunciated in 1845, though before that date the theme namelessly and shamelessly underwrote much of American expansion. It invoked the providential right of the United States to push westward to the Pacific, to take possession of the North American continent. In explaining this process, American historians have often concentrated on the internal debates over slavery and assumed the primacy of the dynamic outward thrust of frontier expansion and territorial aggrandizement. These were indeed important factors. The hardline Polk Administration, whether by war or diplomacy, had northern Mexico's annexation firmly in its sights. Yet multilateral and reciprocal contexts should not be forgotten. When Texas was admitted as a state, the United States inherited the dispute over the boundary with Mexico that brought on the Mexican War of 1846–48. In this way, the war was a legacy of instability created by expatriate American slaveholders on the nation's borderlands. International intrigue added to the complexity. When Texas achieved its independence, Britain had given loans to the fledgling republic, much to the irritation and suspicion of Washington. Potential 'European encroachment' made 'manifest the destiny of continental domination'.[22] The process was reminiscent in some degree to that of later European expansion in Africa,[23] where activities of traders and missionaries created local interests and sources of contention that eventually drew imperial powers in. Lest some advantage be lost, rival empires contended in a vicious circle. European 'inclination to interfere' in the Lone Star State was, some authorities have argued, 'caused chiefly by fear of the growing economic and political ambition of the United States'.[24] As in Africa, the rivalries of indigenous peoples also created opportunities. The political domination of a broad region of the Southwest by Comanche tribes, practising an economy based on raiding and trading backed by the adaptation of European horse technology, weakened Mexican authority and depleted local Hispanic settlement. It is possible that Comanche activity created a power vacuum into which the Americans could step, when allied with the occurrence of drought and the consequent retreat of the Comanche presence.[25]

Though a good many politicians and newspaper editors urged the Polk administration to swallow the whole of Mexico at the end of the Mexican War in 1848, wiser heads prevailed. A more expansive approach would surely have produced cultural indigestion as well as even more intense dissension over the implications for the future of slavery. In the Treaty of Guadalupe Hidalgo, only the more sparsely settled portion of Mexico changed hands. While the treaty gave the United States control of the prize of California and its gold, the carve-up also meant that the non-Anglo population remained fairly insignificant in the portions that the United States gained. Demographic domination rather than multicultural toleration was the aim, in line with the policy that Jefferson had advocated earlier for the Louisiana Purchase. Still, the reality on the ground was persistence of multicultural identities in these borderland regions, and indeed everywhere in the American west an untidy ethnic mixture existed. The acquisition of California brought to the Union a state with one of the highest foreign-born populations in 1850 (23 per cent), a product of both Hispanic influence and the influx of foreigners attracted by the gold rushes. Many different nationalities could be found on the cattle ranches and wheat farms of California in the 1860s, and Californians and other Southwestern states remained greatly influenced by the Hispanic heritage. This was especially true of the counties along the Rio Grande River in New Mexico, where some 150,000 Mexican Catholics lived. Many learned to cooperate by necessity with the new regime, but these Hispanics did not assimilate, nor were they encouraged to do so.

As a way of justifying invasion and retention of the territories, Americans treated Mexicans as an ethnically different and inferior 'other'. They were regarded as lazy, 'sordid and treacherous'. Historian Thomas Hietala shows that Americans disparaged Mexicans as barbaric people that would have to be removed from the path of civilization, just as was necessary for 'savage' Indians. Illinois Congressman Orlando Ficklin spoke of 'a corrupt priesthood, with an affiliated moneyed aristocracy' that had 'waged unceasing war upon the liberties of the [local] people'. But the people themselves were, in American estimates, 'barbarous and cruel'.[26] The United States followed here a de facto policy of *lebensraum*, based on the eventual influx of Anglo-settlers to dominate the area ethnically. Not that this demographic solution took effect quickly. The territories of New Mexico and Arizona remained unassimilated and as long as they were, the United States was reluctant to admit them as states. In fact, these territories were quasi-colonies distrusted because of their Hispanic, Mestizo and Catholic heritage for more than a generation and did not become states until 1912. Only then could the frontier be said to be over. Or could it? The cultural mixing continued, with Hispanic immigration beginning to mount at precisely the same time. The Mexican heritage survived.

7

America's Civil War and Its World Historical Implications

The place of the Civil War within American culture is secure and that place is reflected in the name and the stature of the event in American memory. The very term 'Civil War' suggests an internal conflict, whereas the preferred Southern appellations, the War Between the States or the War for Southern Independence, connote a struggle between two would-be nations. This particular Civil War itself betrays, as a concept, a slight hint of insularity in another way, as it is not in normal discussion preceded by the word 'American'. In American debates, the absent word is taken for granted, whereas the English or Russian civil wars require geographic clarification. The volume of scholarship compounds the problem. Other dirty and bloody civil wars litter the pages of history, but we know so much more about this one fratricidal conflict. This insularity reflects the war's huge dimensions. Six hundred and twenty thousand dead is an impressive number in so far as it dwarfed in its rate of casualties per capita all other American wars, thus supplying a simple but accurate explanation of its importance in American memory. Brother against brother, neighbour against neighbour, so the maudlin legend goes. The awful tragedy cannot be denied. The rate of casualties was, however, not unique. It was no greater than that suffered by armies in the First World War and deaths paled beside the contemporaneous Chinese Taiping Rebellion (1851–64) where some 20 million may have perished.[1]

Not only have Americans wrongly treated the war as unique. Foreigners did likewise at the time. Some Europeans regarded the conflict as an example of the follies of American democracy.[2] Yet the war expressed cross-Atlantic and other transnational connections. External events did not 'cause' the war, but the pressures produced by rapid industrialization in the North Atlantic world contributed greatly through competition for resources to fulfil the demands of that economy. The character of transnational westward expansion was at the heart of the conflict, not the moral evils of slavery. The Mexican War and the territories that the United States took in 1848 exacerbated sectional tensions. Was the new frontier to be dominated by slaves and cotton planters or free farmers? Once the highly unstable concoction that was America's westward rush unravelled, other transnational pressures came into focus. The South's revolt depended on the importance of its raw materials for European manufacturing and on the assumption that Britain would either remain neutral or recognize the confederacy as a new nation. 'Tellingly, Liverpool, the world's largest cotton port, was the most pro-Confederate place in the world outside the Confederacy itself.' In France, too, cotton merchants and manufacturers 'pleaded with Napoleon' to recognize the rebels.[3] The possibility of British and French aid for the South, either politically or militarily, made diplomacy vital for the administration of President Abraham Lincoln. Transatlantic friction was considerable early in the conflict, with British neutrality severely compromised by the Trent Affair (1861) in which the Union Navy took Confederate agents from a British ship, though later released them as Lincoln backed down from a confrontation.[4] Diplomacy had to be supplemented by the private United States Sanitary Commission's work, which established branches in Britain and France to emphasize the Union's superior moral conduct, including on the treatment of prisoners.[5]

Despite such campaigns, sympathy for the confederacy abroad was not limited to cotton manufacturers. In the British dependencies in Canada fears grew of an American invasion in response to United States disputes with Britain over neutrality. Despite the fact that Canada had harboured abolitionists, opinion on the war was greatly divided, partly because Canadians could not see until the emancipation proclamation of 1863 a clear moral purpose for the Union resisting the secession.[6] This position roughly paralleled that of many in Britain itself.[7] For the British, clandestine building of ships for the Confederates to use as raiders was a violation of neutrality, which cost them dearly in damages negotiated after the Civil War in the Alabama Claims legal action, but support for Confederate raiders illustrates that a certain admiration for the South existed. The Alabama's exploits in the Atlantic gave the name to the post-war damages case, but the war touched people on the other side of the globe too. When the Confederate raider, Shenandoah – purchased in Glasgow and refitted on the high seas as a warship – sailed around the world, it entered the port of Melbourne, Australia on January 25, 1865, to be lionized by the colonial establishment. Young Melbourne women dined and danced with the sailors in their steel grey uniforms. The Shenandoah was reprovisioned and repaired by colonials and its captain recruited several dozen extra crewmen from American residents and other would-be adventurers. The vessel went on to sink more than a score of defenceless Yankee whalers in the North Pacific before discovering in August 1865 that the war had been over since April.[8]

From a military viewpoint, the Civil War presaged much that would come to be identified as 'total war' in the European conflict of 1914–18. Waging war against an entire civilian population, as William T. Sherman did in his scorched-earth march through Georgia, qualifies as part of this genre.[9] The technology of an industrial age was also employed for the first time; the firearms factories that pioneered the American System churned out rifles for the Union Army. Generally the North was at an enormous advantage in provisions such as boots for soldiers and in the production of weapons. The telegraph aided rapid communications while railroads moved supplies, artillery and men. Though not important in the military scheme of things at the time, ironclad ships and the first submarines in service gave a glimpse of the future of sea warfare. Even aerial reconnaissance in the form of balloons appeared. New developments in weaponry, especially grooved-bore rifles, made for deadly and accurate firepower over 500 metres compared to 100 for the old-fashioned muskets.

But many of these supposed technological innovations were not entirely new. Europeans had invented the grooved-bore rifle and, moreover, the so-called first modern war had aspects of a more traditional kind, drawn from European military knowledge. Not only did the superficial trappings of Europe's military styles such as uniforms display the derivativeness of the American military of the period but also the tactics in the early part of the war were taken from French military handbooks of Antoine Henri Jomini. They reflected Napoleonic war experience, including the marching of men directly towards the enemy in mass formation, to maximize the power of old-fashioned weaponry by each line firing and then falling back. Faced with appalling carnage, the military altered tactics and trench warfare was one result. Even this was not quite new; the Crimean War had already seen use of trenches. Yet Earl J. Hess correctly calls the Battle of Cold Harbor (1864) 'an ominous precursor of World War I, with massed frontal attacks against determined men armed with modern weapons and protected by a sophisticated system of trenches'.[10]

The military lessons of the Civil War about firepower and casualties were quickly lost upon most European military strategists, however. Those, like some British elitist observers, that did understand the implications were 'appalled by the destructiveness of this struggle'. Convinced that the devastating conduct of the war resulted from 'the limitations of a volunteer army produced by a democratic society', especially 'lack of leadership and discipline', they wished to avoid both democracy and its military implications.[11] Yet the swift Prussian victory over France in 1870–71 obscured the significance of trench warfare, military stalemate and mobilization of industry and civilian populations. Instead, the Franco-Prussian War became the benchmark. Even American strategists – there were several in Europe at the time – were impressed by the speed and efficiency of the Prussian offensive. General Philip Sheridan witnessed the war from the safety of Prussian General Headquarters, though national pride and awareness of the different geographical and strategic conditions prevailing in the United States prevented wholesale adoption of Prussian military reforms.[12]

Far more significant in the longer term than the military side of the conflict was the remaking of the United States. The idea of American nationalism consolidated around the Union as an indivisible nation. The balance of power within the constitution shifted towards the federal government as a result of the South's defeat. This shift paralleled the centralization of power elsewhere in the modernizing world. The period from the 1850s to the 1870s was one of national consolidation not only in the United States, but in Europe and Japan as well. The creation of Italy and the German Empire were both complete by 1870, as was the Meiji Revolution rejuvenating and modernizing that ancient kingdom. Canada achieved its federation and dominion status in 1867, partly as a response to the Civil War, with diplomatic tensions between the United States and the British North American provinces displaying just how vulnerable those possessions would be to annexationist pressure. In Europe, as in the United States, war was a direct agent of political concentration of power. The creation of the modern American industrial nation through war bears more than a passing resemblance to the transition to nationhood in Europe – Lincoln and Otto von Bismarck could each be seen as men who united a nation through blood and iron.[13]

Lincoln's politics of moderate, liberal nationalism and his enunciation of a 'new birth of freedom' in the Gettysburg Address were, however, far removed from the objectives of the conservative Prussian and his authoritarian brand of nationalism. As late as the First World War's beginning, the German Empire lacked a representative let alone a truly democratic form of government. Moreover, the growth of the American nation-state remained remarkably circumscribed. Federalism and Southern resistance to the imposition of Yankee ways during and after Reconstruction were paramount influences. The 'spring of government' was weak.[14] Because laissez-faire prevailed there could be no truly strong central authority. This was made clear in Reconstruction policy. The vast investment of federal resources needed to strengthen the position of the ex-slaves in the South and provide them with land did not transpire. Instead, their advancement was limited to civil and political rights as befitting of a liberal revolution. Even that achievement was rolled back after the mid-1870s as the military occupation of the South ceased and 'Redeemer' governments devoted to white supremacy took charge in the Southern states. While national political unity had been obtained and the potential for an interventionist federal government laid out through the Fourteenth Amendment to the Constitution, the persistence of localism and the contested meanings of the war highlight the weaker state in the comparative perspective of Germany.

Equally important alongside the military outcomes were the immediate economic implications of the war. These lay in the disruption of the cotton trade and its effects on the British and world economy. While cotton merchants had lobbied for pro-Southern policies, they also extended the efforts of abolitionists from before the Civil War to find alternative sources of supply. As a result of the war, cotton growing was promoted in Egypt, West Africa, Brazil and India. While in some places demand slipped after the Civil War as the South reasserted its position, the nature of cotton production had been transformed everywhere, with more diverse sources of world supply and transnational indentured labour replacing reliance on slavery. As Sven Beckert states, by 1883, cotton from Egypt, India and Brazil 'had captured a full 31 per cent of the continental European market or a little more than twice as much as in 1860'.[15] The change in the global economics of cotton production weakened the position of planters internally in the United States and reduced their leverage in the complicated post-bellum quest for political concessions from the North. King Cotton and the South would never again be interchangeable ideas. Cotton's changing geography in turn powered global transformations. In British India more land had to be devoted to irrigation and export crop activity rather than food production, while cotton growing in Turkestan consolidated Russian imperialist ambitions in Central Asia.

The war also disrupted the financial networks described in Chapter 2. Whereas the Mexican War had been financed by a British loan, the US Treasury could not obtain adequate foreign funding from 1861 to 1865. European financiers found the proposition too risky, given the Union's precarious position. The federal government was forced to rely instead on internal resources, which in turn meant higher taxation and the printing of the paper dollars known as greenbacks. Inflation soared, but the growing national debt was 90 per cent held by Americans. The long-term results were to strengthen US finances internationally. United States investment houses took over the brokerage of loans, including foreign loans and symbolically the New York Stock Exchange gained in 1863 a new home in Wall Street. Whilst the US Treasury refinanced much of its debt through cheap British loans from 1871 to 1873, the ground was laid for later US financial pre-eminence in the Atlantic economy.[16]

Direct political impacts abroad were fewer. During the war the international position of the United States was weakened considerably, just as it would have been permanently had the South succeeded. The need to focus on the fight with the secessionists meant that the Union could not resist the French intrusion by Napoleon III, who installed a member of the Hapsburgs as Emperor Maximilian of Mexico in 1864. The Monroe Doctrine seemed under threat. Secretary of State Seward wanted American intervention, but Lincoln ruled that the Union already had enough on its plate. Once the war had finished, Napoleon's project was exposed for the ludicrous vainglory that it contained. He was forced to abandon the hapless Emperor to execution at the hands of angry Mexicans in 1867.

The war's outcome effectively ended French ambitions in the western hemisphere, but not before it had encouraged this one last burst of activity.

The Civil War might have become a turning point in the projection of American power internationally, given the size of the Union Army in 1865 and the accumulation of economic resources to back it up. Yet the army had been mobilized for one thing only and, with the South defeated, most soldiers were quickly sent home tired of war. What army remained had to focus on either policing the Indian frontier or occupying a white South that did not accept the idea of equal status for African-Americans. There was little interest in projecting American power internationally immediately after 1865 because the internal political divisions were too great to expect agreement. But the advocates of expansion persisted. Seward's acquisition of Alaska in 1867 was part of a continentalist strategy enunciated by him in the 1850s, in which Canada would be caught, he hoped, in a pincer movement and tumble into American hands.[17] Dreamy annexationists such as Senator Zachariah Chandler wanted Britain to cede Canada in return for settlement of the Alabama Claims, while Seward and President Grant advocated a takeover of Santo Domingo to secure the approaches to any attempted isthmian canal in the Panama area. None of these schemes came to anything. The Alabama Claims were settled in more conventional fashion, while the internal problems of the Johnson and Grant administrations, congressional–presidential rivalries and Canadian opposition to annexation scotched the more outlandish hopes for new territories.

Political and social reconstruction in the South (1865–77) was, in itself, among the more insular of historical periods. Historians see American Reconstruction as *sui generis*. Nowhere else in which slavery was abolished did the forces of abolition attempt to undermine the political and economic power of the former planters with such a degree of success. Peter Kolchin notes that 'Reconstruction was not only without precedent in the United States; it was also without true parallel abroad'. Elsewhere former owners and their allies determined the political fate of the ex-slaves; in the US blacks were 'the beneficiaries of an unusual political configuration in which their cause was identified with that of the Union'.[18] Though abolitionists drew lessons from comparable post-emancipation societies, Eric Foner argues that labour shortages enabled African-Americans to negotiate a more favourable outcome compared to the West Indies where the colonial rulers could import indentured labour. Ex-slaves had less bargaining power in the West Indies and existed as a peasant farming population. American experience underscored, Foner states, 'the uniqueness of Reconstruction in the history of postemancipation societies'.[19] Steven Hahn has argued that in the South there did not emerge a parallel to the conservative 'marriage of iron and rye' linking the economic power of the Prussian-landed elite and the Rhineland industrialists.[20] Reconstruction essentially dealt the planters out of the American nation's key power bloc.

At the grassroots level, freedmen cared not one whit about international events in the immediate aftermath of the Civil War. Would they get their demands for 40 acres and a mule – the land and the means to farm? Would they get voting and civil rights? Would they be able to live free from the fear of white intimidation? From the North's point of view, punishing the South was a key issue too. As a result of the inept policies of President Andrew Johnson, who favoured leniency in dealing with the South, the Republican-dominated Congress took control over Reconstruction and its imposition of military rule in the defeated Confederacy allowed Congress to force radical Reconstruction governments on the South for a short period after 1867. Black people themselves sought advancement within the Union under this aegis; emigration sentiment that had been building pre-war did not immediately revive. Ex-slaves mostly preferred to be thought of as Americans. Leon Litwack avers that blacks contrasted the advantages they held with those of their 'less fortunate brethren in Latin America and the Caribbean'. African-Americans thought these Latino ex-slaves to be less developed because they lacked traditions of republican government and the tutelage of white civilization.[21]

Even imperfect revolutions in American life are, however, bound to produce consequences spilling into the international arena. So too with Reconstruction. One transnational influence was the emigration of the defeated. The Civil War stimulated an outflow of frightened Confederates fleeing the Union in disgust at the end of slavery. Judah Benjamin, the Confederate high official, moved to England while others went as far afield as Japan. More commonly slaveholders tried to re-establish their plantation way of life in Latin America. Confederate Admiral Matthew Maury – someone with long-held interests in Latin America – helped attract 2000 ex-Confederates to Mexico with the promise that they could import 'laborers' if they were (nominally) paid. Yet far from all Southerners even contemplated deserting the nation. Prominent Confederate leader Robert E. Lee rejected Maury's entreaties to join the Mexican enterprise.[22] Despite the attempt to establish a new form of peonage south of the border, the settlements collapsed after the restoration of the Mexican Republic and the downfall of Emperor Maximilian, and most émigrés returned.[23] Indeed, Daniel Sutherland estimates that 80 per cent came back from all countries by 1868.[24] However, some remained. Confederates in Brazil founded settlements such as Vila Americana where their descendents still celebrated their Southern heritage a century later and had a Confederate symbol on the town flag.[25]

Existing studies underestimate such transnational linkages because they are *comparative* in approach. They do not look at the influence of one national emancipation experience on another. As the largest single slave emancipation in world history, the outcome of the US conflict was bound to influence the fate of the surviving slave regimes in Brazil and Cuba. Though emancipation was not completed in Cuba until 1886 and Brazil in 1888, the process was well underway in the 1860s, with the last known slave imports to Cuba arriving in 1866.[26] A song reportedly sung in the sugar plantation fields of early 1860s Cuba went

Avanza, Lincoln, avanza
Tu eres nuestra esperanza
(Advance, Lincoln, Advance,
You are Our Hope.)[27]

The American example weakened Cuban slavery but, ironically, American citizens continued in the 1870s to hold slave property on the island, a practice forbidden in the United States after 1865, and Congress failed to prevent this hypocrisy though President Grant pleaded for such a prohibitory law. It took the efforts of the Cubans themselves and Spanish abolitionist sentiment to accomplish the final liberation in several stages.

The end of slavery coincided with various emancipationist schemes as the world moved slowly and unevenly from different forms of unfree to free labour. Karl Marx and the emerging socialist movement took note of the 'coeval' nature of the American slave and Russian serf emancipations, the stirrings of working-class protest in Europe and Asian upheavals such as the Indian mutiny of 1857. These could be interpreted as signs of the restiveness of the subaltern classes, Christopher Bayly notes. But Marx ultimately assigned 'Oriental' and European protests to separate boxes.[28] If the connection here was tenuous, it was stronger in the case of the European emancipation of the working class. John Bright and liberal Prime Minister William E. Gladstone set the American struggle in the wider context provided by the Civil War. They 'drew an analogy between American slave emancipation and the enfranchisement of smallholders and working people in Britain' in the reform bills of 1867 and 1884.[29] The emancipation of the serfs in Russia in 1861 also roughly coincided with the agitation to remove slavery. To be sure, the freedom granted to Russian serfs did not include political rights, but neither did the American ex-slaves truly retain such rights beyond Reconstruction's aftermath. Those who wish to validate in the evidence of the Civil War the ideas of American exceptionalism point to the unique outcome of that war – a new birth of freedom, an end to slavery and racial inequality. So finely articulated by Lincoln in his Gettysburg Address, these sentiments remained a noble ideal rather than a fully fleshed out reality.

The transnational dimensions of Reconstruction are even clearer when put into a longer-term framework. Though African-Americans gained their freedom, the fact remains that many civil rights were subsequently taken away in the 1880s and 1890s. In the Plessy v. Ferguson decision of 1896, the Supreme Court declared state segregation legal, provided the test of separate but equal facilities had been met. The case applied to Louisiana railroads, but the principle dominated American civil rights law until the

1950s. Simultaneously, conservative lily-white state governments removed through literacy tests and other subterfuges the right of African-Americans to vote. Compare black voting in Louisiana in 1896 with that in 1904. As many as 130,000 remained eligible before draconian literacy and poll tax laws were applied. Eight years later, only 1342 registered to vote – a decline to less than 1/100th of the former level.[30]

This legal attack upon civil rights occurred in the international context of Social Darwinism and the rise of Europe's formal colonialism in Africa that accelerated in the 1880s. Reconstruction itself had officially ended in 1877. Historians have hardly noted the fact – let alone explored – the implication that literacy tests were being introduced simultaneously in places such as Natal in South Africa (1897) to control non-white immigration from elsewhere in the British Empire.[31] Recall too that Congress pandered to the prejudices of Californians on Oriental customs and behaviour by the exclusion of Chinese labouring-class immigrants in 1882, just 1 year before the Civil Rights cases in which the court opinion written by a Northerner, not a Southerner, ruled that the private racist behaviour of the people could not be counteracted by the courts.[32] The civil rights cases of 1883 not only coincided with anti-Chinese immigration action, but also paralleled efforts to block Asian immigration in other settlement societies in the same period.[33] The precondition of the counter-revolution against Reconstruction was the simultaneous efforts of whites to control non-white people in the European empires. Whites feared the demographic threat that non-white races posed. The decline in the Euro-American birth rate might lead to racial suicide. Future President Theodore Roosevelt was concerned about this in the 1890s and he was influenced in thinking about the strategic position of the white races by the work of the Anglo-Australian racialist and Social Darwinist Charles H. Pearson.[34] Domination of the non-white races of Africa allowed whites in both the American North and the South to conclude that racial oppression via literacy tests was part of the natural order of things. Oppressing American blacks was a justifiable form of internal colonialism in this view, as part of a global effort by the Anglo-Saxon race to keep political control of the world. After 1898, the acquisition of American colonies made it impossible for those imperialist Northern politicians within the Republican Party, who might have had reservations about the abandonment of African-American rights, to criticize Southern disfranchisement.[35]

To exercise this power at home and in the wider world, the United States needed not just national unity, which had been confirmed at terrible cost in the war, but a stronger state apparatus. The Civil War did not achieve this result. The state remained a compromise, a balance of forces with lingering internal divisions and enhanced regional identities. How a strong state developed is the subject of Chapter 9. This nation-state evolution can only become clear by treating the whole of the nineteenth and early twentieth centuries together; we must step back in time and put the United States in still wider historical perspective, but we must move forward as well as back. The struggle to create a strong state would not be completed until the First World War. International imperatives of war, security and military conflict abroad succeeded where the Civil War had failed.

8

How Culture Travelled: Going Abroad, c. 1865–1914

The decade after the Civil War witnessed simultaneous and yet contradictory trends. Freed from the pressures of the possible break-up of the Union and European meddling in Mexico, the United States could complete the removal of the Indians and settle the west. Attention turned towards internal development, with the United States developing a large domestic market by the late nineteenth century and investment in railroads vastly exceeding that in sea transport. The broad lines of the nation's geographical expanse had already been marked out. With the exception of Alaska in 1867, no further additions to American territory were made until 1898. Meanwhile, territory after territory acquired in 1803 and 1848 won admission to the union. Yet at the same time, the 1860s to 1880s saw a pattern of increased contacts abroad in business, tourism, reform and cultural life. Despite the conventional picture of the era as one of continentalism, these were not decades in which the transnational context and connections of the United States were neglected. Rather, Americans prepared the pattern for the more visible global expansionism of the 1890s and beyond.

One way or another, these developments revolved around cultural outreach. Conventionally one thinks of the twentieth century as the era in which American popular culture became ubiquitous across the globe, but the processes were far from new. Well underway in the pre-Civil War decades, the transnational impact of American culture grew after 1865, with reciprocity remaining an important feature. Foreigners invited Americans to export their culture as much as Americans imposed their ideas upon others; and Americans were only able to display their cultural wares on the world stage because they could take advantage of the consolidation of European empires and the economic impact of Western civilization on non-Western peoples. Especially important was the British diaspora. Building upon antebellum dreams of limitless growth and utilizing contacts and infrastructure within the British Empire, American cultural transmission occurred on a global, not just a transatlantic basis.

A large segment of this expansion revolved around experiences of travel. In the late twentieth century, television and film conveyed American culture to the world. In the nineteenth century the physical presence of Americans was more vitally important. American culture was closely tied to the mobility of Americans throughout the world. Travel was undertaken by a variety of groups and Americans abroad engaged in many different activities, but all were involved in 'the journey' itself and frequently they commented on their overseas experiences. Travel and tourism must be the point of departure, as it were, for this chapter. Not only is travel directly important as a manifestation of how Americans culturally penetrated other places. Travellers also wrote letters and published travel books that defined for Americans their own sense of identity. From travellers came the knowledge that Americans gained of foreign places and hence the opportunity for cultural reciprocity that was always part of American transnational experience.

Americans travelled abroad for a multitude of reasons. Missionaries, businessmen, reformers, clergymen, creative artists, government officials and society women, all of these were travellers. What is very noticeable is how in their reminiscences, businessmen and reformers who ostensibly travelled to foreign lands to fulfil specific economic, religious, social or political goals wrote vividly of the places and people that they encountered. The genre of their writing and their experience was the tourist tale as much as social or political reform. Among earnest Christian reformers, for example, the Rev. Francis Clark, the founder and leader of the United Society of Christian Endeavor, one of the largest and most influential Christian organizations, peppered his accounts of religious work with copious and colourful details of foreign travel. He wrote in 1897 the luxuriously titled *Our Journey around the World: An Illustrated Record of a Year's Travel of Forty Thousand Miles through India, China, Japan, Australia, New Zealand, Egypt, Palestine...Spain.* There he described customs, places and people with equal enthusiasm. Even places that he found religiously repulsive such as India he could catalogue as 'gorgeous heathenism'.[1] Business travellers tended to be more focused on opportunities to make dollars, to be sure. George Francis Train, who travelled extensively through Asia and Europe from the 1850s to 1870s, was 'always commenting on ways American businessmen might cultivate profitable relationships with the natives'.[2] But Train too gave colourful detail on the places that he visited, as did peripatetic American engineer and later president, Herbert Hoover, who travelled around the world seven times between 1895 and 1908.[3]

American travel overseas was based on the simple practicalities of improved ocean communications and cheaper fares. This began in the first half of the nineteenth century but accelerated from the end of the

Civil War. Just as immigrants to the United States benefited from cheaper transatlantic passage, so too did American tourists abroad, but in a different way. The first steamships, the *Sirius* and the *Great Western*, arrived in New York from London in 1838. Nonetheless, until the Civil War most crossings were by sail, then competition and technology combined to halve the cost of a one-way cabin-fare to 100 dollars or less between 1860 and 1900.[4] But the special benefit was rather different from that for immigrants. Travel flourished with the regularity and comfort of steamship crossings, better and more passenger cabins and the synchronization of ocean lines with land routes. Steamships became linked by timetable and telegraph communication with rail to expand the network of travel on both sides of the Atlantic. Within Europe, rail track tripled between 1870 and 1914 to allow Americans to tour broadly over the continent. Oceanic tourism, the only type that the American government measured, rose fourfold from 1860 to 1900 in consequence of these changes and the allure of foreign places. Tourism to Mexico and Canada, probably of some importance already, was not registered statistically at the time. Notwithstanding, the official figures for foreign oceanic travel – reaching 100,000 people in 1885 for the first time – remained tiny in comparison with the size of the American population. American tourists were part of a small cultural elite.[5] Such travel was economically sensitive too; it fluctuated markedly with the economy, with the depression years of the early 1890s witnessing a slump. Yet this group had disproportionate significance for the export of American culture. At home, the importance of this travel experience for Americans would lie in the trickle-down effect that returning opinion makers would have and on the accounts that they sent back for the reading public.

Histories of American tourism in this period focus almost entirely on the European connection, numerically the most trafficked route. Mark Twain was one of many writers and stage performers who frequently crossed the Atlantic, but there were also clergymen involved, like the Rev. Clark who visited Britain some 20 times. For reformers, businessmen and wealthy socialites, the Atlantic crossing became commonplace. But it was not just European travel that grew. Whether it was a uniquely American trait is doubtful, but Americans abroad explored the world, not just Europe. When Mark Twain toured the Holy Land as part of his job as a correspondent for the *San Francisco Alta California* aboard the *Quaker City*, he joined a tourist ship full of Americans eager to see both Europe *and* the Middle East. Twain's *Innocents Abroad* (1868) was the result. Travel to the Holy Land could easily be seen as a search for the nation's biblical roots and the emotional appeal would be hardly surprising for evangelical Americans. A few years before he died, the devout and influential evangelist Dwight Moody insisted on visiting 'the scenes of his Master's earthly career' in 1892. Temperance reformer and

Methodist Frances Willard also toured Palestine in 1870 though she found the tackiness of Jerusalem with its relic-sellers disappointing.[6]

Much more unexpected and under-researched is the extent of truly global travel by Americans from the 1870s. Trans-Pacific travel was made easier by the regular steamship routes operating with government postal subsidies to Yokohama in 1867 (later with services to China) and by 1898 six steamship lines were 'crowded with passengers'.[7] The San Francisco–Yokohama trip took 22 days in 1886, but less than 12 by 1898. Meanwhile, many social commentators journeyed to New Zealand and on to Australia in the late nineteenth century, taking advantage of the steamship services via Hawaii that began in 1875. Henry Demarest Lloyd (in 1899) was one. These routes, and the international telegraph network, made possible rapid round-the-world travel feats by the 1870s. George Francis Train made the trip, reputedly in 80 days in 1870 and provided, almost certainly, the model for Jules Verne's fictional Phineas Fogg in the celebrated novel.[8] Many followed. Women joined in, not only as family members when men such as Twain or Clark circled the globe, but also on their own. Elizabeth Cochrane Seaman (writing under a pseudonym) was a New York-based journalist whose *Nellie Bly's Book: Around the World in Seventy-Two Days*,[9] documented her whirlwind global journey of 1890 to show that a woman could do better than Jules Verne had envisioned for a man: 'Her work was covered in Joseph Pulitzer's *New York World*. She became an instant if temporary celebrity.'[10] Yet despite the publicity given to this exploit, Woman's Christian Temperance Union (WCTU) organizer Mary C. Leavitt had already shown that American women could travel alone around the world some years before Bly set out. Leavitt had done so in a path-breaking and epic journey begun in 1884. In fact the WCTU created a special category in the 1880s – its round-the-world missionaries, ambassadors for temperance, who in sometimes whistle-stop tours acted as peripatetic agents for the cold-water crusade, though Leavitt did not seek a record-breaking transit. For the WCTU missionaries that followed in her footsteps, the need to organize temperance societies in the countries they visited made necessary a more extended but no less arduous progress. All the while they sent back to the United States accounts of their voyages and of the peoples they encountered. In other words, they acted as others did, as travellers and tourists, exhibiting an American thirst for knowledge of the wider world and conveyed that knowledge back to Americans.[11]

One notable characteristic of this travel was indeed the role of women. An elite of American women devoted a great deal of energy to foreign trips. This trend could already be detected before the Civil War, when women such as literary figure and transcendentalist Margaret Fuller travelled in search of European culture; the radical Fuller joined in the enthusiasm of Young America and threw her support into the liberal revolution in Rome in 1848. Fuller was unusual, however. More common in antebellum times was the tradition of the Grand Tour. An eastern seaboard elite had sent to drink at the fonts of European culture their daughters and sometimes sons in emulation of the European tradition of the eighteenth century. In the 1860s and 1870s the grand tours continued in more democratized forms. The future temperance reformer Willard spent 1868–70 in Europe, visiting Russia, Turkey, Greece, Egypt and other exotic locations as well as the Middle East, Britain and France with her wealthy friend Kate Jackson. Willard called the trip 'one of the crowning blessings of my life'.[12]

Interesting though the phenomenon was, the role of curious and vigorous American women does not completely explain the post-1870 global dimensions of American travel. One important theme that does is an apparent urge among certain classes of Americans to experience the strenuous life – a quest to find the primitive, the exotic, the savage. Americans who felt their own land was becoming civilized showed a penchant for getting back to nature and to supposedly earlier stages of human development. This drove them to travel to distant lands that were off the beaten path. The irony was that European royalty and aristocracy shared this urge to seek the primitive. As Roderick Nash points out, 'As late as the 1870s almost all the nature-tourists on the American frontier continued to be foreigners.'[13] A good deal of American tourism fitted into this same European drive. John Muir, the great advocate of American wilderness, found natural and spiritual perfection amid the granite of Yosemite, but he toured the world in 1903–04, fearing the disappearing wilderness worldwide. He journeyed up the Nile, admired the tall trees of Australia, the hot, smelly mud-springs of New Zealand's Rotorua and the lush Diamond Head of Hawaii. Muir's tour was relatively sedate; he saw wild places from a distance, often viewed through the tree samples collected in botanic gardens. Not so for some other tourists. Teddy Roosevelt went to British East Africa on a widely publicized safari in 1909–10. The trip involved 200 trackers, skinners, porters, gun bearers and tent pitchers; Roosevelt and his son shot, preserved and shipped back to Washington over 3000 specimens of wildlife. Such strenuous tourism as Roosevelt's was strongly identified with masculinity.

Another reason for the interest in global travel was the fact that many of the United States' strategic and economic activities abroad were not European centred. Missionaries went to China, Africa, the Middle East, Southeast Asia and India – and the reports they sent home were published in missionary magazines. These whetted the appetite for the unusual and exotic.[14] The role of the navy should not be forgotten either. Americans heard the stories of the exploits of their far-flung naval squadrons. Walter Colton, brother of Whig ideologue Calvin Colton, was naval chaplain in the Mediterranean in 1831–32. Through his naval experiences he caught the travel bug and sought to communicate the enthusiasm through travellers' tales, such as *Ship and Shore, in Madeira, Lisbon, and the Mediterranean* (1851).[15] The annexation of California also had a stimulatory effect in broadening horizons westward. California became in the late nineteenth century an important American tourist destination promoted by the railroads, but it also opened up the intriguing prospect of exploring the Pacific and the Orient. For Mark Twain, California became a departure point for a visit to the Sandwich Islands in 1866, when he took a 4-month trip as correspondent for the *Sacramento Union*. On his return he lectured on his experiences and discovered how popular his accounts of travel could be.

International travel not only saw affluent Americans go abroad. Foreigners also travelled to the United States as part of a reciprocal tourist trade. We do not know how many foreigners came, as these figures are only available from 1919, but there were prominent examples, judging from the books written about the experience. Throughout the nineteenth century from Tocqueville to James Bryce to Rudyard Kipling, Europeans of considerable stature visited the American Republic. Some were curious about the social system while others came to worship unspoilt American nature. European travellers' accounts of America began to multiply from the 1830s, later featuring such luminaries as Charles Dickens and Anthony Trollope. Harriet Martineau completed two books on her American travels, starting with her *Society in America* in 1837.[16] After the Civil War came pioneering tours by non-Europeans. One visitor was the Marathi campaigner for the rights of women and children in India, Pandita Ramabai, who was in United States from 1886 to 1888 and covered 30,000 miles. In 1889, she published in Marathi *The Peoples of the United States*. Among other South Asians, Hindu holy man Gopalrao Joshee toured with his high-caste wife in 1884–86 and pronounced the superiority of Indian culture, while Bengali Swami Vivekananda visited the Chicago's World's Fair in 1893 and contended with Ramabai over religion and the status of women.[17] Though travel was a reciprocal process, the balance between foreigners coming and Americans going appears to have been unequal. In the 1920s, the first time that records were kept, foreign travel to the United States was between a third and half that of Americans travelling overseas, a fact which reflected the greater economic prosperity of the United States, but also the apparent lure of both the 'old world' of Europe and the exotic world beyond for Americans.[18]

Travel did not necessarily broaden the minds of Americans, to be sure. For one thing, it showed the elites undertaking it just how much they had in common; it could strengthen national identity.[19] Whether influenced by prior knowledge or not, travellers absorbed the worlds they visited into cultural frameworks privileging Euro-American ways of knowing. A larger part of the literature on this topic views travel from within the theoretical perspectives of post-colonial studies. Critics generally tax Europeans with constructing a subjective self against a colonial Other.[20] In the view of experts writing specifically on American tourists, American women (like male travellers) shared this European discourse. But in this 'othering' of the world, the reinforcement of American exceptionalism was a complicating theme. Americans were involved in a triangulation between Europe, the non-Western world and the United States. Through travel and the letters and books that followed, Americans shaped their national identity in part by journeys abroad. According to literary scholar Mary Schriber, as women wrote home they viewed the foreign as the quaint past and the United States as the face of the future. They presumed 'to remake the world in the image of the United States, which is to say in the image of white, Protestant, middle-class values'.[21] Thus women's travel was 'as much about American exceptionalism and the romance of America as about home and abroad'.[22] In reality, when Americans typecast foreigners, they did so in more complex ways than this. For one thing, their frames of reference broadly differentiated nations and people in a hierarchy of civilizations stretching from the highest form of republican society, the United States, through European civilization and on to Oriental barbarism and simple savagery. Within this framework, issues around the treatment of women and of religion loomed large, with European and especially American Protestantism as a higher form of civilization than Catholicism or eastern Orthodox religion figuring in the calculations.[23]

Moreover, the main problem was not the ideological assumptions of travellers, but the superficiality of their observations, a trait shared almost universally with travellers from other nations. Tourists picked up necessarily thin knowledge, their experience sometimes reflecting – as with Carrie Chapman Catt's tour on behalf of woman's suffrage worldwide in 1911–12 – information gleaned from guidebooks. Rushed travel could be biased in a way hardly inclined to provide sympathy for foreign peoples. Thus Nellie Bly's immensely popular account of her mercurial globetrotting contained chapters such as 'One Hundred and Twenty Hours in Japan'.[24] Like many other travellers, she contrasted a lazy, hapless and filthy Orient with her own progressive country. During a whirlwind tour of Hong Kong, she 'visited two quaint and dirty temples. One was a plain little affair with a gaudy altar. The stone steps leading to it were filled with beggars of all sizes, shapes, diseases and conditions of filth. They were so repulsive that instead of appealing to one's sympathy they only succeed in arousing one's disgust.' An earlier genre showed middle-class women how their sisters, even in Europe, lived lives more restricted than did women in the United States.[25] The superficiality of such tourist observations was noted by the more perceptive. Margaret Fuller had dismissed the opinions of her countrymen and women thus: 'the American, on many points, becomes more ignorant for coming abroad, because he attaches some value to his crude impressions'.[26]

Nor did geographical information available to Americans from other sources necessarily break down ill-informed representations of other cultures. According to one historian, the *National Geographic* magazine became a 'dominant force in establishing American impressions of the world, its inhabitants, and the scientific enterprise'. The National

Geographic Society was composed of a group of scientists in the 1880s, but it increasingly became the vehicle for a popularizing magazine. About four-fifths of the circulation went to such people as industrialists, businessmen of all types and professionals. For this magazine, America stood for industry, scientific wonders and the future; Europe and Asia for integration of peoples into a 'natural' landscape and the past. Neither did the content include any hint of a multicultural America and its transnational encounters.[27]

Post-colonial theorists dwelling upon the obvious arrogances and silences in travellers' tales and geographical literature may, however, be too harsh on nineteenth-century American tourists of the middle classes in condemning superficial perceptions of foreign peoples. Rather, travellers' attitudes were often ambivalent, being both sympathetic and dismissive. Especially in the work of women there was an awareness of possible gender parallels crossing cultures. WCTU round-the-world missionaries appreciated that the view of the West as superior was somehow flawed. These women detected underlying patterns of gender subordination and they qualified racial oppression with awareness of a common humanity. Harriet Clark's impressions and those of her husband Francis in *Our Journey around the World*, differed markedly. A man and a woman so travelling, Harriet stated at the outset, 'are likely to see all things through different glasses. The man may, perhaps, have a clearer vision and a wider outlook; but the woman, with more leisure, and with more opportunities in some directions because she *is* a women, will notice little things which have escaped the larger vision' and yet were 'none the less interesting'. A woman who 'for the sake of taking a journey around the world has given up her own home' could 'not help but feel a sympathy with home life in other lands', Harriet confided. This perspective made women more empathetic towards the downtrodden of their own gender, even though it did entail hints of superiority as well. The Clarks' divergent outlooks were seen most clearly in the depiction of Hindu child brides. For Harriet, 'my heart cries aloud for help to rescue the benighted women and innocent children of India'. Her husband, on the other hand, seemed less troubled – the weddings were 'most gorgeous affairs' and he pronounced it 'pleasant to believe' that in India 'as everywhere else in this old world', there was 'much conjugal felicity'. He failed to comment on the gendered effects of child marriages. Rather, 'matchmaking' to achieve the old custom of arranged marriages was 'an open, honourable, and avowed occupation'.[28]

Tourist responses were highly gendered in this way, but gender did not block men from offering their own complex accounts of the cultures they encountered. A travel book such as Twain's *Innocents Abroad* can be analysed in post-colonial terms depicting the 'Old World' as one of decay, past glory and inferiority.[29] Yet Twain was not unappreciative of foreign splendours,[30] and he criticized the conduct of Americans 'who talked very loudly and coarsely, and laughed boisterously', in one case claiming that an offensive American tourist 'did not mention that he was a lineal descendant of Balaam's ass'.[31] Despite his gentle reproofs of American culture, *The Innocents Abroad* sold furiously and was successful as newspaper copy. Twain also provided in his travel accounts unsettling evidence about American racial prejudices, suggesting that Americans were not fully civilized: 'Negroes are deemed as good as white people, in Venice.'[32]

However it was valued, the impact of tourism came vicariously for most Americans. They experienced the exotic through voluminous travel literature rather than by direct contact. Travel writing exploded as a genre in the nineteenth century. Books and articles became both a stimulus to travel and a response as tourists sought to relate their experiences and cash in on the thirst for knowledge of the foreign. Of 1765 travel books published in the United States from 1830 to 1900, 1440 came after 1860.[33] On top of this was the intimidating number of periodical accounts. Some of this was not tourism pure and simple. Reformers' observations ostensibly on political topics, such as Henry Demarest Lloyd's accounts of New Zealand in *Atlantic Monthly*, were often as much about the place as the ideas and reform practices. Lloyd's account had references to the natural environment, with comments on earthquakes and invasive species. These quasi-travel tales could be as successful as the real thing. Clark's 1897 volume on his round-the-world Christian organizing tour quickly sold in excess of 50,000 copies and made enough money to allow him to plough the profits back to subsidize future trips.[34] The great curiosity about the outside world also showed in the role of missionary magazines promoting work in Africa. A huge interest in what contemporaries called 'the dark continent' was reflected in the career of Henry Morton Stanley. American newspaper readers avidly consumed the stories of Stanley's trip to Africa in 1871, his explorations in subsequent years and the dramatic tale of his meeting with the Rev. David Livingstone.[35]

The same degree of interest can be observed in wider observations of Americans on foreign cultures. According to literary historian Howard Mumford Jones, travel commentary of the antebellum period 'was bellicose, defensive, or propagandistic as embattled American writers sought to fend off influences deleterious to the republic, to democracy, and to Protestant Christianity'. But by 1870, this bluster had waned. Magazines such as *Atlantic* carried 'the most amazing variety of travel articles, critical accounts of foreign masterpieces or current foreign writers', and impressive discussions of foreign politics. While earlier travel books were 'didactic', often 'militantly Protestant', and anti-monarchical, those after about 1870 had, Jones shows, a 'relative absence of condescension' or 'chip-on-the-shoulder' attitudes. A greater cosmopolitanism, at least among the educated classes, was registered also in art and design. Thus, for example, a vogue developed by the 1880s for things Japanese, a trend also evident in Europe with the Japanese influence on European painting through Claude Monet's work. Exhibits on the Orient at the Philadelphia (1876) and Columbian (1893) World's Fairs excited interest, while operas and operetta featuring non-Western themes flourished. The *Mikado* had an 'enormous run' in 1885.[36] Of course much of this enthusiasm could be accused of Orientalism, of perpetuating stereotypes. But the point remains that travel helped create interest. Well-to-do tourists brought back furniture and objet d'art from abroad and set fashion trends. The knowledge that tourism promoted was uneven and warped, but it remained to some degree reciprocal.

* * *

Missionary and religious reform movement impacts were also transnational. American Protestant missionaries abroad numbered 3478 by 1899, though the British still provided more, at 5393. This flies in the face of (false) assumptions concerning the exceptionalism of American evangelical outreach. Areas where the American presence was pronounced and fast increasing after 1870 could be found, however. Methodists established missions in India (1856) and China (1847), but expanded there post-Civil War together with extensions into Japan (1872) and Korea (1885). Meanwhile the Congregationalist American Board of Commissioners for Foreign Missions was dominant in the Sandwich Islands and the Middle East. The latter had a mesmerizing pull for missionaries inspired by both Orientalism and millenarian beliefs. Missions to scattered, mainly Orthodox and Catholic, communities in the Ottoman Empire adjusted to local conditions after unsuccessful early proselytizing in the 1820s in order to bridge the cultural gap. They pioneered modernizing educational institutions, including the forerunner of the American University of Beirut in 1866.[37] At home nationwide missionary boards mobilized congregations to support foreign work and, from the time of the non-denominational Women's Union Missionary Society for Heathen Lands in 1861, sent out single women missionaries to work specifically among Indian and other Asian women in their secluded and segregated spaces called zenanas.

Distinctive American impacts were most felt, however, in non-denominational Christian moral reform societies. The real surge in American missionary activity came from the 1886 founding of the Student Volunteer Movement for Foreign Missions (SVM), an outpouring of millenarian organizing in which teams of evangelists scouted colleges for students to pledge themselves to train for missionary work. With the urgent and galvanizing slogan to evangelize the world in a generation, this work yielded half the US missionaries to go into foreign fields up to 1920.[38] The SVM was, however, but one of several innovative organizations demonstrating new techniques of reform, especially centred on bureaucratic organization, fund-raising, specialization of functions and non-denominationalism. All involved conceptual innovations that made the organizations bearing the new ideas controversial abroad and disruptive of the existing social order. The same characteristics made them popular among foreign nationals seeking to raise the profile of their particular reform enthusiasm. Non-governmental organizations such as the Young Men's Christian Association (YMCA) and WCTU were representative and vigorous proponents of cultural expansion. In each case Americans served in coalition with non-American groups and used these groups to export American ideas and organizational forms; they networked within the British Empire and extended ideas of informal influence within this empire. The reform influence began before the Civil War, but was carried to great lengths from the 1870s.

Temperance movements ceased to be largely Atlantic in scope and became global in achievement. Teetotalism began in Britain in the mid-1830s, but its most successful salesman was John B. Gough, the silver-tongued American orator who became a staple of the mid-century English lecture circuit, telling tales of his resurrection from abject poverty brought on by drunkenness. The temperance pledge was his answer to the temptations of the bottle, but allied to the cause were efforts of American reformers to use law to effect temperate behaviour. After the Civil War, the export of temperance ideas through travelling lecturers accelerated. The mixed sex Independent Order of Good Templars, a temperance lodge first formed in New York in 1852 became prominent across Britain and Scandinavia in the 1860s and 1870s.[39] From its formation in 1874, the WCTU quickly became from 1876 committed to international action, and the World's WCTU was founded in 1884. The Woman's Christian Temperance Union grew in over 40 countries and membership totalled over three-quarters of a million by the 1920s. Its work promoted secular causes such as woman's suffrage around the world as well as moral and religious campaigns.[40]

Just as temperance involved an element of reciprocity of American and non-American reformers, the YMCA also demonstrated the reciprocity of religious benevolence. Founded by George Williams in London in 1844 in the wake of revivalist meetings that were American inspired, the YMCA was soon exported to the United States, where it thrived among middle-class Protestants.[41] In 1866, Americans introduced a complementary Young Women's Christian Association movement whose genealogy could be traced to mid-century female prayer unions in Britain. By the 1880s, the new burst of religious revivalism associated with the SVM created the incentive and energy to expand the American YMCA overseas – to India, China, Japan and other locations. Women soon emulated this feat, after Anglo-American women jointly established the World's YWCA in 1894.[42] Backed by funding from rich businessmen such as John D. Rockefeller and department store magnate John Wannamaker, the Ys from the United

States were able to push impressively into Asia and began an ambitious building programme to house their headquarters in each colonial outpost. In this expansion abroad there was adaptation in the American Ys from the original British model. The British Ys were pietistic, whereas the Americans became after the Civil War aggressively evangelical. American Ys sought bureaucratic uniformity, whereas the British accepted diversity of affiliated structures. This division led to rivalry, with the British for a time competing in sending out their own Y secretaries to India.[43] By the 1890s, the American Ys focused on organizing district and national YMCA groupings across the colonial world. Introducing indigenous YMCA cadre brought the American Ys close to flirting with colonial nationalism and economic modernization in South Asia and China.

The Ys promoted social reform as well as religion and in China attracted young modernizing student leaders to their ranks, achieving for the organization before the revolution of 1911 what one historian calls 'a scope and reputation disproportionate to its size'. By 1907, 8 cities on the Chinese mainland had branches of some sort. YMCA growth was aided by its 'gradualist' approach to the issue of introducing Westernizing changes. Its values 'paralleled those of traditional China', yet it 'contained a dynamic that appealed to modernizers'. The Y took over leadership in 'starting schools, planning opium-control campaigns, providing famine relief, assisting students overseas, and organizing youth activities'. It cooperated with Chinese interest groups among the 'modern merchants and the new student class'.[44] The organization also conformed to the American global aspiration symbolized by the round-the-world trips of Y leaders, especially John Mott. From a Midwestern farm background in Iowa, Mott developed into a quasi-statesman who hobnobbed with presidents, kings and archbishops. He went around the world on Y and Student Christian Movement campaigns many times and eventually won the Nobel Peace Prize in 1946 for his contribution to ecumenical understanding.

As the example of the Ys and their social agenda indicated, moral and social reformers inspired by evangelical Christianity went far beyond the export of single-issue campaigns. They purveyed the wider American culture as well. Coca Cola and Hollywood typify twentieth-century US culture penetration abroad, but before 1914 cultural exports were often high minded. Protestant religious revivalism and sectarian innovations were vital parts of popular culture that Americans disseminated internationally. Antebellum religion established a transatlantic revival pattern pioneered by Charles Grandison Finney in the 1830s and 1840s, and Phoebe Palmer in 1859 took her drawing room meetings to England and, with her husband Walter, conducted 'extended revivals' for 4 years. 'Thousands upon thousands are born again through listening to the appeal of the Doctor and his lady', a contemporary commented.[45] This strong appeal of American religious innovation abroad continued after the Civil War with the work of Dwight Moody and his accompanying singer and organist, Ira Sankey. After a preparatory trip to Britain in 1872, Moody and Sankey, both theatrically gifted showmen,[46] landed at Liverpool in June 1873 and spent 2 years travelling across Britain conducting meetings of 'spellbinding' popularity. The estimated attendance was an astounding two and a half million people. In 1881 and again in 1891 and 1892 they returned to further acclaim. These evangelists and others like them were exporting the dynamic energy of American revivalism, a highly innovative form of religious enthusiasm centred on individual conversion and organizational methods that utilized modern media.[47]

It would be wise to keep in mind a little observed irony of this work. The rise of American revivalism in the nineteenth century paralleled the emergence of religious revitalization within Islam across the colonial world.[48] The innovations of evangelical religion were products of the market revolution in the United States and its peculiar interaction with the emergence of church–state separation in New England completed by 1833. Revivalism contained both liberal, social reformist elements and highly reactionary or restorationist elements and was an unstable product of rapid social change. It would not split into modern American liberal modernism and fundamentalism until the 1920s, when cultural conflict over immigration and urbanization peaked. In the Islamic world, a parallel movement was expanding in the early nineteenth century as religious leaders revitalized their faith in the wake of Western economic penetration, a trend overlaid by the 1870s with the imperialist division of India, Southeast Asia and Africa into European spheres of control. Islamic influence spread south across the Sahara, partly in response to political pressures on the borderlands of their religion but also from the external threats posed by secularization and Western expansion.[49] There would be no clash of two cultures at that time in the Christian homelands of Britain and the United States, but the ground was laid for the conflicts of the early twenty-first century.[50]

Superficially, both the American and the Islamic forms of revivalism were kept far apart. But this did not mean that they failed to influence one another. Evangelical Americans disapproved of Islam as an absolutist and barbaric religion, but they used their Orientalist visions of that faith in the nineteenth century, as Timothy Marr has shown, to challenge intemperance and slavery and to tax Americans that their own vaunted moral superiority had its vulnerable points.[51] Reciprocal effects could also be seen in the case of Western interactions with Buddhist and Hindu revivalism. Through missionary contacts, a transnational cultural exchange occurred. Christian missionary endeavours responded to the religious and cultural changes going on at the borders of European empires. They faced difficulties in having much impact on the non-Christian world without adapting to local conditions.[52] For example, the need for coordination of missionary activities to support field workers in Burma led American Baptists to found one of the earliest general missionary conventions in

1814. Furthermore, the development of American inter-denominational missionary efforts beginning in the 1860s came in the wake of non-Christian criticism that Christians could not agree on their doctrines. In turn the experiences and tactics of missionary work could be applied within metropolitan societies towards organizations for the visitation of the poor and other ways of ministering to the secularized urban proletariat.[53] For Americans, foreign missions stimulated the movement for the establishment of domestic missions for immigrants.

Nineteenth-century America had, due to rapid social change and the competition of Christian sects attendant upon disestablishment of the churches, produced a pot-pourri of religious enthusiasms. With their right to freedom of religion, the choice available to Americans expanded far beyond mainstream revivalists. Groups such as the Mormons, Seventh Day Adventists and Christian Scientists emerged and took their special brands of Christianity overseas. Mormons recruited converts from English factory towns and Swedish villages for their western American settlements, but an equally interesting group was the Seventh Day Adventists. Formed out of the failed Millerite Movement anticipating the second coming in the mid-1840s, the Adventists embodied such antebellum enthusiasms as vegetarianism and the linking of health with spiritual reform. Charismatic leader Ellen White championed child-centred educational reform, temperance and opposition to the military draft. She travelled 'extensively' in Europe from 1885 to 1887 after the death of her husband and then lived in Australia for a decade from 1891. From a vision she learned that the land down under was ripe for the Adventist message. There she established colleges and hospitals, as she had done in Europe, and a flourishing movement that gave rise to the Sanitarium Health Food Company, one of Australia's most important breakfast cereal manufacturers.[54]

These religious and reform activities had a selective impact. They could succeed in the English-speaking diaspora because of the middle-class culture that emerged with Protestantism and the industrial revolution. In a shared Victorianism, temperance and other individualistic reforms flourished.[55] This same cultural explanation meant, however, that moral and social reform movements were more successful in the United States than in Europe, as in America the cultural hegemony of the middle classes was firmer and the labour movement much more fragmented. In Europe, particularly after the 1890s, the development of organized socialism and working-class/trade union activities gave workers an alternative to the self-help ideologies of American reformers. Self-improvement still appealed, especially to middle-class women in Britain and its colonies, but even women's groups' ability to convey American cultural norms was attenuated by class divisions and, particularly, by the upheavals of the First World War.[56]

These disruptive processes and the reaction of the middle classes towards them similarly shaped the appeal of American literary culture. *Uncle Tom's*

Cabin, the Harriet Beecher Stowe novel of 1852 on the evils of slavery became the most popular American literary export of the century, with an appeal to Europeans and the British Empire that lasted into the 1920s. The secret of its success was not just the controversies of slavery and abolition that were technically resolved in the Civil War, but the way that the novel raised alarm about family structures and the survival of middle-class values. Behind the empathy expressed towards slaves whose domestic lives were torn apart by brutal slave traders, one could detect the pressures upon families created by the processes of immigration, rapid industrialization and urbanization in the Euro-American world. Still, it was those of middle-class status or petit-bourgeois aspiration to whom the novel's religiosity appealed most.

The foreign influence on American culture must not be forgotten in all this. As Richard Pells argues for a later period,[57] the United States was 'as much a consumer of foreign intellectual and artistic influences' as it was a 'shaper of the world's entertainment and tastes'. Indeed, it was these 'foreign influences' that made American culture 'so popular for so long in so many places'. That culture 'spread throughout the world' because, Pells argues, it had 'habitually' absorbed, synthesized and re-exported 'foreign styles and ideas'. Americans avidly flocked to hear Jenny Lind, the 'Swedish nightingale' brought across the Atlantic by P. T. Barnum in 1850. Shakespeare was popular entertainment in nineteenth-century America, and touring players included Sarah Bernhardt, the French actress, who in 8 visits made famous her interpretation of *Othello's* Cordelia.[58] Similarly, Gilbert and Sullivan's operas came to New York, including *HMS Pinafore* in 1878, and provided smash hits for Broadway entrepreneurs. Just as American evangelists went abroad, in popular religion the United States became home to certain foreign charlatans. Scottish-born John Alexander Dowie came to the United States from Australia in 1888 preaching faith healing and insisting on strict prohibitions against alcohol and tobacco. His biblical restorationist philosophy garnered followers in Chicago, where he founded the 7500-strong Zion City, a venture that 'ranks among the largest and most grandly conceived utopian communities in modern American history'. Despite attracting derision when he immodestly proclaimed himself the final incarnation of the prophet Elijah, the 'Prophet Dowie' continued to deceive the spiritually restless until scandal and economic incompetence embroiled his autocratic rule before his death in 1907.[59]

Like much of the foreign culture upon which Americans drew, the export of American culture was more firmly centred on popular than highbrow forms. Even in the antebellum years, American popular entertainment reached Britain and Europe and produced fascination. Circus promoter P. T. Barnum toured England successfully in 1844 and 1846, and the painter George Catlin lectured to the English on Native-Americans in 1840. To make his visit financially viable, Catlin was forced to incorporate

Native-American routines in which actors performed dances and chants as illustrations of his themes.[60]

Americans tried to export their sports as well as prize ethnographic exhibits. Chicago White Sox player and sporting goods promoter Albert G. Spalding made two self-styled 'missionary' endeavours to make baseball a world, not just a national, pastime. Inventor of the term 'America's national game', he first took part in Harry Wright's exhibition tour to England in 1874 and then in 1888–89 toured the world with his own troupe of exhibition players almost a century before satellite television made such sports as basketball globally popular.[61] Memorably sketched against the Pyramids, Spalding's American all-stars tour was nonetheless aimed primarily not at the Middle East but at the Pacific as a field of American cultural and economic expansion. After 1898, the US occupation of the Philippines, Cuba and Puerto Rico also popularized the game there.

It was, however, Buffalo Bill (William F. Cody) in 1887, replete with Native-American warriors re-enacting Custer's last stand to European royalty and the working class alike, who provided the most celebrated example of the export of nineteenth-century American show business. The American Wild West had a transnational appeal because the theme was rooted in encounters between European civilization and savagery. As Joy Kasson has remarked, Buffalo Bill provided an 'example of the wild world of exotic others brought under the control of white, civilized authority'. Europeans were interested in the American exotic, as indeed were urban Eastern Americans. 'The enthusiasm of foreign spectators' made Buffalo Bill 'a worldwide celebrity' linked to the idea of 'personal heroism'.[62]

'Worldwide' perhaps, but the overseas impacts of reformers, missionaries, businessmen, artists and other purveyors of American culture were far from uniform. Class and tradition played roles. It was primarily the masses that were affected by the export of American culture and conservative elites in Europe who worried first and foremost. Here were the roots of anti-American sentiment. Starting in the nineteenth century as a conservative distaste for American democracy and its import to Europe, it became by the time of the introduction of mass consumer culture to the United States in the twentieth century a broader opposition to American hegemony over the working classes. Unevenly by the 1920s, radical and labour movements whose nineteenth-century ancestors celebrated American democracy now denounced American plutocracy and economic penetration while still applauding those Americans who protested against capitalism's domination. This ambivalence about American culture was already evident earlier, because popular culture had penetrated long before the advent of American movies and the Ford T-model car. The reception of the United States in Europe in the nineteenth century involved both sneaking sympathy for American cultural innovation and critiques of it as subversive of tradition.[63]

The impact also varied from culture to culture and country to country as in the case of Buffalo Bill. Not surprisingly the English were sympathetic, viewing Buffalo Bill as part of the expansion of the Anglo-Saxon race, Italians (and Spaniards) 'saw offending braggadocio' in Americans who proclaimed themselves 'the world's greatest riders', while Germans assimilated Cody to their romanticized view of Nature.[64] In similar fashion baseball's spread was uneven and problematic. Spalding did not convince the English to substitute baseball for cricket in 1874. Though Australians flocked to baseball games during Spalding's 1889 visit, cricket still ruled. Partly people came out of sheer curiosity, but also because of the carnival atmosphere. Spectators found enticing a pioneer parachutist, one 'Professor Bartholomew', who was injured jumping from a balloon in Melbourne. When Australians toured the United States to play America's national game in 1897, they could not compete; the tour was a flop and baseball in Australia languished though it continued to be played.[65] In some other places the game caught on much better, such as Japan and Korea where it was spread by college teachers, YMCAs, missionaries and visiting US sailors. In his 1911 recollections, Spalding rejoiced that 'baseball follows the flag' in the 'island possessions' of the Philippines; clearly the cultural import had an easier passage where Americans influenced geo-politics, as they did in East Asia.[66]

The receiving cultures selectively incorporated what interested them and reinterpreted American cultural artefacts. The appeal of Wild West shows was, it must be reiterated, to the exotic, not specifically to the 'American content'. In Europe, the shows included a mishmash of displays; thus in Bradford, England, the crowd was treated to the daring horsemanship of Cossack and Arab riders, while American Indians stayed behind after the show's departure and joined sideshows that blended them into the observation of all the freaks and wonders of the world.[67] For baseball too, the import could be subtly changed. Spalding admitted that there were differences in the way the game was conducted in the Philippines and other island possessions, such as in the treatment of umpires.[68]

As the case of Buffalo Bill indicated, foreigners above all imagined America before they experienced it. Fascination for things American grew as part of a European project of American exceptionalism quite apart from any exposure to the realities of American culture. As early as the 1860s, 'advertising' of tobacco and other American products drew upon the imagery of 'an allegorical female figure, a version of Columbia with stark Indian features', with feathers and wrapped in the Stars and Stripes.[69] Long before the roaring 1920s, commerce 'appropriated the allegorical repertoire of the American dream' wherein Europeans could connect an imaginary west with 'the world of trite consumption goods'.[70] An example of this American west as a space for dreams was the work of German writer Karl May, who from the 1870s wrote cowboy novels without so much as setting foot in the country before 1908. Even then, May never went to the American west. His westerns were virtually unknown at the time in the United States, but sold millions in Germany with the young Albert Einstein and Adolph Hitler among his fans. Today this European fascination has mutated into the spaghetti western tradition,[71] but May wrote with a distinctively German slant. His heroes were not white, native-born Americans but Winnetou, a brave Apache chief, and Old Shatterhand, a German-born frontiersman. Critics have detected here German romanticism. Interestingly, his work was translated into many languages. Thereby, American culture was mediated through German culture as far away as China in an elaborate transnational circulatory system. For Europeans the western was the ideal vehicle to express urges that recapitulated, at least in part, older concepts of bravery and chivalry, but the United States provided other cultural stimuli too.[72]

A prominent theme in the foreign imagination of America centred on race. In the export of certain American commodities, especially tobacco, both slavery and negritude figured highly, as did wider images of Southern tropicality. After all, tobacco was a product of what for many people was a highly romanticized culture of the South, a culture whose appeal was not dinted in the post-bellum years, when it could become teary nostalgia, or jell with the imperialist racism of European colonization of Africa. An early example of this overseas receptivity to racism was the great popularity of the black and white minstrels. Nate Salsbury took his Troubadours to Europe in the 1830s; and the American 'Ethiopian Serenaders', another group of blackface performers played to packed houses in London in 1846.[73] By the 1850s, blackface minstrels had spread beyond Europe with American performers journeying from California to New Zealand, India and Australia. In Australia they took advantage of gold rush conditions to play to packed audiences; after 1865, the Christy minstrels based in Britain further developed the popularity of the genre within the British Empire.[74]

The images of the black and white minstrels, with their caricatures of happy, down-home African-Americans singing and dancing illustrated another theme – the conflicting images that cultural exporters could convey abroad. Touring minstrel shows in 1848 competed with and to some extent subverted African-American abolitionist Frederick Douglass's attempts to create a serious debate over the evils of slavery. Against the singing pseudo-'darkies' of the Deep South legend, abolitionists could, however, export to England wholesome white abolitionist singers such as the Hutchinsons, a popular New Hampshire group converted to the cause during Englishman George Thompson's 1838 visit to the United States.[75]

* * *

The transnational exchange of culture was real, but it was increasingly unequal in one particular area by the late nineteenth century. Europeans began to debate an 'American invasion' in business. Three books on this subject appeared with similar titles in 1901–02. While the English lamented Yankee success in sport and aspects of cultural life, the alarm was mostly over business competitiveness. Though Americans had opportunities at home, their commercial activity was also ubiquitous abroad. Tapping into the business networks of the British in South America, they supplied entrepreneurial talent. Transport was a speciality. American businessmen journeyed abroad to supervise steamship routes, build railroads and run stagecoach lines. Usually they brought 'skills and talent' rather than much capital.[76] New Yorker W. H. Webb developed steamship transportation across the Pacific in the 1870s to 1890s. Freeman Cobb, originally from Massachusetts, came from California during the gold rush era with other Americans who had experience with Wells Fargo to establish one of several highly successful American-run stagecoach businesses in Australia. Later he operated 'deluxe' coach services in South Africa before his death in 1878.[77] The colourful entrepreneur and associate of Elizabeth Cady Stanton, George Francis Train, introduced the first 'horse-drawn tramways into England in the early 1860s'.[78] Some, such as Train himself, were given to harebrained schemes, but the practical experience of others in improvising transportation development in the American west served them well in South America, where distances were greater and climatic conditions often harsher than in Britain.

American businessmen went abroad for a variety of motives, good and bad, accidental and deliberate. They often began simply as travellers and saw business opportunities on the way. At times, as in Hawaii and China, their businesses were the outgrowth of Christian missionary links. Some were ex-naval personnel or the children of missionaries. Among the entrepreneurs were legitimate businessmen, while others were simply snake-oil salesmen. Indeed, the purveyors of American patent medicines spread to the goldfields around the Pacific Rim from the 1850s to 1890s. Sometimes opportunities abroad allowed young men to recompense for failures at home through careers that strangely mimicked the achievements of domestic American contemporaries and were intimately connected to these in trade and finance. One such was New England-born Henry Meiggs, who fled gold rush California in 1854 in scandal. Meiggs was one of a number of American businessmen who, along with British traders and bankers, promoted European investment in South America. A forger and swindler, Meiggs resurfaced in Chile and later built railways in Peru. There he became known as the 'Yankee Pizarro', employing Chinese coolies to construct track across some of the most challenging mountain terrain in the Americas. Meiggs also sold Springfield rifles to the Bolivian government and acquired extensive guano deposits off the South American coast that he exported as fertilizer. His career paralleled those of many executives of the American railroads in the 1870s in his entrepreneurial excesses and rugged individualism, corruption and financial mismanagement, with the costs of building over 1200 kilometres of Andean railroad involving the Peruvian treasury in large, ill-considered loans from London's money markets. Though he died in his South American exile in 1877 still mired in controversy, Meiggs retained loyalties to California and had supporters in the United States. A group of 'Old Californians' had held a celebration for him in New York in 1875 praising his work in Chile and Peru 'in the introduction of the great modern civilizer, the rail-road and the locomotive' and toasted his 'energy and enterprise'.[79]

American entrepreneurs became equally active in the export of American farm technology and know-how. Experience in technological improvization in the American west favoured American enterprise just as it did in the case of transport. This was illustrated in irrigation practice. George Chaffey, an immigrant Canadian engineer had developed Ontario, California, as a planned 'colony' based on advanced irrigation technology, irrigation company finance and intensive subdivision of land. Establishment of certain moral and civic improvements such as agricultural colleges and alcohol prohibition were also integral to the original scheme. An environmental aesthetic based on prescribed tree plantings and a geometric street layout produced the image of a model township, conveying a sense of middle-class order and progress. Rather than a purely economic or technical advance, the scheme was closely reflective of popular culture and its image of an ideal garden landscape. Visiting Australian politicians declared the achievement impressive and they enticed Chaffey in 1887 with the offer of land from a Victorian colonial government anxious to develop the dry interior of Australia. There he introduced special machinery including patented pumps to lift water from the Murray River to irrigate fruit farms being established in his Mildura 'colony'. Though Chaffey's venture was in receivership by the mid-1890s, the towns and fruit industries he established survived to become the heart of Australia's leading irrigation area.

Meanwhile, American engineers mostly drawn from California flocked to the Australian goldfields and became prominent in the mining industry in South Africa as well. In the latter case they applied their knowledge developed in the arid American west to the provision of water for the Witwatersrand mines. The leading figures included William Hammond Hall, first State Engineer of California and his cousin John H. Hammond. Hall and Hammond were part of a group of Americans who worked for the British diamond and gold mining companies in the 1890s, providing mining engineering technology as well as water.[80] Herbert Hoover served the same function in a number of locations, including in Western Australia in 1897–98 before he left for a stint in China. Until 1912 he followed mining interests around the world and became extremely wealthy in the course of his work.[81] Like others, he took advantage of the spreading tentacles of British capitalism. A firm started by Californian mining engineers, the Exploration Company of London 'served as an import–export agency for capital and expertise'.[82] It introduced American 'mining securities into the British market' and 'secured British financing for mines in Mexico, Venezuela, Alaska and South Africa and formed partnerships with international companies'. It also supplied engineers globally.[83] Hoover reported that because of more practical and extensive technical training in the United States there were by 1900 over 1000 American engineers in the British Empire 'occupying top positions'.[84] It was not just better technical training, however, that distinguished this group but the way Americans transformed the profession 'through the inclusion of administrative work as part of the engineer's job'. Many in South Africa worked for Cecil Rhodes' companies and became unhappily caught up in the fiasco of the failed Jameson Raid (1895) and the subsequent outcry against British imperialism and the Boer War. Similarly, American businessmen in China feared for their lives as anti-foreign sentiment swelled in the atrocities of the Boxer Rebellion of 1900.[85]

These American engineers were not simply technocrats. They were exporting American culture. Hoover praised the work of American missionaries in China and hoped to bring economic and cultural modernization to the Orient and parts of the British Empire alike. In his account of his early life, written in 1915–16, Hoover waxed lyrical about possibilities for global progress, centred on trade and development opportunities in the Far East.[86] Similarly in South Africa, American engineers thought they were bringing, Jessica Teisch notes, 'tools of progress', yet the outcome diverged from the engineers' own frontier experience in California. While a 'vibrant mining economy' emerged under American technical impetus, 'agriculture remained undeveloped'. The capitalist modernization that these mining engineers optimistically promoted did not produce an 'equitable and prosperous society' but served instead to foster British imperial goals and the role of big mining companies.[87] Americans still worked within the British Empire and had not yet established their own hegemony.

The transnational enterprises of such men as Train and Webb, engineers such as Chaffey and renegade businessmen like Meiggs represented an individualistic form of capitalism common in new industries in newly exploited areas on European peripheries. In a way, these entrepreneurs reproduced the conditions on the American frontier. They had fled from organized life, but their flight would be in vain. With the development of American corporations entailing the organization and vertical integration of production, pioneer entrepreneurs were pushed to the margins by the 1890s.[88] Having developed national marketing, American corporations then applied these skills to international expansion as a means of gaining new sales for productive enterprises. The case of tobacco was typical. A variety of entrepreneurs such as Cameron Bros. and T. C. Williams of Richmond, Virginia had sent representatives or established branches and allied firms throughout the British Empire in the 1870s and 1880s. Some used relatives in distant ports to represent their interests. But in the 1890s the integration of the American tobacco industry into a monopoly led by James B. Duke saw the world's tobacco industry divided, with the American and British cartel sharing the spoils of much of the world. The small independents and their business connections were squeezed out. [89]

American business had matured in this phase of global mergers. Immensely profitable and yet vulnerable, its export performance had to be improved. Vast quantities of American consumer goods already poured into British Empire markets, but elsewhere, trade barriers often checked the commercial advance. The nation would need to modify its policies of political isolation and bring foreign policy more closely into alignment with economic expansion. Herein lay the origins of the American push to expand trade with the aid of politics, particularly through the adoption of the Open Door approach of the turn of the century. Herein, too, lay the beginnings of American formal empire. Contributing to this shift were the diverse but ubiquitous activities of Americans who had travelled or lived abroad for extended periods since 1865.

Among these groups, one category has so far gone unnoticed and is little studied – the expatriates. After the Civil War, more Americans chose not simply to tour overseas but to live there. Not only did some Confederates temporarily depart after the Civil War and small groups of black Americans resume their search for a better life in Africa after 1878 but also Americans intellectuals such as the great novelist Henry James settled in England in the 1870s. The Anglophile James eventually became a British citizen in 1915, while others such as the American artist Mary Cassatt moved to that Mecca of late nineteenth-century painters, France. Less well known were the missionaries and numerous business people who simply ended up living abroad in places as far flung as Turkey, India and the Pacific Islands. [90] The expatriates included not only representatives of American business houses, but also the leftovers from the trans-Pacific gold-rushes, whaling crews, sailors jumping ship and travellers who simply found somewhere pleasant to live, aided perhaps by a business opportunity or romance. These were a largely invisible group, though their status agitated the State Department and Congress. American overseas residents raised issues of the extent of American power and government defence of its citizens' interests. In a number of countries, the United States, like Britain, successfully asserted full extra-territoriality – the power to dispense justice to its own citizens, even though they were resident in a foreign country. Missionaries and ne'er-do-wells alike took advantage of the special status, but the aim was mainly to facilitate the smooth spread of American commerce. In all, the United States signed 13 extra-territorial treaties in the nineteenth century with places as far afield as Turkey (1830) and Tonga (1886), but most notably China (1844). [91]

The American business communities in many instances centred on the activities of the consuls. Even though these were political patronage appointments, the continuity of Republican regimes through most of the period from 1865 to 1913 gave opportunities to remain at one post for fairly long periods without being removed for political reasons. Moreover, the absence of adequate consular salaries and a career service encouraged the awarding of jobs to people who mixed their own business activities with that of the government. These appointments included, for vice-consuls, many foreign nationals or long-term American expatriates.[92] Among political patronage appointments was that of George Seward, nephew of the Secretary of State to the position of consul in Shanghai in 1862, a post he held from the age of 21 and where he stayed for 15 years while gaining a name for shady commercial dealings. He had to rule upon extra-territorial matters of law despite no legal training or college degree. More scandalous was the nephew of the powerful politician Benjamin Butler, George Butler, who in Egypt developed a 'dissolute reputation' for kickbacks and fondness for nubile Egyptian women. This was not an entirely unusual though exceptionally well-publicized case. The businessmen consuls were often regarded as a rather dissolute lot who had succumbed to the sexual and other moral temptations of their temporary lands of residence. Episcopal Bishop Charles Brent of the Philippines, who toured the Far East extensively in the first decade of the twentieth century, urged the government to clean up the 'disgrace' of the consular service. It did not do so properly until the Rogers Act of 1924, which created merit appointments to replace blatant and inefficient political office seeking.[93]

The activities of the consuls and businessmen illustrated the problem of defining American boundaries as US residents abroad often considered themselves inhabitants of American intellectual space. Just as it was not uncommon for immigrants to the United States to preserve the culture of their youth and homeland, American emigrants were no different abroad. Fourth of July ceremonies in the nineteenth century were held wherever expatriate communities were large enough, and these usually celebrated American achievements both economic and democratic, with over-the-top republican oratory and a good deal of alcohol. They also became occasions on which business contacts could be made. The spread-eagle conduct of some American representatives abroad fed common foreign perceptions about the American Republic and so had potential to promote both admiration concerning larger-than-life American material success and anti-American feeling.[94]

A more serious issue was the way that the widespread presence of Americans implicated the United States in the foreign entanglements that traditional isolationism forbad. In the nineteenth century the government sometimes intervened to put pressure upon governments in South America or the Far East, usually to respect the rights of its citizens. In the most extreme examples, the navy bombarded the coasts of Aceh in the 1830s and Korea in 1871 and the United States landed troops in Panama in 1885 to protect American property. In the 1890s extra-territorial rights would become more urgent as the Cuban Revolution against the colonial yoke of Spain threatened American property and lives. The cultural and economic expansion of the American people beyond its borders created diplomatic, political and military problems that drew the nation to the edge of formal imperialism and simultaneously strengthened the nation-state.

9

Building the Nation-State in the Progressive Era: The Transnational Context

Traditionally, historians have either neglected American nationalism or treated it as unproblematic and fundamentally different from its European cousins. This sharp divide may reflect the impact upon conceptions of that nationalism drawn from ideas of American exceptionalism. But the inconvenient fact remains that many nations have seen themselves as unique. In recent decades, historians have emphasized the contingency of nation-state formation, rather than simply accept its development as self-evident.[1] In making any reassessment of the American case, an important distinction must be made between the growth of nationalism and the growth of the state. Put schematically, the nineteenth-century American state was relatively weak on the federal level, while popular nationalism rooted in republican ideology was stronger. In contrast, European nationalism tended to be the creation of central states and their intellectuals proclaiming mythical national pasts. Yet despite this difference, the two systems tended to converge in the late nineteenth century with the consolidation of European nation-states and the rise of imperialism.

Though the Civil War provided changes in state formation and the issue of pensions for the Union's veterans created a larger bureaucratic apparatus, the modern American state began to take shape in the Progressive Era. It had to be built incrementally over many decades. Never 'finished', as no state structure can be, it grew haphazardly upon the inherited institutions of dispersed governmental power. Existing studies focus on internal factors and the regional, political and administrative sources of the peculiar configurations of state structures that emerged in the nineteenth century.[2] Yet the growth of the *nation-state* fusing nationalism and state structures coincided with international competition over resources and political influence from the 1880s and in response to transnational economic and cultural pressures such as immigration. After a brief review of the pre-Civil War legacy, this chapter concentrates precisely upon the ways that the American state was transnationally produced.[3]

After the American Revolution, popular nationalism developed and a variety of national symbols conveyed American identity. The District of Columbia stood as the ultimate embodiment of the nation, once planned and occupied by the government from 1800. The layout of the city of Washington betrayed grandiose pretensions. Frenchman Pierre L'Enfant's plan envisaged fine boulevards featuring geometric precision, and English-born architect Benjamin LaTrobe supervised the design of elegant classical buildings. This sweeping conception predated the nineteenth-century reshaping of the great capitals of Europe, notably Paris under Louis Napoleon and Germany's Berlin. Yet the splendour of the nation's capital remained unrealized until much later than the time of L'Enfant. Washington was not literally a monumental city in the early antebellum period. It was not until the construction of the Washington Monument began in 1847 that the modern trend to memorialize the heroes of the nation took notable architectural form. In the 1850s Washington was still an unfinished city plagued by fever and poor drainage. Nor was it a national focal point for Americans. Unlike today, relatively few had the chance to visit it. Nationalism developed instead from the combined and yet uncoordinated activities of local elites and the wider populace across the nation.

The practice of nationalism was local and that was both its strength and its weakness. Fourth of July celebrations in the smaller towns and hamlets featured fairs, greased pig catching, bands and logrolling; more important, orators retold the stories of the Revolution. Election contests reproduced a veritable spectacle of democracy as citizens turned out in festive style not only to listen to candidates, but also, consciously or not, to celebrate a nation where (white male) people could vote.[4] Schoolhouses served as a vital conduit for nationalist sentiment through the patriotic history displayed in school textbooks. The national flag gave American citizens a symbol of their shared identity and the 'Star Spangled Banner' reinforced this symbolism when composed as a national anthem during the War of 1812 by Francis Scott Key.[5] Also valuable were the institutions of civil society, especially the law. The Supreme Court under Chief Justice John Marshall established the principle of judicial review in 1803 through the Marbury v. Madison case, though it was not until the Dred Scott decision of 1857 that a law of Congress was declared invalid. Use of the court as a national arbiter of law had been asserted, but law touched the citizenry mainly through state, not national, courts in this period. Appeals to the Supreme Court were rare.

Our image of American nationalism comes down to us from the numerous texts of Fourth of July orations and vivid surviving reports of congressional contests including that of Abraham Lincoln versus Stephen Douglas for the election to the senate from Illinois in 1858. Popular interest in democracy avidly followed by a considerable section of the people was reflected in the relatively high (by modern American standards) voter turnout of up to 80 per cent. Yet the strength of popular nationalism – its localism – exposed the allegiances of Americans to severe parochial divisions and sectional conflict. Allegiance to the nation was through the state governments. Robert E. Lee chose which side to support in the Civil War, so the story goes, by the decision of Virginia. To say 'I am a Virginian' first and an American next, as Lee reputedly did, was common enough. The terminology of 'these' United States stemmed in legal terms from the position that many in the South took – that the states had voluntarily joined the Union and had surrendered their sovereignty only conditionally; they could, so this position went, take their consent to the compact of government away. Yet even in the North, the institutions of individual states rather than federal power were strongest and reinforced localistic sentiment. Volunteers to the Civil War joined 'New York', 'Massachusetts' or some other state regiment, just as Lee commanded the Army of Northern Virginia for the Confederacy. Though there was a national flag, state flags competed for the allegiance of individuals. In perhaps the most extreme example, the United States did not present a united face to the rest of the world in its border control policies. State passports were valid until 1856 and citizenship derived from the laws of each state, a position very unfavourable to racial minorities.[6] One must conclude that despite the appearance of nationalist strength, American allegiances were diverse and fragmented. In the early years of the Republic, 'a weak but popular national state loosely connected a fragmented, ethnically heterogeneous society', historian John Higham judiciously observed. '[C]ultural nationalism, in the sense of a deep popular consciousness of being a single people, hardly existed.'[7]

The secession of 1861 was preceded by several challenges to federal authority. The Whiskey Rebellion (1794); the Virginia and Kentucky Resolves against Federalist power (1798); the Hartford Convention, when, tables turned, the minority Federalists of New England protested against the War of 1812 (1814); and, most seriously, the Nullification Controversy of 1828–33 where South Carolina refused to accept the federal tariff on items that the South had to import such as manufactured goods. The Jackson administration had to threaten military force to get a compromise, but it was a compromise in which key concessions on federal economic policy were made to the South.

The Civil War did not adequately resolve the position of ex-slaves in American society, but did settle the issue of secession. Lincoln's insistence on the indissolubility of the Union prevailed through warfare. National unity was backed up by the passage of the Fourteenth Amendment to the Constitution in 1868. This not only gave civil rights to the

African-Americans freed by the Thirteenth Amendment (1865), it also created national citizenship for the first time. Most important, it gave the federal government the power to enforce these rights against the states. This reversed the position of the pre-Civil War period, where the Bill of Rights had restrained federal government power over individual liberties. At the time of the Revolution, the centralization of power had been feared. Now it was recognized that the central government would need power to enforce basic civil rights. Yet the balance of political power only allowed such enforcement so long as the South remained under the control of the Republican Party, the party of the Union that had won the war. In turn, this political position depended upon occupation of the South during Reconstruction by Northern troops. The South became in effect a set of 'colonies', as historical geographer Donald Meinig has pointed out,[8] but this army of occupation could not remain in the South indefinitely. The power of the state apparatus was hamstrung after 1870, not only by Southern opposition, but also by the increasingly laissez-faire and conservative Supreme Court. By 1883, enforcement of the Fourteenth Amendment had been undermined by the legal rulings that only government institutions, not private institutions such as clubs could be subject to the 'equal protection' clause. On the other hand, by 1886 the use of the amendment to protect 'persons' had been extended to corporations; thus the Court shifted the focus of the amendment's purpose. The regulatory power of state legislatures over business had been weakened and a laissez-faire no-man's-land created in which corporations flourished.

The westward expansion of the United States from the 1840s upon the acquisition of the Mexican territories had also recreated centrifugal forces produced by physical geography and different economic interests. Distances were vast. Because they were so far away, western states developed their own regional identity through mottos, flags, songs and even their own local celebrations of their founding. Citizens used pioneer and historical societies to cultivate a sense of local and state history. Thus Admission Day for many years rivalled the Fourth of July as a quasi-national day in California.[9] Political economy fundamentally drove regional feelings too. Angry farmers in the American west through the Grange Movement (the Patrons of Husbandry) protested against economic forces in Washington and New York that seemed to shape their lives. They chafed at control by railroads and banks and campaigned to use state regulation to combat distant power. But state legislation was checkmated by the interstate commerce power. It was necessary to change Washington. By the 1890s the Populists were seeking to win the presidency and to introduce federal control over communications nationwide. This was the early advocacy of a stronger state, but it was not grass roots protest that eventually overcame local divisions; nor was it the centralizing economic and political forces discussed by Robert Wiebe in *The Search for Order*.[10]

Rather, the external threats to the United States prevailed. The nation-state was produced transnationally.

Only when the United States again faced external military foes did the necessary conditions for the emergence of a strong state fall into place. The great wars of the twentieth century effected the change, but the growth of the nation-state was anticipated in the Spanish–American War of 1898. The United States acquired colonies and had to put an occupying army in the Philippines. Political leaders were also aware of growing imperial rivalries and sought military bases abroad. It was from the 1880s that a modern navy was developed as wooden ships were replaced. From 1880 to 1914 the United States went from having the world's twelfth-ranked to third-ranked fleet. In direct response to the inefficiencies exposed by the Spanish–American War, Secretary of War Elihu Root introduced substantial army reforms as well. These included streamlining control through a Chief of Staff and creation of the War College and the General Staff. American tradition under the Constitution had been against a standing army, but now the focus shifted to an 'expansible Regular Army as the keystone of an effective military establishment'. Root quickly instigated 'steps to reshape the American Army into an instrument of national power capable of coping with the requirements of modern warfare'.[11]

At the same time, social and moral reformers favoured national government intervention in the lives of the people to an unprecedented degree. The American state structure would be morally intrusive as well as militarily competent. First introduced at the state level, laws against abortion, contraceptive devices and alcohol prohibition reinforced a strict middle-class, Protestant morality. But as in economic regulation, interstate influences corroded state efforts to protect communities and demonstrated the need for federal legislation. This came first with the Comstock Act to prevent the passage of obscene material through the mails, passed in 1873. Campaigns against prostitution led federally to the passage of the Mann Act (1910) to prosecute the taking of women across state lines for 'immoral' purposes. Prohibition, a major phenomenon in the Northern states in the 1850s, was also resurgent, especially after the formation of the Anti-Saloon League in 1893. From the passage of the Wilson Act of 1890 through to the Webb–Kenyon Act of 1913 the states sought to use federal law to protect their local communities against liquor imports. But prohibitionists also used this system as a tactic to build support gradually for wider national prohibition.[12]

The period from 1880 to 1917 also witnessed concerted attempts to develop a positive and reformist state. Liberal and radical reformers and many trade unionists had learned the lessons of anti-radical repression in the 1880s. They wished instead to develop, through incremental improvement, a new state structure that incorporated labour as a counterweight to revolution.[13] The loose coalition of reform interests we know as Progressivism developed in response to the 1890s depression and took shape first in state and city politics. Progressivism had grass-roots appeal and stemmed from local issues such as transit company charges, city government corruption, urban pollution and labour exploit-ation. Colourful reformers like Mayor Samuel 'Golden Rule' Jones of Toledo proclaimed the gospel of what amounted to a moderate Christian socialism. Yet there were other strands. The inability to frame adequate regulation of the economy as much as reformers' agitation led to demands for improved national efficiency and much business/corporate cooperation with government developed as Progressivism moved to a national level after 1900. In this search for both social justice and national efficiency, the Progressive Movement did not draw upon its own internal energies alone. It was influenced by an international discourse of reform.

Generally speaking, historians have only recently accepted that the Progressive Era was more than a response to the growth of industrial-ization and urbanization within the United States; it was also part of American attempts to strengthen the nation's social fabric in an interna-tional context. Especially through the efforts of Daniel Rodgers, historians have come to realize the importance of European stimuli upon develop-ment of American Progressivism. The United States lagged in many areas of social and economic reforms, such as in providing insurance against industrial injuries, even though the nation had an extremely high rate of accidents. In social insurance, it was Germany that took the lead in modernizing the older political economy. Americans, too, began to develop accident compensation schemes, with special interests trying to limit the costs of rising levels of industrial accidents, and business sometimes threw its weight behind regulation. But the international struggle to strengthen the nation – the transnational production of the nation – was integral to Progressivism. President Roosevelt noted in 1908: 'It is humiliating that at European international congresses on accidents the United States should be singled out as the most belated among the nations in respect of employers' liability legislation.'[14] For models, reformers drew on both British and German examples to provide compensation systems.

Women reformers contributed to the growth of a welfare state by agit-ating for the adoption, beginning in many individual American states, of mothers' pension schemes before the First World War. The extent to which such schemes drew upon the intellectual example of European maternal welfare schemes influenced by Swedish theorist Ellen Key has been under-rated, with most historians emphasizing comparative national difference rather than transnational connections.[15] Such cases could be conceptu-alized as 'Atlantic crossings'. Yet the pattern of Progressive borrowings was more global than purely Atlantic. The state accident compensa-tion scheme introduced in California 'borrowed' from New Zealand, for example.[16] Indeed a wide variety of ideas filtered from Australia and New Zealand into American progressive schemes. In *Newest England*, social reformer Henry Demarest Lloyd wrote that New Zealand democracy was 'the talk of the world today', and looked for inspiration in settling the competition of capital and labour through systems of industrial arbitration.[17] Peter Coleman has demonstrated the international circulation of ideas concerning Progressivism, focusing on the influence of New Zealand on American reforms. Reformers such as irrigation promoter William E. Smythe in California proclaimed the need for 'New Zealandizing' America.[18] The role of the labour movement in Australian social democracy was studied with equal interest by social reformers as well as academics such as economist Victor S. Clark. The secret or 'Australian' ballot was one reform widely adopted.[19] Less well known is the antipodean influence in irrigation policies and objectives through the work of Elwood Mead. The National Reclamation Act of 1902 set an important early benchmark for the federal government's role in the building of dams and distribution of water for power, farming and flood control. These activities would become major points of federal intervention in the lives of ordinary people in the American west. The Progressive Mead, who would go on to serve as Commissioner of the Bureau of Reclamation in Washington (1924–36), became an advocate of national regulation of water as a result of his work as Chief of the Victorian Rivers and Water Supply Commission in Australia from 1907 to 1915. There he experienced the inefficient competition between states under a federal system, and when he returned to the United States he advocated national cooperation in the regulation of irrigation and water supply questions. He also urged quasi-socialist schemes to aid closer settlement by providing state aid to farmers, not just the traditional American policy of supplying them with small quantities of cheap land. Rodgers has noted Mead's influence as part of 'fashioning a new physical frame for agricultural settlement',[20] even though this case reveals not an Atlantic exchange, strictly speaking, but a global pattern of interconnections. Irrigation policy in America drew upon the experience of British India as well as Australia and included reciprocal global influences. Mead was involved as an expert doling out advice for irrigation policy in Palestine, Australia and South Africa, just as he learned from his experience in those places.[21]

The regulation of business and finance also grew after 1900 in ways that strengthened the state structure. The desire to control monopolies spurred the shift to reform at the federal level because state governments could not effectively combat these vast economic combinations. By 1912, Progressive reformers and politicians were pushing hard for a stronger federal state. In Woodrow Wilson's Democrats they found a party poised to implement key financial changes that Progressives across all political parties advocated. The Federal Trade Commission of 1914 regulated corporations, and the Federal Reserve Act became in 1913 the first federal banking legislation since the Civil War and the first to introduce real federal regulation of banking since the 1830s. Federal power was on the march. The shift was also shown by the introduction of an income tax in 1913. Though the measure raised little revenue at first, it enabled the Democrats to reduce tariffs (the main alternative source of revenue) and to set up a steady and convenient revenue stream that would be vital during the First World War. International factors both directly connected to the war and indirectly influenced by it aided the expansion of this federal power. Ever since the Spanish–American War and the need to enlarge the navy and army demonstrated the inadequacies of the government's existing revenue system, reformers and politicians had been seeking greater federal taxing power in this area. Corporate taxes had already been introduced in 1909. As revenues from tariffs dropped due to wartime trade restrictions after 1914, Congress ratcheted income tax up.[22] The financial basis for a stronger federal state had been laid at last.

On the eve of the First World War, the rise of Progressivism had not, however, produced a state structure identical to that developing in Europe in the same period. Federalism, as the banking reserve legislation organized along regional lines indicates, limited centralization of power. The distinctiveness partly resulted from the way that the nation's innovators could borrow ideas eclectically from many countries to suit their own purposes. They had no one European model in mind. The very way so many social reform ideas had to be imported suggested that the United States lagged behind both Australasia and Europe in the approach to reforms designed to transcend the rugged individualism of the nineteenth century. The growth of the American state remained incomplete. Public ownership of the means of production did not become a serious part of the national agenda, despite the emergence of a Socialist Party formed of both native-born reformers and urban immigrants, a party that gained a respectable 6 per cent of the presidential vote in 1912 at its first serious attempt. The expansion of the national state in economic regulation reached a temporary peak during the First World War, but the leviathan of government regulatory organizations and corporations created to prosecute the war effort was mostly cut back thereafter. Not until the 1930s did serious growth of the federal state resume. Even then, the activities of the Liberty League and other New Deal opponents showed how suspicious of big government many Americans still were.

Social democracy was not, however, the only way that state power could grow in the Progressive Era. Far more neglected is the way the nation defined itself not economically through attachment to the material benefits of the state but culturally. The era of Populist upheaval and Progressive reform witnessed changed notions of national citizenship and rights, wherein the markers of American cultural identity were defined more sharply. Borders and boundaries that hardly existed prior to this time sharpened to mark status as an American.

Immigration and its discontents spurred more rigid national boundaries and a bigger government. New border controls were created, as a product of the increasing international pressures upon the United States. Exclusion of immigrants was not simply an issue for immigration history, but for the definition of the nation and the nation-state bureaucracy required to enforce that definition through restrictions upon unwanted people. The beginnings of this exclusionist policy can be dated to the late nineteenth century, when Congress mollified Californians protesting about the social customs and job taking that they attributed to Chinese immigrants. The latter were largely excluded in 1882, but the states still remained responsible for other immigration restrictions. Not until 1891 did the federal government take formal control of the nation's borders. Congress had initially barred Chinese labourers in 10-year renewable laws, but in 1902, as fears of a more general kind over immigrants mounted, the law excluding them became permanent. Restriction of Japanese immigration was added in 1907–08 under the so-called Gentleman's Agreement with Japan.

In the same period, Americans began to debate new barriers against European migrants. The massive influx of Southern and eastern European immigrants moving into the North and Midwest after 1880 accompanied economic disruption and brought much social discontent, with workers trying to organize collectively against business opposition and state repression. Moreover, many Americans feared that the new European immigration might channel anarchist and other radical political beliefs. Pre-Civil War immigration had been capable of introducing or exacerbating labour violence, but that phase of immigration occurred before the emergence of an international socialist movement and before the widespread industrialization of Europe. Immigrants arriving from the 1880s were different. Though in fact the newcomers were often conservative peasants, fears spread that immigrants might have been influenced by the growing European interest in anarchism and socialism, spurred by new labour, populist and anarchist parties and revolutionary agitators. Anxieties about increased exposure to immigrant violence importing terrorist tactics from abroad were highlighted in the Haymarket bombing and riots of May 1886 in Chicago. A bomb exploded in a demonstrating crowd of workers killing 12 people, including policemen. Eight 'foreign born anarchists'[23] were convicted, not because the prosecution could prove they had thrown the bomb, but because they were held to have incited the bombing. The courts imposed death sentences on 7, an outcome that spurred international labour protests. This state-sponsored repression of radicalism was not new, but it increased in the years after 1886.

Alarm over radicalism produced more than stiffening business and government resistance to labour's demands. It stirred efforts to provide symbolic concessions to workers, for example the Labor Day holiday. The movement of immigrants back and forth across the oceans raised the spectre of a developing international working class in the minds of businessmen and their political representatives in the state. The conflicts that ensued were ideological as well as industrial battles. Immigrant radicals introduced, at the same time as the Haymarket Affair, the idea of the May Day celebration as an expression of international working-class solidarity. First held in Chicago in May 1886 just days before the Haymarket bombing, this event linked May Day with anarchism and communism, and when the International Socialist Congress met in Paris in 1889, delegates designated use of this date internationally from 1890.[24] Meanwhile, labour unions in New York had celebrated with a September Labor Day demonstration in 1882. After 1886, anti-radicals feared that the use of May Day would be enshrined as a commemoration of Haymarket and an incitement to anarchism. Therefore, politicians supported efforts to celebrate labour's contribution that would be in line with American, not foreign, traditions. After the Haymarket riots President Grover Cleveland moved in 1887 to support an alternative date. With half the states having legislated already, Congress passed in 1894 an act establishing a federal workers' holiday in the first week of September. Business continued to oppose Labor Day in many states, but labour had been symbolically incorporated in the American nation-state with the AFL (American Federation of Labor) favouring this 'legally sanctioned' celebration.[25]

Despite these complex moves, fear of foreigners persisted and led to demands for reassertion of 'American' values to dominate the political system through further restriction of immigration. Closely associated with resurgent nativism, anti-Catholic feeling revived in the 1880s and the new nativism gave rise to the American Protective Association (1887) and the Immigration Restriction League (1894). A variety of patriotic and veteran organizations such as the Grand Army of the Republic and the Daughters and Sons of the American Revolution also gained in strength and offered a 'statist version of national loyalty'.[26] Anti-immigrant groups pressed in the 1890s for exclusion of immigrants on a variety of grounds, though the category of 'anarchists or persons believing in the overthrow by force or violence of the government' and 'the assassination of public officials'[27] was not added to the immigration restrictions until Leon Czolgosz shot President McKinley in 1901. Whether or not immigrants were anarchists or socialists, the mobile and propertyless lifestyles of a good many engendered further political concerns. Could or would the new immigrants ever be wedded to the nation-state? The Dillingham Immigration Commission appointed by Congress in 1907 questioned the loyalty and efficacy of European immigration because so many newcomers seemed not to set down roots within the United States; instead they moved back and forth as transnational migrants and did not take out citizenship.[28] Congress added several additional restrictions to the immigration act in the first two decades of the twentieth century, but presidents continued to oppose proposals that would totally exclude the poorer classes of Europeans. Taft, Wilson and Cleveland all vetoed literacy tests on entry. Despite the presence of nativist groups, concern over immigration waxed and waned because business benefited from cheap labour and restrictions were politically unpopular in urban areas where immigrants wished to promote family migration. Not until 1917 was a literacy test – first proposed in the early 1890s – passed. By then the stage had been set for the post-First World War reordering of immigration priorities. [29]

An important indication of these hardening state boundaries was the use of passports. This was an international trend. The United States was one of many governments placing increased emphasis on the regulation of passports after 1900. In the nineteenth century immigrants had arrived with a variety of papers; they often did not have recognized passports. Nor did Americans when they went abroad. So small were the numbers, the US government had not bothered publishing data on the numbers of passports it issued to its own citizens prior to 1905. The change to stricter border controls in several countries came partly as a result of American concern over the numbers and types of immigrants entering the United States. In response to American anxieties about anarchists, socialists and transient immigrants, Italy (and some other European countries) began to introduce passports after 1901 to make it easier for their citizens to move to and from the United States.

The First World War completed the transnational revolution of the passport system begun around 1900 and effected more rigid boundaries across Europe and the Americas. National security threats from without defined the nation within, thus demonstrating once more how the American state was made transnationally, that is, shaped by transnational pressures. John Torpey's *The Invention of the Passport* highlights how passport controls came to play 'an important role', though controls for the Mexican border remained largely ineffective. An executive order in 1915 required 'all persons leaving the United States for a foreign country to have a passport visaed by American officials before departure'. This was a prudent measure due to the renewed insistence on such documents at many destinations because of the world war. A May 1916 act prevented wartime 'departure from or entry into the United States contrary to public safety' and gave legislative teeth to the 1915 executive order. [30]

Another factor prompting Americans to take a stronger stance on border controls in the Progressive Era was environmental. The spread of cholera and yellow fever epidemics in the late nineteenth century came as the result of improved transportation and expanding European imperial rule of peoples in Asia and Africa. Congress therefore strengthened quarantine law. Some individual state governments had imposed their own health checks on foreign travellers for decades, and even though the first federal human quarantine legislation dated from 1878, it did not immediately stop the states' own regulation. With the arrival of cholera from abroad, the Federal Government law imposed stricter quarantine requirements in the 1890s, but these were still executed (sometimes differently) by the states. [31] The final centralization of national health quarantine policy came as a result of the First World War and the even more intense circulation of peoples that the war brought. Disease was more easily and rapidly communicated by the mass deployment and close contact of troops. Indeed, the Spanish Flu outbreak of 1918–19 spurred alarm with at least 20 million deaths worldwide and over 600,000 in the United States. Public health authorities advocated quarantine of sick people and, by 1921, all quarantine stations had been placed under federal control. Meanwhile, health concerns about not only communicable diseases but also a physically defective population had been linked to immigration policy. The Immigration Act of 1891 denied entry to 'persons suffering from loathsome and contagious diseases' that could include venereal infection and empowered federal officers to exclude medical defectives.[32] These health concerns had undoubted nativist and political dimensions. Anxieties about foreign immigrants melded with those about the contagion of physical affliction, and of morals too.

As with microbes and morals, federal power extended over plant imports in the Progressive Era. Here again, laissez-faire and states rights ruled through most of the nineteenth century. Individual states, most notably California, introduced their own pioneering quarantine regulations governing plants, even though these rules arguably interfered with interstate commerce. Federal officials viewed such fragmented policies as dangerous to the national interest, particularly in regard to insect importations. Reorganized as a Bureau in 1904, the US Bureau of Entomology clashed with officials in California, where the State Board of Horticulture drew upon Pacific Basin regional experience in combating plant pests to introduce from abroad so-called 'beneficial' insects that would control unwanted species. These primitive efforts at biological control served as an embarrassment to federal authorities. In addition to the challenge faced by the fact that California was already making cross-national alliances to control pests, the increasing awareness of advances in entomology on an international level led scientists to develop national plant quarantine policies. The depredations of the European gypsy moth after the 1890s and the boll weevil in the South which had come from Mexico at about the same time intensified efforts to establish federal regulation over plant and insect importations. The Plant Quarantine Act of 1912 brought these matters under federal control.[33]

The reinforced boundaries of the nation-state in immigration and scientific policy complemented the growth of popular nationalism. Though hardly a new American phenomenon, nationalism now became more clearly identified with the state. State regulation of boundaries promoted national distinctiveness and pride in American exceptionalism. An important regulatory development connecting people with the state was the nationalization of nature. While Americans had usually thought of their natural world as different and superior, American nature was not defined purely as national before the late nineteenth century. True, the material abundance of the frontier underlay American concepts of exceptionalism. Paintings often associated the richness of the American west with manifest destiny, but these did not clearly distinguish between US nature and the nature of the Americas. Traditionally the idea of natural abundance had been applied prior to the nineteenth century by European explorers to the Americas as a whole, not the British colonies alone, the assets of which had been seen as somewhat deficient in comparison with the gold, tropical fruits and other precious items found elsewhere. Even in the mid-nineteenth century, the paintings of Frederick Church showed an expansive appreciation of New World environmental abundance in his representations of the Amazon. This perspective chimed in with entrepreneurs' plans to exploit these regions and with an ambitious version of Manifest Destiny taking in the whole of the western hemisphere. At a microcosmic level the chief American philosophers of nature treated the physical world as transcendent and God given. Nature was rooted in particular places as well as the nation and all showed, as in Henry David Thoreau's *Walden*, that the immanence of God's creation could be found everywhere in nature. [34] The appreciation of Yosemite as an American icon stemmed in no small part from the publicity given by John Muir, who, it is often forgotten, was Scottish-born. His sensibility was derived from the rugged grandeur of his homeland when applied to the American west. Granite he could appreciate at a time when most Americans preferred the more manicured landscapes of farms and gardens. [35]

Nor was nature yet part of the state. The nationalization of nature had to be carved from these broader transnational traditions. The beginnings of federal regulation of nature came through the creation of national parks. The first of these dated from 1872 when Congress acted to preserve Yellowstone. But it was in the 1890s that moves to create national parks spread, as part of the quest to sharpen American identity. This was precisely the moment that a wide reformation of American nationalism began. This nationalization of the spaces of nature accelerated with the 1906 National Monuments legislation under President Theodore Roosevelt, and in 1916 the National Park Service gave the parks a unified system. Concern with preservation of the wild in the United States was closely tied to fears that the primitive struggle with wilderness was over and that the tides of new European immigrants would lack American pioneering values and had in some way contributed to an environmental crisis. [36] As William T. Hornaday, a famous naturalist and director of the Bronx Zoo warned in regard to native-bird extinctions: 'All members of the lower classes of southern Europe are a dangerous menace to our wild life. . . . The Italians are spreading, spreading, spreading.'[37] In response to this perceived if irrational crisis in national identity and the possible extinction of iconic wild life, the regulation of nature in the parks emphasized American exceptionalism. Yellowstone was the first designated 'national park' in the world, though in colonial Africa as well as Australia, and Canada, the American example was often copied. [38]

The Progressive Era also witnessed the beginnings of attempts to control the rampant destruction of forests practiced in the previous 200 years. Signalled by the appointment of Gifford Pinchot as Chief Forester in 1898 and the inception of the US Forest Service in 1905, national conservation policy became allied to Progressive concepts of national efficiency and vigorous government. Pinchot changed the name of the federal forest reserves (first established in 1891) to 'national forests'. His policies implied not only protecting them from use but also focusing Americans' national pride on their natural heritage and its conservation.[39]

This nationally distinctive policy of Progressive conservation was the product of an international sensibility that stemmed from the impact of European colonial expansion. Strategists in all major European countries feared a worldwide shortage of resources. Roosevelt was typical of world leaders in becoming deeply concerned about the stock of global forests and the implications for national power and efficiency, as reflected in his appointment in 1908 of a National Conservation Commission. This body took part in an inventory of American resources measured against a world of heightened national economic competition. The commission's effort to make the case for more conservationist use of resources marked the culmination of several decades of debate. George Perkins Marsh's classic text *Man and Nature* (1864) signalled the beginning for Americans of a concern with the over-reaching impact of humans on other species. Yet Marsh was the long-term American Minister to Italy and his work was influenced by his observation of forest destruction in Europe. The appointment in 1876 of Franklin Hough as an agent to investigate the rate of consumption of forests and the best methods for renewal was the first action by the federal government towards developing a forestry policy. Hough went to Europe to study this issue, thus emphasizing the European impact on American policy. Most of the pioneer American foresters were German born or trained and brought with them the concept of state responsibility for resource stewardship.[40] German Bernard Fernow had become the first Chief Forester in 1886. American national practice and national regulation developed in this context of a transnational discourse over the struggle for resources.[41] The objective was to maintain the privileged and superior American position derived from the era of early frontier abundance.

Pride in a specifically American nature complemented other state nourishment of nationalism. New rituals of nationhood emerged, often not state sponsored, but soon incorporated in the symbols of the state. These rituals of patriotism had a popular basis in civil society spread by the institutions of the 'organizational society'.[42] A key example was the Pledge of Allegiance. Baptist clergyman Francis Bellamy wrote the Pledge for the public schools' quadricentennial celebration of Columbus Day in 1892 and, in the midst of labour, radical and anti-immigrant turmoil in that decade, its adoption quickly took a conservative turn and spread across the nation's school boards.[43] The monuments of the American nation-state and the public celebrations surrounding their commemoration similarly proliferated.[44] While the Civil War divided the nation emotionally, by the 1890s Americans began to reunite. Reconstruction's end had left a white racial consensus that African-American equality was not worth fighting for, provided slavery had been abolished. The nation became reconciled at the time of the Spanish–American War, when both Northerners and Southerners could serve together against an external enemy and contemplate acquisition of an empire of little brown brothers in Asia. This North–South alliance was signalled with interment of dead Confederate veterans in Arlington National Cemetery from 1901, an event of national reconciliation directly attributable to the role of the Spanish–American War in 'bringing troops from the North and South together in a common cause'.[45] With the commencement of the Arlington National Cemetery Memorial Amphitheatre (authorized 1913), a focal point for a national commemorative structure honouring the nation's war dead had been marked out. It was finally dedicated in 1920, followed in 1921 by the interment of the Unknown Soldier, an event that symbolically unified the nation around the wars that Americans had fought. This theme was played out with various local valences as communities constructed their own commemorations of the nation's war dead in cities across the United States.[46]

During the Progressive Era, new patriotic anthems of national significance achieved wide dissemination through the improved national means of communication that press and, in the 1910s and 1920s, film and radio made possible. The addition by Katherine Lee Bates of *America the Beautiful* in 1893 came in a significant year. It is telling that this song was composed at a time of increased immigration, when the anti-Catholic American Protective Association was influential and when labour unrest was rife. The APA was strongest in and began in the Midwest and the upper Mississippi Valley where the song first became popular in the 1890s. *America the Beautiful* synthesized nationalism with the appropriation of the landscape. Nation and people were drawn together in venerating a patriotic cultural heritage.

State structures had come a long way towards national consolidation by 1917, but they were not identical to those in other countries as they bore the marks of history and piecemeal development. Nor did these structures work with particular efficiency. Federal and state powers still squabbled over such matters as the division of constitutional and political authority on alcohol control, and immigration policy remained a controversial matter. Borders were not sealed by anything other than the war itself, because immigration policy was an uneasy compromise between pro-immigrant and restrictionist camps. The latter remained unhappy because people regarded as undesirable, such as Slavs and Jews, were not effectively excluded. The literacy test of 1917 could be taken in any language, including Yiddish.[47]

The First World War would vastly, if temporarily, augment state power. Frenzied hatred of things German, attempts to root out aliens and promotion of Americanism proliferated. One result would be to strengthen the nationalistic aspects of the federal state through wartime propaganda identifying the nation with the extension of federal power, another to focus on the repressive possibilities of the state as an agent of national security. The Espionage Act of 1917 and the Sedition Act of 1918 gave extra government powers to suppress dissent during wartime. All this and more lay in the future, but it was not simply a future that happenstance thrust upon the United States. The nation's deeper involvement in great power politics preceded the war. A stronger state had developed in part to deal with all that the nation's growing interests in the world created. Among other influences, the outward thrust of American formal imperialism spun intricate connections that brought the nation to the doorstep of war.

10

The Empire That did not Know Its Name

Empire is one of the most transnational and commonplace aspects of human civilization. Though independent from Britain, the United States of the nineteenth century did not escape imperial history. Formally and informally, the nation acquired colonies, annexed territories and took de facto control of other areas. Yet American Empire displayed differences and ambiguities that one would expect from a country so professedly opposed to empire and so favoured by material circumstances to avoid its overt manifestations over much of the nation's history. If the United States became an empire in the nineteenth century, its exact borders were difficult to determine. Historically, they were flexible, permeable and constantly changing. These 'borders' shifted as a result of constant pressures within the United States to expand, both culturally and economically. That said, it is important not to depict American Empire as purely a process of informal commercial penetration of other lands. This chapter's focus will not be simply upon 'expansion' as is common in the literature under the legacy of the work of William Appleman Williams and the Williams school, which saw economic and ideological motives of trade and the open door policy of equal access to markets of all nations as critical.[1] Empire was multilateral and reciprocal. It involved ruling as well as expansion and cultural exchange rather than simple outward thrust. The acquisition of empire had consequences for domestic culture and politics that will be considered here. The approach will involve analysing the ruling of empire; the way that continental territorial status obscured the lineages of and lineaments of empire; the influence of international imperialism on the United States, including the role of race theories in the promotion of empire; and, not least, the impact of economic abundance on the growth of American power worldwide.

One oft-neglected aspect is the status of territories acquired within the continental United States. While the nation did not have formal colonies until 1898, a continental empire existed much earlier. It was in the territory acquired after the Louisiana Purchase, especially in the Mexican cession, through to the Spanish–American War that US colonial practice was born. The continuity between 'overseas' and 'continental' expansion illustrated in that experience has not been sufficiently stressed. The Filipinos were not the first people that the US government ruled as subjects rather than citizens. Though Alaska had been acquired in 1867, no territorial government was established until 1912 because too few European peoples lived in the possession, which remained unincorporated. Below the forty-ninth parallel, the pattern was similar. Amerindians, unless assimilated, were treated purely as wards of the nation-state after 1870. In each of these cases race clearly became closely allied with empire. Only European peoples could join the republic as self-governing territories admitted as states and, even then, the nation's legislators and presidential administrations were selective in their treatment. New Mexico remained excluded from statehood until 1912 essentially because too many Hispanics and Catholics lived there. Formally a territory, New Mexico remained effectively a colony, though one with internal territorial government. It became, with its expanding mining industry, an economic colony of eastern state and transnational capital as well.[2]

The continental frontier also saw the genesis of strategies and tactics later used for policing the overseas colonial territories. The army that guarded Indian reservations and conducted the Indian wars on the Great Plains in the 1870s learned techniques for pacification of rebel tribes, techniques that were directly transferred into practice in the Philippines after 1898.[3] Twenty-six of the 30 generals in the Philippine War, such as Nelson Miles, and a good many of the soldiers had seen service on the American frontier and some came from the massacre of old warriors, women and children known as the Battle of Wounded Knee in 1890. Such know-how they utilized in the Philippines.[4]

The continental empire not only provided useful experience, it gave American imperialism its distinctive cover of assimilation and incorporation of colonies in a nation-state. Nation was coterminous with empire. In fact the 'empire' in question was not a dirty word in the nineteenth century. It connoted dominion over an expanding area of republican government under the Jeffersonian formula of an 'empire of liberty', but this view was blind to the violence and demographic consequences of Western impacts on indigenous peoples. As empire came increasingly to mean after 1870 dominion of a few European nations over many non-whites, the image of empire began to sour. Added to the basic inequality of power was the inconvenient fact that unlike American Indians, the subject peoples of other potential colonies could not be so easily wiped out or marginalized. Empire's unpleasant connotations could be erased or occluded within the continental US, but not if territories were acquired overseas in the mould of European expansion.

Increasing connections between the elites of Britain and the United States aided the functional transition to formal empire at precisely the same time. American reformers, businessmen and missionaries already worked within the British imperial possessions and relied upon them for protection and communication. Members of the Anglo-American financial and social elites had begun through the phenomenon of transatlantic marriages to blend as well. The arrival in the United States of southern European peoples as part of the great streams of migration emphasized the need to preserve Anglo-Saxon superiority. The nation's elite, backed by academic reinterpretation of the American Revolution, stressed the shared racial heritage of the Anglo-Saxon peoples across the Atlantic and indeed in the British dominions. Unlike the early nineteenth century, this Anglo-domination spread around the world with colonies of English-speaking white settlement societies in Australasia and South Africa as well as North America to provide racial leadership. Signs were that Britain had become reconciled to (white) colonial independence within the empire. Within this context, an Anglo-American rapprochement grew intellectually and politically, backed by Social Darwinist doctrines. Opinion makers such as naval strategist Alfred T. Mahan and clergyman Josiah Strong spread these views. Christianity and Anglo-Saxonism under an increasingly American-centred leadership constituted the very pinnacle of civilization according to Strong and Mahan.[5] While neither unequivocally supported large-scale territorial acquisitions before 1898, Strong believed that the demographic dominance of the race was the most important factor for the 'commanding influence in the world's future', with the 'exact nature' of that domination still 'undetermined'. Mahan understood that force might, as a 'last resort', be necessary to assert Anglo-Saxon power but until 1898 concentrated on the idea of the United States acquiring the rights to coaling stations and ports rather than subject peoples.[6]

By the 1890s, the United States could no longer confine its de facto colonialism under the rubric of 'internal' manifest destiny. In part, the trajectory of American Empire was similar to that of other imperialist powers. The perceived threat from each other led to pre-emptive acquisitions of territory by all. In this way, European imperialism increasingly encroached on American attitudes, because political leaders and opinion makers ambitiously favoured the global outreach of the nation's civilization, whether or not they favoured formal empire. European and American imperialisms were intimately connected with the expansion of global communications and the spread of capitalism's mode of production. After 1870 the European powers divided Africa, Southeast Asia and the Pacific and took proprietary concessions in China. Afghanistan remained as a buffer zone between the Russians expanding south in Central Asia and the British consolidating their hold on the northwest frontier of India in present-day Pakistan. The Japanese flexed their muscles and showed in the acquisition of Formosa (Taiwan) after the Sino-Japanese War of 1895 that imperialism was not a phenomenon limited only to Westerners. Imperialism had become a trans-global fashion as much as a strictly economic need. Prestige spurred the French to take the sands of the Sahara in the name of Frenchness and civilization and extend their domain in the jungles of Indo-China. Germans felt their late arrival as a unified nation had disadvantaged them in the struggle for world power and sought belated recognition of their naval strength and token settlements in the Pacific and in East and West Africa, together with political and economic influence over the decaying Ottoman Empire. Political economists such as England's John A. Hobson saw in all of this an emerging economic struggle for control of the world. Later Vladimir Lenin would add his own gloss and depict financial imperialism as the last stage of capitalism.

From the 1890s, the United States entered increasingly upon this world stage, sometimes locking horns with overtly imperial powers, at other times cooperating with them. Some historians have detected a rising cosmopolitanism as political elites warned of the need to relate more vigorously to the rest of the world, to strengthen incipient American greatness through a muscular foreign policy.[7] This stance was seen most clearly in the presidency of Theodore Roosevelt after 1901. For all his vigour, however, Roosevelt accentuated trends already visible in the 1890s. The United States intervened in the internal affairs of Latin America, particularly in the Caribbean in the name of the Monroe Doctrine. Increased US economic interests stimulated the growing assertiveness. A new benchmark was set in the Venezuelan border dispute with Britain in 1895. Secretary of State Richard Olney declared Latin America a virtual sphere of American influence and reserved the right to oversee the drawing of Venezuela's border with British Guiana. The extension of American power in Latin America went forcefully further in the way President Roosevelt's administration engineered in 1903 a regional revolt in the Panamanian section of Columbia, a revolt aided and abetted by the presence of an American warship. Here the Americans followed a tradition of gunboat diplomacy and intimidation established by the British. The ambition to exert control was now extended beyond protecting the security of American businessmen and other nationals. The US fashioned not only Panamanian independence but also administrative control of the zone in which to build the Panama Canal. The Canal would prove after its opening in 1914 a potential boon to American strategy, giving the nation in effect a two-ocean navy, and turning it into a potentially global military force. This outcome mimicked the British interest in the Suez Canal route, though in fact American control of the Canal Zone was more direct than Britain's at Suez.

To this control of key waterways was added substantial formal imperialism. In 1898, the United States had joined the supposed final stage of world imperialism by acquiring its own portfolio of colonial possessions. It acquired an empire overseas as a result of the short Spanish–American

War. Precipitated by American humanitarian outrage over Spanish atrocities in putting down the festering Cuban rebellion after 1895 and the sinking of the USS *Maine* in Havana Harbour in February 1898, the unequal struggle ended with the comprehensive defeat of the outdated Spanish navy by July 3. The United States found itself occupying Cuba and Manila as well as Guam and Puerto Rico.

What was the nation to do with these spoils? President McKinley reputedly prayed over whether to hold these possessions in the name of civilization. Europeans such as Rudyard Kipling urged the United States to embrace the white man's burden alongside the British. While clearly uncomfortable over joining the imperial powers, American military and political strategists valued the bases in the Pacific that Manila and Guam provided. In turn, the demands of sea power backed the drive for overseas markets in East Asia for US industry in the wake of the 1890s depression. No matter that the actual market for American goods in China was slight at the time. The dream of the China market was an old and powerful one going back to late eighteenth-century American commerce there. Whether the major motive be economic or God's mission – McKinley was an overtly devout if politically pragmatic Methodist – the outcome was the same. The United States kept the whole of the Philippines rather than risk its falling into the hands of Germany or any other imperial power and assumed a protectorate over Cuba. Though Cuba was 'freed' in 1903, thereafter it remained under American economic and political domination, and Guantánamo Bay became a US base by treaty rights renewed in 1934. At the same time, American influence over the Sandwich Islands (Hawaii) had grown after the Reciprocity (trade) Treaty of 1876 and pressures from American sugar interests in the islands backed the successful annexation of the still independent country in 1898; in Samoa great power rivalries stretching back two decades were solved by a tripartite division of the territory between Britain, Germany and the United States – almost simultaneously. Once again, the advantages of a naval station boosting US strategic and trading potential in the Pacific loomed large in the decision to acquire a colony. The United States had become manifestly a world power.

These acquisitions posed problems for a nation born anti-colonial. A tradition of ideological opposition discouraged direct engagement with the world politically in so far as that process involved implication in the dealings of European empires and their anti-democratic policies. As David Reynolds has observed, the United States had developed an 'intense anti-imperial ideology'.[8] The deeper origins of this tradition can be traced to the American revolt against empire in the form of British rule in 1776 (no taxation without representation). Early on the United States also sided rhetorically with revolutions against imperial rule across the western hemisphere. The Monroe Doctrine (1823) was designed to keep European empires from meddling in the affairs of the western hemisphere. The acquisition of the Philippines and the bloody insurrectionary war that followed as Filipinos sought independence called this anti-colonial tradition into question. Americans at first bitterly divided among themselves; imperialists such as Senator Albert Beveridge not only frankly urged that the United States recognize its role as a new imperial colossus, but also drew upon the legacy of the Louisiana Purchase and Alaska to provide an impeccable imperial pedigree. As the historian Frederick Jackson Turner observed at the time, the United States had a colonial history and policy 'from the beginning of the republic; but they have been hidden under the phraseology of "interstate migration" and "territorial organization" '.[9] Yet naturalizing American imperialism was going too far not only for anti-imperialists but also for a wider body of American opinion. Thus, for example, some senators sought to distinguish between global and hemispheric imperialism, accepting the annexation of Puerto Rico but not the Philippines. But once the annexations were fact, debate shifted to the way Americans ruled other peoples. Politicians, governments and their colonial functionaries sought to overcome divisions over empire by working to distinguish US colonialism from European. They soon re-emphasized that even within the experience of empire, the American version would be benevolent and enlightened. It would work towards giving self-government for the Philippines, though the explicit aim of independence was one that American policy-makers did not take seriously prior to at least 1913.[10]

Because of this anti-colonial legacy, the United States did not establish a colonial office in the government. It called its key territories 'Insular Possessions', administered euphemistically through the Bureau of Insular Affairs, in tacit embarrassment over the holding of subject peoples. In 1901 the Supreme Court established that the nation's rule over these peoples as subjects, not citizens, was indeed legal. The Philippines, Guam and Puerto Rico were 'foreign to the United States in a domestic sense'. Not fully part of the Union, they were just as clearly American possessions.[11] In the decisions surrounding the status of the possessions gained in 1898, a racial compromise prevailed despite dissent. Imperialists regarded the Filipinos as little brown brothers in need of uplift, while Southern racists railed against incorporation of yet more non-white peoples as citizens. Either way, the new possessions were excluded, with the exception of Hawaii, from full territorial status. White demographic ascendancy in these lands seemed far-fetched. Tropical places were thought to be unhealthy for Euro-Americans rather than for the indigenous inhabitants. The collapse of indigenous populations that had aided the empire of liberty internally threatened to operate in reverse. Europeans could not dominate demographically and therefore the acquisitions were deemed unsuitable for full assimilation.

Despite this apparent distinctiveness, Americans drew upon European colonial experience in administering its new possessions. Colonial officials and other Americans in positions of influence visited such places as Burma, Singapore and Egypt in search of inspiration for details of public health policies, agricultural practice and botanical exchanges and to view drug regulation. As historian Laura Briggs notes, medical regulation of prostitutes was common throughout the European empires and the system initially adopted in the Philippines 'anything but exceptional'.[12] Borrowing was noticeable also in Samoa, where the territory had been put under the control of the US navy. With the rapid turnover in administrations, the officers in charge tended to draw upon German and British precedents established in the parts of the island group under the control of those imperial governments. The American naval commandants found in German Samoa 'a model which could serve as a basis for planning'.[13] Some people in the Philippines wanted to go further, however, and advocated a more expansive colonial state; they read widely in the literature of British imperialism such as the works of Lord Cromer, British Consul General of Egypt, and saw their task as Rudyard Kipling did. This group included American resident businessmen, administrators, missionaries and military people, including Charles Brent, Protestant Episcopal bishop of the Philippines, Governor-General W. Cameron Forbes and General Leonard Wood. Pro-colonialists had contacts with Filipino lobbies in the United States through the Episcopal Church and the Committee for Uplifting the Moro Wards of the Nation. They also had links to the Republican Party, including to the pro-Charles Evans Hughes wing of Republican Party during Hughes' 1916 presidential bid. Forbes, Brent and others worked with and within the administrations of Roosevelt and William Howard Taft to retain the islands under United States control, convinced that the date of Philippine independence must be kept distant. In the minds of the pro-consul group, the Filipinos were a primitive, indeed, savage people, fragmented by race, religion and stages of economic development; on no count were they considered material for an independent nation within the foreseeable future.

Nevertheless, American officials wished to blunt anti-colonial criticisms, assuage guilt and distinguish their empire in two ways. One was by seeking to modernize the colonies. To that end, the American administration introduced widespread schooling in the Philippines and public health reform to combat tropical diseases. Officials worked to stop the spread of malaria, cholera, yellow fever and other scourges, a policy that was also adopted elsewhere through the work of army sanitation experts Walter Reed and William C. Gorgas in Cuba and Panama. Tackling yellow fever, Gorgas reduced the death rate on the isthmus to such an extent that he came to be 'regarded as the foremost sanitary expert in the world'. So much so that in 1913 the Transvaal Chamber of Mines invited him 'to study pneumonia among mine workers'.[14] It has been argued that this imperialist modernizing activity was a uniquely American phenomenon[15]; but as Gorgas' secondment to South Africa suggests, it was part of a wider modernizing project within European empires. The discoverer of the carrier of malaria was not an American but a British Indian army doctor, Ronald Ross.

Much exchange of information occurred among the European powers on the control of tropical diseases. In the wake of a worldwide cholera epidemic, an International Sanitary Convention had been held in 1892 and within a few years an International Office of Health was established in Paris.[16] As an official US representative, Gorgas himself took part in an Egyptian Medical Congress and familiarized himself with sanitation problems 'encountered in the construction of the Suez Canal', though these proved to be quite different from the problems experienced in Panama.[17] Americans were more diligent and forthright in pursuing health measures whereas the British in India dragged their heels for the indigenous, but the first objective for all colonizing peoples was to protect themselves against tropical diseases before venturing to help the colonized. American colonial health official Victor Heiser's testimony confirms that priority number one was to safeguard the American officials and military in the new possessions.[18] While Americans were often more vigorous in applying new sanitation policies, Gorgas himself complained that his superiors, who were trying to cut costs in Panama, did not give him enough financial support.[19] Moreover, sanitation measures were not simply medical interventions but measures functionally controlling the local populations, particularly in the case of the Philippines.[20] Nor were Americans the only colonial rulers to change traditional societies by building roads and dams and fostering scientific forestry. In India, much infrastructure was built, though directed towards export industries rather than improving the lot of subsistence farmers.

A second area in which Americans strove to distinguish the position of their own empire from European rivals was in the provision of moral reform. Opium policy quickly became a cause célèbre. US missionaries in the Philippines declared the Chinese smoking of opium to be an unacceptable custom. They felt it blocked Christian evangelizing. When the US regime in Manila in 1903 proposed to licence opium and tolerate its import, the missionaries rose in righteous alarm and through their effective lobbying in Washington had the policy changed. An Opium Commission was established to investigate alternatives. It toured the Far East and recommended a policy of restricting use to purely medical cases. This prohibitionist approach in turn became the basis for American policy in the region. The government saw advantages in advocating opium prohibition for the entire South and East Asian region because it put the United States on the side of the Chinese government. A new generation of mission-educated Chinese dreamed of modernizing China and at the same time strengthening independent Chinese action to discard Western influences, including British opium imports. The United States supported the attempt of the Chinese government to reform China in this way. In so doing, the United States might gain economically, as a modernizing China dealing squarely with the opium problem would be a better target for free trade under the Open Door policy. American missionaries in the region emphasized that an opium-free nation would have more money to spend on legitimate imports. Free trade and moral improvement would be mutually reinforcing.[21] The US government may also have supported moral policies such as anti-opium policies because these legitimized American forms of empire. As Anne Foster remarks, 'By 1909, Americans comfortably employed the rhetoric of moral superiority of U.S. rule in the Philippines when compared with other colonial powers, not least because the United States was the only power to give up the lucrative opium revenue voluntarily'.[22] Missionaries drew favourable contrasts between the United States and several other European governments on the opium issue and also on the restriction of imports of alcohol into the Pacific Islands, another issue on which the nation took a moral stance from 1902.

These moral projects of empire had reciprocal effects at home that historians have often ignored. The island possessions in the Far East had a domestic impact through missionaries, church magazines, lantern shows and exhibitions like the St Louis World's Fair of 1904. Exhibitions were a major vehicle through which government tried to assert its view of American colonialism's benevolent uplift of non-European peoples. The effect of such media-savvy events was, however, to increase the amount of information available on colonial subjects rather than to deepen understanding of the American possessions. At the World's Fair, exotic themes predominated, where the Philippine pavilion, with near-naked native Filipinos exhibited in prurient fashion for the wide-eyed Midwestern gaze, reinforced a sense of America's burden to civilize, stirred curiosity in the Orient and justified recent atrocities.[23] Yet the image and the impact were far from uniform. World's fairs were contested spaces and the images of steady European progress disputed by groups sympathetic to the Filipino and subverted by the carnivalesque atmosphere of the fairs themselves.[24] Soon government officials began to modify their attempts to use world's fairs for such overtly imperialist propaganda, though they still used these events, as in the Pan-Pacific Exposition of 1915, to celebrate American commercial expansion and technological superiority.[25]

On the pro-empire side, it was not just government proclaiming the virtues of imperial uplift for the savage peoples of the world. The wider public exhibited a degree of enthusiasm for the white man's burden that historians have not fully appreciated. Youth groups such as the YMCA were supportive of American tutelage in the Philippines; young people's publications such as the *Youth's Companion* of 1909 rejoiced at the spread of 'greater America' and told boys' own annual tales of the fall of Manila.[26] *National Geographic* saw an unprecedented surge in membership post-1898 and the acquisition of the Philippines became a major topic for coverage through exotic pictures of the new possessions and their 'savage' peoples. The impact of the colonies on the metropole thus came not simply through events which governments tried to stage-manage, but through popular culture as well.[27]

Empire affected not only attitudes at home, but also domestic policies. In order to combat problems in the new territories exposed by colonial rule and military action, it would become necessary to reform American policies on drug use, drinking and sexual conduct in the army. These changes then provided opportunities for reformers to import to the metropole the lessons of colonial rule for regulation of morals. The spur to convert imperial attitudes and practices on the use of alcohol into domestic policy came from the response of reform groups to the Spanish–American War and especially the war in the Philippines. The American occupation meant more military forces and more conspicuous action by the military. This action conflicted with the civilizing mission proclaimed by American policy-makers. Despite all the talk about trade possibilities and the white man's burden, the exports of American culture up to 1902 had, critics maintained, mainly been soldiers and the imports from the Philippines mainly the dead and their coffins. Moral reformers argued that an American Empire should be different, moral and upright. A campaign developed to oppose drinking by army personnel in the military canteens in the Philippines. Alcohol abuse was said to contribute to diseases, death and poor military performance, and drunken soldiers also gave a bad example for the natives. Immediately after the Spanish–American War began, the Woman's Christian Temperance Union successfully lobbied for a law to make the military canteens dry. The WCTU and the churches also wanted the Philippine government to shut down American-style saloons freely operating in Manila and vicinity, though in this latter demand they had only partial success.

One effect of this agitation was to assuage domestic American anxieties about imperial responsibility and to buttress pro-imperial attitudes at home. The WCTU sought to discover what reformers could do 'toward righting the atrocious conditions in the Philippines' where 'under supervision and sanction of American authorities' liquor interests flourished.[28] The canteen issue helped to discharge evangelical concerns about the imperial adventure – to cleanse it and provide a good moral purpose. The WCTU thus helped to legitimize empire. The controversy contained overtones of the correct example to be set internationally and the need to develop a morally superior position to that of other empires in order to provide world leadership. The effects upon the WCTU developed thereby an alliance (partly unconscious) with the military occupiers. Though reluctant to endorse empire openly because the temperance ranks contained a good many pacifists and anti-imperialists, the WCTU organ, the *Union Signal*, now in effect endorsed the Philippines administration, but only insofar as its practices could turn 'barbarism into civilization'. However, the WCTU remained uneasy about empire and enough in tune with anti-imperialists to rule out any wholehearted endorsement of American policy. Lillian Stevens, the WCTU's national president, urged the United States to avoid a permanent occupation of Cuba and charged that special economic interests were likely to subvert humanitarian endeavours there and in the Philippines.[29] Moral imperialism was thus an unstable force, at once supportive and critical of formal colonialism.

Disquiet over the acquisition of empire also touched upon another matter. How could the United States avoid the possible moral contamination of the American population that exposure to the ideas and practices of foreign nations might bring? Imperialism's repercussions on the homeland were important in this sense. The WCTU could experiment with prohibition policies abroad and utilize the sense of guilt over the conduct of American troops to extend those policies at home. To achieve a liquor-free army in the Philippines, the temperance forces stressed the need for a liquor-free canteen in the entire American army. As half of the American army regiments were stationed in colonial outposts at any one time as late as 1907, this equation was both easy and essential.[30] Thus one of formal imperialism's impacts was to gird the loins of moral reformers at home, to stimulate their efforts to cleanse American society of evil assumed to be born of moral contagion abroad.

Like most other American temperance organizations, the WCTU had by this time begun to rally around the campaign for national alcohol prohibition. This was not an inevitable result. In fact anti-alcohol reformers had argued over the issue in the 1890s, but the discovery that young men could become corrupted in the army overseas hastened reformers' efforts to instigate prohibition at home. Specifically, the campaign against the military canteen in the Philippines became a covert way to experiment incrementally with small-scale forms of prohibition legislation. Increasingly the Anti-Saloon League of America and its allies took this approach after 1900. The impact was destabilizing as temperance reformers adopted the controversial and divisive objectives of national prohibition – objectives that were not purely a product of conditions within the United States.

From the Philippines occupation came another unwanted side effect of empire – in the spectre of sexual contact with the indigenous and consequence dangers of venereal disease and racial impurity. The WCTU took a central part in the purity crusade against the official inspection of prostitutes undertaken in the Philippines by military doctors for the health and safety of the American army in the field. The WCTU was concerned that the United States' version of empire should not be morally stained, as was the British Raj, which had sanctioned licensed prostitution. WCTU lobbyists obtained an official medical book of inspection and used it to great effect in embarrassing the US military. Secretary of War Elihu Root was inundated with hostile petitions, letters and personal callers. He reversed US policy and banned inspections. The official regulation of Filipino prostitutes in this way stopped, though informally the army still allowed doctors to report on the condition of suspect women. Like the sale of liquor, prostitution defied the attempts of reformers to eradicate it, but the moral exceptionalism of American colonial rule had been asserted.

The WCTU stressed the need to remove the stain from the American flag – to make it, as one reformer later observed, 'stand in the Far East as the symbol of righteousness'. [31]

The unease of missionaries and reformers helped to make American Empire distinctive. The other notable aspect was the readiness, relative to European empires, to promise independence. Yet this feature should not be exaggerated or simply seen as a product of an American anti-colonial tradition. There was no guarantee that the Philippines would get self-government at all in the early years, nor was a policy of working towards independence a uniform one between political parties. More important than American benevolence in moving in this direction were protests and armed resistance in the colonies. At home anti-imperialists argued, though unsuccessfully, the incompatibility of empire and republicanism. Bostonian mugwumps, socialists, intellectuals and others joined a motley de facto coalition with Southern racists, some western populists and opportunist Democrats to oppose the acquisition of colonies. [32] The defeat of William Jennings Bryan, the anti-imperialist Democratic Party candidate at the presidential election of 1900, temporarily put paid to the political impact of the domestic crusade against colonies. In the Philippines, however, the US government faced opposition much stiffer and longer in duration. A resistance movement developed under Emilio Aguinaldo after the Americans refused to recognize a Filipino declaration of independence made at the time of the Spanish–American War. The American occupation force could only succeed in pacifying these opponents gradually and at great loss of life. Atrocities were committed on both sides. Some 126,000 US troops served in the islands, where they received an unwelcome introduction to the real world of colonialism's transcultural 'exchanges'. About 4000 died, while 16,000 Filipino combatants were killed and as many as 200,000 Filipino civilians lost their lives. By 1902 the United States declared the war over, but even though the mission had been theoretically accomplished, fighting continued for several years. The resistance helped by the pressures it put upon American financial and military commitments and upon the American self-image as an anti-colonial nation to limit the imperial adventure. The government needed to introduce measures to show that the American commitment was not to be infinite. Already in 1907 a constituent assembly, though very much advisory and administration controlled, had met.

Resistance to empire from the Filipinos and their allies in the United States gained further traction through an American political system that differed sharply from the British or French. Appointments to the colonial bureaucracy were political patronage jobs, as in the territories of the continental United States. No substantial colonial office power existed to lobby for continued control, for adequate numbers of administrative personnel in the field or to stand above party politics on the issue of imperialism. Philippines administrator and later US Secretary of War William

Howard Taft, though on the side of a long-term tutelage, had his eye on
the presidency after Roosevelt and the election of 1908. American elections determined a 4-year cycle to phases of American Empire. Within
that framework feverish efforts had to be made to show progress towards
a measure of self-rule. Moreover, anti-imperialism still lingered within
the ranks of the Democratic Party. The pro-colonial lobby's influence
dipped sharply in 1913 when Woodrow Wilson took the White House.
With Wilson's Democrats in charge, a new pro-independence Governor-
General, Francis Harrison, was appointed to Manila and a course set in
the 1916 Jones Act for self-government through 'Filipinization' of the
civil service; the act established a fully elected Filipino legislature with a
house and senate. This predated serious efforts from the British to decol-
onize India. American anti-colonial credentials were also shored up by the
case of Cuba, where the United States did not maintain a formal colonial
regime. Under the Platt Amendment (1902), Cuba received its nominal
freedom in a victory for the anti-colonialists.[33] Hawaii, on the other hand,
had been admitted as a territory and did not qualify as a colony, though
it was to be 1959 before it was admitted as a state, partly because the
influx of Japanese plantation workers made the islands seem ransomed to
expanding Japanese power in the Pacific.[34]

While the government moved some colonies towards independence,
others, particularly Puerto Rico, were kept on a very different track – in a
political no man's land – not bound for either independence or statehood.
The Foraker Act of 1900 retained Puerto Rico as a non-incorporated
territory. This uncertain status would cause tensions with nationalists in
subsequent years. Puerto Rico remained essentially a colony, but one with
close and growing economic and demographic ties to the mainland by the
1920s as Puerto Ricans gained entry permits to the United States, where
they could earn money to remit back to relatives. Under the circumstances,
independence became as impossible for the United States to give as it was
for Puerto Rican nationalists to accept the alternative of statehood. Puerto
Rico had been essentially bought off, with too large an economic stake in
retaining American links. The United States applied a highly assimilationist
social and educational policy that aimed to indoctrinate Puerto Ricans
with pro-American attitudes.[35] This programme could succeed, however,
partly because there was a strong collaborationist element within political
factions among Puerto Ricans from as early as 1900. Thus indoctrination
and collaboration combined, but resistance to and dissent from American
rule was not inconsiderable, peaking in the 1930s, an era of violence and
economic discontent. The United States would not countenance independence at this time, precisely when the Filipinos were offered their freedom.
The reason for the retention of Puerto Rico was its potential to help guard
the approaches to the Panama Canal and provide a naval base. It was, as
Samoa and Guam were, valued for its strategic potential.

Puerto Rico's anomalous position put the alleged American generosity towards the Philippines into perspective. The United States promised eventual self-government and independence to the Philippines partly because the resistance of the Filipinos immediately after the acquisition had been so strong, but also because the number of Filipinos was so large that assimilation was impossible and because by the 1930s the islands were simply vulnerable to Japanese expansionism and aggression, a position only too well confirmed in the Second World War. Moreover, by promising Philippine independence in 10 years after 1935, the United States could divest itself eventually of the need to support the islands' agriculture, which was in sharp competition with US sugar beet and other interests. Cuba was similar. There the nation was too close for the United States to contemplate an acquisition that might eventually open immigration to Afro-Cuban peoples. Nor was strategy so important an issue in the Cuban case, because Puerto Rico more efficiently and conveniently provided bases in the Caribbean.

The key questions everywhere in the rule of American Empire were thus racial and geo-political, not anti-colonial. Strategy determined the exertion of power, and race the manner in which the new relationship with the United States would be deployed. The decision whether to apply principles of formal control, informal control or territorial incorporation rested upon the demographic composition of the would-be colony and the racial threat incorporation as a territory would pose for the United States. The United States shared this racial exclusiveness and racial ideologies with several other imperial powers.

Territorial acquisitions were classic pawns in the American strategy, which was not about the glories of taking land. Colonial outposts were merely the means to an end – commercial expansion and security backed by naval power. The influential naval strategist and historian Mahan understood how to achieve this goal. In his book *The Influence of Sea Power Upon History*, he studied how British naval superiority not only aided that nation directly in a militarily sense but also facilitated British domination of world commerce. Mahan believed by the 1890s that Britain could no longer rule single handedly but that an Anglo-American consortium of the seas should claim control.[36] He therefore urged a larger navy, de facto domination of the Caribbean and construction of the isthmian canal. Mahan's arguments won – or coincided with – political support in regard to a strong navy and pro-imperialist policies from such influential Washington figures as Senators Henry Cabot Lodge of Massachusetts and Albert Beveridge of Indiana, as well as Theodore Roosevelt, who became Assistant Secretary of the Navy in 1897 and the victorious vice-presidential candidate in 1900. These and others like them constituted a foreign policy elite within the Republican Party developing the architecture of empire.

Nested in this architecture was the policy of increased opportunities for American trade and investment abroad. The Open Door Note of Secretary of State John Hay in 1899 asserted the non-violability of China and equal access to markets under the most-favoured nation principle. Hay's position became a key prong in American policy, though it was actually derived from British policy. Another string to the expansionist bow was so-called dollar diplomacy in which American laws encouraged the nation's banking houses to invest in Latin America and then act as de facto government agencies reordering the local economies through fiscal changes such as central banking and gold standard currency stabilization. The policy was in effect a forerunner of the International Monetary Fund of the post-Second World War period.[37] The US government used this financial power backed by the state to leverage trade and political interests in Latin America and East Asia. The government also intervened increasingly in Latin American affairs under the Roosevelt Corollary to the Monroe Doctrine (1905), which made the United States the enforcer within the hemisphere of intergovernmental financial transactions.

Missionary and reform lobbying functioned within the *real politic* of these American strategic objectives. It could serve the assertion of a new American form of anti-colonial hegemony over other empires in order to gain influence and concessions within the European struggles for world power. But the hard power policies of economics and military necessity were closely related to the 'soft power' of moral influence and cultural hegemony in a specific confluence of values as well. Hard power policy makers and the advocates of moral reform thought alike and influenced one another. Soft power, a term invented by political scientists late in the twentieth century to describe the post-Cold War world, was hardly new.[38]

It is not sufficiently understood how important religion and the idea of the spread of 'civilization' were in the motivations for American expansion. American imperialism had a strong tone of evangelical moral reform – even officially as seen in President McKinley's pious reflections on the acquisition of the Philippines. There is a strong case for historians to reinvestigate the impact of evangelical religion upon American policy makers. One thinks of Theodore Roosevelt and other architects of empire such as Mahan as tough realists, but they had thoroughly religious as much as strategic views. It is little known that Mahan served 10 years on the Board of Missions of the Protestant Episcopal Church and told Theodore Roosevelt in 1901 that it was important for the European powers to provide 'simple, entire liberty of entrance for European thought as well as European commerce'.[39] Both Mahan and Roosevelt justified the use of force in international relations in terms of the spread of Christian civilization. God was 'the power who works in us to sanctification', Mahan stated. Mahan was one of the contributors to the 1910 World Missionary Conference in Edinburgh. Through Seth Low, head of the American advisory group to the conference, Mahan had a major influence on the conference's deliberations.[40] Mahan also published in 1909 a devotional book, arguing in part that the English racial advance, like Israel's entry into

Canaan, had been authorized by God to redeem American territory from the (Amer-)'Indians' and set it apart for a distinctive mission of universal salvation.[41] Events such as the annexation of the Philippines were seen as part of 'a divine strategy for the incorporation of East Asia within Christianity'. Mahan welded commerce and Christianity together and predicted danger in China gaining European material wealth without the 'higher ideals, which in Europe have made good their controlling influence over mere physical might'.[42] The threat of an East–West clash could only be averted by 'the extension of American power and its corollary, Christian civilization'.[43]

From 1913 to 1919 the shape of this new power became clearer under the foreign policy of a president with an anti-imperialist pedigree, Woodrow Wilson. Friend of missionaries such as John Mott (the peripatetic leader of the Young Men's Christian Association and the Student Volunteer Movement), the Presbyterian moralist Wilson took American diplomacy further in the direction of defining American self-interest as a form of cultural hegemony through American internationalism. American missionaries and Wilson shared a similar philosophy, perhaps hardly surprisingly as the president was the son of a clergyman who had once been a missionary to Quebec Indians. Christianity and manifest destiny reinforced American exceptionalism and reconciled Americans to empire at the same time. But it would not be the formal empire that prevailed.

The imperial burst of 1898–1902 had demonstrated the power of America, but not its source. In order to understand this point we must do more than look for economic explanations of either formal or informal imperialism. We must appreciate the implications of the rise of American economic power as a political fact in global politics and culture. In order to do this we must step back and consider the topic of imperialism from the perspective of the American economy. The secret of American economic and political strength globally was created in the previous century of continental development. The country's internal assets provided a platform upon which business and government could project economic muscle as well as political influence across the globe. American economic power also had enormous cultural appeal at home and abroad. The nation's fast-growing influence and interests abroad in turn explain how the nation was drawn into the formal imperialism discussed above. The economic and ecological 'footprint' of the United States had widened, with vast consequences for other countries and for Americans.

The most important accessory to American power was material abundance. The land and its attendant treasures partly explain how and why the United States could be self-sufficient in many products. The United States could supply most of its own foodstuffs and energy requirements in the nineteenth century. Indeed, the nation was a major exporter of wheat, cotton and corn, providing Europe with vital grain supplies through to the 1920s. Equally important, the major resources needed for industrial development – such as wood, coal, iron and many precious minerals – were all found in ample quantities within the United States. For example, in forests only Russia had a larger supply in 1900. These elements of self-sufficiency helped the American economy grow when combined with the injection of international labour, capital and transport improvements. Not only did the United States hold supplies of raw materials for industry within its vast borders but these were also effectively exploited for industrialization from the 1870s to the 1920s in a process of resource use more intensive than was true of other industrializing economies of the time.[44]

The very abundance of resources, however, tended to project American appetites outward upon the world. The initial largesse of forest, prairie grass, water and soil created a sense of spaciousness to American Empire; the reality was, however, increasing scarcity produced by frontier conditions specifically as a result of the way the low labour to land ratio worked. One effect of land and other resource largesse was a culture of waste. Alarmingly the annual per-capita consumption of timber was more than 10 times that of France, Britain and other industrializing countries. As the National Conservation Commission concluded in 1909, 'History clearly showed that in countries with abundant natural resources and sparse population there is no thought of the future, and all energy is directed to the exploitation and reckless use of what nature has abundantly provided.'[45] The labour–resource trade off was particularly noticeable in agriculture. To create farmland easily, forests had been burned rather than cut down because of labour shortages and had also served as a major source of railroad ties, bridges and engine fuel because wood could be conveniently harvested close to railroad lines. Wood for housing, furniture and home fuel was used with equal profligacy. Instead of bringing in stone fences (except in New England where rocks had to be moved to make farming possible), settlers in the East erected cheap and easily constructed wooden fences, even though these would not last. Once land was cleared for farming, precious soil was used to enhance the agricultural economy and produce abundant supplies of grain. Again land was worked with profligacy because of the shortage of labour. Little attention was paid to soil conservation. Rather, quick gains were made before moving on. Wheat and cotton yields were initially high, but diminishing economic returns inevitably followed bumper crops in older communities as people moved west. As the National Conservation Commission noted, 'The universal custom in new regions has been the continuous taking of crops from the soils without putting anything back in the way of manure etc.'[46]

Because of the shortage of human labour, farmers and factory managers tended to introduce machinery to overcome problems of labour scarcity. This meant the need for more energy to run machines, at first in the nineteenth century with water power or wood and increasingly after the Civil War in the case of factories with fossil fuels. During the First World War mechanical tractors largely replaced horses on farms as the conversion reached its logical conclusion. Yet the United States had already turned to fossil fuels for lighting in the late nineteenth century, then for automobiles after 1900. The nation was again fortunate in having suitable fuel, with oil discovered in Pennsylvania in 1859, then New York and later in other states such as California and Texas by 1900. The great monopoly of John D. Rockefeller's Standard Oil Company emerged and supplied crude to the rest of the world, controlling 70 per cent of the world market. As historian Howard Zinn comments, 'Oil was now second to cotton as the leading product sent overseas.'[47]

In the meantime the profits from cotton and wheat that had flowed to transportation companies and to cities could be used to develop a 'second nature', reorganizing the resources of the frontier into the built environment.[48] However, the urban/consumer economy developing by the late nineteenth century created demands for raw materials and export markets that could not be satisfied completely within the boundaries of the nation. Frederick Jackson Turner proclaimed the end of the frontier, but the mass production of the second industrial revolution upped the stakes and transferred the realization of American abundance with all of its contradictions into new realms. From the early twentieth century, manufacturers sought to produce larger qualities of consumer goods for the urban middle class and even mass markets, using advertising, corporate reorganization of marketing and a revolution in the production process soon known generically as Fordism. At the fulcrum of these changes was Henry Ford. He replaced a largely craft-based manufacturing system with assembly lines. Whereas skilled workers had exerted substantial control over their work practices, the new system featured large-scale manufacturing processes centred on chain-driven moving lines that supplied parts to assembly teams. Therein semi-skilled workers performed management-specified tasks. The process accelerated the pace of work and realized large productivity gains.[49] The price of automobiles fell sharply, allowing the motorization of America in the 1920s. The upside in the adoption of these processes was the way the older ideas of abundance of resources could be transferred into the consumer cornucopia that mass assembly-line production supplied. Ford did not hide the sources of his improvements, which were quickly copied by other manufacturers. The scientific management ideas of Frederick Winslow Taylor had already stressed measuring work practices and developing optimum times for specific tasks, but Ford's insight lay in the broader need to change the entire system of production.[50] The motorcar magnate's methods were more effective and underpinned prosperity for the middle classes between 1914 and 1929. Though US workers did dull, repetitive work and were discouraged from joining unions, they were better paid than their counterparts in Europe.[51]

The downside of this consumer-oriented society was the widening economic and ecological footprint of the United States. The nation already dominated the late nineteenth-century world demand for several tropical commodities. Americans had sugar interests in the Caribbean, Hawaii and (after 1898) the Philippines, and their fruit companies in Central America turned parts of the region into 'banana republics'. The United States was not the only coffee market in the world; much was consumed in under-developed colonies, continental Europe and the Islamic world, but the American was already the largest. By the 1880s the United States consumed over a third of all the coffee exported from producing countries and almost half by 1900. This thirst for caffeine had considerable environmental and social impacts in hill regions of South America, as forests and subsistence farms were converted for cash crop exports. Burned by fluctuating supplies and prices for Java coffee, American coffee merchants had abandoned that source after decades of trade with the Orient and turned to Brazil.[52] Meanwhile, interest in range cattle spread from the American west through Central and South America, and in the early twentieth-century American foresters began to harvest through principles of scientific management the tropical timbers of Filipino and Central American rain forests. Later, in the 1920s, the US possession of 90 per cent of the world's cars meant considerable call upon the Malayan rubber industry for tires, though in Liberia and Dutch Sumatra, US companies such as Firestone bought up large chunks of land for rubber plantations to satisfy the automobile industry's heavy demands. These 'insatiable' appetites, as one historian has termed them,[53] were certainly not unique to Americans. Thus British India's white rulers cleared forest in Assam for teak products and replaced the landscape with tea plantations. Such changes were social and cultural transformation of immense significance, as they substituted monocultures that discouraged biodiversity in a variety of European empires, but the fact does not gainsay the extensive ecological and economic impacts of American consumers.

The American market was like a giant steamship swallowing up small boats in its powerful wake. Both Hawaii and Puerto Rico were in this category, but a key case of the effects of the American giant was the Cuban Revolution of the 1890s. Americans had substantial investment in Cuban sugar plantations and railways. This economic interest was well known to the US government and a cause of concern in the light of the simmering revolt on the island. As President Grover Cleveland pointed out in 1896, '$30,000,000 to $50,000,000 of American capital are invested in the plantations and in railroad, mining, and other business enterprises on the island. The volume of trade between the United States and Cuba, which in 1889 amounted to about $64,000,000, rose in 1893 to about $103,000,000.'[54] More significant was the way the vagaries of American demand for Cuba's products drew the nation directly into the island's social conflicts. Americans took the bulk of the sugar crop, but these imports adversely affected the domestic beet sugar industry. American farm interests lobbied successfully for increased import duties on foreign sugar. The Cuban economy suffered in consequence and the resultant economic discontent stimulated the outbreak of the new phase of rebellion against Spanish rule in 1895.[55] As conditions in Cuba deteriorated and Spain's fierce repression of the rebellion dragged on, Americans feared a power vacuum into which another European power could step, but also expressed a moral urge to intervene. The nation's financial interests in the island underpinned these anxieties. When Cubans damaged foreign property on the island, that action implicated the United States. Some Cubans fled to the United States where they lobbied for intervention, smuggled arms back and returned to fight, hoping for American support. As Cleveland put it, the US government was being 'constantly called upon to protect American citizens' and 'to claim damages for injuries to persons and property'.[56] The United States did intervene, though not until the USS *Maine* incident precipitated the war. The whole episode demonstrated that American 'space' had spread with the de facto boundaries of the nation far beyond the official ones. The footprint of American power abroad had drawn the nation into war and contributed to the policy of formal imperialism adopted by McKinley.[57]

Before 1917 the political and military impact of American economic power was felt only to a limited extent, but was already important in Latin America, especially Mexico. US investors built railroads in Mexico, acquired land and developed resources industries such as oil. These economic interests and their impact on Mexican politics contributed powerfully to the destabilization of the Mexican government in a turbulent era. One example was the Texas (Oil) Company. Faced with falling production of crude in its American holdings, the Texas Company moved into Tampico, Mexico. From there its involvement worked its way into American policy. The company had strong links with the Texas Democratic Party and through the Texan Colonel Edward House, adviser to President Wilson, to the White House after 1913. These oil interests came under threat from the Mexican Revolution of 1910–11 and the turmoil that followed. Wilson approved, according to historian John Mason Hart, an armed invasion to stabilize Mexico and protect strategic interests in 'oil, rubber, copper, and zinc'.[58] The tangled details of the Vera Cruz intervention of 1914 need not detain us here. Conservative strongman Victoriano Huerta had murdered the Mexican president and seized power. Partly for this reason and partly because Huerta was thought to favour European rather than American financial concessions, Wilson withheld recognition and engineered overthrow of the Huerta government only to find that his successor proclaimed a far more radical policy inimical to foreign penetration of the economy. Friction continued until the First World War intervened to distract American attention. This was the first time that the United States had refused to recognize a foreign government on the moral grounds of its allegedly anti-democratic politics. The action set a precedent for the moralistic foreign policy that was to follow.

Outside of Latin America, the nations of the world experienced American power economically, not politically. At the turn of the twentieth-century Britain and its colonies felt the growing impact of American technology. Fifty-three per cent of American trade was with the British Empire in 1900, but that trade was unequal. For every dollar Americans received from exports Britain got back 31 cents from its trade with the United States. The torrent of imports came not only from food now, but also from steel and a host of other industrial items. Underground railways, at first British in construction, were now built or augmented by American technology and funded by J. P. Morgan's financial house. Even the English press was supplied with American printing machinery. In his book, *The American Invaders*, contemporary commentator Frederick McKenzie noted the effects and the possible future for all of Europe: 'America has invaded Europe not with armed men, but with manufactured products. Its leaders have been captains of industry and skilled financiers, whose conquests are having a profound effect on the every-day lives of the masses from Madrid to St. Petersburg.'[59]

While this account registered a certain exaggeration and alarmism, American economic penetration abroad would move steadily in the 1920s into consumer goods, and many other economic changes anticipated in the period 1900–14 would be carried much further. However, American external expansion would not favour permanent acquisition of additional new territories, but economic and political policies to enhance a new world order. The architect would be Woodrow Wilson, who denounced an anti-democratic regime in Mexico while simultaneously pursuing Machiavellian policies in regard to American business there. He would combine after 1914 the economic interests of the United States abroad with moralistic diplomacy and advocacy of democracy for other countries. This approach was partly based on his missionary background and the experience of American cultural expansion. But it would take a seismic shift to develop something more than an economic interest in flexing American political power beyond the Caribbean. Europe's war did that.

11

The New World Order in the Era of Woodrow Wilson

The summer of 1914 was calm enough along the eastern seaboard. The Boston Braves, ancestor team of the Atlanta Braves, were on track for the baseball world series and all was apparently well with the world of Americans. Nevertheless, the diplomatic and political impact of the fatal shots at Sarajevo on June 28, 1914 was quickly felt across the Atlantic. True, the outbreak of the First World War in August 1914 did not directly affect the United States. After all, the nation had a long tradition of non-involvement in European power politics. President Wilson at once proclaimed neutrality, highlighting, interestingly enough, not the precepts of George Washington against foreign entanglements but the transnational allegiance of Americans. Drawn as they were from many nations opposed in the conflict, the American people must of necessity practice non-involvement.[1] To do otherwise would tear the country apart. Yet as a trading nation with a strong international commerce, the war was bound to affect the United States. The war intensified conflicts within American society just as Wilson feared, but also strengthened the American state and a sense of national exceptionalism and spurred a vigorous projection outward of new forms of cultural, economic and political expansionism in the period after 1919. This expansion was based upon an altered relationship with Europe and the world. Woodrow Wilson would be at the centre of this new influence through his articulation of a new American 'internationalism'.[2]

Though the United States departed from its political isolation towards Europe, the results of the war would be contradictory. The pattern of American transnational connections became more uneven, characterized by both involvement and resistance to involvement and, building upon the achievements of the Progressive Era, by further tightening of national borders. The nation-state continued to be produced transnationally in these ways. As a result of the wartime experience the United States erected new political and trade barriers against transnational influences in the name of security and prosperity. At the same time, the world war and its aftermath pushed the United States into greater political and economic involvement, in search of wider markets and investments. The result was the very unstable new international order of the 1920s that collapsed in the Great Depression. In many ways the 1920s represented a harbinger of the growing yet still inchoate American hegemony set to replace the old European empires. As such it would owe much to earlier American experience and to the cultural stresses of wartime. The increasing role of (American-led) transnational organizations, the policy of formal and ideological anti-colonialism and the extension of American media and communications pointed towards this new post-imperial world order. At the same time, international forces accentuated the tendencies of Americans to retreat behind a cultural as well as political wall of their own making. The significance of the 1920s for the new international order of the American Century would not be revealed until another world war had been fought.

The effects of the European war upon American society were evident well before the nation joined as a belligerent nearly 3 years later. At first the economic impacts were positive. The conflict perpetuated the long period of prosperity that, despite several financial panics, extended from 1897 to 1919. European demand surged for American goods, including armaments and foodstuffs. To finance the war, the British were forced to take out massive loans in New York and to liquidate their American assets. For the first time the United States became a creditor nation, owing the world less than it lent.

Another effect was demographic change with profound social implications. European emigration to the Americas was cut off as armies deployed their young men in battle and as U-boats made the crossing of the ocean more perilous. As a result of the disruption and the war-driven economic boom, unemployment dropped and factories searched for cheap labour from the American South and Mexico rather than from the Mediterranean. This shift in labour supply changed the complexion of American racial relations. No longer could race be shuffled off as a problem for 'the South'. Large numbers of African-Americans moved permanently to Northern cities and whites reacted with prejudice and violence. Riots occurred in cities such as East St Louis in 1917 and in the notable case of Chicago in 1919. De facto real estate segregation rapidly transformed neighbourhoods. Each week, blocks of Chicago's south side shifted from being white neighbourhoods to being predominantly black. With race relations deteriorating, the Ku Klux Klan revived – helped along by the 1915 film *Birth of A Nation*, which depicted the outcome of the Civil War in racial terms and treated Klansmen as heroes. Meanwhile tens of thousands of Mexicans streamed into the Southwestern states, accelerating a movement begun in the 1890s when the railroad between the United States and Mexico had been completed. They worked on farms replacing the now excluded

Chinese and Japanese and also increasingly moved to cities. Thus events far away in Europe shifted the demographic balance in the United States and caused racial and ethnic convulsions that reverberated in the 1920s and beyond.

Try as President Wilson did to keep the nation neutral, the insistence of Americans on trading with belligerents and the equal determination of the German U-boat commanders in attacking that shipping inevitably brought the United States and Germany into conflict. Sympathies among the elite towards Germany as an important centre of European culture and Anglo-Saxon racial civilization gave way to stereotypes of barbarians. The society still divided over this depiction, however. Opinion in the Midwest among those of German descent was hostile to entering the war. They were joined in their opposition by socialists, feminists, pacifists and some labour unions. Wilson sympathized with Britain's rule of law and parliamentary democracy, while many young Americans volunteered for the Red Cross and others joined the Canadian Army or those of their homelands in Europe. But Wilson was still set upon a course of principled neutrality. American attitudes towards Europe became ones of thinking Europe inferior because such a conflict had occurred.

Americans began to die in the conflict before the nation entered the war. The attack upon the *Lusitania* in 1915, an unarmed British ocean liner on which 128 Americans perished, inflamed American opinion. Pushing Wilson towards hostilities was also Germany's intrigue in Mexico, with the Zimmerman Note in January 1917 threatening US dominance in the region. Audaciously, the Germans offered to back Mexican claims for return of the huge territory seized by Washington after the Mexican War of 1846–48. This maladroit intervention brought simmering border security issues with Mexico, the Monroe Doctrine and the European conflict together in a potent mix, inflaming public opinion. It was, however, the increased submarine attacks upon American shipping by a Germany desperate to strangle Britain of supplies that caused relations to deteriorate to breaking point. On April 6, 1917 Congress declared war, triggering the greatest military undertaking in American history to that time. The eventual mobilization of millions of men was certain to have profound cultural impacts across national boundaries as much as it would influence the outcome of the war.[3]

Until the main body of troops disembarked in the summer of 1918, the United States did not directly influence the battles. The Germans, freed by the end of the war on the eastern front after Russia's capitulation, threatened to push through to Paris in March 1918 but their progress was halted and fresh American troops helped drive the enemy back decisively towards the German frontier. The United States had not won the war, but it had tipped the balance in terms of allied morale and materiel. Meanwhile, over 2 million Americans, including over 40,000 African-American troops, had landed in Europe; 53,000 American men died on the battlefield and many of these lay buried in war graves in France that were administered post-war by the United States as a poignant reminder of the human consequences of the expanding American world role.[4] Soldiers were disappointed by what they saw of war-torn Europe and many returned disillusioned and cynical about the causes of American involvement. A bout of emotional isolationism set in but, all in all, the war remained the most extensive exposure to Europe that Americans would undergo until after 1941. Any mentality of isolation could not be secure henceforth. Soon middle-class tourists flocked to Europe and intellectuals such as Ernest Hemmingway, Gertrude Stein, Max Eastman and Lincoln Steffens headed for Paris to escape American Babbittry as the nation entered on a new phase of cultural conflict over sex, religion and prohibition. Perhaps the lyrics of 'How you gonna keep 'em down on the farm, after they've seen Paree' (1919)[5] were correct after all.

Wilson was determined that American participation should not lead to more of the same old imperialist rivalries. He was a liberal in the nineteenth century Anglo-American tradition of free trade, moderate reform and nationalism – his politico-economic views were akin to those of Victorian era-prime minister W. E. Gladstone. Wilson drew upon these liberal convictions and synthesized them with growing American power and the new world situation of collapsing multinational empires to produce a new diplomacy. The result was the Fourteen Points enunciated on January 8, 1918. Guaranteed freedom of the seas, disarmament, an end to secret treaties, and rights of national self-determination – these were some of the principled demands of the nation's high-minded president.

Noble though the Fourteen Points seemed, very significant in their development was the threat that Wilson felt from the Bolshevik Revolution. He articulated an alternative vision to socialism and revolution, one based on liberal individualism. Thus the Fourteen Points should not be seen in isolation. They were a product of the international political conjuncture rather than simply an American-derived idea projected upon the world stage and they signalled a *real politic* commitment to American interests. Wilson proposed a new form of international relations that would go beyond imperialism, because he, like V. I. Lenin, saw the war as a product of imperialist rivalries. Not for nothing did American troops take part in the allied invasion of Siberia in 1918 in defence of the White (anticommunist) Russian forces in the Russian Civil War, though the objectives were murky and the outcomes only demonstrated Japanese preponderant power in the region and the failure of the anti-communist counter-revolution.[6] At the Versailles Peace Conference, Wilson advocated national self-determination for Europe's peoples. His approach went against the old tradition of allowing different ethnicities to mingle within multinational empires. Rather, he proposed national units that would be relatively homogenous, though in fact the lines drawn on the map in post-war Europe still mixed many different nationalities inevitably together and would be the cause of further trouble. This was one problem. Another was the colonial world beyond.

Wilson could not extend self-determination to the peoples of the European empires. His failure to do so stemmed partly from European imperial machinations, but he also held back from the nationalist idea's logical implications because of his own (racist) view of non-European social development and racial potential. Prominent African-American intellectual W. E. B. Du Bois was one who, on behalf of a Pan-African Congress in Paris, lobbied Wilson's advisors for moves towards self-government in the former German colonies in Africa. As a compromise, Wilson took up from the swirl of ideas circulating within the Western democracies and at Versailles the notion of Japanese, British imperial and French 'mandates' under League supervision, rather than independence, for forfeited territories in the Middle East, Africa and the Pacific.[7] The agreement at Versailles did not touch but in fact enhanced the empires of the successful allies. Only Germany and the Ottoman Empire suffered loss of colonies. Wilson's answer to the imperfections of the treaty was the proposed League of Nations to settle international disputes. This idea drew upon American reform traditions. Since the 1870s individual Americans had been proposing a system of international arbitration and, in fact, an International Court at The Hague had been established in 1905 as the result of diplomatic efforts by several governments and transnational agitation among peace reformers, including Americans. But Wilson could not bring the Senate and the American people along with him to accept the League, nor join the Court. The former, in particular, offended the idea of entangling alliances and the pro-League Democratic candidate lost the 1920 presidential election.

In one of his famous mangled expressions, new President Warren Harding promised a return 'to normalcy', but his inelegant term did not describe reality. The United States did not retreat to political isolationism but rather to what some diplomatic historians now call 'independent internationalism'.[8] Regarding the Pacific, the government hosted the meetings that led to the Treaty of Washington in 1922 regulating the size of great power navies. Moreover, American leaders still aspired, despite the rejection of the League, to a new world order. The 1920s Republican Party administration of Calvin Coolidge co-sponsored the Kellogg–Briand Pact of 1928 to 'outlaw' wars. Though idealistic in retrospect, this treaty must be seen in the context of American internationalists' commitment to peace, self-determination and commercial intercourse. Internationalism was therefore extended through a vigorous pursuit of American export opportunities. Herbert Hoover as Secretary of Commerce (1921–28) saw to this, with the government supplying as much information and incentive as possible to manufacturers to develop American trade in Latin America and across the globe.[9]

Not only was the United States diplomatically involved in Europe in the 1920s; its economic foreign policy had repercussions there. US financial pre-eminence post-war meant that the government became inevitably involved with European diplomacy because of the war debts problem. The United States insisted on payment of these debts owed by the allies and in turn the allied nations, particularly the French, demanded German reparations to square their finances. Germany defaulted on its payments in 1922–23, France occupied the Ruhr, and the basis had been laid for German nationalist denunciations of a punitive and unjust peace. Americans bore no little responsibility for this situation, which the Dawes Plan to reschedule war debts only partially retrieved. American economic power had been exerted abroad and enmeshed the country in reciprocal relations of credit and trade, but not in an equal way. Tariff policy in the 1920s showed how unequal the relationship was to be. Despite the huge trade surplus and prosperity, protectionist interests in Congress secured, through the Fordney–McCumber Act of 1922, prohibitive duties shielding domestic industries against foreign competition while congressional laws encouraged US exports and farmers lobbied for the dumping of their produce on world markets. Despite the Open Door policy, economic expansion remained contradictory in practice, serving only American trade, not reciprocal commerce.

These cross-national extensions of US economic influence at the expense of foreign countries were equally noticeable in the cultural arena. American films had been a minor item internationally before the First World War, but with the French otherwise preoccupied after 1914, the war allowed the American industry to consolidate internally and overcome French competition. Aided by the activities of the Department of Commerce, Hollywood achieved worldwide pre-eminence even before the arrival of talking pictures in the late 1920s. The film industry was helped by the Webb–Pomerene Act, which promoted such collusive trade practices abroad as block booking systems for exhibition of movies, while outlawing these at home. French films could not use such practices in the United States.[10]

Flush with the moral power of a nation that had intervened to bring victory and peace in Europe, the United States sought to resume its older efforts to export many of its institutions to that continent.[11] Already during the world war the American Red Cross and the YMCA were very active in Europe. The latter undertook essentially political roles spreading the values of democracy. It became in effect an agency of the American government's war effort. Post-war a host of other organizations set out to change Europe as well. Moral reformers tried to expand prohibition and at the same time to defend the United States against corrupting foreign influences. The World League Against Alcoholism (WLAA) was established in Washington, DC, in 1919 to spread information worldwide about the benefits of alcohol prohibition. Coming after the Eighteenth Amendment had made the sale of liquor in the United States unconstitutional, the

League had a partly utilitarian purpose. A dry world would make it easier to defend national prohibition against foreign liquor smugglers. However, the WLAA also had an idealistic side. It resembled Wilsonian internationalism in remaking the world in the aftermath of war. It was strongly evangelical in its roots and reformist in its motivation to cleanse the world of the stain of drink. From offices in London the League worked ultimately in over 100 countries and sent lecturers to campaign for prohibition in Sweden, New Zealand, India and Britain. Though the League had friends in many nations and nearly achieved prohibition in a number, only Finland and Iceland became totally prohibitionist. The organization was, however, symptomatic of a new form of cultural hegemony, in which middle-class people abroad looked to the United States for models of economic and social modernization. European advocates of prohibition praised Henry Ford for his economic success and business efficiency.[12]

By the 1920s, the model of American business was mass production and consumption. Assembly-line mass production identified with Ford through the Model T soon spread in Europe and the British Empire as well as America. 'Fordism', as it became known, was introduced in branch plants of prominent American manufacturing companies established in Canada, Australia and Europe; simply to survive the cheaper competition, European car manufacturers had to 'Fordize' their own plants.[13] American business advertising followed this intrusion with J. Walter Thompson becoming a global company, in the wake of its American clients' success in Europe. Fordism's equivalent also applied to retailing. In the 1920s Woolworth's opened across Europe cheap mass retailing stores based upon a socially mixed clientele and reduced service. Woolworth's was to the five-and-dime store what 'the Model T was to mass mobility'.[14]

A key linkage between the expansion of business methods and the older tradition of moral and social reform was Rotary. No longer were America's 'missionaries' mainly Protestant clergy and temperance reformers. A novel movement of businessmen fused service and economic efficiency and promoted American business culture abroad in hegemonic fashion. Founded in Chicago in 1905 as a businessmen's club, Rotary quadrupled in size and businessmen soon introduced affiliates in Canada and then Europe and other parts of the world in the 1920s. By 1929, the club had about a quarter of its affiliates overseas. Rotary International became an important arena in which European businessmen worked to modernize their national economies and social relations in the war's aftermath. It also promoted international understanding and cooperation to foster 'good will, and international peace through a world fellowship of business and professional men, united in the ideal of service'.[15]

The identification of the United States with modernity spilt over into social life. Jazz as well as American cinema became popular in Europe and, indeed, Asia. Outposts such as China's most Europeanized city of Shanghai saw modern American culture, including nightclubs and jazz, flourish in the 1920s. In Europe the presence of an American literary elite and the memory of the First World War soldiers helped spread American culture. The Parisian avant-garde obsessed over 'le hot jazz', equating the new musical forms with modernity and defiance of convention. Josephine Baker, the voluptuous and erotic African-American dancer became a star in Paris. The fusion of risqué entertainment and sexuality abroad was a variation on the pattern of the 'flaming youth' culture of 1920s urban America. The evidence suggested that American and modern culture had almost merged. It was not simply Americanization that was occurring in Europe, but cultural modernization at the same time.

From the perspective of the late 1920s, the new cultural expansion seemed to contribute to a new world order, but not an empire like the British, French or pre-war Russian. Underlying the expansion of American influence was, instead, deterritorialized economic and cultural power. With the United States identified with modernity rather than a purely national cultural expression, even Communists saw opportunities for appropriating American methods and institutions to undermine traditional class structures. Italian Communist Antonio Gramsci wrote how the masses could embrace the modernization of culture and economy and so challenge aristocratic hegemony. Class mobilization would occur in the social upheaval that cultural change was expected to bring. Within the Soviet Union, American films were not banned but, on the contrary, highly popular in the 1920s. Soviet leaders saw Fordism not as United States imperialism, but as an engine of modernity that could aid a socialist revolution based on technology and progress.[16]

Enticing though the promise was for many, the new cultural hegemony was not fully achieved at that time. Europeans picked and chose aspects of American influence that appealed. They turned American influences, as they had before the First World War, into their own cultural products as part of the expression of modernity. The obsession with jazz among the avant-garde, for instance, merged with Europe's long interest in North and West Africa as part of their own colonial regimes; the cult of Negrophillia reflected a modernist and Parisian version of Orientalism.[17] Evident too was outright European resistance to American cultural penetration. Both the older style of cultural expansion and the new Fordist mass consumerism faced anti-American criticism. Cultural nationalists saw to that, particularly after the late 1920s, but many of the American moral projects were suspect for opposite reasons. They were not enough in tune with the consumer-oriented age. Much of continental Europe, except Scandinavia, resisted prohibitionist moves and European opposition presaged American abandonment of the policy. Indeed, European wines smuggled into the United States added to Scottish and Canadian whiskey and Mexican tequila to confound the hopes of prohibitionists at home. Soon American prohibition would be abandoned (1933), and abroad the World League against Alcoholism became moribund. Meanwhile, cultural conservatives in Europe criticized not only new-fangled American prohibition, but also its American nemesis, the permissive culture of consumerism. Jazz the cultural conservatives condemned as a form of moral disease, just as they did in the United States. But European resistance to American institutions extended to German and French attempts to rescue their film interests in the 1930s and Rotary's efforts at international understanding floundered in the wake of the emergence of totalitarian states. In Germany, Nazis marginalized and eventually disbanded Rotary clubs even though the latter tried to comply with the racist regime by expelling Jewish members. [18] Fascists campaigned to strip supposedly impure influences such as Jewish–American business practices from their societies. Nazis picketed Woolworth's in Berlin and some American businesses underwent facelifts to survive. But American big business had penetrated in profound ways. Germans were happy that their cars bore German names, even though in the case of Opel, it was an American subsidiary of General Motors; General Motors was happy, too, despite the fact that Ford's German plant built trucks for the Wehrmach.

American businesses faced more conventional opponents too. They had to contend with traditional buying patterns and status symbols, particularly among the poor and the upper classes. Five-and-dime stores still made up only a tiny percentage of the consumer market in France, Italy and Germany as small retailers and traditional elite department stores steeped in class distinction fought back. Chain stores accounted for 23 per cent of retail turnover in the United States, 7 in Britain and just 1.3 in France in the 1930s. [19] Contributing to the reaction against American influence in Europe was the collapse of the international political and economic order in the Great Depression, events conditioned by the failed policy objectives of the United States (and others) in the 1920s. The modernizing process and American cultural influence had been checked, but the world would not be the same again. The development of mass consumption as a transnational process had well and truly begun.

* * *

The impact of the Great War within the United States had been just as important in promoting social upheaval as the influence of American post-war expansion was upon European societies. While externally the United States had to project its power and become involved in European diplomacy, the effects at home accentuated pre-war conflicts and reignited the nation's self-perception as exceptional. The domestic significance of the war lay in the social dissent and dislocation that accompanied it. But this internal dissension was externally connected. Even before the formation of the American Workers (Communist) Party in 1919, many Americans assumed the Bolshevik seizure of power to be connected to socialism within the United States, a view apparently confirmed by the Soviets' own

initial expectation of a world revolution. American Progressives in this
era, such as social reformer Jane Addams, did respond to the revolutionary
upheavals of Europe and its transnational ideologies, supporting socialism
and internationalism and opposing war.[20] Yet they were also influenced
by the multicultural nature of America's immigrant-filled cities. Addams
wrote before the First World War of immigrants in the slums of Chicago
'laying the simple and inevitable foundations of an international order'
through the cosmopolitan 'intermingling of the nations'.[21] This reformist
cosmopolitanism clashed head-on with majority xenophobia during the
war and after – and lost.

The wartime situation cannot be explained without recalling what
the country was like immediately before the war. Only a minority of
the articulate Anglo population agreed with Addams' sanguine assess-
ment. The huge influx of immigration had brought millions of people
with strange customs, religions and languages. Serbs, Italians, Jews and
Russians seemed to the Anglo majority a threat because they did not
assimilate. Cities were growing and changing under the impact of immigration and industry – they were becoming more alien places in the eyes
of rural people. The nation also faced severe class conflict and economic
change before the war, a condition intersecting with immigration patterns.
Strikes were common and unions organized across the landscape of labour.
The Industrial Workers of the World (established 1905) had emerged
as a quasi-syndicalist union strong among Western miners, some factory
workers and transient labourers.

When the war came to America in 1917 these pent-up pressures intensified. With some labour groups, socialists and immigrants hostile, concern
about anti-war advocacy could be easily tapped by adroit politicians and
by citizens groups that took posse-like actions. The war also allowed
diffuse pre-war feeling against immigrants to be focused – with anxieties psychologically discharged, as it were, into anti-German action. On
the serious side, authorities sent suspect Germans to internment camps
and distorted the facts about the war's origins; on the comic, American
anxieties over cultural pluralism led to name changes, such as sauerkraut
being labelled liberty cabbage. When the Bolshevik Revolution began in
November 1917, concern over the power of labour and immigrants easily
turned into fear of working-class agitation against the war effort. Recall
that the Bolsheviks sued for peace with Germany in the Treaty of Brest–
Litovsk in March 1918. The Russians had reneged and socialists seeking
world revolution now led them. Politicians could channel hostility towards
foreigners into hatred of supposedly unpatriotic American socialists such
as Eugene Debs and anarchist Emma Goldman. The war gave the opportunity for ambitious individuals like Attorney General A. Mitchell Palmer
to start in 1919 the Red Scare through the Palmer Raids on dissidents.
Over 1500 aliens were arrested and 249 deported to Russia, while native-
born dissenters against the war were also jailed.[22]

In reaction to the external threat, new institutions re-emphasizing national difference were created. Formed in 1919 among the returning veterans, the American Legion extended anti-radical xenophobia. It agitated against subversion and plied anti-Bolshevik propaganda to government and community alike. The war also stimulated the production of a more nationalist American history, with academic historians enlisting in the propaganda campaigns of the government's Committee on Public Information. A new national mood of self-righteousness surfaced in popular culture. Songs of the war depicted Americans entering on a holy war for democracy against autocracy. George M. Cohan wrote the most famous wartime song, *Over There*, indicating that the nation was needed to come to the rescue of old Europe. In the case of *Pershing's Crusaders*, a military march by E. T. Paull, the sheet music cover depicted General Pershing and his men accompanied, as they marched to battle en masse, by two armoured figures from the Crusades replete with crosses on their shields.[23]

Not only was nationalism strengthened by the war and fused with religious moralism but the war also enlarged the American state's economic role. The government was able to get congressional support for projects unimaginable before. Measures to help mobilize the entire economy such as temporary nationalization of the railroads under the Railroad Administration, a government shipping corporation to build a proper merchant marine to carry troops and supplies and regulation of energy by a Fuel Administration, all these and more became possible. Many of the wartime agencies utilized voluntary labour by business leaders – the so-called 'dollar a year men' doing their patriotic duty. The establishment of this government–business cooperation presaged the early New Deal agencies of government economic intervention, though this trial leviathan was turned back temporarily during the demobilization and depression of 1919–21 that followed post-war cutbacks in government expenditure.[24]

More important than the economic and administrative growth of the state was its infusion with moral reform. Reformers assumed the stature of a Christian coalition in alliance with the state, a move with international implications. Allegiance to the nation-state of reformers previously international in their focus grew and the activities of these groups were then projected outwards in the 1920s in tandem with American power to produce the lop-sided cultural expansion of that era. Reformers used the war to get measures passed that they only dreamt of before. The prime example was national prohibition. The Anti-Saloon League had succeeded in getting almost half the states to ban alcohol prior to 1917 and then used military circumstances to achieve its national aims by claiming that to drink was to be pro-German. With the major breweries bearing German names and many saloons immigrant dominated, the message tapped wartime xenophobia effectively. Moreover, grain used in whiskey was needed to feed the allied nations. The case for wartime prohibition was strong and the prohibitionists could use their early successes under the necessities of mobilization to make the change permanent through a constitutional amendment in 1919. The state was being reshaped as a moral entity.

An alliance also developed between women reformers and the state. Before the war, activist women had felt excluded from the nation and many were attracted to internationalist organizations. The International Council of Women (founded by May Wright Sewell and others in Washington, D.C. in 1888), the International Woman's Suffrage Association (1902), the World's WCTU and peace societies gave American women platforms to promote international solidarity on suffrage, opposition to war, and equal rights. Some found the achievements of the British suffrage movement worthy of emulation by Americans.[25] But suffragists were able to use the world war to gain political support for their cause at the national level. As a result they became more closely aligned with patriotism. Though some women formed the Woman's Peace Party in 1915 and travelled to Europe to aid the peace negotiations as part of Henry Ford's quixotic effort to end the fighting, most in the woman's suffrage movement threw themselves behind the war effort in the hope of getting the vote as a reward for their patriotic sacrifices. They succeeded in 1920. Post-First World War, the Sheppard–Towner Act (1921) saw advocates of maternalist social policy lobby successfully for federal child welfare legislation for the first time. The state and social feminists had become more closely attached, a trend that would accelerate in the 1930s. But voting rights did not bring economic equality. While women temporarily benefited from the war by getting better access to some 1 million jobs in boom conditions, the post-war employment situation was grimmer. Women were still expected to give way to male workers. The outcome illustrated that the war was too short to transform gender and other social relations for Americans.

What the war did do was intensify contradictions in American society, especially over prohibition, labour and radicalism. Farmers displayed their discontent with low agricultural prices by supporting radical populist parties across the western states in the early 1920s. The Socialists had still received an impressive vote in the 1920 presidential election on the back of anti-war sentiment. These politico-economic conflicts exacerbated by war not only continued into the 1920s, they also had international reverberations. When Italian immigrant anarchists Nicola Sacco and Bartolomeo Vanzetti were arrested in 1920 for a payroll robbery and murder in Massachusetts, several years of radical protests against their trial and conviction followed. Rallies in favour of the two condemned men – who protested their innocence – were held as far away as London, Paris, Tokyo and Sydney before their execution in 1927.[26] This was a major episode in international labour solidarity linking elements of the American working class to the international labour movement. Liberals as well as socialists joined in radical protests too and these links got American social reformers into trouble. The case was best illustrated in the peace movement. Though women received voting rights as a result of the war, women's groups were also accused sometimes of being both anti-war during the conflict and too radical after the war – as with the peace advocate and women's reform leader Jane Addams, who was denounced as a friend of Bolsheviks in the 1920s.[27]

Pressures for social and ideological homogeneity grew precisely because of intensified conflicts and continuing dissent within American society. These conformist pressures were felt in a variety of ways, such as the revived Ku Klux Klan's spread across the nation. No longer limited to the South and to attacks on African-Americans, the Klan paraded openly in Washington, DC, and intimidated Catholics, Communists and Jews. Though the Klan did infiltrate into Canada, it was marginal there. Its ideology was intolerant of other peoples and not suitable for export, in contrast to other more progressive social movements of the time. The organization's rise was symptomatic of a national exclusiveness revealed notably in the pressures to conform to the ideological precepts of 100 per cent Americanism, a popular political cliché of the era.

This cultural conflict within America exposed a growing cleavage between old stock Protestants and rural and small town Americans on the one hand and a new cultural elite on the other that looked outward towards the world. The Klan and Christian fundamentalist groups campaigned against cosmopolitanism. For rural Americans modernism and the theories of Charles Darwin represented dangerous foreign views, whose influence was allegedly centred in New York, a city said to be 90 per cent alien. That an alien could be popularly defined as one with immigrant parents or grandparents spoke volumes for the way many Americans now conceived of ethnic difference as the proxy for foreign political subversion. New York, too, was the home of the intellectual class – previously Anglo, New England and mugwump – that began by the 1920s to develop distinctively modernistic, pro-urban and anti-rural sentiments. Journalists and critics such as H. L. Mencken lampooned prohibition and the Scopes or 'Monkey' Trial on the teaching of evolution (1925), while the publishing industry came under the influence of those perceived to be foreign. Bennett Cerf of Random House and Alfred Knopf, the most innovative publishers of the 1920s represented cosmopolitanism and transnational influences. Both were of Jewish background. The academic world was still largely Anglo, but figures such as anthropologist Franz Boaz at Columbia imported new ideas of cultural relativism. These views were vastly different from the America of the Klan or the Scopes Trial fundamentalists, who accepted economic progress and used the new communications medium of radio and film that helped them to recruit more widely, but not the cultural divisions over modernity that war hastened.

Cultural conflict affected African-Americans differently, causing them to consider once more getting out, rather than attempting to move into the American mainstream. This time, however, emigration sentiment developed on a mass level rather than remained predominantly the work of agitators or intellectuals. The 1920s marked the nadir of American race relations. Faced with such pressures as the Klan, Marcus Garvey's Universal Negro Improvement Association organized a commercial venture to return disillusioned African-Americans living in Northern ghetto cities to Africa. Garvey claimed Ethiopia, one of the few still independent countries in Africa, as the spiritual motherland of Africans. A West Indian hostile to European colonialism, Garvey harboured strong Pan-African beliefs that linked the African diaspora to an Africa-driven future.[28] Despite his movement's demise amid financial scandal in 1925 and Garvey's own imprisonment, these attempts to use Pan-African beliefs to forge a new path to racial uplift did not end. They would resurface in the 1940s. But equally interesting was the way Garvey's ideas mirrored the Klan's racial exclusiveness. Cultural separatism seemed the answer to the cultural conflicts that the war generated.

The majority white tendency towards racial homogeneity and intolerance had parallels in the field of immigration policy after the removal of wartime restrictions abroad produced one last burst of southern European arrivals. To counter the threat of entry by supposedly inferior ethnic and racial groups, patriotic societies such as the American Legion and the Immigration Restriction League lobbied successfully for new immigration acts in 1921 and 1924. The latter reduced permissible immigration from Europe and Asia to just 150,000 annually, down from the already restricted 350,000 in the Act of 1921. The 1924 Act was racially and ethnically biased through a quota system favouring the Nordic races that helped to create a more exclusive American identity.

Rather than being a product of endogenous conditions, however, this new exclusionary policy stemmed from transnational conditions. It paralleled European trends and those in the white dominions of the British Empire, with the Great War marking a 'seminal change in the world order', as Mai Ngai points out. The war entrenched national boundaries, 'ushering in an interstate system' that sanctified 'the integrity of the territorial nation-state' and ideas of self-determination. An illegal alien problem emerged in many countries as the turmoil of war and post-war revolution produced stateless citizens and refugees. Ostensibly reflecting, in the American case, activism's domestic political struggles, the context for the shift in policy was international through 'the specter of millions of destitute European war refugees seeking entry into the United States'.[29]

Behind immigration borders resembling those simultaneously erected in many countries, the nation was able to take stock of the rapid population changes of the 1890–1914 and 1919–24 periods. Together with the surrounding social agitation, the 1924 act helped create a national identity more firmly grounded in race. That revised national identity still did not include Asians or Mexican-Americans, whose inflow was, respectively, excluded and limited by the new laws. The labour of immigrants was now less desired than was the purity of Nordic blood. The legislative capstone to immigration restriction sentiment had created a 'raced' nation. The coming of the New Deal and the Second World War would further strengthen this racialized nation-state.

12

Forces of Integration: War and the Coming of the American Century, 1925–70

In 1943, Wendell Willkie, the defeated Republican Presidential candidate of 1940 wrote a book telling the story of his 49-day goodwill mission around the world as an emissary for the US government in the depths of the Second World War. *One World* emphasized common human aspirations for economic development, an end to European empires, and self-determination as the basis for peaceful cooperation between peoples. A publishing juggernaut selling over 3 million copies, the book demonstrated growing American awareness of the nation's new international leadership. Translated into many languages, Willkie's book was an important turning point at which Americans accepted the global interconnectedness that had become obvious as early as the First World War. As Willkie put it, 'There are no distant points in the world any longer.'[1] War and aeroplanes had seen to that. Yet Americans would use that moment in history to project an asymmetrical version of their relations with the wider world. In 1941, publisher Henry Luce had proclaimed 'An American Century' in *Life* magazine. That phrase and its implications were much discussed too. Luce urged an expansive, missionary approach to political and cultural relations, in which the world would be rewritten in the image of the United States. The attempt to engage the world explicitly and remake it was not new; it was well underway in the 1920s. It would be a phase of American power not completed until the 1970s. Though controversial and contested by Progressives such as Franklin D. Roosevelt's Vice-President Henry Wallace from 1941 to 1945, Luce's mindset tended to prevail in government policy. One world turned out in the American vision of the future to be an American world.

The nation experienced a bewildering variety of transnational contacts in this period. The approach in this and the following chapters is not to emphasize the year-to-year shifts in these contacts. To do so would be to obscure long-term patterns. Political events and transnational forces drew the United States into international affairs in a way that could not be easily reversed; these forces centred around the internationally shared crises of the Great Depression's financial collapse, the rise of autarchy or self-sufficiency among nations, the spread of fascism, the transformative politico-economic effects of the Second World War on American power and the activities of non-governmental agencies. This and successive chapters analyse in turn structural, long-term trends in American transnational engagement and disengagement. These patterns defy any precise chronology as they were building from the 1920s onwards. But they centre on the high noon of American hegemony from the early 1940s to the late 1960s.

During this period, American social and political influence abroad expanded far beyond levels attained in the late nineteenth century and promoted further 'Americanization' of European as well as non-European cultures such as Japan. In turn, anti-American reactions stirred among intellectuals and the political left.[2] Ironically, the process was partly a shared one of modernization or Westernization across national borders as urbanization, technological change and consumer-oriented capitalism spread. Nevertheless, the post-Second World War projection of American power provided vectors for the export of American cultural values, social institutions and transnational organizations, even though these 'exports' were often solicited from abroad and invariably mediated and reshaped through local circumstances. The reciprocity of transnational exchanges continued, though the exchanges were unequal and influenced by Cold War power politics.[3]

The growing international involvement of the United States was not based upon the weakening of national boundaries, but rather the development of a stronger American state structure fitted to its political and economic role in the world. Anticipated in the war mobilization of 1917–19, the growth of a federal regulatory state resumed in the 1930s under the New Deal promoted by Roosevelt to combat the depression. Now government embraced interventionist welfare policy as in Europe and aimed at full employment, though this goal was not completely achieved until the Second World War's military necessity made massive deficit spending essential. From this position, the United States projected its power outward, especially from 1941 to 1973. The period from the 1920s to the 1970s was not therefore one of weakened nationalism but paradoxically of heightened boundary making that some have called hyper-nationalism.[4] This period broadly corresponded to the expansion of consumerism and the export of Fordist methods of mass production. The emphasis was on globalizing the American dream.

* * *

This rise of the American nation to world power after 1945 paradoxically had its immediate origins in a decade in which the United States sought protection from the vagaries of the changing international system through greater self-reliance. This was the time of the Great Depression and New Deal. The pattern of national consolidation begun in the First World War and in the Immigration Act of 1924 resumed with the onset of the 1929 stock market crash and the ensuing depression. Though this economic catastrophe started in the United States, it soon spread to Europe when American banks called back funds that they had lent abroad in the 1920s. The domestic downturn also contributed to a dramatic contraction in international trade exacerbated by the high Smoot–Hawley Tariff of 1930 against imported goods, a tariff that was intended to protect American industries and jobs. As trade slumped, even free trade Britain tried to protect itself and its imperial possessions from the vicissitudes of the economic upheaval by imposing an Imperial Preference Scheme favouring trade with its colonies and dominions. The autarchy or self-sufficient trade blocs adopted in central Europe similarly contracted world trade. By 1933, more than 30 million people were unemployed in the major industrialized countries, with a higher rate of unemployment in the United States than in any except Germany.[5]

Only with the election of the Democrat Roosevelt as President in 1932 and the inception of the New Deal programmes of government employment after 1933 did the United States resolutely respond to the deteriorating world economic situation. Even then, policies were sometimes conflicting and hesitant as well as controversial among the American public. New legislation gave greater protection to organizing rights of labour through the Wagner Act (1935) and Congress passed in the same year the now famous Social Security Act to provide social insurance for many categories of workers. Agricultural price supports and production controls were also established to end the farm product glut that resulted from reduced exports. Both Germany and the United States used public works programmes to alleviate unemployment, the New Deal by establishing a variety of so-called alphabetic agencies, such as the Civilian Conservation Corps (CCC) planting trees and doing other conservation work. In Britain, economist J. M. Keynes challenged the orthodoxy of balanced budgets and advocated deficit spending in economic downturns, but this theory was not adopted in the United States before 1938, when a second downturn produced by the Roosevelt administration's budget cutting drove home the need for calculated fiscal stimuli. Generally speaking the New Deal programmes were more successful than British efforts in reducing unemployment, raising hopes of saving capitalism and rescuing millions from despair, but less successful than the German solution of stimulating growth through massive rearmament and tighter central control over the economy. True, corporate–government cooperation in the National Recovery Administration and the tactics used to mobilize workers in support of the early New Deal were not unlike schemes seen in Germany. A visiting British Labour Party member concluded, from watching the National Recovery Administration's 'Blue Eagle' parades of workers cooperating with business and the state, that 'he might well have been in Nazi Germany'.[6] Yet the resemblance was superficial. Fascism of the Italian or German variety remained marginal in the United States, though populist demagogues such as Senator Huey P. Long of Louisiana and rightwing radio broadcasters and politicians Gerald K. Smith and Father Charles Coughlin were hardly absent from public debate.

The New Deal had its own distinctive national configuration, but it was influenced by several decades of transnational Progressive theorizing, planning and policy examples from abroad. European advocates of social welfare influenced American bureaucrats and policy makers in this decade. Social security legislation embodied the principle of social insurance that had long been debated in America but implemented only in one state – it drew upon European experience and ideas. For all its 'compromises and limitations', writes Daniel Rodgers, the Social Security Act was 'a social insurance variant, unmistakable in its European progeny'. The system 'came into the crisis' of the 1930s 'premade and pretested, its arguments fully formed and elaborated'. That was its advantage in providing a readymade response to the long-term challenge of securing people from the fear of losing their jobs that the depression had underlined in no uncertain terms.[7]

Though American governments were now more receptive to international progressive ideas, the effect of the economic crisis was, as in other countries, to diminish interest in international affairs temporarily and to build higher cultural walls of containment against external pressures. Immigration slumped along with the economic decline, and this reinforced culturally the effects of the 1920s restrictive immigration legislation. Immigration slowed to a trickle and even reversed at times. Federal authorities deported 400,000 alien Mexican workers no longer needed to fill labour shortages that had appeared in the Southwest during the 1920s. In foreign relations too, the more hostile international climate of the 1930s compromised the American version of internationalism of the 1920s and drove the United States into the shell of isolation, though the isolationist desire essentially meant isolation from Europe, not the world as a whole. Not only did the Neutrality Acts of 1935–37 bar the United States from involvement in foreign wars. In addition, the Senate inquiry into the armaments industry in 1934–35 unearthed allegations of venal economic motives for US entry into the First World War and effectively labelled the Du Pont Company, Anglo-American financiers, J. P. Morgan and Co. and others as 'merchants of death'. The message was clear. Stay out of Europe's wars.

There were exceptions in attitudes, of course, particularly on the left, where international communism had an impact. Though small in terms of the major political parties, the Communist Party of the United States of America (CPUSA) was strong in the intellectual centres of the urban east in the 1930s and was building its power within the growing industrial unions. Its 'popular front' policy adopted in the mid-to-late 1930s, in line with the worldwide policy of the Moscow-controlled Comintern, allowed it to work alongside socialists and other radicals not actually in the Party. The Communists and their allies campaigned for racial equality, raising funds and protesting against racism, emphasizing in the process the 'global nature of social and economic problems'.[8] Left-wing popular front groups provided the basis of American volunteers to fight in the Abraham Lincoln Brigade and other units in the Spanish Civil War for the Republican (leftist) government against the fascist General Franco's nationalists, who were aided by Hitler. Convinced that capitalism and racism went hand in hand, some 3000 idealists served, including African-Americans. But for the vast majority of Americans, the war was a distant and little-understood conflict. A 1937 Gallup poll found that two-thirds of the American public 'had no opinion about the events in Spain'.[9]

Isolationism did not apply to events south of the border, culturally, economically or politically. In fact, interest in Latin America rose, produced in part by Roosevelt's Good Neighbor Policy adopted in 1933 and the consequent abandonment of military intervention in Latin American affairs. American hegemony would henceforth be enforced by economic means, as Washington negotiated reciprocal trade deals and relied on the power of its foreign investments in the region, which already topped 4 billion dollars. These economic interests could, however, test the new neighbourliness. When Mexico nationalized its oil supplies in 1938, the United States protested and demanded reparations, but did not intervene militarily in the way that Woodrow Wilson had done after the Mexican Revolution. A settlement of US companies' claims was effected in 1940. Accompanying the greater political interest in Latin America was enhanced US cultural interest in the region; Pan-American Airways gained a postal contract subsidy in 1927 that speeded communications by the carrying of the mails and other news by air, and rich American travellers were soon 'Flying Down to Rio' for holidays, while the envious and titillated could watch the phenomenon in films such as the Fred Astaire–Ginger Rogers motion picture of the same name (1933). The US government at the Buenos Aires Inter-American Conference of 1937 (opened by Roosevelt) adopted a cultural exchange programme between the United States and other American nations that the government sponsored, the first programme of its type.[10] Educators urged school syllabi to address Hispanic affairs as part of Progressive education (as well as encouraged interest in China and Japan). A federation of Pan-American clubs was established in the schools of New York to spread knowledge of Hispanic culture and language, and scholars began to advocate a western hemispheric history – what historian Herbert Bolton called a history of 'greater America'. The Carnegie Institution fostered (1937–45) collaborative multivolume studies, too, of Canadian–US relations, as cooperation with the northern neighbour under the government of Prime Minister William Mackenzie King grew. The opening of the Thousand Islands Bridge in 1938 across the St Lawrence River symbolized cooperation, while the Ogdensburg Agreement (1940) between King and Roosevelt created the Permanent Joint Board on Defence that oversaw the defence of North America and tied Canada into US strategy thereafter.

Knowledge of foreign affairs grew after the mid-1930s as momentous events changed the face of politics in Europe and the global balance of power. Radio, the television equivalent of its time, weakened intellectual isolation because it was the first truly mass medium to penetrate the home. The appeal of radio was its immediacy and intimacy; it brought foreign events quickly, even instantaneously, to the American people. During the 1938 'Anschluss', in which Hitler annexed German-speaking Austria, the Columbia Broadcasting System's Edward Murrow broadcast by short wave and commented on the events directly from Vienna in a radio first. American listeners also heard British Prime Minister Neville Chamberlain proclaim 'peace in our time' in 1938 at the Munich Settlement. But the broadcasting of the *War of the Worlds*, in October of the same year, in which precocious actor Orson Welles frightened radio audiences with a fictional portrayal of an invasion by aliens, was certain to raise American anxieties over the potential of external forces to do harm.

Not surprisingly, popular desire to remain free of political and military entanglements in Europe still prevailed and was stimulated by pacifist sentiment precisely because of the memory of harm that a real world war had done just two decades before. Ironically, support for peaceful resolution of international conflict was a transnational phenomenon. The Oxford Union had voted not to fight for king and country in a landmark debate in 1933. The United States similarly sought to avoid war, responding to rather than setting the international agenda for the European and Asia-Pacific regions in the depression decade, due to the expansionist aggression and intentions of Japan and Germany, respectively.

Yet commerce complicated political isolation, producing circumstances that took the United States eventually to a new world war. US economic resources and trade policies in the Pacific were linked to the events of the Sino-Japanese War, after Japan annexed Manchuria in 1931 and then in 1937 extended its hostilities into a full-scale war against China. The Japanese military effort led to growing dependence on US scrap iron and oil. The export of oil and other potential war materials made the United

States in a de facto sense complicit (among other nations) in Japanese expansion at the same time that the nation continued to support China, a country to whose independence the United States had since missionary days a strong emotional commitment. Though trade with China was not large, the Open Door policy had attained sacrosanct status for American administrations and the United States refused steadfastly to sanction Japanese aggression. Roosevelt did not invoke the Neutrality Acts against China in 1937, an action that allowed the Chinese to buy such equipment even though this antagonized Japan. A series of US decisions in 1940–41 that halted provision of war materiel to Japan pushed the latter further into its aggressive policies as it sought alternative supplies in Southeast Asia, helping to bring about the Japanese decision to strike pre-emptively at Pearl Harbor in December 1941. Most historians argue that the United States did not deliberately provoke a Japanese attack, but nevertheless the American government showed little understanding of Japanese strategic imperatives and psychology prior to the war, just as the Japanese miscalculated the American response to the Pearl Harbor bombing. The declaration of war in the Pacific soon brought the United States into the war against Hitler as well, a war that for France and Britain had already begun in 1939.[11]

Until that time, Americans remained strongly divided over the need for or the desirability of taking sides in the emerging conflict across the Atlantic. After Germany overran the Netherlands, Belgium and France in 1940 and threatened Britain, the American administration worried about the implications of enhanced German domination of Europe, but public opinion still split on whether to aid the allies. Nevertheless, the controversy over whether to support Britain or not raised foreign policy debates to new heights of passion and enhanced the depth of discussion. One lobby group with wide support, America First, stressed isolationism. Its iconic hero of the first Atlantic air crossing, Charles Lindbergh, served as a spokesman. His mid-western background and Nordic ancestry reflected also the major political and social sources of the isolationist sentiment. On the other side, the Committee to Defend America by Aiding the Allies reflected eastern, urban and more Anglophile groups. Led by people self-consciously labelling themselves as internationalists, the Committee argued that the United States must become more involved in world affairs. But these lobby groups argued not over the necessity for military intervention, but over whether complete isolationism or material aid short of war to the allies was the best way to keep Americans out of the European conflict.

* * *

The war transformed American society after 1941 and ensured the end to formal isolationism. During the war Americans agreed that they must learn more about the wider world. News broadcasts naturally covered the march of military and political events, and historians called for greater knowledge of world history. 'World War II', as Neil Smith remarks, 'brought the populace face to face again with geography'.[12] But external events also transformed the United States internally in many material ways. Some 6 million women were drawn into the paid workforce to replace males in factories, shipyards and other blue and white-collar employment. African-Americans moved into Northern cities in even larger numbers than during the First World War. They also fought in the military. Though this occurred in segregated regiments, it would be difficult to turn from a fight against fascism to restore the inequality in racial matters which had characterized race relations in the American South the 1920s and 1930s. Meanwhile ethnic groups were consolidated into Americans as part of the fight against fascism. There was no recurrence of the widespread xeno-phobia in the First World War concerning foreigners, and prohibition was not reintroduced though some temperance reformers argued that it should be. Even wartime propaganda was at a lower key.

American attitudes towards Asians underwent more contradictory paths of change, however. Because the United States was allied in the Second World War with China against Japan, the war enhanced the legal status of Chinese in the United States. Chinese Americans worked hard for the war effort and a higher percentage than in other ethnic groups enlisted in the armed forces. As a reward and to improve relations with its ally, the Chunking (Nationalist Chinese) government of Chiang Kai-shek, the United States drafted in 1943 a new immigration quota for Chinese. The latter were no longer part of the racial exclusionist policies of earlier decades. Simultaneously the position of the Japanese deteriorated, with the internment as enemy aliens of Japanese residents, whether or not they were born outside the United States, and whether they were loyal to the United States – as almost all were.

The Second World War was to have a far more transformative polit-ical and economic effect than the First World War. Its military spending gave a huge boost to the economy, and prosperity prevailed until after the 1946 demobilization. Alone of all the anti-Axis powers, the United States escaped physical damage to its continental heartland, and thus its indus-trial capacity and transport infrastructure emerged able to support the nation's enhanced economic and political power. The United States ended the war the de facto successor of the European empires in its world role, dwarfing its worn-torn competitors in industrial production, with 50 per cent of the world's GNP in 1945 and holding 70 per cent of the world's gold reserves in 1947.[13] Extending its imposing military performance in both Western Europe in 1944–45 and the Pacific from 1942 was the atomic bomb, from its awesome first application at Hiroshima, in August 1945. Until 1949 the United States alone had this weapon. Though the American position was almost immediately challenged by the alternative Soviet bloc of state-run economies, communism was not a direct economic threat but rather a political one. Communism in China, North Korea and North Vietnam after 1945 showed the political power of Marxism as a revolutionary motivator and alternative to capitalism in the under-developed world.[14]

Its central position the United States maintained thereafter not through colonies but access to markets and cultural prestige stemming from the Second World War. It 'ruled' an empire of sorts under the system described by historian Geir Lundestad as 'empire by invitation' in which allies courted and acceded to American hegemony.[15] This time the United States would not seek political isolation from Europe. The victorious allies led by the United States were also relatively magnanimous. Americans were more worried about the potential for Soviet aggrandizement in Europe and Asia than in punishing Japan and Germany, and both were aided in reconstruction. Western Europe recovered from its wartime chaos with the ample financial aid of the Marshall Plan and joined in defence of the 'free world'.

In international relations there came a new commitment to international political and economic institutions. The United States spearheaded policies of multilateralism in foreign affairs. Gone was the insistence on no entangling alliances. The United Nations was formed as the new supranational body charged with ensuring world peace and international social and economic cooperation after a San Francisco conference established its charter in 1945, and the United States took the lead in its deliberations. Post-war alliances were established with the North Atlantic Treaty Organization (NATO) in 1949, the Baghdad Pact in the Middle East (1955) and the South-East Asia Treaty Organization (SEATO) in 1954, and the American government partly bankrolled the United Nations. The United States also used supranational organizations, when suitably influenced by its own policies, to regulate the world economy as well as the global polity. Foreign economic policy became centred on replacing the gold standard that had failed after 1929. The allied powers created a new international monetary system based on the dollar as a reserve currency at the Bretton Woods Conference of 1944 and established the International Monetary Fund and the World Bank as instruments of global development and economic regulation. These bodies reflected American recommendations on market economies, fighting inflation and control of third world debt. With varying degrees of enthusiasm, the United States joined the political, social and cultural activities promoted by the United Nations, but American foreign policy also encouraged transnational initiatives of its own through cultural diplomacy.

The Cold War prompted a cultural offensive for the minds of people around the world.[16] The most prominent instrument of American outreach was the United States Information Agency founded in 1953 to promote foreign knowledge of American society. The government had already in the Second World War period used cultural diplomacy aimed at influencing other states through the provision of programmes to stress the benefits of 'free' civilization and the American way of life, but these efforts expanded in the 1950s.[17] Further Cold War cultural initiatives covered specific groups. The United States encouraged a free trade union movement in Western Europe to combat communist influence, and the 1950s saw the peak activity of the Congress of Cultural Freedom, a transatlantic intellectual forum that sponsored *Encounter*.[18] This organization achieved notoriety when it was shown in the 1960s to have been secretly funded by the Central Intelligence Agency. James Burnham, the former Trotskyite turned Cold War warrior, who advocated a US struggle for world hegemony, served as a consultant.[19] Some of these government initiatives involved educational and cultural exchanges such as the Fulbright Scheme (1946) and other activities of the Institute for International Education (IIE) that were not directly tied to the Cold War, but rather reflected the desires of American policy-makers to combat the causes of war – as shown in the rise of fascism. Senator William Fulbright, a critic of American foreign policy over-reaching was a key figure in the promotion of this broader view. Another part of this approach had been the Voice of America. Founded in 1942 to counter Axis propaganda over the airwaves, the VOA was nearly disbanded after the Second World War, due to ideological opposition to government involvement in media and communications. Revitalized in the Cold War, the organization joined in a battle for the world's hearts and minds that entailed the export of American intellectual culture. The VOA added music to its broadcasts and began in 1955 'Music U-S-A'. This programme was credited with making jazz, considered by the communists to be a decadent Western influence, hugely popular in Eastern Europe; it brought Louis Armstrong, Duke Ellington and Charlie Parker to millions of foreign listeners.[20] Like other elements of cultural diplomacy, such programming reflected the belief that liberal ideals and enhanced international cooperation between peoples otherwise divided by political ideologies could be achieved through education, information and entertainment.

The Cold War cultural offensive linked home and abroad. It portrayed global geo-politics starkly divided between slave and free, and through McCarthyism – and the wider anti-communist push which many Democrats as well as Republicans supported – sought to cleanse American society of alien radicalism at the same time that it used cultural policy to counter communism's appeal abroad. These two tendencies were closely linked, marking the United States off against its allies while projecting American cultural power internationally. The fact that the United States had avoided revolution, war on its own soil (except for Hawaii) and serious internal political strife during the Second World War led many US intellectuals to praise American society in comparison with European. The old idea of American exceptionalism gained new recruits even while in academic circles Americans promoted comparative analyses of political development. In this way, the projection of power was asymmetrical – the United States influenced other countries and exported its culture, but simultaneously celebrated American uniqueness and wished to guard American culture from foreign contamination. The American image of the ideal world incorporated one-world ideas of an end to isolation, but also reflected the US-driven and missionary-like vision of Henry Luce.[21]

Another internationalizing influence was in economic policy. Here too, global relationships were asymmetrical. The First World War altered American dependence upon foreign capital and immigrant labour, with the nation now able to rely on its internal supplies of these factors of production. The United States produced for many decades thereafter a trading surplus, as its exports gained ground in world markets. But from the 1920s dependence upon foreign raw materials entailed critical changes in international relationships. The nation had to become steadily more involved internationally, not to develop balanced and equitable trade, but to fulfil the demands of the American economy. By the Second World War the United States imported about 60 different minerals and 23 came exclusively from foreign sources. This dependency had military implications. Roosevelt sent troops to Dutch Suriname to safeguard Alcoa's interests for the production of aluminium even before the United States entered the war in 1941, while oil supplies provided another case of growing dependency. If there were to be a Third World War, Secretary of the Interior Harold Ickes wrote in 1943, it would have to be fought with somebody else's oil. US reserves were dwindling. From the 1940s onwards the administration engaged in diplomacy for access to Arabian petroleum. Economic integration increased from the 1950s still further as Cold War defence industries scoured the planet for key metals such as titanium.[22]

The second aspect of economic policy that pushed the United States towards global engagement was the drive for open markets. The catastrophes of the 1930s depression and the Second World War strengthened free trade arguments, because policies of national self-sufficiency had contributed to the economic turmoil and Hitler's rise. Recall the long history of trade barriers, especially in agriculture, which peaked with the heavily protectionist Smoot–Hawley Tariff of 1930. In the Roosevelt administration, Secretary of State Cordell Hull argued for the link between trade and peace, and liberal trade doctrines began to gain ascendancy through reciprocal deals, particularly with Latin America after 1934.[23] By 1945, freer trade had become a touchstone of US foreign policy, though protectionism for many industries still made American policy inconsistent. The introduction in 1947 of the General Agreement on Trade and Tariffs (GATT) began a long series of initiatives culminating in 1995 in the World Trade Organization that brought greater synchronization of American foreign trade initiatives with internal economic policy. True, sectional interests continued to command Congressional support, through farm subsidy programmes (first introduced under the New Deal) and from import quotas.[24] The struggle between advocates of open trade and those of protectionism within the government, and among labour unions, farmers and political parties, indicated how complicated United States international engagement could be in an era of increasing globalization. Yet forces favouring global integration gradually gained the upper hand from the 1950s. As economist Douglas Irwin has noted, 'The importance of the GATT and the agreements it has fostered cannot be measured in terms of reducing U.S. tariffs', but rather 'in strengthening the vested interests that have a stake in perpetuating open trade policies. The GATT has provided an institutional means of giving stability and credibility to such policies by making their reversal more costly'.[25]

* * *

Engagement with the wider international community was also aided by non-government organizations. Among these groups the most prominent were the missionaries. While Americans had sent foreign missionaries to Burma, China, the Middle East and other destinations since the early nineteenth century, American missionary numbers did not approach the British until the twentieth century. In fact the greatest growth in American missionary activity occurred after the Second World War, with American numbers doubling from the 1920s to the 1960s, after dipping during the great depression. In 1925, 'slightly less than half of [world] Protestant foreign missionaries were from the United States'. By 1957, two-thirds were Americans, with four-fifths of missionary funds coming from that source. From the 1920s to the 1960s, American missionaries made many efforts not only to evangelize non-Christian peoples but also to develop them economically and socially. They built agricultural colleges, did education work among women and girls, brought and trained missionary doctors and built hospitals. In India, for example, American missionaries built upon late nineteenth-century efforts, and 'formed medical and nursing schools for women' because local customs 'forbade the medical care of women by men'.[26] These modernizing activities were also important because in the main they occurred outside the patterns of formal imperialism. Except in the Philippines and the other 'insular possessions', American missionaries could operate with greater independence from the state and, as was the case with ancillary service groups such as the YMCA, were often modestly sympathetic to nationalist claims and anti-colonial movements. American missionaries strongly supported, as did the YMCA, the development of indigenous control 'to bring into being self-governing, self-supporting, self-propagating churches'.[27]

In the late nineteenth and early twentieth centuries American missionary efforts had been concentrated in East Asia and in 1925 this region still accounted for 43 per cent of missionaries from the United States, with another 16 per cent in India. The Sino-Japanese conflict of the 1930s, the subsequent world war and the coming of the Chinese Communists to power in 1949 ultimately drove American missionaries out of their most important target nation, China, but not before a cultural and political impact on the United States had been felt. Many American families were touched by the Chinese missionary experience. Pearl Buck, the daughter of Southern Presbyterian missionaries grew up in China and wrote of her impressions in *The Good Earth*, the best-selling American novel of 1931 and 1932. As Robert McCaughey has noted, Buck's work 'did more to shape American views of China in the 1930s than any other publication' – and that before it became the basis of a major MGM movie in 1938.[28] Buck returned to the United States permanently in 1934, and though she repudiated missionary work under the influence of the growing Chinese nationalist movement, her missionary background continued to influence her. In 1942 she and her second husband established an 'East and West Association' to promote trans-Pacific intercultural understanding. Such sympathy for Asian peoples was not uncommon among missionaries and their families. They generally protested against legislation or customs hostile to Asians, such as discriminatory immigration laws. Thus Sidney Gulick, born into a missionary family in the Marshall Islands became at the age of 28 in 1888 a Protestant missionary educator in Japan after education at Yale University. After decades lived almost entirely abroad, he returned to the United States in 1913 where he opposed racism and advocated better treatment and understanding of Japanese and Chinese people in California. Gulick especially criticized the harsh immigration restrictions of the 1924 immigration law and favoured peace between Japan and the United States in the tense time of the late 1930s, but he was not successful in attempting to reverse the discriminatory laws.[29]

From the missionary lobby came other important feedback effects upon domestic American society in the mid-twentieth century. Missionaries had long promoted cultural awareness of China, but academic study of the 'Far East' developed as a specialized field by the 1920s, partly under missionary influence. Several pioneer students of East Asian history and culture came from missionary backgrounds. A prominent example was Edwin O. Reischauer, born in Japan of Protestant missionaries, who became doyen of Japanese studies in the United States after the Second World War and, under President Kennedy, American Ambassador to Japan. Another, Kenneth Scott Latourette, Sterling Professor of Missions and Oriental History at Yale, had been a missionary himself.[30] A second area of feedback was in government service, where some missionaries' offspring born in China found employment during the Second World War in the Office of Strategic Services. Later some worked for its successor, the CIA, as American relations with Communist China demanded experts in Chinese culture and languages. Apart from missionaries who had been educated or lived in China, such expertise was in short supply in the 1940s and 1950s. A more telling example was the author of the American

Century concept itself. Born in China of a Protestant missionary couple, Henry Luce's American Century articulated the mission-like concept of the nation's historical destiny in a secularized form.[31]

The missionary influence was, however, not restricted to East Asia. With China out of bounds from the late 1940s, American churches stressed in succeeding decades missions to Southern Africa, India and Latin America, though both India and Africa had long been important missionary fields. Along with this globalization of American effort, missionaries went diversification of the churches involved in missionary work. For the first time the American Catholic Church sent out large numbers of missionaries. (Not until 1916 did any American Catholic missionaries go to China, for example). By 1966 there were 7170 US Catholic missionaries abroad, of whom 2516, the largest number, were in Latin America.[32] Many of the missionary orders involved from the Catholic Church were transnational not only in the sense that Catholics owed spiritual allegiance to Rome, but also in the way the missions were run by Americans affiliated with internationally prominent Roman Catholic holy orders such as the Jesuits. Of lay people, about two-thirds were Papal Volunteers for Latin America, an organization set up by the Pope in 1960 that had 'as its objective aiding in the vast social revolution' affecting Latin America at that time.[33]

The 1920s to 1960s also saw expansion in more secular fields of endeavour. Scientists participated in the Pan-Pacific Science Congresses inaugurated at Honolulu in 1920 and held triennially around the Pacific Basin until 1938 and then again after the Second World War. The Institute of Pacific Relations (IPR) established in Hawaii in 1925 was a body formed originally by the YMCA but also embraced academics, social reformers and government officials in a search for a cross-Pacific dialogue.[34] American non-governmental action abroad flourished as part of the new American internationalism that was based on bringing economic and social modernization to the world and thereby promoting peace and stability.

Some of these prominent activities were associated with American philanthropic foundations. The Carnegie Corporation founded in 1911 on the fortune of steel magnate Andrew Carnegie promoted international education and peace studies. Carnegie Libraries were built across the English-speaking world, not only in Carnegie's native Scotland, but also in places as far flung as New Zealand until 1929. However, the most important foundation of the inter-war years was that established by John D. Rockefeller, Jr. From its inception in 1914 the Rockefeller Foundation promoted programmes in social and economic development. The Rockefeller family themselves had already backed heavily the YMCA's efforts in Asia, but now the foundation turned to more scientific and secular programmes. One line of work was in health. Building upon the American public health achievements in the Philippines, the foundation established an International Health Board to promote public health and eliminate endemic diseases by tackling such problems as hookworm and yellow fever in the tropical countries of Asia, Africa and the Americas.[35] Foundation involvement in non-governmental outreach by Americans intensified in the climate of the Cold War, prompted in part by changes in American tax laws and in line with the growing prosperity of American capitalism. Though established in 1936, the Ford Foundation became the largest private philanthropic entity in the early 1950s under the leadership of Paul Hoffman. It emphasized international programmes such as cultural and student exchanges, development grants for agricultural improvement in poor countries such as India and post-Second World War rehabilitation in Europe. Thus, for example, the foundation financed key buildings for the Free University of Berlin.[36]

The network of transnational organizations grew after the Second World War – but these operated in a very different context from nineteenth-century moral and cultural expansion. Post-colonial nationalism had replaced the formal European imperialism swept away by the results of the First and Second World Wars and this complicated the transnational diffusion of new movements and techniques of economic and social development. The new American hegemony supported supranational organizations and decolonization of European empires, as shown in the American repudiation of French and British attempts to maintain their hold upon the Suez Canal by interfering in Egyptian politics in the Suez Crisis of 1956. At the same time, the enhanced power of nation-states (especially the American) and their bureaucratic apparatus regulated what could be done across national boundaries. War itself was a key expression of the action of sovereign states and, in the case of war in East Asia in the 1930s and the world war following, was a great impediment to voluntary transnational action whether religious or secular. Not only were transnational organizations checked by such interstate turbulence but those organizations closely associated with the League of Nations either ceased to exist or suffered severe setbacks in the 1930s. After the Second World War the impact of transnational organizations in promoting greater global integration was limited by the bipolar Cold War context of the Soviet Union and its Eastern European satellite states versus the United States and the Western alliance.

To be sure, new transnational organizations arose to contest the dominance of such great power rivalries, and Americans joined and created organizations to enhance opportunities for peace. Thus concerned scientists founded in 1945 the Federation of Atomic Scientists, typified by its most famous spokesman, J. Robert Oppenheimer, and others associated with the Manhattan Project that produced the first atomic bomb. The Federation warned of the dangers of nuclear war and argued against new weapons systems,[37] but American and Soviet arsenals continued to grow in the 1960s and 1970s in a spiralling arms race. Oppenheimer himself lost his government security clearance during McCarthyism and was politically discredited. Other transnational groups promoting international understanding, such as the Institute for Pacific Relations, also came under attack in the 1950s from McCarthyists as harbouring dangerous leftist elements in the struggle with communism. The Institute was accused of sympathy with 'Red' China and wound up in 1960.

While external constraints upon transnational organizing did exist, the NGOs themselves reflected the changing political economy of the post-war world. Much of the growing NGO activity was now highly institutionalized through government, corporations, foundations and supranational bodies. Even those that were not funded in this way failed to avoid the ideological effects of a divided world. Foundations genuinely expressed the desire for global progress and were generally advocates of liberalism rather than conservatism. Right-wing groups often sharply criticized them. Yet the key foundations such as the Ford also wished to ensure that the United States' distinctively capitalist economic system be presented to the underdeveloped world in a positive light through benevolent action by NGOs and governments.[38] Amid such Cold War interventions, the role of American civil society in global outreach was compromised by great power politics. More than in the period to the 1920s, American voluntary society action abroad was unavoidably judged against or implicated in the growing political, military and economic might of the United States. American NGOs had always to some extent promoted American cultural values, but after the Second World War this ideological content had a different political freight associated with US international hegemony.

* * *

Against the tendencies for closer integration with the wider world were obstacles still promoting difference. Despite expanded non-government activities, transnational relationships at the people-to-people level diminished in the period from the 1920s to the 1960s. Indeed, the change occurred in part *because* so much of that non-governmental activity was now highly institutionalized or mediated through government, corporations and foundations. Robert McCaughey has noted the tendency for international studies and American awareness of the wider world to become more professionalized post-Second World War.[39] Community engagement decreased. Certainly many obstacles to integration were beyond American control. Yet other obstacles reflected internal development; they came from structural changes in American demography, society and economy that cannot be analysed with the tools of international relations theory.

A longer-term perspective is required to detect these structural trends. Within the general pattern of greater global integration over the 'American Century', there occurred a reversal of roles between state and society. Until 1914 the population maintained transnational linkages primarily due to immigration, while the state remained politically (through opposition to entangling alliances) and economically (through tariff policies after 1860) relatively detached from the international community. By the middle of the twentieth century, however, the American population had become more insular in outlook. Meanwhile the state had become more integrationist, despite temporary political isolation from Europe between the two world wars. This paradoxical development can best be traced from the 1920s in parallel to the growth of the American Century.

13

Insular Impulses: Limits on International Integration, 1925–70

While elites and governments preached multilateralism in alliance, military and trade policies, less integration occurred on the people-to-people level. The American population came to know less of foreign countries in this period as education and travel patterns changed to more nation-centred ones, as media interest in things foreign changed scope and content and as immigration and other transnational links inherited from before the First World War diminished. The cultural impact of the Cold War had a similar insular effect through fear, though it also revealed, as shown in succeeding pages, how great power rivalries affected the Civil Rights struggle at home. Ironically, the rituals, traditions and laws that government had deployed for several decades enhanced insularity. The heightened tension over insularity versus integration was a product of history – notably through the impact of immigration policy. Our departure point takes us back to the 1920s. The restructuring of nationhood around racial exclusions in 1924 made the middle decades of the twentieth century very different from the nineteenth.

These restrictions on the movement of peoples promoted more rigid intellectual as well as political borders and had implications both for knowledge of the rest of the world and for the consolidation of national identity. This restructuring must be seen especially in the transnational context of the First and Second World Wars. The determination of the United States to control entry to its borders was tested briefly by the arrival of refugee intellectuals from fascism in the 1930s, by the poignant story of Jews trying to escape from totalitarian Europe to the United States in the early part of the Second World War and by the continual pressures of immigration from Mexico that fanned, for example, riots in 1943 between Mexican gangs wearing their distinctively outlandish 'Zoot Suits' and American soldiers stationed in Los Angeles. Yet the racial reordering of the population giving preference to Nordic elements continued until 1965.[1] It would take the social upheaval of the 1960s to break these barriers down seriously. Only then would this national consolidation truly unravel with renewed immigration from Latin America and the Asia-Pacific region. The issue of multicultural diversity and identity returned to the domestic political agenda by the 1980s in response to this renewed challenge to national exclusiveness. Even then, nation-state control and surveillance imposed in 1924 would continue to define population policy despite the growing flood of illegal immigration.

Not only did the Johnson–Reed Act (the Immigration Act of 1924) create a rigid quota system for Europeans and Asians, it also shaped the racial construction of national identity. The new law drew distinct racial lines between European and non-white immigration, Mae Ngai has argued, treating all Europeans as 'part of a white race, distinct from those considered to be not white'. With tiny quotas for Chinese, Japanese and other Asians, it functionally excluded non-whites because it stated that they were racially ineligible to become naturalized citizens. 'These developments resolved the legal ambiguities and conflicts over the racial status of Asians' vexing the law 'since their arrival in the mid-nineteenth century'.[2] In turn the legal and bureaucratic moves altered the mental 'map' of racial discrimination. Race had been previously marked by 'contours of white and black' that had 'denoted race as a sectional problem'. Now with the Great Migration of rural African-Americans and Mexicans to urban areas post-1917, immigration policy became 'part of an emergent race policy' more comprehensive and 'national in scope'.[3]

These new immigration policies did not create an ironclad restrictive policy – demand for labour in the southwest and fears of offending Latin American countries kept the western hemisphere out of the quota system altogether. But entry from that quarter became more closely supervised. Mexicans, the chief group at issue, had to fulfil new visa requirements, taxes on entry and medical inspections designed to limit undesirables and those likely to be a burden on the state. These screening procedures were conducted at US consulates abroad, not at the nation's borders. Creating categories of illegal aliens, with sharp distinctions between them and citizens, the new laws provided for much harsher treatment through deportation. Attention focused on people who would formerly have been ignored or allowed to enter legally. These included some who had entered before 1924 without record, such as deserting seaman or entries from Canada, but especially from the mid-1920s the illegal immigrant problem became closely identified with Mexican-Americans. Many would-be Mexican immigrants could not pay the increased head tax and dodged the immigration entry points – entering illegally in much larger numbers after the mid-1920s. These Mexican aliens faced the deportation dragnet of the newly established border control police. Not something simply decided at the border itself, the border patrol's enforcement policies reflected anxieties over the presence within the American population of aliens. In a mark of new racial categories closely linked to their alien status, 'Mexican' became a racial group designated in the census. When the economy turned downward in 1929, local communities in the southwest mobilized to seek removal of unwanted illegal immigrants. The deportations of some 400,000 Mexicans in the next 10 years were underpinned by the racial stereotyping of these people as a burden upon the community. This 'racing' of the nation also informed the internment of Japanese-Americans in the Second World War, an action that clearly coupled immigration and security policies. Though 65 per cent of the 120,000 Japanese sent to wartime camps were citizens, all were assumed to be potential instruments of a hostile power.[4]

This racial reordering of immigration should not be separated from the wider cultural shifts that merged patriotism and the nation-state in the same era. The ideology of patriotism provided an enhanced sense of American difference and national superiority drawn from the wartime experience. Creation of new popular rituals of nationalism had, so an earlier chapter argued, begun in the 1890s, but the process was completed in this period. Though penned in the crisis of the First World War, Irving Berlin's *God Bless America* was rewritten and released in 1938 where it took on a religious sanction for US exceptionalism as sung on Armistice Day by Kate Smith while war clouds loomed over Europe once more. On a political level, too, overt rituals of patriotism were strengthened. At the same time that bureaucrats and politicians proclaimed new categories of aliens, the pledge of allegiance took on a stronger form. In 1923–24, the ritual had become linked more explicitly to the American state, with adoption of the pledge to 'the flag of the United States of America' rather than to 'my flag', a term that some argued could have applied to any nation from which immigrants came. The change came after lobbying from the National Flag Convention in which the American Legion and the Daughters of the American Revolution were prominent. With the addition of 'under God' in 1954, at the height of the Cold War, the modern pledge – conceived as both 'patriotic oath' and quasi-prayer – became complete.[5]

Changes in the landscape of patriotism emphasized the national political heritage and the scope for world leadership. Mount Rushmore (dedicated in 1927 and completed in 1941) etched the pantheon of American political heroes directly onto the environment through the carving of mountains in the image of four revered presidents.[6] But the impact of the Second World War, with the erection of the US Marines Corps War Memorial in Washington in 1954 carried the identification of people and patriotism still further by fusing symbols of democratized war and American power. Based on the marines' heroism in the struggle against the Japanese on Iwo Jima, the mountaintop raising of the flag photographed in wartime by cameraman Joe Rosenthal symbolized in its reproduction the United

States' rise to its hegemonic position; indeed the mountaintop photo snap consciously or not resembled the top of a globe; the collective straining of the individual soldiers emphasized the will of the American people and the movement of the flag forward the progressive realization of democracy. No wonder that the image became a war loan poster and a ubiquitous postage stamp before its final realization in sculptured form. War, the state and democracy were linked in the Iwo Jima monument to American power.[7]

Though American involvement in the world had shifted in revolutionary ways as a result of the Second World War, American knowledge of that world had in some ways shrunk since Woodrow Wilson's time. The role of geography as a subject in schools declined in the inter-war years. After Pearl Harbor, a nationwide poll revealed that 60 per cent of Americans were unable to locate either China or India on an outline map of the world.[8] True, the involvement of American armed forces in the Second World War prompted a renewal (of sorts) for the discipline, yet intellectual priorities had shifted. Americans must learn about other regions and peoples not on their own terms, but as part of advancing American political and strategic objectives. Maps were redrawn to emphasize American 'proximity' to threats.[9] Geography could play a part in high policy, too, in the quasi-imperial rethinking of the world in the phases of free market expansionism.[10] Similarly, schools gave greater attention to American history and fostered less knowledge of things foreign after the First World War under the influence of the Progressive historians. At the same time the lessening of immigration meant that more people lacked intimate knowledge of foreign places – knowledge that came from having been born in or having immediate kin born in a foreign country.

Equally troublesome was the declining place of foreign languages. Study of these had weakened over the course of the twentieth century, but in an uneven way. In 1915, 36 per cent of American students studied modern foreign languages in high school; by 1966 the figure was below 15 per cent. This, despite the fact that the Soviet launching of the Sputnik satellite in 1957 produced self-searching concerning American education. The National Defense Education Act (1958) provided for increased foreign language instruction in American schools. Money for language training and area studies followed in the 1960s as American sought to understand the countries of South and Southeast Asia. On this foundation centres for area studies, for example, Cornell University in Southeast Asian Studies, sprang up in the 1960s. Yet the late 1960s saw American priorities turn to domestic ones in response to civil unrest at home. Illinois congressman Paul Simon noted in 1980 the decline of interest in foreign language study post-1968. In 1974 there were there 'one half a million fewer United States high school students enrolled in foreign languages' than 6 years before and only 5 per cent of those graduating to become teachers had taken 'any course which expose[d] them to the culture of another country or to the international political arena'.[11]

Travel could in some circumstances compensate for the failures of formal education. American travel abroad had started to move away from its elitist foundations of the nineteenth century in the 1920s, when prosperity and cheaper transport took intellectuals and the middle class to Europe and Latin America in larger numbers than ever before. The figures for American overseas tourists in the 1920s rose from around 300,000 a year to over half a million by 1930 but dropped back under the impact of the Great Depression to early 1920s levels,[12] as did the number of passports issued. The rise of totalitarian regimes in central Europe together with the Second World War meant that Americans would get their most significant foreign travel experience in the 1940s as members of the military.

Certainly the enforced travel of wartime and the Cold War 'educated' a great many young military service personnel. American soldiers were exposed in the millions to Japanese culture in the Pacific, mostly as combatants and (some) as occupiers of the defeated empire after the Second World War. This experience was not inclined to endear the Japanese to them, but rather tended to reinforce racial stereotypes of fanatical and barbaric Orientals.[13] Military encounters overseas were far from being entirely negative, to be sure. Veterans brought back European, Asian and British Commonwealth war brides – undeniable evidence of intercultural contact. Reported numbers of the military marrying foreigners vary wildly, indicating gaps in the historiography of transnational history. Yet war brides represented the largest single case of legal migration to the United States since the mid-1920s.[14] At least 150,000 made it to the United States in the first 5 years after the war. Where non-white war brides were concerned, the cultural exchange potentially threatened racial boundaries. But only a few thousand Asian brides came into a nation of 140,000 million people.[15] These immigrants by marriage were absorbed as a one-off immigrant flow, and their impact on American society was minimal. The process was, moreover, almost entirely one-way. Rare were the examples such as Robert Lincoln O'Neill, from Madison, Wisconsin who married a Russian-Australian woman and stayed for the rest of his life as part of the small American community in Brisbane, Australia. But O'Neill did not give up his American roots. He remained an American citizen for more than 20 years before proclaiming his Australian citizenship with the words, 'Now I'm one of you'. He celebrated Fourths of July with his American 'pal' Rocky by getting well and truly drunk.[16] The comparative fates of those women who stayed in Europe while their sisters went across the Atlantic with GI husbands similarly enforced the cultural and economic power relationship. Young Italian girls swooned at victorious American troops in Naples in 1943. As much as political liberation, these uniformed men represented there and in many other countries material relief from wartime austerity. They brought food, as well as cigarettes and other luxuries to a destitute people. Back in America, war brides faced the same struggle of adjustment as other more conventional immigrants in earlier periods, but with the added complications of post-war housing and job shortages during the dramatic demobilization just before the Cold War set in. Much later, brides valued how their personal opportunities had been advanced. Some war brides recalled how fortunate they had been to marry Americans. In the longer run the cultural exchange reinforced American exceptionalism.[17]

This lopsided process continued through the stationing of troops in Europe. Once again American men became potential marriage partners, but also good business helping to lift spirits and bringing money into war-devastated communities. Young Americans were drafted to serve in Germany and elsewhere, among them Elvis Presley, whose 2-year army stint in the 1950s interrupted a stellar pop music career but inspired the film *GI Blues* and helped turn the rock star into an international movie idol as well. But a balanced cultural exchange between conquered and conqueror could not occur, especially in the immediate post-war occupation, when German women seemed willing to sell their sexual favours for money or food, so desperate was their situation. For their part, the US army discouraged fraternization as inimical to their democratization mission, believing that women attracted to the GIs might be Nazi or (later) communist spies. Commanders also worried about contact between African-American soldiers and white German women.[18] Whether with white or black Americans, sexual contact caused great friction within German society during both the 1940s occupation and the Cold War deployments of the 1950s. German churches and conservative social commentators deplored the spread of venereal disease, the undermining of morals and the insidious Americanizing influence that fraternization brought.[19] On top of this, Germany could not yet compete with the material largesse of 1950s America, with its huge cars and mod cons. The armed forces' experience abroad reinforced stereotypes of American material superiority.[20]

Equally ambiguous for a process of cultural interchange was the story of 'normal' foreign travel for peaceful purposes. This did not revive until the mid-1950s. Shipping carried most tourists to Europe and this form of travel still limited sojourns abroad. Air offered new opportunities, but commercial passenger aviation was still in its infancy. Not until 1957 did airborne passengers overtake the number going by ship, and it was not until the late 1960s brought mass cross-Atlantic transit that the international tourist market became democratized.

When mass overseas travel began, the exposure of Americans to foreign cultures did not necessarily increase. Overseas travel now tended to be of shorter duration – by 1966 the average European holiday had already dropped in 10 years from 6 to 4 weeks – as the trip of a lifetime became affordable in the prosperity of the 1960s. Time spent abroad was even less for the Caribbean. Two to four weeks meant a whistle-stop tour, or a stay highly packaged. When they did travel, Americans could increasingly stay in American-style accommodation and eat American food with an American travel section under the Marshall Plan used to encourage, for example, modernization of the French tourist industry in the 1950s.[21] Though American hamburger chains did not invade Europe until the 1970s, Europeans already offered American food after the Second World War. Hotels sprang up to provide American-style service and familiar brands. The spread of American hotels abroad began in 1949, when the first 'international' chain was founded with Hilton setting up in Puerto Rico, and Hilton built its first hotel in Europe in 1953 at Madrid.

More important than the conditions for foreign travel was the growth of domestic tourism. Cheaper flights and better roads meant that Americans could spend more vacation time within the United States or close by. Travel to Hawaii meant staying literally within American space while seemingly encountering the exotic. Moreover, 'international' travel often meant, even earlier in the twentieth century, cross-border forays into Canada and Mexico or going to the Caribbean, where Cuba, until 1959, had become an American gambling, nightclub and beach haven.[22] North American travel boomed in the 1950s with the rise of the interstate National Defense Highway system. Americans did go 'abroad' but a significant percentage of them chose to go just across the border. Expenditure on travel to Canada and Mexico constituted 46 per cent of total international tourist expenses by 1956.[23] Though earlier figurers are undoubtedly incomplete, this compared to 4.8 per cent of recorded expenditure in 1900.

American business had much to gain from the expansion of domestic rather than foreign tourism. A dollar spent abroad was one lost to the economy, and fewer foreigners travelled to the United States because they did not have the money to do so. From beginnings made by the railroad companies in the first decade of the twentieth century, Americans were encouraged by road improvements in the 1920s and the expansion of the national park system to 'see America first'. Visitors to National Parks reached 1 million in 1921, 10 million by 1947, 20 million by 1957 and 45 million by 1970. Until 1957, this was double the increase for foreign travel, though the latter then boomed to reach 4 million travellers abroad by 1970. Tourism helped solidify the modern nation-state by tying nationalism to iconic places and by encouraging citizens to identify nationalism with their experiences of those places. For the expanding middle class, tourism reconciled the gap between American nature and the urban–industrial nation, defining 'an organic nationalism that embodied the essence of America'.[24] Visits to national parks and monuments reinforced a sense of the United States as a place of great natural beauty and the imprint of 'the national' on the park and monument system arguably reinforced – by making routine – a sense of American exceptionalism.

Theme parks such as Disneyland worked in similar ways. Opened at the height of the Cold War in 1960, the most famous Disney exhibit was 'America the Beautiful', which featured a stunning circular depiction of the physical beauties of the landscapes of all states, set movingly against the playing of the Katherine Lee Bates' patriotic song. In these ways, the rise of mass travel strangely failed to educate Americans about the rest of the world, in comparison with nineteenth-century elite travel. At the same time, modern American experience abroad reinforced hierarchical relationships, particularly in non-Western countries. For Cuba and American dependencies such as Puerto Rico, travel (and gambling by tourists) became major economic support mechanisms.[25]

Media worked in similar ways to express and reinforce American power. The global importance of the Hollywood film industry – and its role as a purveyor and a representative of distinctive views about American traditions – grew. This dominance was not based simply on rolling over competitors and imposing American culture, however. American film moguls in the 1930s paid attention to lucrative foreign markets by modifying racial and ethnic stereotypes in an exercise of cultural hegemony rather than raw power. Yet the stories told were pure American. Ruth Vasey aptly states the hegemonic transnational content. 'Hollywood *constituted* its audiences as "American" in a remarkably literal fashion. By involving audiences in its particular vision, which was characterized by bourgeois and consumerist behaviour, it influenced attitudes and behaviour both inside and outside the United States' and produced a skewed, 'homogenized picture' of the larger world.[26] Because the European-born or those of recent immigrant stock largely dominated the industry, it was in the 1920s deeply suspect to nativist Americans. This was one reason why motion-picture moguls strove to Americanize and sanitize their product's content. The pull of Hollywood was strong for European actors and directors and the industry maintained a transnational dimension with such luminaries as German director Fritz Lang coming to make pictures in California. Iconic Hollywood films had vital European contributions. Almost all the stars of *Casablanca* (except Humphrey Bogart) as well as the director were European immigrants or political refugees.[27] But European artistic innovation was assimilated into American mass market-oriented themes. After the coming of the talkies in the late 1920s, Americans saw few foreign films. They did see British productions, but these were a small minority of pictures that tended to feed stereotypes of Britain as a class society or drew upon interest in historical nostalgia.[28] The trade in films had become more unequal across the Atlantic. Germany, especially after the coming of the Nazis, stood out against the trend until victory in the Second World War gave the US dominance of (free) central Europe's film exhibition as well.[29] Because this American supremacy undermined the foreign product, the effects were felt back in the United States as foreign films became harder to obtain. In 1960 only 10 per cent of the films Americans saw were foreign and the figure would drop thereafter.

Other media changed too, though the general pattern of increased insularity was punctured by periods of greater transnational interest. In journalism, the rise of fascism and the events of the European and Pacific war theatres strengthened interest in foreign events and produced an impressive foreign press corps that continued to influence American newscasting. Foreign correspondents supplied in the 1940s riveting news on radio under the leadership of CBS's Edward Murrow. William L. Shirer, who wrote for the *Chicago Tribune* and the *International Herald Tribune* in Paris, was another of note. The decline in this tradition began only after the advent of television in the 1950s. Television's rise encouraged the dominance of images over trained journalists operating on the spot. Commentators have identified an inward-turning news service apparent in the 1980s, yet the seeds were sown three decades earlier.[30] By the end of the 1960s, foreign news in American newspapers and on the new medium of television featured mainly countries relevant to American policy or ethnic groups of significance within the United States. Thus events in Vietnam understandably dominated foreign news in the 1960s and the Middle East and Eastern Europe received more striking coverage than those of, say, close neighbours Canada and Mexico.

International education offered more hopeful transnational exchanges. Americans were leaders in this field. The custom of attending universities in Europe for graduate training in the nineteenth century established an early tradition of cosmopolitanism. The PhD based on the German model became standard. Universities grew as research-intensive institutions and German practice influenced many American disciplines, including history and economics. In the twentieth century the patterns of overseas study changed. By the 1920s the practice of undergraduates taking a semester or year to study in Europe began for some students at the best universities, though it was far from a mass programme. The Institute for International Education (IIE), founded in 1919 with a Carnegie Corporation grant, established a student visa system in 1921 and became active in exchanges with European universities.[31] After the Second World War, IIE programmes assumed global dimensions, but the focus changed as the flow of students into the United States increased. The US role shifted to being an education provider. The IIE took on administration of Fulbright scholar exchange programmes initiated in 1946 with US war credits to allied countries. In 1952 the Institute began to administer Ford Foundation Grants that assisted US diplomatic efforts to supply education for likely leaders in the underdeveloped world. Education had become part of the Cold War. Non-immigrant students coming into the United States rose 70-fold to 98,000 by 1970 from 1925, with almost all the increase occurring from 1953.[32] Undergraduate study abroad also expanded, but the programmes never concerned more than a small minority of American students, and their educative role in acquiring knowledge about the world was seriously questionable. The United States was now an exporter of educational culture rather than a receiver. This pattern matched the shifts in the economy and the political power of the United States, but the result was to reduce the chances of such exchanges reorienting American academic priorities, which were increasingly drawn from within American culture.

Popular culture as well as education became more globally oriented. This phenomenon disseminated American values, but pop culture quickly revealed how difficult it had become to distinguish modernization from Americanization. In both the United States and Western Europe, cultural elites shuddered at these effects in transnational unison. The 1950s witnessed the spread of American rock and roll to Europe, begun officially by Bill Haley and the Comets and their 'Rock Around the Clock' in 1955; Elvis Presley followed soon after, but by the 1960s, reciprocal effects were felt as British youths refashioned American R and B into a new musical trend. The Beatles rather than American groups became the face of 1960s popular music, and spearheaded a British 'invasion' of the United States that demonstrated how interlinked modern youth culture in Western societies had become. The tendency of youths to stay longer at school and college accompanied the rise of mass consumer society and laid the groundwork for such a culture across the modernizing Euro-American world, though the trend had first been noticeable in the 1940s when Frank Sinatra tapped the teenage girl phenomenon known as bobby-soxers. Pop culture was transnational by the 1960s with the youth of Paris as well as New York (1964) and Tokyo (1966) experiencing Beatlemania. In the 1970s other European countries such as Sweden (through ABBA) would provide popular musical competition for American stars on a global level.

The feedback effects of American popular culture and the cross-national phenomena of pop pilgrimages recall how difficult it was by the 1970s for the United States to remain bordered off against foreign influences. But one did not need to look at the ephemera of pop culture to see this. The very pattern of American political and military involvement in the world made it almost impossible to compartmentalize the domestic and the foreign. It was the Cold War struggle that lay, for example, behind future President John F. Kennedy's plans for a 'New Frontier' in domestic policy in 1960. Cold War rivalries produced during the Eisenhower and Kennedy administrations global competition over the space race, changes in Civil Rights and novel foreign policies initiatives in the cultural realm. Kennedy's Peace Corps harnessed the idealism of American youth to change the world in a non-violent and democratic way, with thousands sent across Latin America, Asia and Africa to engage in projects of social and economic aid to poor nations.[33] Seven thousand had departed for overseas by 1963, though the movement was criticized as providing a positive gloss on Cold War realities of American foreign policy. Yet internally Civil Rights provided the clearest example of transnational effects and here the images conveyed to the world contradicted the message of the Peace Corps. The transnational connections in the modern American struggle for equality did not begin with Kennedy, however.

Cold War politics, which cordoned off the United States, simultaneously exposed the nation and its people to the international spotlight in the 1940s and 1950s. That attention accelerated changes in race relations. In the landmark Brown v. Board of Education of Topeka, Kansas case, the Supreme Court declared segregated schools unconstitutional in 1954, but a long and bitter struggle followed to implement desegregation policies in education, transport and housing policy and to achieve vital federal legislation removing racial discrimination in such matters as employment and accommodations (the Civil Rights Act of 1964) and in suffrage (the 1965 Voting Rights Act). This struggle of African-Americans and their white liberal allies has been typically conceived as part of a domestic reform tradition. Yet the international context vitally shaped issues. In analysing this topic it is crucial not to weigh internal versus external factors as the two were interactive. [34]

The struggle for world power after the Second World War influenced attempts to broaden Civil Rights at home. The military provided a key case. African-American troops had fought against Hitler's genocidal regime in a segregated army. This policy was awkward and embarrassing, but it reflected the state of Civil Rights in the United States. The change did not begin until 1948, when political campaigning for the presidency necessitated a policy shift. Faced with the need to galvanize black voters to replace Southern whites who deserted for Strom Thurmond's Dixiecrats over the (mild) Civil Rights agenda of the Democratic Party, President Truman issued during the campaign in July 1948 an executive order calling for 'equality of treatment' in the armed forces. Yet Truman set no timetable, and it took the larger military and political imperatives of the Cold War and the subsequent 'hot war' on the Korean peninsular in 1950 to bring a complete change in army policies. African-American leaders such as A. Philip Randolph lobbied Truman that 'Negroes would not shoulder a gun to fight for democracy abroad while they were denied democracy here'. [35] Practicalities aided these protests. Though the army had resisted desegregation, when troops were needed at the front, it was administratively and logistically difficult to replace troops by colour.

The Civil Rights conflict became not merely a series of momentous struggles in American history, but events seen, within a day or two, in many countries thanks to jet aircraft carrying television footage. By the late 1960s, satellites further sped the transmission of visual messages. The effect was startling to international audiences with the spread of television through the developed world. Pictures of police with truncheons, water-cannon and dogs attacking Civil Rights protesters flashed around the world nightly on screens in Europe and as far away as Australia in the 1960s. In places such as India and Fiji, too, newspaper editors noted ill treatment of African-Americans. Chester Bowles, US Ambassador to India, called racial discrimination 'the number one question' in Asia concerning American power and prestige. Foreigners flooded Alabama governor James Folsom with letters urging him to show clemency towards a robber and accused rapist sentenced to death in 1958. The American example stimulated such foreign struggles as that against apartheid in South Africa and affected foreign visitors in the United States. Non-white students faced discrimination and went back to their home countries to become political and administrative leaders while remaining appalled by the treatment of African-Americans. Faced with such pressures, the United States adopted a Civil Rights policy as part of its 'international agenda to promote democracy and contain communism', as Mary Dudziak has pointed out. President Eisenhower did not personally believe in federal enforcement of desegregation in the South, but worried about the impact of the defiance of desegregation in Little Rock in 1957 and feared the incidents there would feed 'the mill of Soviet propagandists'.[36]

The movement towards Civil Rights was not only stimulated by the Cold War but also limited in ways that rigidified the nation-state and reinforced exceptionalism. First, there was the reaction against such foreign censure. Some conservative Southern politicians viewed desegregation as a communist plot. Even Martin Luther King was accused of being pro-communist in order to undermine his position and closely monitored by the FBI. Second, while Civil Rights were promoted, broader African-American radical and progressive efforts to develop a 'politics of the African diaspora'[37] came under censure as being communist inspired. Historian Penny Von Eschen shows how radical and progressive blacks not only embraced domestic Civil Rights in the wartime and immediate post-war years. They also supported Pan-Africanist solidarity and championed global decolonization of non-white peoples as part of the same struggle as American Civil Rights. They looked forward to the time when 'the colored peoples of the world will no longer be exploited and expropriated by the Western world'.[38] Communists and 'fellow travellers' such as W. E. B. Du Bois and singer Paul Robeson worked in the 1940s through the International Committee on African Affairs to achieve these goals.

This work drew upon the deeper traditions of the African diaspora as an alternative to intellectual and cultural integration within a nation thought to be profoundly racist. The tradition was carried forward in the twentieth century in the new context of formal political control over most of Africa by the European powers. Whereas Marcus Garvey reflected lower middle-class aspirations for uplift of the ghetto population through business activity,[39] proletarian as much as race sentiment motivated Du Bois. In his works on Africa and African-American history as well as in his political actions he sensed the transnational pressures of classical European imperialism surrounding the race issue in the 1930s and 1940s.[40]

While the Cold War inspired liberal Civil Rights agitation as a marker of superiority to communism, it created after 1948 an inhospitable environment for such radicalism. The impact was to detach Civil Rights from this African diaspora approach. The radical anti-imperialist project became tainted. People like Robeson were denied passports and therefore could not travel to address the Bandung conference of the Non-Aligned Movement in Indonesia in 1955. McCarthyism silenced the anti-colonial struggle in America, with links between 'international and domestic politics' in race issues severed.[41] Radicals had tied racism to the political economy of colonialism, but now racism was reconceptualized as a psychological or moral problem 'confined to the limited horizons of U.S. "race relations."'[42] Mainstream African-American identity changed to emphasize the gap between American blacks and their compatriots in Africa and elsewhere in the diaspora. In this exceptionalist reading, African-Americans could succeed through moderate, incremental Civil Rights, while Africans were regarded as primitive and in need of modernizing through liberal reform. Moralism overtook the discourse of race, representations of Africa, and Civil Rights alike.[43]

For all that, diasporic discontent against the nation did not go away in the 1960s. Long fascinated by Africa, Du Bois took exile in newly independent Ghana in 1960, where he died soon after. He renounced his American citizenship after the government refused a renewed passport because he had joined the Communist Party. Others took refuge metaphorically in the Nation of Islam, which provided an emotional rather than physical space for attacking American racism.[44] Transnational travel picked up with an easing of passport restrictions and improved air transport. Many civil rights activists, including Malcolm X actively engaged with Africa and travelled there in the 1960s.[45] Still, it must be remembered that these sentiments were those of articulate minorities. Intellectual interest in Africa there was, but seeking improvement of conditions at home took precedence for most African-Americans.

The Civil Rights movement (and the contradictions that its history produced internationally) was part of a much broader intellectual shift post-Second World War centred on the development of human rights doctrines.[46] This concept had its origins in eighteenth-century Enlightenment thinking about the rights of man. Though always part of the American political tradition,[47] it had been honoured mainly in the breach of practical politics. Anti-slavery crusaders in the Anglo-American world had campaigned strongly for the rights of African-Americans and against the Atlantic slave trade. But the explicit expression, 'human rights', was not common and as a concept was dwarfed in late nineteenth-century discourse by racist and Social Darwinist ideas. When Woodrow Wilson proclaimed the doctrine of national self-determination at the end of the

First World War, human rights took different shape. Early twentieth-century conceptions presented rights as the collective properties of ethnic or national groups, not freestanding individuals.

The horrors of the Second World War revitalized action to recognize the rights of individuals. Diplomats and political leaders framed a new political and legal regime of human rights to avoid recurrence of genocide. The Nuremberg trials of Hitler's henchmen established legal precedents of accountability and recognized the category of 'crimes against humanity'. The conventions and codes of earlier human rights practice were transformed in the UN Universal Declaration on Human Rights in 1948. This was not a legal convention but a statement of principles influenced by the Declaration of Independence. President Truman and such Democratic political strategists as Hubert Humphrey referred to the UN Declaration as modelled on the rights Americans took for granted and began in 1948 to use the language of human rights to fight for Civil Rights for African-Americans.[48] Truman's rhetoric also invoked the Cold War as justification for broadening human rights claims to include other peoples. He used Americans' affinity with this tradition to distinguish their political system from that of the Soviet Union. Liberals therefore subsumed not only the struggle for African-American freedom, but also human rights as a philosophical principle, into the geo-political struggle against communism.

For all its difficulties, the 1950s and 1960s was in some ways the high point of American hegemony, but US power was simultaneously challenged on many fronts. By the late 1960s an Asian guerrilla war showed how a small country could defy the might of the American military, pinning the world's greatest army down to a stalemate in the jungles of Vietnam. Meanwhile, Soviet and Chinese Communist influence grew in Africa, and the small nation of Cuba conducted its own revolution (completed in 1959) and then became a socialist thorn in the side of the United States providing inspiration to revolutions elsewhere in Latin American in the 1960s. The stationing of Soviet missiles in Cuba brought the world to the verge of nuclear war in 1962, reminding Americans how the physical space promoting national security had shrunk. At home the assassination of John Kennedy in 1963 and of Martin Luther King and Senator Robert Kennedy in 1968 showed the world the fragility of civil order when accompanied by riots in the ghettos of American cities that followed. The United States was already entering a crisis of confidence in the system that accelerated in the early 1970s with the slowing of world economic growth and, at home, perhaps the greatest scandal to affect the presidency in a hundred years. The 1970s would not be happy times, but in that decade, the beginnings of a new phase of globalization connecting America to the wider world was clearly underway. This new globalization would simultaneously threaten American national identity and provide enticing new avenues for extension of American economic and cultural influence abroad.

14

From the 1970s to New Globalization: American Transnational Power and Its Limits, 1971–2001

What shall we remember of the millennium's last 30 years? Most likely for Americans the personal world of family and community will be recalled first, but sometimes the personal and the political come together in images of national experience. The passage of time in these years evokes strong memories. Imagine a fast-forward compilation of television clips concerning the United States in the wider world. A president's rapprochement with China; American helicopters leaving Saigon as the North Vietnamese advance; long lines forming at gasoline pumps as fuel from the Middle East runs short; the nation's chief of state on screen resigning; a hostage crisis in Iran; an ex-movie star president denouncing the Soviet Union as an 'evil empire'; a wall tumbling in Berlin; burnt out tanks on the road from Kuwait to Baghdad; stock market charts indicating a dot-com revolution; a terrorist-damaged American ship; a blown-up embassy; an Israeli and a Palestinian leader shaking hands at the White House; and much more. Some of these images would not make a similar list in 200 let alone 2000 years. Yet behind surface events, United States national power and its global position were intertwining, and it is important to discern the structural changes underlying commonplace headline stories.

This chapter first charts key moments in the transitional decade of the 1970s and the American response to challenges posed by international reversals and domestic turmoil, then goes on to analyse so-called 'new globalization' as it affected the United States, especially through the role of the Reagan administration. In this period American cultural, economic and political influence spread transnationally in striking ways. Finally, the chapter examines new cross-national influences constraining and shaping the United States. Just as the United States influenced other nations, transnational influences changed the nation's social and economic fabric and challenged national power. These changes set the scene for the dramatic events of September 11, 2001.

Many academics, government officials and media commentators agree that the world grew closer together in the last three decades of the millennium. Some theorists call this shift new globalization. While historians dispute the extent, unidirectional nature and irretrievability of the change, there can be little doubt that changes in political systems, economics, media and communications brought a more interdependent world. For the United States, the relationship to that growing interdependence of peoples has been contradictory. In some ways the United States became a key agent of the forces making for greater global integration. At the same time, new globalization did not mean all nations were equal. The United States exhibited powerful capacities for independent action, as the nation rose in this period to unprecedented military power and economic prosperity. Moreover, historical circumstances left the United States at first as a beleaguered nation. Strong impulses to turn inward were evident in the 1970s, a critical period in the realignment of the United States internationally.

The 1970s was a difficult decade for Americans and many of the troubles that emerged in that period were linked in some way to the transnational consequences of the Vietnam War. That conflict temporarily weakened national economic and political power and affected American prestige internationally. Unlike the Korean War, very few countries joined as allies (Britain, for example, stayed out) and US troops faced the brunt of the fighting along with the South Vietnamese. Demonstrations against the Vietnam War were not only held in the United States, but also became a regular feature of life in other countries. Anti-Americanism grew in the Third World on this basis. The My Lai Massacre of 1968 in which an army officer was convicted (1971) of ordering the slaughter of unarmed Vietnamese villagers showed the American and international publics that US troops were as capable as their enemies of atrocities against innocent civilians. Economically the impact of war was serious too. Costing some 150 billion US dollars, the war accelerated the rise of budget deficits and spurred inflationary pressures that were already gathering from enhanced labour organization bargaining and the welfare programmes promoted by President Lyndon Johnson and his Great Society reforms of the 1965–69 period.

Militarily and strategically the Vietnam adventure ended in defeat with 58,000 American lives lost and 150,000 wounded. In January 1973 the administration of President Richard Nixon agreed to withdraw financial and military aid, leaving South Vietnam to its own devices. Two years later, at the collapse of the South, images of American helicopters leaving the US embassy in Saigon for the last time provided powerful symbols of American defeat in world eyes. Refugees that had collaborated with the Americans clung to the craft, while others were of necessity pushed away.

At home, division already had grown in American society over civil rights, feminism, drug culture and the military–industrial complex. Student dissent rocked the universities, as it did during this era across the Western world including Germany, Mexico and France. In part the protests stemmed from the discontents of the baby-boomer generation of youth. In France, the anti-war agitation coincided with the teething troubles of the expansion of university education. Burgeoning student numbers (up from 170,000 to 514,000 in 10 years to 1968) led to discontentment with bureaucratic interference, though French revolutionary traditions and class-consciousness also served as motivating factors. In the United States, the war's role was crucial in sensitizing a college generation to radical protest and in fostering sharp internal divisions between blue-collar families and well-educated dissenters on university campuses. Richard Nixon exploited these divisions to restore the power of the 'silent majority' of patriotic Americans. When the US Air Force bombed Cambodia to destroy Communist supply lines into South Vietnam, the action spurred a new round of student uprisings leading to the Kent State University protest incident of May 1970 in which the Ohio National Guard shot 4 students dead. The state had turned upon its own people, as it had already on the national level when the Nixon administration wiretapped and engaged in other illegalities in surveillance of radicals.[1]

Though college campuses soon returned to calm, the cultural impact of the war remained. One permanent feature was the arrival after 1975 of Vietnamese refugees and other Vietnamese and Cambodians post-1975. Over 100,000 Vietnamese evacuated South Vietnam at the fall of Saigon in 1975, many being accepted into the United States. Then in 1978 came a wave of so-called boat people, often ethnically Chinese, who had been discriminated against by the new Vietnamese regime. As a result of the flood of refugees and economic immigrants, people-to-people links were established with Vietnam despite the US government's political isolation from the new Communist rulers, and further Vietnamese immigration in the familiar chain migration pattern occurred. By the century's end, 988,000 foreign-born Vietnamese lived in the United States, making this the fifth-largest immigrant group. The influx brought greater ethnic and cultural diversity but the demographic effects were largely limited to seven states – especially California – that together had nearly three-quarters of the total number of Vietnamese refugees and other Southeast Asian immigrants.[2]

Despite the domestic repercussions of the war, with the arrival of refugees and the Eurasian offspring of American servicemen conceived with Vietnamese women serving as visible symbols to remind the public, one striking result was for Americans to wish to put Vietnam behind them. This outcome was difficult to achieve, however. The existence of more than 700 American prisoners of war in Vietnam had agitated public opinion in the period before the American pullout in 1973, and even after the release of these, many Americans persisted in believing that others in their thousands were missing in action (the MIAs) and kept in secret confinement by the Communists somewhere in Indochina.[3] The MIA syndrome became just one more irritation, complicating internal American recovery from the social and cultural impact of the war. Nevertheless, the war produced a definite inward turning, culturally speaking. Americans saw the Vietnam War in terms of its effects on the United States alone. Films, for example *The Deer Hunter* and *Coming Home*, emphasized the impact upon returning soldiers and the wounds psychological and otherwise that the conflict brought. Americans wished to heal and many hoped to remember the war in a low-key way through the subdued Vietnam Veterans Memorial designed by Maya Ying Lin and dedicated in 1982. The losses of the Vietnamese both north and south were largely forgotten; but the war was not and the Memorial did not help. Even the Vietnam veterans felt slighted and unwanted, as the American flag was missing from the design. Moreover, only the dead, not those who served, were registered on the memorial wall's solemn stone. The war as remembered was a festering 'wound', as some put it, on the body politic. In this way, the Vietnam War did not bring about greater engagement with the world culturally, but rather the opposite.[4] A similar inward turning occurred politically and diplomatically. While in foreign policy Nixon travelled to China in 1972 and began the process of cultural and economic exchange that led to full diplomatic recognition 7 years later, the trend of US policy in the 1970s was to emphasize the limits of American power in the Pacific and the need for East and Southeast Asian countries to shoulder the burden of self-defence.

In these years the United States became preoccupied with internal events in a way that shook confidence in the system. Ironically these 'internal' events were closely linked to the Republican administration's attempts to control information on the most important 'external' event of the time, the Vietnam War. The effects were to weaken the power of the presidency temporarily and to undermine Nixon's foreign policy strategies. Following the break-in to the Democratic Party headquarters, the Watergate scandal of 1973–74 unleashed a chain of events that produced the resignation of Nixon from the Presidency. American politics was in the mid-1970s firmly focused on Watergate's collateral damage to the domestic political system. Watergate was one challenge to American confidence, but there were several other issues raising the possibility that the American system was in decline globally.

The unhappiness of the 1970s went far beyond the embarrassing withdrawal from Vietnam. Not only had Soviet power in the Middle East and Africa grown, with Cold War-inspired civil wars spreading to places such as Angola but for the first time the United States confronted a discourse of limits on a broad front. An environmental movement born in the post-1950 period out of well-educated, middle-class concern with the quality of life in cities and the destruction of nature became in the 1960s radicalized and sensitized to environmental constraints. The phrase 'limits to growth' expressed alarm at the accelerating degradation of planetary resources. Though the key report of that name was commissioned by the 'Club of Rome' and was international in scope, its main authors were Americans. Earth Day, established in 1970, and the American-inspired group Friends of the Earth played on the combined association of Nature with earth and the whole globe. The special abundance of America had limits after all.

In economic terms, the 1970s were years of low economic growth and high inflation. Most Western powers, especially Britain, suffered from these problems, though the worsening trade position and high budget deficits of the United States made the nation particularly vulnerable because of the dollar's role as the de facto reserve currency. To make US industry and exports more competitive and so redress the trade deficit, the United States pressured its allies to agree to a lower dollar exchange rate in late 1971, but the currency's fall continued soon after. So seemingly limitless post-1945, US economic power faced the challenge of imports from Japan in a wide range of manufactured goods, but especially automobiles. Equally startling was the impact of rising energy prices and shortages of oil. The energy crisis produced by the OPEC oil cartel reacting against Israel's Yom Kippur War in 1973 combined with spiralling inflation and a cyclical downturn to end the long post-war economic prosperity. Speed limits on roads were introduced as one of many measures to conserve fuel, rationing was introduced and long lines of automobiles gathered at the gas stations in the winter of 1973–74. Accustomed to abundance, Americans were flustered and though the alarm subsided by 1975, this was not to be the last oil shock. The Iranian Revolution of 1978–79 removed the American-backed dictator, the Shah, Mohammad Reza Pahlavi, and soon after an Islamic fundamentalist regime took charge. A second energy crisis ensued as civil unrest in Iran made the output of the world's second largest oil producer unreliable. This circumstance was combined with the Iranian hostage crisis, in which radical Iranian students held 52 Americans at the US Embassy in Teheran in late 1979 in payback for decades of American support of the Shah. They were not released until January 1981 and became a thorny issue in the Presidential election of 1980 because of the president's inability to resolve the problem. The hostage crisis ruined Jimmy Carter's already weakened presidency and he was to be remembered as a chief executive who presided over declining political power and rising economic austerity.

Yet the gloom of the late 1970s concealed the beginnings of a revival. The external shocks produced a reordering of the American economy and the political landscape. A vigorous movement to restore American patriotism and self-assurance was already underway from the conservative side of American politics. The growth of American power resumed soon after, ushering in another 25 years of largely prosperous times. The change

came about ostensibly because of one man, Ronald Reagan, but the reality
was far more complex.

During Reagan's 1984 re-election campaign, Republican advertisements
credited the popular president with having brought a 'new morning' to
America. After the tumult of the 1960s social divisions and the economic
doldrums of the 1970s, the national mood had certainly revived. A large
part of the revival stemmed from the political change. It is tempting
to think that the United States was simply reasserting control over its
own destiny, courtesy of a tough leader. Reagan's foreign and defence
policies encouraged this renewal of national exceptionalism as the president prosecuted the Cold War struggle with vigour, acted against socialist
revolutions in Central America, intensified the arms race and proclaimed
the Soviet Union an evil empire. The domestic impact of Reagan as president also supplies evidence for an American-centred regeneration of the
nation. Reagan's tax cuts and deregulation helped make the 1980s prosperous years, at least after 1982, though prosperity was hardly shared
fairly under trickle-down economics. The long boom punctuated by the
recession of the early 1990s gave way to a stock-market bubble and much
lower unemployment. To some extent Bill Clinton's presidency was a bene-
ficiary of the more dynamic and prosperous economy that emerged from
the 1970s trough. Yet the 1980s reflected deeper pressures than the flux
of presidential politics. The changes that we now call new globalization
influenced domestic American decision-making. Satellite communications,
the computer revolution culminating in the World Wide Web of the 1990s,
freer flows of capital, floating exchange rates, a myriad of transnational
NGOs and the discourses of environmentalism and human rights were
just some of the signs of global integration.

The rise of new globalization was not, however, the result of inexorable
technological forces outside human influence. It was spurred by changes
in the economic and political relations of modern capitalism, which were
in themselves truly a transnational phenomenon. From the 1940s to 1970,
the impact of Keynesian economic spending had boosted global economics.
But labour-capital competition and rising prices for raw materials, particularly with the oil shocks of the 1970s, brought a crisis in this cycle of
capital accumulation globally, not just in the United States. The reassertion
of corporate and financial strength against union power and government
regulation in the 1980s was the response. The reinvigoration of capitalism
and free markets across the entire Anglo-American world brought a new
cycle of growth peaking in the 1990s under the impact of cheaper labour,
credit and the new technologies of the third-wave industrial revolution
through computerization. The patterns of deficit spending, income tax
cuts and stimuli to corporations differed from the Keynesian Revolution
of the post-war years. The state was now being downsized. Free-market
economists urged liberalized rules of trade, unfettered global circulation of
capital and an end to bureaucratic regulation of business. Under Reagan

these ideas were introduced into government. Free-market policies were seen in environmental issues where Reagan attempted to cast off national assets such as US public lands, relaxed red tape on pollution regulation and encouraged a return to higher gasoline consuming cars. In 1986, the administration rolled back the 1978 automobile fuel economy standards, ostensibly because market forces would work better to control gasoline use. The change contributed to a marked increase in global greenhouse gas emissions by the 1990s.[5] In the energy issue, domestic and foreign policies became intertwined. The United States encouraged oil producer competition abroad through diplomatic leverage upon Middle Eastern oil states in the Persian Gulf and fostered foreign oil exploration by multinational companies. With the end of the oil crisis, larger cars became more common again and higher energy consumption was registered.[6]

The efforts of the right in the United States to restructure under Reagan were paralleled by a move to anti-union policies in Britain under Prime Minister Margaret Thatcher. Like Reagan, she pursued a vigorous foreign policy as shown in the Falklands War (1982). By the 1990s European countries were also downsizing government and selling off state assets such as telephone companies. The American version of capitalism had become more and more an international model. The transnational political moment of neo-conservative politics as well as global economic pressures brought about these changes, not just the personality of Ronald Reagan and his popularity among the American people.

The United States remained as it had been since 1945 at the centre of the world's economic activity, but its global economic relationships changed after the 1970s. Ever since the early 1950s the United States had run down its gold reserves through financial aid to Europe, the war in Vietnam and other overseas troop commitments, but by 1971–72 the nation was also running trade deficits. The reduction in gold reserves was dramatic and the post-war international economic settlement began to unravel. For one thing, the Bretton Woods agreement's provision tying the dollar to gold collapsed in 1971 and free floating exchange rates became the norm. This benefited some sectors of the American economy. The dollar remained the de facto reserve currency and the effect of the financial shake-up by the 1980s was to boost global capital flows, which proved advantageous to American investors abroad and the American stock market that could draw more easily on European money. American investment in foreign countries increased in the 1970s and 1980s and the Reagan administration extended trade liberalization. Even though Reagan stressed American nationalism and political dominance, the American economy became more integrated with the world economy. Foreign trade rose from around 11 per cent of GDP in 1970, to 20.5 per cent in 1980 and 26 per cent by 2000,[7] with the United States being more generous towards others in opening markets than some of its key competitors were in return. For the first time since the First World War the United States became a debtor nation in 1985. Americans sucked in imports to fund their high standard of living and foreign moneylenders profited; the United States stayed afloat with European and, increasingly, Asian capital investments and treasury bond purchases. Backing these changes in the economy was the emphasis in public discourse and mainstream politics on globalization's advantages. In the early 1990s the George H. W. Bush administration pushed through the North American Free Trade Agreement (NAFTA) and officials during the Clinton presidency talked up free trade and supported the World Trade Organization (WTO, established 1995). The brave new world of modern globalization in which the United States participated in the game rather than orchestrated the rules had almost arrived in an economic sense.

Though the American economy boomed until 2 years after the stock market crash of 1987 and then again from 1993, the effects of globalization on the regional economies of the United States were uneven. Deindustrialization became a phenomenon from the 1970s as high labour costs drove American companies to relocate to the developing world, including Mexico, South America and East and Southeast Asia. The converse was the closure of factories and the loss of population in so-called 'rust belt' industrial towns, particularly the Northeast and Midwest. Heavy industry in states such as Ohio came under pressure, with Youngstown's steel mills part of the rust belt phenomena of decaying cities and towns. Employment in the US steel industry fell from over half a million workers in 1973 to 240,000 by 1983. With unions weaker than in Canada and policies more free market oriented, old US industries went downhill more easily.[8] Meanwhile other regions such as California and Arizona benefited from defence industry contracts or tourism – or both – and grew exponentially to become the 'sunbelt' of the 1980s and 1990s. The growth of the computer industry in California in the 1980s transformed the American economy further and led to a hi-tech rebirth of certain regions. As in the nineteenth century, vast fortunes were made and gleaming cities mushroomed such as Dallas–Fort Worth and Houston along with Seattle and Silicon Valley towns such as San Jose. This global economic impact had class and racial aspects too, with corporate globalization disproportionately hurting non-white people through loss of low-skilled job opportunities and disruption to communities.

Regional or class disparity within the American economy was hardly a new phenomenon. In the nineteenth century the South's economic development was skewered by its external focus, which made it difficult to introduce secondary industries and which favoured cotton and other agricultural exports. Similarly the American west was export oriented and essentially a colony of the East in the late nineteenth century. The textile industry of the Carolinas had migrated from New England in the 1880s only to move on to the third world in the Reagan years. Nor were the dislocating effects of globalization only felt in the United States. Rust belts existed in other countries such as Britain and in the dilapidated industrial towns of the former Soviet Union and its Eastern European allies in the 1990s. Nor would the process of globalizing national economies end there. Though the United States had been continually reindustrializing since 1981 for the new 'information economy', a white-collar rust belt seemed possible after the collapse of the stock market bubble in 2000–01. Centres of the new tech-related economy experienced, for instance, loss of jobs to India, with its good universities and where English was readily spoken among the highly educated and growing middle class.[9]

The disparities within the economy had political and cultural consequences. The power of the Southern states and the Southwest in American politics grew. Prosperous areas tied to defence industries were more conservative, especially in the Bible Belt of the South. Elsewhere, the blue-collar politics of the 1930s and 1940s Democratic Party as well as trade union membership suffered through the decline of traditional manufacturing industries. Liberal and more cosmopolitan peoples huddled along the east and west coasts and large metropolitan areas were also those after the 1970s more internationally oriented. San Francisco and New York had always been international cities,[10] but immigration now made others such as Los Angeles and Seattle much the same. These areas continued to support relatively liberal politics, while the heartland moved in the 1980s in a conservative Republican direction. These apparently internal effects with profound implications for the balance of power in the nation were products of uneven integration in the new globalization phase since the 1970s.

Integration with the world's economy was not just economic. It also had cultural implications. Potential American influence in the world was extended, especially through American media with the cable television news channel CNN developing in the 1980s and cable networks spreading internationally in the 1990s. Media and communications had begun many of the key globalization changes earlier. These could be traced back to the pioneer Telstar satellite transmissions from 1962. By 1969, global coverage already allowed over half a billion people around the world to watch live as two American astronauts walked upon the moon. In the 1980s and 1990s, satellite television and the rise of video spread American pop culture, with basketball growing in popularity in Asia and Latin America. At the same time, Hollywood reinvented itself in the wake of television's challenge by focusing on blockbusters and action films. Overseas markets supplied up to half the profits of the movie industry in the 1990s, up from around a third from 1950 to 1980. In Anglophone Africa, for example, American films accounted for 70 per cent of the market. Hollywood's domination was slowly starving out its competitor national film industries. By the late 1990s, the European film industry was one-ninth the size of what it was at the end of the Second World War.[11] Even the relatively healthy French film industry snared just 26 per cent of its home market. Outside Europe, Asian film industries did better, particularly in India and Hong Kong, but in Australia, a successful, state-subsidized local industry did little more in the long run than supply a training ground for future Hollywood stars and directors.

In yet another area of international influence, the 1980s spread of American business in the service industries fed upon and furthered the pattern of new globalization. With the freer movement of technology and money, American multinational corporations extended their reach and duplicated in services changes that had earlier occurred in the production of consumer goods. From small European beginnings in Britain in 1974, McDonalds rapidly expanded its business in the 1980s and saw erection of the first golden arches in Moscow in 1990. The main expansion of fast food in continental Europe had to wait until then because, as Victoria de Grazia states, only then did similar conditions to those in the United States appear, such as patterns of commuting long distances to work rather than being able to return home for lunch.[12] From the mid-1980s the tendency to internationalize production and distribution processes saw American food and beverage chains begin to affect the way large parts of the world ate and drank, though this spread of American techniques did not go unchallenged. In reaction, the 'slow food' movement stressing traditional preparation and dining was started in France and Italy.

The consequences of this diffused cultural product for American knowledge and international experience were important. American space had become by the 1990s 'globalized'. With the spread of American business it was far easier for Americans to travel abroad while remaining within familiar territory. It was in the 1980s that automatic credit card transactions allowed US hotel chains to make great headway in many overseas countries. In the 1990s, coffee chains such as Starbucks, as well as films, cable television and the Internet enabled people more easily to duplicate their American experience while abroad and keep in touch with home. Of course this desire to seek out comforting symbols of home was a human characteristic not unique to Americans. Canadians migrated to winter 'colonies' in Florida and Mexico while the English and German tourists transformed parts of Southern Spain and France in their own image. But the American impact was greater because the absolute number of Americans travelling was larger, as was the dollar value of American tourism as a percentage of the global total; 20 per cent in the 1960s, it was still 12.2 per cent of a very much bigger cake in 2002.[13]

In the United States, the role of the media had a similar effect in narrowing knowledge and creating an American intellectual space that occluded competitors. Film scholar Toby Miller notes, 'In the 1960s imports accounted for 10 per cent of the US film market' compared to only 0.75 per cent by 2000, leaving foreign films 'essentially excluded from the US, as never before'.[14] In reality, marginalization of foreign movies was not new, but the economics of the blockbuster phenomenon and increasing cross-media ownership over the 30 years since the 1970s squeezed out foreign movies to an unprecedented degree. The same constraints have, according to Christopher Jordan, also changed the nature of movie production and narrowed the ideas they present, to re-emphasize traditional American values, including nationalism, the work ethic, 'rugged individualism and self-help'.[15]

American influence also spread through 'neo-liberal' ideas in which the works of American economists and other policy makers were prominent. The most famous was Milton Friedman. Like a nineteenth-century missionary, Friedman toured the world preaching the virtues of free markets and the sins of big government. No country in the developed world did more to implement the free-market philosophy in this period than New Zealand. Yet the most famous case was of Chile, where Friedman lectured in 1975 during Augusto Pinochet's military dictatorship. Neo-liberal professors from the so-called Chicago School of Economics advised the Chilean government, in whose ranks served a group of PhD graduates known as 'the Chicago boys'.[16] Neo-liberal ideas took root because the international financial institutions such as the IMF and World Bank favoured them and rewarded governments needing loans and other assistance to stabilize their economies in a period of high inflation and stagnating trade.

Other American ideas were more obviously linked to the earlier history of nineteenth-century cultural expansion. Alcohol prohibition had been decisively defeated in the United States in 1933, but late twentieth-century drug policy was in some ways an attempted reincarnation. The US prohibitionist approach to narcotic control began in the decades before the First World War and was closely connected to the drive against alcohol. A pioneer in the 1920s and 1930s was Richmond Hobson, President of the World Narcotic Defense Association and the man who had first proposed the alcohol prohibition amendment to Congress. Within the US government, leadership came from Harry Anslinger, head of the Federal Narcotics Bureau from 1930, who came to the job after working in the Federal Prohibition Bureau enforcing the Eighteenth Amendment in the 1920s. But not until after the Second World War did the American approach to narcotic control gained political ascendancy internationally. The 1953 Opium Convention bore the marks of Anslinger's influence, and Anslinger also proposed a so-called 'single convention' to bring all narcotic controls under one prohibitionist convention and authority. The 1961 Single Convention on Narcotic Drugs under the United Nations (ratified 1964) had 180 member states by 2000 and an International Narcotics Control Board was established to monitor and enforce prohibition (except for regulated and prescribed medical uses) of heroin and other hard drugs.

Yet buoyed by decolonization and the ability to play off east and west in the Cold War, producing countries dragged their heels on ratifying the various conventions. Some countries could be swayed by promises of military and financial aid to comply with standards under the comprehensive treaty of 1961, but a few nations ignored the treaty regime entirely, and others, such as Iran and Turkey played hard to get and sought to manipulate US aid and political support in return for compliance. Clearly the United States (and the other industrialized countries) did not have their way entirely.[17]

Just as with alcohol prohibition, US policy still met resistance both at home and abroad. War was a more important stimulus to the opium traffic than was the power of international conventions to prohibit it. A heroin epidemic in the 1960s followed upon the US military intervention in Southeast Asia. American servicemen took the addiction back home, while American prosperity and the rise of youth culture championing drug use in the 1960s created still more lucrative markets. Ironically, most American hard drugs came from the famed golden triangle around the borders of Thailand, Burma and Laos where hill tribesmen, who had cooperated with and been protected by the CIA in the struggle against Communists, cultivated the poppy.[18] President Nixon escalated the rhetoric by proclaiming illicit drugs as the nation's public enemy in 1971 and established a Drug Enforcement Agency to deal with the problem in 1973. He was to be one of several presidents who tried to protect Americans against this foreign invasion by declaring 'war' on drugs. The 'war' was to last indefinitely and had considerable effects on American connections with foreign countries in the 1980s and 1990s.

This transnational aspect of the drug problem became especially clear when attention shifted to the flood of cocaine imported from Latin America from the late 1970s. Authorities at first underestimated the threat, perhaps because cocaine was a drug reputedly beloved among well-to-do young urban professionals and the glitterati. But in response to the emergence of cheap crack cocaine and accompanying crime as a severe problem on the streets of American ghettoes in 1985, the Reagan administration introduced in 1986 a policy of zero tolerance towards drugs and adopted the 'Just Say No' slogan for American youth.[19] US foreign policy became involved because cocaine smuggling had grown into a lucrative transnational business. When the United States overthrew Panamanian strongman Manuel Noriega in 1989, one of the ostensible reasons for intervention was his role in the flow of cocaine destined for American shores. Yet Noriega's trial and imprisonment by US authorities did not significantly stem the tide. In fact cocaine was probably as widely available in the period after the US intervention as before. By the late 1990s the United States became convinced that intervention at the source – the cultivation of coca leaves in Columbia – was necessary. The Clinton administration entered into an agreement in 2000 to supply the Columbian government with military aid to suppress the cocaine cartels. This billion-dollar plus 'Plan Columbia' intervention was highly controversial in Latin America because of the long history of US political and military interference on that continent. American intrusion in the affairs of foreign countries was in the case of drug wars a transnational extension of domestic politics and policies. Only the military and the economic power of the United States allowed these policies to be introduced, however ineffective they may have been in their implementation. [20]

American economic and moral reform practices along with cultural influences spread in such highly visible ways from the 1970s to the 1990s. Did this cluster of changes usher in a new deterritorialized American Empire? Certainly the course of drug policy suggested a deterritorialization process in which American domestic and foreign policy objectives were intertwined. The porousness of national borders became obvious, in terms of drugs pouring into the United States and in terms of economic, diplomatic and military action abroad to enforce an American domestic social policy on nation-states lacking the authority to police their own territory.

Transnational power exhibited in these ways had limits that must be clearly charted, nonetheless. Military force, international agreements and American government money lavished on solution of the drug problem did not bring about international compliance any more than diplomacy and law enforcement did in the area of alcohol prohibition decades earlier. [21] Outside influences now shaped American policy responses in a reactive fashion as successive American administrations struggled to counter every new twist of the drug traffic saga. Other areas in which the extension of American influence appeared at firsts glance to be considerable on closer inspection also revealed limits to American transnational power.

In no area of cultural affairs was American influence abroad so ostensibly large as in the cinema, yet even here Americanization was a complicated process. Audiences selectively interpreted American films. The problem of reception is a difficult one, but we cannot assume a simple process of absorption as in the case of a blotting paper culture. Japan accounted for up to 20 per cent of Hollywood revenues at the end of the twentieth century, but there can be little doubt that much of the content was, to apply the words of a clever film, 'lost in translation'. Michael Jordan may have become the most recognized sportsman on the planet and served as a symbol of the new global capitalism, [22] but figures such as Ronaldo Luíz Nazário de Lima and Diego Maradona rivalled him. Football, or soccer as Americans called it, was the most prominent world game, not basketball, and the United States remained marginal in that sport. Despite the influence of mainstream American films globally, in Asia alternatives flourished. Bollywood made more films than Hollywood, and began to influence international film styles as well as video clips with its distinctive dance sequences. Al-Jazeera challenged CNN as a television network in the Arab world as did the BBC globally. Palestinian teenagers and Iranian youths wore Nike T-shirts as they chanted anti-American slogans. Terrorists used the Internet to proclaim their causes and exchange bomb-making information. The means for resisting were found in the interstices of globalization itself and these systemic changes could still be both localized and refracted through other identities.

New globalization's effects shaped the United States itself, most notably in the way that immigration was changing the nation's ethnic composition. The restricted immigration policy that had structured a raced nation from the First World War was replaced in 1965 in an act of Congress influenced by the political climate of the Cold War, the Civil Rights movement and the concomitant desire of government to demonstrate an end to racial intolerance. The new law removed previous restrictions that favoured Caucasian, Western European immigration, while maintaining a strict limit on the total numbers of immigrants admitted at 170,000 for the eastern hemisphere (with a limit of 20,000 per country) and 170,000 a year for the western (no country limit). Asian immigration was no longer subject to special restrictions as under the Chinese Exclusion Act of 1882 and its successors. In 1965, 90 per cent of immigrants still came from Europe, but under the new act, by the 1980s only 10 per cent did so (though a flurry of Russian and other Eastern European immigration followed the collapse of the Soviet Union in 1991).[23] The major result of the changes of 1965 was the steady stream of migrants from Latin America, who constituted more than one-third of all immigrants in every year since that time. Not only were Hispanics heading for the American Southwest but states such as Illinois, Florida and New York developed strong concentrations.

This was only the beginning. According to the Census Bureau, by 2100 a quarter of the population would be of Hispanic origin, as both legal and illegal immigration from Mexico, Cuba and elsewhere in Latin America grew. A large Pacific Island and Asian influx would augment this diversity. In the 1980s and 1990s Asians had also poured in, and by 2001 made up 4 per cent of the total population. The very face of America would change along with other countries of the Pacific Rim such as Canada that experienced similar Pacific basin immigration. But though the bureau projected the foreign-born proportion of the nation's population to rise from 10 per cent in 1999 to 13 per cent in 2050,[24] the figure would not be higher than at certain times in the nineteenth century. This simple fact testifies to the earlier multicultural history of the United States that had been forgotten in the late twentieth century – as if globalization was something entirely new. Once more the United States was becoming a multi-cultural nation even while conservative citizens groups and state policies sought to avoid this result through stricter immigration surveillance. Once more, too, the United States became part of an international pattern. Most of the developed European nations, particularly France and the United Kingdom, confronted the difficulty of policing borders and managing a more diverse citizenry, as the poor and what might be termed the 'aspirational' classes of the developing world voted with their feet and moved to the rich countries of the north. Globalization now had marked feedback consequences everywhere. The United States faced huge challenges in resisting the reciprocal demographic effects of the economic globalization that the US government supported. In response, anti-immigration forces grew in such states as Florida and California. Conservatives sponsored or supported legislation requiring that bilingual education programmes be dropped, that the printing of election ballot papers in different languages cease and that English be the official state language. By 1995, 22 states had legislated thus.[25]

Environment was yet another aspect of how 'outside' influences affected the American 'inside'. After the Second World War the exploitation of resources had shifted increasingly overseas; the already prodigious appetite for coffee, rubber and tropical fruit products was supplemented by dependence on developing countries for strategic materials needed by military defence industries. Oil, a commodity that encompassed both defence and civilian uses, was the most important commodity desired from abroad. Especially important was the expansion of the automobile industry that, along with industry, fuelled rapid growth in energy use. The United States consumed 45–50 per cent of world's energy in 1945. This proportion dropped to 33 per cent by 1973, but only because other nations had boosted their manufacturing capacity and car ownership. The absolute volume of American energy told a different story. As the population expanded by 89 per cent from 149 million people in 1949 to 281 million in 2000, total energy consumption rose 208 per cent to 98 quadrillion British thermal units and per-capita energy consumption climbed 63 per cent.[26] Though historically almost self-sufficient in oil, the United States had become by the 1970s vulnerable to Middle Eastern oil shocks for the first time, with imports supplying 46.5 per cent of 1977 consumption. This figure had dropped back to 27.3 per cent in 1985 as US exploration in Alaska and elsewhere opened new domestic sources, but imports again supplied almost half of US petroleum by the mid-1990s. In 1995, the United States used 25 per cent of world energy with only 5 per cent of the world population. As a government report noted, 'By comparison, Japan – ranked 4th in energy use – used 6 percent of the world energy while having 2 percent of the world population.'[27]

Profligate energy use contributed to the climate change that scientists increasingly prophesized in the 1990s. The transnational political agenda arising out of global warming conflicted with inherited American traditions. The nation's economic abundance rooted in its heritage of resource richness underpinned economic growth and consumerism and created increased dependence on world markets. Yet this very pattern since the 1960s made the United States unwilling as the greatest fossil fuel user to disrupt the American economy to support United Nations' attempts at limiting planetary climate change through countermeasures. The failure to sign after 1997 the Kyoto Protocols on climate control through reduction of greenhouse gas emissions became a prime example of the emerging conflict between global environmental imperatives and American political and economic objectives.

The United States faced criticism and constraints upon many of its environmental policy actions from transnational non-governmental organizations. The latter were a marked feature of the new globalization, with numbers increasing rapidly. Environmental organizations such as the Worldwide Fund for Nature (established in Britain in 1961), the Friends of the Earth (formed in 1969 by Sierra Club Executive Director David Brower with its first international division in France in 1970) and Greenpeace (formed in Canada in 1971), became international organizations with affiliates in many countries. All lobbied against any government – including the United States – that opposed the Kyoto Protocols. The leaders of such groups flocked to the conferences such as the United Nations Conference on Environment and Development (the Earth Summit) in June 1992 in Rio de Janeiro. Delegations from 178 countries attended the meetings. From the Rio Conference came a biodiversity treaty and other statements of policy agreement but the conference also provided global forums for publicizing the plight of the planet and potential solutions. This was not the first such conference; meetings stretched back to the 1972 United Nations Conference on the Human Environment held in Stockholm, 'the first major modern international gathering on human activities in relationship to the environment'.[28] NGOs lobbied the United Nations for international conventions and the US Congress adhered to some of these, such as the Ramsar Wetlands Convention of 1971 (acceded to in 1987). Most notably, the United States proposed the World Heritage Convention 'as an extension of the American national park ideal', and was the first nation to ratify, with a 95–0 Senate vote in 1973.[29]

Still another example of NGO influence transnationally was the prominent role of humanitarian aid groups responding to increased global poverty and both human and 'natural' disasters. Poverty was indeed a severe social and economic problem that developed countries had to take into account. With the end of French and British colonialism, the ideological splits of the Cold War severely affected ex-colonial countries by the 1970s. Civil war became endemic on the continent of Africa. Angola, Zaire (the former Belgian Congo) and much more of Africa experienced political strife. This together with droughts and the failure of international aid to address fundamental problems of poverty spelt disaster. By 1984 a large part of the southern Sahara (the Sahel) was enveloped in drought. Recent research suggests that climate change contributed to African calamities, but so too did development policies.[30] In the early years of new globalization, assistance tended to be directed under the World Bank and IMF programmes towards exports rather than subsistence food production in underdeveloped countries.

As the world's wealthiest country, the United States had an important role in alleviating these problems and since 1961 had contributed through the US Agency for International Development (USAid). But the government did not help matters by its opposition in the 1980s to population control policies. The Reagan administration responded to the domestic lobby on Christian Right causes by refusing aid to poor countries and non-governmental organizations that gave abortion advice or undertook abortions. This was called the Mexico City Policy, named for the site of the international conference at which the policy was announced in 1984.[31]

The world would end, wrote famed Anglo-American poet T. S. Eliot, not with a bang but a whimper. In the crises of global poverty and environment, the developed world faced such a prospect in the era of new globalization. In response, new NGOs rose to the challenge. Britain's Oxfam, started during the Second World War but coming to prominence in the crisis over the Bangladeshi Civil War in 1971, and the French group Médecins sans Frontières (1971) both established affiliates in the United States and campaigned worldwide. Aid groups also joined transnational events such as the Live Aid Concert (1985) for Ethiopia to raise global consciousness. An estimated one and a half billion people worldwide watched the telecast featuring prominent rock groups. Such activity shaded into the realm of social protest, a phenomenon that had retreated somewhat in the 1970s but revived in the 1980s. The role of transnational protest groups and their effects on American foreign and domestic politics must be considered seriously.

Civil protest made a dramatic international return in the 1980s. However, the key issue was not the death that might occur through 'a whimper' but that which many people feared from the 'bang' of nuclear annihilation. Protesters took this judgement as self-evident and campaigned vociferously against the threat of nuclear war in that decade. Ronald Reagan had from 1981 stepped up the arms race as part of the reassertion of US national power. This muscle flexing included the search for an anti-missile screen, the Strategic Defense Initiative popularly known as Star Wars as well as the development of the Cruise and MX missiles. The former were to be deployed in Europe. In response, a transnational anti-nuclear campaign developed in tandem across the Atlantic. In Britain the Campaign for Nuclear Disarmament grew around left-wing labour, trade union, church and feminist support. In the United States, the CND was paralleled by, and cross-fertilized with, the Nuclear Weapons Freeze Campaign, the Committee for a Sane Nuclear Policy, and other anti-nuclear groups. Prominent in the English anti-nuclear campaign were women camping on Greenham Common from 1981 in protest against the nearby installation of a lethal nuclear arsenal. Women's activism was vital in the American case too. An Australian anti-nuclear campaigner living in the United States, Helen Caldicott, joined Physicians for Social Responsibility, an anti-nuclear group dating from 1961, and founded in 1982, the Women's Action for Nuclear Disarmament (WAND). Caldicott and her husband were soon seasoned media campaigners on all nuclear issues including testing and peaceful nuclear power. The globetrotting doctor argued that spending money on nuclear weapons was not only dangerous, but also socially irresponsible because it took potential funds from a large range of social welfare initiatives. [32]

Influenced by quasi-evangelical and well-organized leaders such as Caldicott, protesters held mass demonstrations against the nuclear arms race with 'nearly a million participants' turning out for a June 1982 rally that stretched three miles down New York City streets. This was, historian Lawrence Wittner argues, 'the largest political rally in American history'. [33] Partly in response to awareness of international opinion, especially among Western European allies, the administration offered to forgo deployment of Cruise and Pershing II missiles in Western Europe if the Soviet Union removed its own SS-20 missiles based in Eastern Europe. This idea, claims Wittner, came 'directly from the banners of the European peace movement'. [34] Responding to the public alarm registered in polls in which some 70 per cent of Americans opposed augmentation of nuclear arsenals, Reagan announced plans in 1984 to negotiate further reductions in nuclear weapons, reversing earlier policy. The arrival upon the scene of Mikhail Gorbachev, who became Soviet Communist Party General Secretary in 1985, then transformed Soviet policy by unilaterally halting Soviet nuclear tests. More importantly, he made negotiation of an intermediate-range nuclear weapons agreement separate from any US concessions on the Strategic Defense Initiative. Soviet strategy was based on the assumption that without an escalating nuclear arms race, the Star Wars project would lack support in Congress. This action by Gorbachev was influenced, according to Wittner, by transnational anti-nuclear groups and spurred Reagan to match the Gorbachev initiative against the advice of hawks in his administration. [35] Thereby the Soviet leader's actions had set in motion the most important nuclear disarmament measure of the era. This was the US–USSR Intermediate-Range Nuclear Forces (INF) Treaty, signed in 1988, which removed all Cruise, Pershing II and SS-20 nuclear missiles from Europe.

Any assertion that anti-nuclear campaigners spurred Soviet and American leaders to change direction needs qualification, however. After all, massive anti-war demonstrations and even unfavourable public opinion polls did not deter an American president and his British prime ministerial counterpart, Tony Blair, going into an unpopular war against Iraq in 2003. A more conventional approach holds that the pressure of American nuclear expansion brought Gorbachev to the unilateral changes that he made because the Soviet Union could no longer stand the arms race and its effects on the Soviet economy. But this view, too, must be qualified. Gorbachev's struggle to reform communism and the consequent challenge to the Soviet military establishment should not be underestimated in changing the climate of negotiation. [36]

Whatever its precise impact, the transnational peace movement had been aimed at limiting the independent actions of both superpowers and indeed at all countries that brandished an expanded nuclear capability. It was not simply a movement directed at the United States. In some other areas, such as human rights, transnational action similarly cast a wide net and was often directed not at great powers, but at the dictatorships and authoritarian governments that still controlled much of the developing world. Nonetheless, the US role was called increasingly into question by the developing global discourse on human rights.

Non-governmental organizations in the human rights field were active in criticizing the United States' place within that tradition. The nation had taken a leading role in placing human rights in the 1940s and 1950s upon the international agenda. But the government did not make human rights a central plank of its own foreign policy until the ill-fated Carter administration in 1977–81.[37] While the Carter administration's efforts were unprecedented, the link with Cold War competition established in the 1950s remained. Not only did successive administrations use human rights as a stick with which to beat the Soviet Union and its satellite states in Eastern Europe but the United States supported regimes in Central America that abused human rights, provided they were allies in the Cold War. Even for the Carter administration, 'The major emphasis...was rhetorical and its principle impact was on domestic politics.' The administration did not 'significantly withdraw material support from repressive United States friends'.[38] If this was the outcome of Carter's efforts, what could one say of Reagan, who criticized Carter's policy as hurtful to America's foreign allies? Under Reagan, the government supplied aid through shadowy groups to anti-leftist forces in Nicaragua (as revealed in the Iran-Contra scandal of 1986) and to a variety of right-wing governments in Latin America. Though successful support of such regimes removed the perceived threat of communism, patent hypocrisy on human rights began to be turned against the American government by transnational organizations.

Important in developing criticisms of American achievements on human rights was Amnesty International, founded in Britain in 1961, and opening in the United States 3 years later.[39] Amnesty criticized American support for repressive regimes abroad such as Chile where the Central Intelligence Agency had encouraged the military overthrow of an elected Socialist government, as well as the US Government's imprisonment of Vietnam-era conscientious objectors at home.[40] As Amnesty moved from its focus on political prisoners to a wider concern with economic and social justice, it brought American domestic human rights issues under the spotlight by the 1990s. US human rights advocacy abroad was, critics stated, unmatched by remedial action at home in areas such as the racialized criminal justice system.[41] Supporters of the United States argued that only in a free country could prison and judicial abuses come to light, but the point remains that the transnational context of human rights generated embarrassment abroad for the American political system long before the Abu Ghraib scandals of the 2003 Iraq War.

The web of intergovernmental organizations posed more contradictory opportunities and possibilities. On the one hand, treaties that the United States signed and organizations that it joined could implement liberal development and other free-market policies. Thus the World Bank and the IMF became in the 1980s agents for the stricter supervision of internal policy-making in third world countries. Economic and political object-ives were closely aligned here. President Clinton was reported as saying that with the Cold War's ending and the emergence of new democracies, especially in Eastern Europe in the 1990s, 'the best way of securing the markets in a lot of these former communist developing countries was to integrate them into a global economy through trade'. Trade was also 'the leading edge to creating a more secure, peaceful world'.[42]

International agreements and supranational organizations could effect trade liberalization, but they placed limits on American power and domestic policies as well. Other countries could use NAFTA, the WTO and its predecessor (the General Agreement on Trade and Tariffs), to gain entry to American markets because import restrictions that the US Congress imposed were open to litigation under international agreements. This power threatened US domestic policies in terms not only of job protection, but also of environmental standards. After Congress in 1990 introduced labelling laws on canned tuna to protect dolphins from drift net fishing, Mexico threatened a WTO challenge to remove the ban on its tuna exports that did not conform to the 'dolphin-safe' label. A compromise deal was brokered in 1995–98 and the ban on Mexican tuna eventually lifted in 2000.[43] NAFTA also led to increased competition from Cana-dian forest industries. Labour unions and lumber companies protested and lobbied Congress, which in response imposed discriminating tariffs. A series of squabbles with Canada over this issue ensued through the 1990s.[44] In the light of the experience of such competition, labour lobby-ists threatened to stymie further free trade initiatives for the whole of the Americas. First proposed in 1994, the Free Trade Area of the Amer-icas (FTAA) faced objections within the United States, but opposition to free trade was transnational too. Just as unions within the United States feared loss of jobs, foreign governments and workers in Latin America saw the possibility of American domination in the FTAA and opposed its implementation.

The fears of globalization extended to investment as well as the trade in goods. Changes in the international economy and the growth of bilateral investment arrangements made a comprehensive investment deal rationally desirable for the opening of free markets. The Clinton administration supported the Multilateral Agreement on Investment, which had its origins in the Organization for Economic Cooperation and Development, a UN agency. But by 1998 the OECD backed off because of great dissension within member countries. Opposition came from both developed countries such as France and developing countries in Latin America, all of which feared a new round of invasion by American culture.[45]

Within the United States, opposition to changes in global trade and investment spawned new protest movements. Among the leaders was Lori Wallach, a lawyer who founded Public Citizen's Global Trade Watch in 1995. By 2001, Wallach was a leading figure in an activist network of what she called 'cross-sectoral country-based coalitions'. These groups were 'linked internationally with their counterparts around the world'.[46] She and fellow activists fought the tendency for objections to environmentally dangerous trade liberalization to get lost in the interstices between national governments and the WTO. Wallach had worked in trade law and brought middle-class values and special expertise to what was a highly technical field, but the more emotive and visceral effects of transnational anti-globalization protests at the street level should not be forgotten either. Environmental and labour groups demonstrated both in the United States and abroad against the movement for free trade enshrined in the WTO and in international meetings held annually after the WTO's founding. The WTO meeting in Seattle in 1999 was severely disrupted by protesters, as were succeeding meetings in Geneva and other foreign cities.

Different challenges came from the pressures of the immigrant diasporas. Refugees from Cuba formed in Southern Florida a lobby hindering a possible thaw in relations with Fidel Castro's Cuba. Equally, the transnational Jewish Diaspora complicated American Middle-Eastern policy. Though only a tiny minority of American Jews migrated to Israel and made up only 4 per cent of immigrants there,[47] private aid from the Diaspora flowed back to Israel and political support in important states such as New York influenced domestic political debates, senate contests and even Presidential elections. The United States provided massive military and economic aid of 3 billion dollars a year according to pro-Israeli US sources,[48] without which Israel's strategic position and economic development would be seriously compromised. American Middle-Eastern policy was not determined by a Diaspora effect, it must be emphasized, as oil and other strategic conditions played powerful roles and Israel pursued its own national self-interest as well. In the Cold War, Israel stood as a bastion of Western values against the perceived threat of Soviet expansion and remained one of the United States' most reliable allies.[49] From 1991, the first Iraq War and the challenge of militant Islam to American domination of the Persian Gulf region provided additional reasons for continuing strong support. But the consequent difficulties that the world's most powerful government faced in being an honest broker in the conflict over Palestinian statehood contributed seriously to Islamic unrest in the entire region.

While the United States faced demographic, economic, environmental, anti-nuclear and human rights criticism and constraints upon its actions and its power, its political and military position was very different in the last decade of the twentieth century. In the Middle East, Saddam Hussein's ill-fated seizure of Kuwait in 1991 underlined the preponderance of the American military. Quickly the Iraqis were swept back by an American-led force, leaving only the smouldering ruins of Iraqi tanks and trucks in the desert. Geo-politically, the United States stood supreme too. Globally, the collapse of the Soviet Union removed the major alternative power block. American politicians and opinion leaders believed the United States had 'won' the Cold War. But what was to replace it? At first the concept of an end to history as a struggle for liberty became fashionable through the ideas of Francis Fukuyama; in this reading of history, liberal democratic civilization had triumphed in the main and only pockets of resistance remained to be mopped up. The spread of the World Wide Web of the 1990s underlined the idea that commerce had triumphed over ideology and that with commerce went relative peace. The prosperous Clinton years of 1993–2001 were characterized by still greater integration into the world economy, the stock market boomed and GNP expanded for an unprecedented period. But internecine wars in the Balkans suggested that history of the older type in which divisions and struggle prevailed had not ended. Old ethnic scores remained unsettled there and religious intolerance threatened between Muslims and Christians as well. The new world order of globalization had begun to emerge, but its full implications for the American place in the world did not become clear immediately. That would have to wait until September 11, 2001.

Epilogue: 'Nothing will Ever be the Same': 9/11 and the Return of History

According to the conventional wisdom, the world changed irrevocably on September 11, 2001. 'Nothing will Ever be the Same', shouted the headline from a Philadelphia newspaper.[1] Evidence of new policies on civil liberties, the treatment of prisoners, the impact of global terrorism, a more assertive sense of national identity and novel foreign and military policies abounded. But the response to the event displayed important continuities with the past and expressed longer-term shifts in Americans' transnational relationships. The nature and repercussions of the attack showed how interconnected the world had become economically and culturally. The attackers had been foreigners, resident in the United States as students. The attack had been planned transnationally and represented the efforts of a wing of the global Islamic diaspora discontented with American Middle East policy. More broadly, Islamic militants resented the huge challenges that globalization had brought to their religion, societies and traditional worldviews – against which they violently reacted. The results of the attack were likewise multicultural and transnational. Among the roughly 2700 people killed at the World Trade Center, about one-tenth were non-Americans and still others were Americans of recent foreign origin or multicultural descent. The World Trade Center's very workforce indicated how American capitalism had become globally connected with the attack disrupting global stock markets and commodity trading. The media event, too, was of global reach and significance. Front-page news for months everywhere, the sight of planes flying into buildings was beamed instantaneously through CNN and Fox News into living rooms on the other side of the globe in the middle of the night. Non-Americans, with the exception of sections of the Islamic communities of the world, joined in condemnation and seemed sympathetic to the United States in its unusual role as the victim of a terrorist attack.

Politically and militarily, the Bush administration's responses broke sharply with the main approach of the Cold War decades, when allies were all important. After several decades of multilateralism came the reassertion of a vigorous unilateralism across several fields, especially on military, environmental and juridical grounds. The administration refused to support the International Criminal Court opened in 2002, continued to spurn the Kyoto protocols, attacked the United Nations and, though belatedly cobbling together a 'coalition of the willing', went to war in Iraq in 2003 without clear UN backing. The exertion of unilateralism in Iraq matched a pronounced intellectual change. The United States was officially anti-colonial, but Americans and observers outside the country began to talk openly about the 'E' word, even though Secretary of Defense Donald Rumsfeld and President George W. Bush denied US ambitions as an empire. Commentators such as conservative columnist Max Boot suggested that the nation needed to assert its own power more vigorously and recognize in word what was already clear in deed.[2] In apparent confirmation of imperial status, administration figures arrogated to themselves the right to decide on issues of self-determination for other nations and threatened regime change in several, including Iran and North Korea. The Bush administration seemed to synthesize, in the early post-September 11 phase, Wilsonian moralism and idealism for democratic reform abroad with Theodore Roosevelt's big stick and assertive nationalism.

Terrorism replaced Cold War demons as the nation's enemy. To be sure, transnational terrorism was not new, as Britons familiar with the Irish Republican Army's American finances knew. Yet the terrorist post-9/11 was a new kind of enemy, shadowy and without a specific territory that could be conquered. This deterritorialization in the form of Al-Qaeda ironically mirrored the globalization trends towards transnational corporations that knew no allegiance to nations and the global franchising of brands, with Al-Qaeda as the Kentucky Fried Chicken of terrorism. Flexible transnational terrorist networks with proliferating cells, specialized operatives and training centres threatened the economic and political interests of the new globalization.

These external threats had profound impacts upon Americans by threatening their civil liberties through the Patriot Act of 2001. Thousands of suspect resident aliens and some citizens were detained, people of Muslim belief or Middle-Eastern appearance suffered suspicion and intolerance, and abroad the United States established at Guantánamo Bay a nether-land prison outside of American law where the government could hold foreigners indefinitely without trial. Deterritorialized terror produced deterritorialized law, beyond Anglo-Saxon traditions of justice, beyond the Geneva Convention. Captured Taliban and Al-Qaeda operatives in the Middle East were handed to authoritarian governments or proxy armies where human rights abuses occurred. The moral murkiness troubled lawyers and many in America, but the whole episode revealed that globalization brought severe challenges to traditional American legal ideals and constitutional positions.

In response to the unprecedented attacks, Americans also embraced a newly vigorous nationalism – as seen in the American flag lapel badges, which became an almost compulsory part of bodily attire for politicians, government officials and many ordinary Americans. The rhetoric of leaders on such ritualistic occasions as State of the Union and Fourth of July addresses reaffirmed the idea of the United States as a special place. On Independence Day, 2004, George W. Bush proclaimed that 'this Nation under God is still free, independent, and the best hope of mankind'. Bush also used American exceptionalism to justify American foreign policy in Iraq and Afghanistan because 'America is a nation with a mission...we understand our special calling: This great republic will lead the cause of freedom.'[3] The iconography of American patriotism in popular culture became fused with the response to the Al-Qaeda attack. A calendar put out by COMDA, The Calendar People celebrated American exceptionalism while mourning the losses of September 11. In this artefact, the image of the now destroyed twin towers of the World Trade Center stood outlined behind images of stoic firemen and flights of fighter aircraft, as well as fields of amber grain and other images drawn explicitly from *America the Beautiful*.

The reception of 9/11 obscured multiculturalism and transnational influences. Ironically the commemorative calendar registered only in small print that a Canadian-based company published it in Ontario. The fact that a proportion of the deaths on 9/11 were of non-Americans was lost upon the media and the public debate. Later losses by foreign nations in terrorist bombings in Bali and elsewhere received less fulsome coverage. Rather, government, media and public initially treated the new terrorism as a problem for the United States and September 11 as an American tragedy. The attack and the nation's response reinvigorated an American insularity. The initial choice of the term 'crusade' to describe the action in Afghanistan – later discretely dropped – indicated insensitivity towards Islamic cultures that prevailed in influential circles. The world would be remade in the American image. Thereafter the United States had to go to great lengths to be seen coming to terms with Islam and to distinguish between good and bad Muslims. Whether American multiculturalism could truly encompass this very different religion remained seriously questionable.

Militarily the conflict highlighted the new face of war in the era of new globalization. The United States would fight primarily through decisive airpower. The use of troops would be sparing in Afghanistan. The military action would rely on the proxy armies of the Northern Alliance together with highly trained and relatively small numbers of CIA operatives and Special Forces. Thus American casualties would be kept to a minimum. Even in the case of Iraq where a ground war had to be mounted with a sizable invading army, the land campaign was preceded by 'shock and awe' bombing assaults, and the United States assiduously cultivated proxy forces among the dissident Kurds of the North and expatriate Shiite communities to make the invasion easier.

The reliance on bombing came with a new political spin and promises of a more justifiable kind of warfare. This war would be highly techno-logical, restrained, limited and professional. Bombing must be targeted, using global positioning systems and so-called smart weapons that would hit enemy military targets, not civilians. The new world of war would be sold to the public as surgical and computerized. Though the reality turned out to be different on almost every count, the bottom line was not that smart war would stop civilian casualties but that it would render these largely invisible to the American public. The media involvement was unprecedented in the way that the government tightly controlled inform-ation on outcomes, including the almost total erasure of non-combatant deaths and sanitized reporting of the deaths of American service personnel.

Despite the administration's rhetoric and several obvious ways in which change was registered, September 11 did not simply usher in a brave new world. Those events encouraged forces growing before that time. The attack on the World Trade Center enabled the assertion of a new kind of American quasi-imperial power that had been building since the demise of the Soviet Union in 1991. None of this, least of all the military changes, occurred overnight. Aerial bombing had been integral to Amer-ican military strategy since the 1940s. The reason for the tactic even then had been to minimize land force casualties. The dropping of nuclear bombs in 1945 was designed in part to reduce the horrific toll expected upon a land invasion in Japan. But the civilian losses, as in the Hiroshima and Nagasaki attacks, were immense and, in retrospect, unacceptable to the domestic publics of Western nations. This unwelcome contradiction between military tactics and the media effects of seeing innocent civilians die was reaffirmed in the Vietnam War. As Martin Shaw has argued, 'The new Western way of war' was 'a clever reinvention...It transcends the fundamental degeneracy of earlier bombing' but created new contradic-tions 'through multiple transfers of risk, particularly to civilian popula-tions'. If bombing-led warfare did enter 'a distinctive new phase,' however, this came after 1991, not 2001. The first Gulf War in response to Iraq's invasion of Kuwait and the subsequent ethnic nationalist conflicts in the Balkans already showed NATO reliance on the strategy of 'virtual war' using 'smart' weapons and strict rules of engagement.[4]

The new face of war was in other ways not entirely new either. Nineteenth-century Americans had fought many small wars. They had battled Indians repeatedly and sometimes used gunboat diplomacy; they had violently punished Indian tribes who became allied with their enemies and/or attacked American settlers. They acted punitively against recal-citrant minor powers from the Barbary pirates of 1801–15 onward. In these 'savage wars of peace', to use the Rudyard Kipling phrase command-eered by Max Boot, a number of features resemble the post-9/11 world.

American borders in the nineteenth century were permeable amid rapid and uncontrolled economic and cultural expansion. The agents of such expansion were in civil society more than the state, as they have been with the new globalization since the 1970s. This nineteenth-century expansion exposed Americans and their interests abroad to risks countered by the state through punitive military expeditions, as today. Earlier expansion was closely related to technological shifts in communications, through railroads and the telegraph, just as the world of satellites and global positioning systems shapes communications and empires of the post-9/11 world. American settler colonialism was achieved through collaborative alliances with other groups – Indian tribes, Hispanics or rogue American settlers outside the nation's borders. Proxy armies, as in the case of the (Afghan) Northern Alliance since 9/11, were not unknown before 1900; indeed, Andrew Jackson's use of Cherokee Indians to destroy their mutual enemy, the Creeks, provides an early example.

Nineteenth-century traditions of cultural and economic expansion backed by military force have in some respects been revived since the 1990s. In the intervening years, American policy was rendered different through the necessity of responding to the total wars of 1917–18 and 1941–45. The war with the Axis powers was considered just. Though over 400,000 Americans died in the Second World War, this was a price that had to be accepted, no matter how terrible. Thereafter, the unpopularity of wars and particularly wars based on a conscript army in a demo-cratic society where citizens can vote produced greater efforts to find new techniques of fighting. Military adventures after the Vietnam War would be different. The attack on tiny Grenada in 1983, a painless assault to stop an alleged Communist plot in the Caribbean, set the tone and was uplifting to American morale post-Vietnam. In the meantime the army, air force and politicians had considered ways to distance Americans from war. This led to the abandonment of the draft, more intensive voluntary recruitment strategies, the introduction of high-tech weaponry and the media-dominated campaigns of the 1990s beginning with the coverage of the first Gulf War.

Even though the Defense Department presented American military tactics overseas as new, American attitudes towards foreign military involvement continued to be influenced by memories and tradition. How struggles on American borderlands were presented in history and popular culture shaped the way Americans came to think about their international relationships in the early twenty-first century. History weighed upon the conflict in representations of 9/11 and of the shadowy enemy. George W. Bush's vocabulary suggested a Christian heritage and appeared initially to endorse Samuel Huntington's idea of a clash of civilizations. 'Operation Infinite Justice' indicated Bush's ability to dispense the judgement that Muslims believed only Allah could. The language reflected the way General John J. Pershing's 'crusade' to save Europe in the First World War had been popularly represented. With this European heritage of the centuries invoked, the administration turned to American republican traditions. The United States did not want colonies. It would free the Iraqi people from 'tyrants' in 'Operation Enduring Freedom'. Whereas Europeans spoke of limiting or controlling evil, influential American strategist Richard Perle called in evangelistic mode for 'an end to evil'.[5] In comic book style, the bad people must be punished. The realist strain of the Cold War era had been at least temporarily abandoned in favour of traditional American ideologies rooted in millenarian religion, republican political ideals and frontier traditions. In addition to the resort to such revolutionary-era concepts as freedom and liberty, policy-makers chose the nineteenth century for their rhetoric and defined the enemy as an Indian or outlaw 'other'. Frontier labels such as 'smoke them out' and 'wanted, dead or alive' abounded. This echoed the earlier terms of policy analyst and former State Department official Richard Haass in his description of the United States as a 'reluctant sheriff' dispatching posses against rogue elements.[6] These phrases suggest that the traditions of Euro-American civilization and its small wars on the frontiers of American expansion were influential in the way the events of the twenty-first century were represented.

American difference, even exceptionalism, is rooted in popular culture and media. Yet this tradition is misleading. The nation was deeply connected in the nineteenth century to world history and remains so today. Just as the United States contributed to the world's cultural heritage and its economic and technological resources, so too did it draw upon that heritage to enrich American society. There have been ups and downs in this story of transnational connection, as the power of the American state has changed. Yet the contradictions of American power and sense of national distinctiveness on the one hand and its deeply enmeshed cultural and economic relations globally on the other have not been resolved. These have indeed grown since the time of Woodrow Wilson and have been further accentuated by the events of September 11.

Economically the United States was now more dependent on the world than ever, with a vast trade deficit and near-addiction to Chinese, European and other foreign capital. At home, the budget deficit grew alarmingly, continuing an upward trend since the Reagan years punctuated only by the more restrained fiscal outcomes of the Clinton administration. Internationally, the nation maintained a military presence more globally comprehensive than at any time in history, taking bases in the former Soviet Union's old strategic strongholds in Central Asia and seeking out new oil supplies there. But the United States still needed allies, as unilateral military force of any kind short of nuclear annihilation could not realize the modernizing, free-market world that its leaders wanted. Though American military and political power remained dominant, the war in Iraq could not be easily won, let alone military conflicts elsewhere in Asia. The messiness of war intervened, and concern over American causalities mounted. By 2004 the US was following a more considered, multilateral approach to its foreign policy in an attempt to retrieve lost ground. Much of the goodwill generated for the United States internationally after the World Trade Center attack had been squandered and new resentments created over the expanded American presence across the globe. In all this the world was not a blank slate upon which American cultural, economic and foreign policies could be written. History does not stop, does not end, at least not yet.

Notes

Introduction

1. For the concept of 'free security', see C. Vann Woodward, 'The Age of Reinterpretation', *American Historical Review*, 66 (October 1960), 13–19.
2. On the recent trend of textbooks to incorporate transnational perspectives, see Mary Beth Norton et al., *A People and a Nation*, 7th edn (Boston, MA: Houghton Mifflin, 2005); Alan W. Brinkley, *American History: A Survey*, 11th edn (Boston, MA: McGraw Hill, 2003).
3. Thomas Bender, *Nation Among Nations: America's Place in the World* (New York: Hill & Wang, 2006); Eric Rauchway, *Blessed among Nations: How the World Made America* (New York: Hill and Wang, 2006); Edward Davies, *The United States in World History* (New York: Routledge, 2006).
4. American historiography until the 1920s had important writing in which the imperial context of US history had been developed. See Ian Tyrrell, 'Making Nations/Making States: American Historians in the Context of Empire', *Journal of American History*, 86 (December 1999), 1015–44. Modern studies of colonial relations between North American and Britain are legion. For these, see especially the *William and Mary Quarterly*. For Native Americans and African-Americans, see Chap. 7 below. An important intercultural study of the colonial period is Richard White, *The Middle Ground: Indians, Empires, and Republics in the Great Lakes Region, 1650–1815* (New York: Cambridge University Press, 1991). For both the theory and practice of transnational history, see David Thelen, ed., 'The Nation and Beyond: Transnational Perspectives on United States History', *Journal of American History*, Special Issue, 86 (December 1999); and Thomas Bender, ed., *Rethinking American History in a Global Age* (Berkeley, CA: University of California Press, 2002). On comparative history, see Micol Seigel, 'Beyond Compare: Comparative Method after the Transnational Turn', *Radical History Review*, 91 (Winter 2005), 62–90.
5. Catherine Hall, *Civilising Subjects: Metropole and Colony in the English Imagination, 1830–1867* (Cambridge: Polity Press, 2002), p. 9.
6. Frank Thistlethwaite, *America and the Atlantic Community: Anglo-American Aspects, 1790–1850* (1959; New York: Harper & Row, 1963).

7. Gary Y. Okihiro, *Common Ground: Reimagining American History* (Princeton, NJ: Princeton University Press, 2001), p. 17.

8. Gordon Greenwood, *Early Australian-American Relations: From the Arrival of the Spaniards in America to the Close of 1830* (Melbourne: Melbourne University Press, 1944).

9. Herbert E. Bolton, 'The Epic of Greater America', *American Historical Review*, 38 (April 1933), 448–74.

10. Gerald E. Poyo and Gilberto M. Hinojosa, eds, 'Spanish Texas and Borderlands Historiography in Transition: Implications for United States History', *Journal of American History*, 75 (September 1988), 393–416. So common has this approach become that there is now even an Association for Borderland Studies and a *Journal of Borderlands Studies*.

11. See Frederick Cooper, 'What is the Concept of Globalization Good For? An African Historian's Perspective', *African Affairs*, 100 (2001), 189–213.

12. A. G. Hopkins, ed., *Globalization in World History* (London: Pimlico, 2002).

13. Scott Burchill, 'Marx on Globalization: Contemporary Resonances', http://www.zmag.org/sustainers/content/1999-07/24burchill.htm (20 September 2005).

14. Arjun Appadurai, *Modernity at Large: Cultural Dimensions of Globalization* (Minneapolis, MN: University of Minnesota Press, 1996).

15. Kevin H. O'Rourke and Jeffrey G. Williamson, *Globalization and History: The Evolution of a Nineteenth-Century Atlantic Economy* (Cambridge, MA: MIT Press, 1999).

16. The literature on American exceptionalism is large. For an introduction, see Jack P. Greene, *The Intellectual Construction of America: Exceptionalism and Identity* (Chapel Hill, NC: University of North Carolina Press, 1993); Seymour Martin Lipset, *American Exceptionalism: A Double-Edged Sword* (New York: W. W. Norton, 1996); Byron Shafer, ed., *Is America Different?: A New Look at American Exceptionalism* (Oxford: Clarendon Press, 1991); Ian Tyrrell, 'American Exceptionalism in an Age of International History', *American Historical Review*, 96 (October 1991), 1031–55.

17. What follows has been influenced by Michael Geyer and Michael Bright, 'Where in the World Is America? The History of the United States in the Global Age', in Bender, *Rethinking American History in a Global Age*, pp. 74–5.

1 Born in the Struggles of Empires: The American Republic in War and Revolution, 1789–1815

1. *Thomas Jefferson: Writings* (New York: Library of America, 1984), p. 98.

2. Jefferson to Rabout de St. Etienne, ibid., p. 954.

3. Thomas H. Adams, *The Paris Years of Thomas Jefferson* (New Haven, CT: Yale University Press, 1997), pp. 207–9.

4. *Jefferson: Writings*, p. 97.

5. Christopher Brown, *Moral Capital: Foundations of British Abolitionism* (Chapel Hill, NC: University of North Carolina Press, 2006), pp. 456–7.

6. David Brion Davis, *The Problem of Slavery in the Age of Revolution, 1770–1823* (Ithaca, NY: Cornell University Press, 1975), especially p. 167.

7. Matthew Rainbow Hale, 'Neither Britons nor Frenchmen: The French Revolution and American National Identity', PhD dissertation, Brandeis University, 2002, pp. 14–15.

8. Mary Beth Norton et al., *A People and a Nation*, 7th edn (Boston, MA: Houghton Mifflin, 2005), p. 202.

9. On the formation of parties, see Noble E. Cunningham, *The Jeffersonian Republicans: The Formation of Party Organization, 1789–1801* (Chapel Hill, NC: University of North Carolina Press, 1957); Joseph Charles, *The Origins of the American Party System* (New York: Harper & Row, 1956); Harry Ammon, 'The Genet Mission and the Development of American Political Parties', *Journal of American History*, 52 (March 1966), 725–41; Paul Goodman, *The Democratic-Republicans of Massachusetts: Politics in a Young Republic* (Cambridge, MA: Harvard University Press, 1964). For the interrelations of external and 'internal' events, see Hale, 'Neither Britons nor Frenchmen'.

10. Linda Kerber, *Women of the Republic: Intellect and Ideology in Revolutionary America* (Chapel Hill, NC: University of North Carolina Press, 1980), pp. 282–3.

11. Winthrop Jordan, *White over Black: American Attitudes Towards the Negro, 1550–1812* (Baltimore, MD: Penguin, 1969), p. 380.

12. Ibid., p. 381.

13. Norton et al., *People and a Nation*, p. 209.

14. James Sidbury, 'Saint Domingue in Virginia: Ideology, Local Meanings, and Resistance to Slavery, 1790–1800', *Journal of Southern History*, 63 (August 1997), 534, 551; Alfred N. Hunt, *Haiti's Influence on Antebellum America: Slumbering Volcano in the Caribbean* (Baton Rouge, LA: Louisiana State University Press, 1988), p. 118. See also Eugene Genovese, *From Rebellion to Revolution: Afro-American Slave Revolts in the Making of the New World* (New York: Vintage, 1979).

15. E. Wilson Lyon, *Louisiana in French Diplomacy, 1759–1804* (1934; Norman, OK: University of Oklahoma Press, 1974), p. 206.

16. *Jefferson: Writings*, p. 1137.

17. Ibid., p. 1143.

18. Anthony F. C. Wallace, *Jefferson and the Indians: The Tragic Fate of the First Americans* (Cambridge, MA: Belknap Press of Harvard University Press, 1999), pp. 206, 207.

19. *Jefferson: Writings*, pp. 1120, 1119.

20. John M. Murrin, 'The Jeffersonian Triumph and American Exceptionalism', *Journal of the Early Republic*, 20 (Spring 2000), 11.

21. Wallace, *Jefferson and the Indians*, pp. 276, 20. This would be an 'ethnic homeland' for 'a culturally homogenous' American people (pp. 17, 18).

22. Murrin, 'Jeffersonian Triumph', p. 4.

23. The republic's geographic development would multiply factions so that they would counteract domination by any one group.

24. Jefferson to John C. Breckinridge, 12 August 1803, *Jefferson: Writings*, p. 1138.

25. Peter S. Onuf, 'Review of Anthony F. C. Wallace, *Jefferson and the Indians: The Tragic Fate of the First Americans*', H-Law, H-Net Reviews, May, 2000, http://www.h-net.org/reviews/showrev.cgi?path=24409959285535.
26. Jefferson to Breckinridge, 12 August 1803, *Jefferson: Writings*, p. 1137.
27. Local American supporters used the technique of what would become known as the 'filibuster' – a form of grass roots expansionism condoned, in some cases, by American authorities.
28. Murrin, 'Jeffersonian Triumph', p. 12; Frank Lawrence Owsley, Jr and Gene A. Smith, *Filibusters and Expansionists: Jeffersonian Manifest Destiny, 1800–1821* (Tuscaloosa, AL: University of Alabama Press, 1997).
29. Marcus Rediker, *Between the Devil and the Deep Blue Sea: Merchant Seaman, Pirates, and the Anglo-American Maritime World 1700–1750* (Cambridge: Cambridge University Press, 1987), deals with this plebeian world for an earlier period.
30. James A. Field, *America and the Mediterranean World, 1776–1882* (Princeton, NJ: Princeton University Press, 1969), pp. 49–69, 138, 209. For a celebratory portrayal, see Max Boot, *The Savage Wars of Peace: Small Wars and the Rise of American Power* (New York: Basic Books, 2002), Chap. 1.
31. Jefferson to Pierre Cabanis, 12 July 1803, *Jefferson: Writings*, p. 1136, italics added.

2 Commerce Pervades the World: Economic Connections and Disconnections

1. J. T. R. Hughes, *American Economic History*, 2nd edn (Glenview, IL: Scott Foresman, 1987), p. 365.
2. Douglass C. North, *The Economic Growth of the United States, 1790–1860* (Englewood Cliffs, NJ: Prentice-Hall, 1961).
3. Hughes, *American Economic History*, pp. 367–8.
4. Ben J. Wattenberg, *The Statistical History of the United States from Colonial Times to the Present* (New York: Basic Books, 1976), p. 887; J. Potter, 'Atlantic Economy, 1815–1860: The U.S.A. and the Industrial Revolution in Britain', in A. W. Coats, ed., *Essays in American Economic History* (London: Edward Arnold, 1969), pp. 14–48. However, it is much harder to assign precise weighting in this pre-1860 period, which more than one economic historian has described as a 'Statistical Dark Age' so far as the Gross National Product is concerned. Paul A. David, 'New Light on a Statistical Dark Age: U.S. Real Product Growth Before 1840', *American Economic Review*, 57 (May 1967), 294–306.
5. Peter L. Bernstein, *Wedding of the Waters: The Erie Canal and the Making of a Great Nation* (New York: W. W. Norton, 2005), pp. 375–7.
6. Hughes, *American Economic History*, p. 368. The biggest increase was not from South or Central America, but from Asia, from which imports doubled over that period. Exports also more than doubled but were only a third of the level of imports. This partially explains American interest in increasing exports to Asia, as a way of balancing the trade without resort to specie payment.

7. George Francis Train, *Young America Abroad* (London: Seth Low, 1857), p. vii.
8. Ibid., p. v.
9. Ibid., p. 58.
10. Paola Gemme, 'Imperial Designs of Political Philanthropy: A Study of Antebellum Accounts of Italian Liberalism', *American Studies International*, 39 (February 2001), 19–26.
11. Jacques M. Downs, 'American Merchants and the China Opium Trade, 1800–1840', *Business History Review*, 42 (Winter 1968), 418–42; David F. Long, ' "Martial Thunder": The First Official American Armed Intervention in Asia', *Pacific Historical Review*, 42 (May 1973), 144.
12. Melvyn Stokes and Stephen Conway, eds, *The Market Revolution in America: Social, Political, and Religious Expressions, 1800–1880* (Charlottesville, VA: University Press of Virginia, 1996); Charles Sellers, *The Market Revolution: Jacksonian America, 1815–1846* (New York: Oxford University Press, 1991).
13. Calculated from Sven Beckert, 'Emancipation and Empire: Reconstructing the Worldwide Web of Cotton Production in the Age of the American Civil War', *American Historical Review*, 109 (December 2004), 1408–9.
14. Lloyd Mercer, 'The Antebellum Regional Trade Hypothesis', in Roger Ransom, Richard Sutch and Gary M. Walton, eds, *Explorations in the New Economic History: Essays in Honor of Douglass C. North* (New York: Academic Press, 1982), pp. 444–5; Richard Sutch, 'Douglass North and the New Economic History', ibid., p. 21; North, *Economic Growth of the United States*. On staple theory see Morris Altman, 'Staple Theory and Export-Led Growth: Constructing Differential Growth', *Australian Economic History Review*, 43 (November 2003), 234, which reaffirms the importance of staples.
15. C. A. Bayly, *The Birth of the Modern World, 1780–1914: Global Connections and Comparisons* (Oxford: Blackwell, 2004), p. 132.
16. Hughes, *American Economic History*, p. 204; Daniel Headrick, *The Invisible Weapon: Telecommunications and International Politics, 1851–1945* (New York: Oxford University Press, 1991), pp. 6, 28–49.
17. Tom Standage, *The Victorian Internet: The Remarkable Story of the Telegraph and the Nineteenth Century's On-Line Pioneers* (New York: Walker and Co., 1998), p. 83.
18. Albert Boime, *The Magisterial Gaze, Manifest Destiny and American Landscape Painting, 1830–1865* (Washington, DC: Smithsonian Institution Press, 1991), p. 72.
19. Hughes, *American Economic History*, p. 204.
20. Richard E. Ellis, 'The Market Revolution and the Transformation of American Politics, 1801–1837', in Stokes and Conway, eds, *The Market Revolution in America*, p. 163.
21. Hughes, *American Economic History*, p. 208.
22. Peter Temin, *The Jacksonian Economy* (New York: Norton, 1969), p. 22.
23. Richard Sylla, 'Review of Peter Temin, *The Jacksonian Economy*', Economic History Services (17 August 2001), http://www.eh.net/bookreviews/library/sylla.shtml; John Joseph Wallis, 'What Caused the Crisis of 1839?' NBER Working Paper Series, Historical Paper 133, April 2001.

24. D. C. M. Platt, *Foreign Finance in Continental Europe and the United States, 1815–1870: Quantities, Origins, Functions, and Distribution* (London: G. Allen & Unwin, 1984), p. 142.

25. Harvey H. Segal, 'Cycles of Canal Construction', in Carter Goodrich, ed., *Canals and American Economic Development* (1961; Port Washington, NY: Kennikat Press, 1972), p. 191.

26. Wattenberg, *Statistical History*, p. 869.

27. Platt, *Foreign Finance*, pp. 163, 165; Raymond W. Goldsmith, 'The Growth of Reproducible Wealth of the United States of America from 1805 to 1950', in S. Kuznets, ed., *Income and Wealth of the United States: Trends and Structures* (Cambridge, MA: Bowes & Bowes, 1952), p. 285.

28. Hughes, *American Economic History*, p. 160.

29. Segal, 'Cycles of Canal Construction', p. 179.

30. Ibid., p. 191.

31. Platt, *Foreign Finance*, p. 156; George Taylor and Irene Neu, *The American Railroad Network, 1861–1890* (Cambridge, MA: Harvard University Press, 1956), p. 6.

32. Platt, *Foreign Finance*, p. 157.

33. Ibid., p. 165.

34. Quoted ibid., p. 162.

35. Albro Martin, *James J. Hill and the Opening of the Northwest* (New York: Oxford University Press, 1976), p. 393.

36. Harold U. Faulkner, *The Decline of Laissez-Faire, 1897–1917* (New York: Holt, Reinhart and Winston, 1951), p. 87.

37. The specific impact of these changes on American national power are considered below, Chap. 7. Jay Sexton, *Debtor Diplomacy: Finance and American Foreign Relations in the Civil War Era, 1837–1873* (Oxford: Clarendon Press, 2005), pp. 130–3, 240–1.

38. John Madden, 'British Investment in the United States, 1860–1880', PhD dissertation, Cambridge University, 1957, cited in Platt, *Foreign Finance*, p. 144.

39. William Weisberger, 'George Peabody', *American National Biography Online* (23 March 2005).

40. Peter Way, *Common Labour: Workers and the Digging of North American Canals, 1780–1860* (New York: Cambridge University Press, 1993); Sucheng Chan, *Asian Americans: An Interpretive History* (Boston, MA: Twayne, 1991), pp. 30–1.

41. Leland H. Jenks, *The Migration of British Capital to 1875* (New York: Alfred Knopf, 1927), p. 363.

42. Platt, *Foreign Finance*, p. 164.

43. Thomas Cochran, *Pabst Brewing Company: The History of an American Business* (New York: Oxford University Press, 1948), pp. 113–21.

44. Frank Thistlethwaite, *America and the Atlantic Community: Anglo-American Aspects, 1790–1850* (1959; New York: Harper & Row, 1963), pp. 30, 32.

45. David J. Jeremy, *Transatlantic Industrial Revolution: The Diffusion of Textile Technologies between Britain and America, 1790–1830s* (Oxford: Blackwell, 1981), pp. 78, 93.

46. Seventy-four per cent of immigrants in the industry were weavers – almost certainly handloom weavers. Ibid., p. 255.

47. Ibid., p. 254.
48. Quoted ibid., p. 95.
49. Ibid., p. 259.
50. Ibid., pp. 253, 254. On the Lowell Mills, see Thomas Dublin, *Women at Work: The Transformation of Work and Community in Lowell, Massachusetts* (New York: Columbia University Press, 1979).
51. Jeremy, *Transatlantic Industrial Revolution*, p. 260.
52. Alan Dawley, *Class and Community: The Industrial Revolution in Lynn* (Cambridge, MA: Harvard University Press, 1976).
53. Faulkner, *Decline of Laissez-Faire*, pp. 92–3.
54. See Bray Hammond, *Banks and Politics in America, from the Revolution to the Civil War* (Princeton, NJ: Princeton University Press, 1957).
55. Robert Remini, *Andrew Jackson and the Course of American Empire, 1767–1821* (New York: Harper & Row, 1977), p. 25.
56. Richard Hofstadter, *The Age of Reform: From Bryan to F.D.R.* (New York: Knopf, 1955), p. 74.
57. Mira Wilkins, *The History of Foreign Investment in the United States to 1914* (Cambridge, MA: Harvard University Press, 1989), p. 608.
58. Jeffry A. Frieden, 'Monetary Populism in Nineteenth-Century America: An Open Economy Interpretation', *Journal of Economic History*, 57 (No. 2, 1997), 367–95.
59. Hughes, *American Economic History*, p. 138.
60. David A. Hounshell, *From the American System to Mass Production, 1800–1932: The Development of Manufacturing Technology in the United States* (Baltimore, MD: Johns Hopkins University Press, 1984), pp. 34–5.
61. Peter Temin, 'Free Land and Federalism: American Economic Exceptionalism', in Byron E. Shafer, ed., *Is America Different?: A New Look at American Exceptionalism* (Oxford: Clarendon Press, 1991), p. 75.
62. John K. Brown, *The Baldwin Locomotive Works, 1831–1915: A Study in American Industrial Practice* (Baltimore, MD: Johns Hopkins University Press, 1995), pp. 44–7.
63. Arthur M. Schlesinger, Jr, *The Age of Jackson* (Boston, MA: Houghton Mifflin, 1945), p. 423; Robert Remini, *Andrew Jackson and the Course of American Freedom, 1822–1832* (New York: Harper & Row, 1981), pp. 68–71, 360–1.
64. Douglas A. Irwin, 'Historical Perspectives on U.S. Trade Policy', http://grove.ship.edu/econ/trade/Irwin_on_us_trade.html (14 August 2004).
65. Brown, *Baldwin Locomotive Works*, p. 45.
66. Faulkner, *Decline of Laissez-Faire*, p. 244; Benjamin W. Labaree et al., *America and the Sea: A Maritime History* (Mystic, CT: Mystic Seaport, 1998), pp. 7–8.
67. Faulkner, *Decline of Laissez-Faire*, p. 247.
68. Wilkins, *History of Foreign Investment*, p. 608.
69. Faulkner, *Decline of Laissez-Faire*, p. 78.
70. Richard P. Tucker, *Insatiable Appetite: The United States and the Ecological Degradation of the Tropical World* (Berkeley, CA: University of California Press, 2000), pp. 188–95.

3   The Beacon of Improvement: Political and Social Reform

1. Alexander Keyssar, *The Right to Vote: The Contested History of Democracy in the United States* (New York: Basic Books, 2000), Table A.3.
2. John A. Phillips and Charles Wetherell, 'The Great Reform Act of 1832 and the Political Modernization of England', *American Historical Review*, 100 (April 1995), especially pp. 411–12, stress the modernizing effects against revisionist interpretations.
3. Christine Bolt, *The Women's Movement in the United States and Britain from the 1790s to the 1920s* (Amherst, MA: University of Massachusetts Press, 1993); Jane Rendall, *The Origins of Modern Feminism: Women in Britain, France and the United States, 1780–1860* (Basingstoke: Macmillan, 1985), pp. 300–2; Bonnie Anderson, *Joyous Greetings: The First International Women's Movement, 1830–1860* (Oxford: Oxford University Press, 2000), pp. 168–72, 195–6.
4. Arthur Schlesinger, Jr, *The Age of Jackson* (Boston, MA: Little Brown, 1945), pp. 118, 318.
5. Quoted George D. Lillibridge, *Beacon of Freedom: The Impact of American Democracy on Great Britain* (Philadelphia, PA: University of Pennsylvania Press, 1954), p. xiii.
6. David Paul Crook, *American Democracy and British Politics, 1815–1850* (Oxford: Clarendon Press, 1965).
7. Jamie L. Bronstein, 'The Homestead and the Garden Plot: Cultural Pressures on Land Reform in Nineteenth-Century Britain and the USA', *European Legacy*, 6 (No. 2, 2001), 159–75; Bronstein, *Land Reform and Working Class Experience in Britain and the United States 1800–1862* (Palo Alto, CA: Stanford University Press, 1999).
8. Ray Boston, *British Chartists in America* (Manchester: Manchester University Press, 1971), pp. xiii, 80.
9. Daniel Walker Howe, *The Political Culture of the American Whigs* (Chicago, IL: University of Chicago Press, 1979), p. 77.
10. Calvin Colton, *Four Years in Great Britain* (New York: Harper & Bros., 1835).
11. In American parlance, the term has in more recent times been appropriated by the legislative procedure of stalling legislation by the tactic of conducting interminable speeches.
12. T. P. Dunning, 'The Canadian Rebellions of 1837–38: An Episode in Northern Borderland History', *Australasian Journal of American Studies*, 15 (December 1995), 35–9. For the rebels, see Cassandra Pybus and Hamish Maxwell-Stewart, *American Citizens, British Slaves: Yankee Political Prisoners in an Australian Penal Colony 1839–1850* (Carlton South, Vic.: Melbourne University Press, 2002).
13. Robert E. May, *Manifest Destiny's Underworld: Filibustering in Antebellum America* (Chapel Hill, NC: University of North Carolina Press, 2002), p. xv.
14. George W. Pierson, *Tocqueville and Beaumont in America* (New York: Oxford University Press, 1938), p. 358; *Essex Register*, 15 September 1831.
15. Harold Murraro, 'Garibaldi in New York', *New York History*, 27 (April 1946), 184.

16. Ibid., p. 182.
17. David Herreshoff, *American Disciples of Marx* (1967; New York: Monad Press; distributed by Pathfinder Press, 1973), pp. 57–9, 70–1.
18. Donald S. Spencer, *Louis Kossuth and Young America: A Study of Sectionalism and Foreign Policy, 1848–1852* (Columbia, MO: University of Missouri Press, 1977), p. 135.
19. Paola Gemme, 'Imperial Designs of Political Philanthropy: A Study of Antebellum Accounts of Italian Liberalism', *American Studies International*, 39 (February 2001), 34.
20. Edward L. Widmer, *Young America: The Flowering of Democracy in New York City* (New York: Oxford University Press, 1999), p. 16.
21. Ibid.; Merle Curti, 'Young America', *American Historical Review*, 32 (October 1926), 34; Thomas Hietala, *Manifest Design: Anxious Aggrandizement in Late Jacksonian America* (Ithaca, NY: Cornell University Press, 1985).
22. Tocqueville journal, 10 October 1831, http://www.tocqueville.org/ny5.htm (1 May 2005). The 'last word in the way of an association seems to me to be the temperance societies.' Their effects were 'one of the most notable things in this country.'
23. J. F. Maclear, 'The Idea of "American Protestantism" and British Nonconformity, 1829–1840', *Journal of British Studies*, 21 (Autumn 1981), 68–89; Richard Carwardine, *Transatlantic Revivalism: Popular Evangelicalism in Britain and America, 1790–1865* (Westport, CT: Greenwood, 1978), pp. 68–9.
24. Thomas Haskell, 'Capitalism and the Origins of the Humanitarian Sensibility, Part 1', in Thomas Bender, ed., *The Antislavery Debate: Capitalism and Abolitionism as a Problem in Historical Interpretation* (Berkeley, CA: University of California Press, 1992), especially p. 153.
25. W. J. Rorabaugh, 'Edward C. Delavan', *American National Biography*, http://www.nysm.nysed.gov/albany/bios/d/ecdelavananb.htm (14 December 2004).
26. Arthur Bestor, 'Patent Office Models of the Good Society: Some Relationships between Social Reform and Westward Expansion', *American Historical Review*, 58 (April 1953), 505–26.
27. See, for example, William Crawford, *Report on the Penitentiaries of the United States* (1835; Montclair, NJ: Patterson Smith, 1969).
28. Norman B. Johnston, 'V. John Haviland', in Hermann Mannheim, ed., *Pioneers in Criminology*, 2nd edn (Montclair, NJ: Patterson Smith, 1972), p. 98.
29. Frank Thistlethwaite, *America and the Atlantic Community: Anglo-American Aspects, 1790–1850* (1959; New York: Harper & Row, 1963), p. 89.
30. Robert G. Waite, 'From Penitentiary to Reformatory: Alexander Maconochie, Walter Crofton, Zebulon Brockway, and the Road to Prison Reform – New South Wales, Ireland, and Elmira, New York', *Criminal Justice History*, 12 (1991), 92–3, 96–7; John Vincent Barry, 'Alexander Maconochie, 1787–1860', in Mannheim, ed., *Pioneers in Criminology*, p. 69.
31. Johnston, 'Haviland', pp. 100–2.

32. Rendall, *Origins of Modern Feminism*, pp. 219–22; Thistlethwaite, *America and the Atlantic Community*, pp. 52–5; Barbara Taylor, *Eve and the New Jerusalem: Socialism and Feminism in the Nineteenth Century* (London: Virago, 1983).

33. Thistlethwaite, *Anglo-American Connection*, p. 94.

34. Frederick Hale, 'Marcus Hansen, Puritanism, and Scandinavian Immigrant Temperance Movements', *Norwegian-American Studies*, 27 (1977), 18, http://www.naha.stolaf.edu/pubs/nas/volume27/vol27_2.htm.

35. J. K. Chapman, 'The Mid-Nineteenth Century Temperance Movement in New Brunswick and Maine', *Canadian Historical Review*, 35 (March 1954), 43–60; Brian Harrison, *Drink and the Victorians: The Temperance Question in England, 1815–1872* (London: Faber & Faber, 1971), p. 196; Elizabeth Malcolm, *Ireland Sober, Ireland Free: Drink and Temperance in Nineteenth Century Ireland* (Dublin: Gill & MacMillan, 1986).

36. Harrison, *Drink and the Victorians*.

37. Carl J. Guarneri, 'The Associationists: Forging a Christian Socialism in Antebellum America', *Church History*, 52 (March 1983), 42.

38. Catherine Beecher, *A Treatise on Domestic Economy* (1841; New York: Source Book Press, 1970); Ian Tyrrell, *Sobering Up: From Temperance to Prohibition in Antebellum America, 1800–1860* (Westport, CT: Greenwood Press, 1979), pp. 78–9.

39. Timothy L. Smith, *Revivalism and Social Reform: American Protestantism on the Eve of the Civil War* (New York: Harper & Row, 1957), p. 42; Ernest R. Sandeen, 'The Distinctiveness of American Denominationalism: A Case Study of the 1846 Evangelical Alliance', *Church History*, 45 (June 1976), 222–34.

40. Carl Guarneri, 'Introduction' to Christine Bolt, 'Abolitionism and Women's Rights in the United States and Britain', in Guarneri, ed., *America Compared: American History in International Perspective*, Vol. 1: *To 1877* (Boston, MA: Houghton Mifflin, 1997), p. 316.

41. Elizabeth Heyrick, *Immediate not Gradual Abolition; or, An Inquiry into the Shortest, Safest and Most Effectual Means of Getting Rid of West Indian Slavery* (London: J. Hanshard, 1824), pp. 15–18, 35–6; Betty Fladeland, *Men and Brothers: Anglo-American Antislavery Cooperation* (Urbana, IL: University of Illinois Press, 1972), p. 178.

42. Fladeland, *Men and Brothers*, pp. 275, 299, 301.

43. Ibid., pp. 226, 283.

44. Walter Merrill, ed., *The Letters of William Lloyd Garrison*, 6 vols (Cambridge, MA: Belknap Press of Harvard University Press, 1971–81), Vol. 3: *No Union with Slaveholders, 1841–1849*, pp. 350, 56–7; Garrison to George W. Benson, 22 March 1842, ibid., pp. 61–2.

45. Fladeland, *Men and Brothers*, p. 300.

46. William McFeely, 'Frederick Douglass in Great Britain', in Guarneri, *America Compared*, p. 301.

47. Guarneri, 'Introduction', ibid., p. 299.

48. McFeely, 'Frederick Douglass in Great Britain', p. 301.

49. George Shepperson, 'Thomas Chalmers, The Free Church of Scotland, and the South', *Journal of Southern History*, 17 (November 1951), 517–37. The donation partly evidenced trans-Atlantic denominational solidarity, but may

also have been a calculated propaganda exercise – to show Southerners' benevolence toward the less fortunate, and to draw attention to the argument that Britain's factory owners were less solicitous of their 'free' workers' human welfare than slaveholders were of their human chattels.

50. R. J. M. Blackett, *Building an Antislavery Wall: Black Americans in the Atlantic Abolitionist Movement, 1830–1860* (Baton Rouge, LA: Louisiana State University Press, 1983), pp. 120–3, 143–4; Lawrence B. Glickman, ' "Buy for the Sake of the Slave": Abolitionism and the Origins of American Consumer Activism', *American Quarterly*, 56 (No. 4, 2004), 889–912.

51. R. J. M. Blackett, *Divided Hearts: Britain and the American Civil War* (Baton Rouge, LA: Louisiana State University Press, 2001), pp. 119, 230–1.

52. Gustave de Beaumont, *Marie; or, Slavery in the United States: A Novel of Jacksonian America*, translated by Barbara Chapman (Stanford, CA: Stanford University Press, 1958).

53. Alexis de Tocqueville, *Democracy in America*, transl. Henry Reeve, 2 vols (1835, 1840; New York: Schocken Books, 1961), I: 393.

54. Ibid., 426.

4 People in Motion: Nineteenth-Century Migration Experiences

1. For studies of migration historiography reflecting the newer approaches, see Jan Lucassen and Leo Lucassen, eds, *Migration, Migration History, History: Old Paradigms and New Perspectives* (Bern: Peter Lang, 1997).

2. Adam McKeown, 'Global Migration, 1846–1940', *Journal of World History*, June 2004, http://www.historycooperative.org/journals/jwh/15.2/mckeown.html (5 June 2005). See also McKeown, *Chinese Migrant Networks and Cultural Change: Peru, Chicago, Hawaii, 1900–1936* (Chicago, IL: University of Chicago Press, 2001), pp. 43–5.

3. Donna R. Gabaccia, *Italy's Many Diasporas* (Seattle, WA: University of Washington Press, 2000), p. 43.

4. Charlotte Erickson, *Leaving England: Essays on British Emigration in the Nineteenth Century* (Ithaca, NY: Cornell University Press, 1994), pp. 167–73.

5. Ibid., pp. 143–4.

6. Sucheng Chan, *Asian Americans: An Interpretive History* (Boston, MA: Twayne, 1991), pp. 105–7; Sucheng Chan, *This Bittersweet Soil: The Chinese in California Agriculture, 1860–1910* (Berkeley, CA: University of California Press, 1986), pp. 389–93.

7. Brinley Thomas, *Migration and Economic Growth: A Study of Great Britain and the Atlantic Economy* (Cambridge: Cambridge University Press, 1954); Thomas, *The Industrial Revolution and the Atlantic Economy: Selected Essays* (London: Routledge, 1993).

8. Stephan Thernstrom and Peter R. Knights, 'Men in Motion: Some Data and Speculations about Urban Mobility in Nineteenth-Century America', *Journal of Interdisciplinary History*, 1 (Autumn 1970), 7–35. See also Knights, *The Plain People of Boston, 1830–1860: A Study in City Growth* (New York:

Oxford University Press, 1971); Knights, *Yankee Destinies: The Lives of Ordinary Nineteenth-Century Bostonians* (Chapel Hill, NC: University of North Carolina Press, 1991).

9. Hartmut Kaelble, *Historical Research on Social Mobility: Western Europe and the USA in the Nineteenth and Twentieth Centuries* (London: Croom Helm, 1981). On the unsatisfactory state of comparative studies of social mobility, especially between the United States and European societies, see ibid., p. 57.

10. William H. Sewell, *Structure and Mobility: The Men and Women of Marseilles, 1820–1870* (New York: Cambridge University Press, 1985), pp. 11, 252–3.

11. Leslie P. Moch, *Moving Europeans: Migration in Western Europe since 1650* (Bloomington, IN: Indiana University Press, 1992).

12. Dirk Hoerder, 'Introduction', in Dirk Hoerder and Jörg Nagler, eds, *People in Transit: German Migrations in Comparative Perspective, 1820–1930* (Washington, DC: German Historical Institute; Cambridge: Cambridge University Press, 1995), p. 1; Karl Marten Barfuss, 'Foreign Workers in and around Bremen, 1884–1918', ibid., pp. 201–24; Susan Meyer, 'In-Migration and Out-Migration in an Area of Heavy Industry: The Case of Georgmarienhutte, 1856–1870', ibid., p. 178ff.

13. Gabaccia, *Italy's Many Diasporas*, p. 44. The Americas did not attract more than 10 per cent of the Risorgimento exiles. See also Donna R. Gabaccia and Fraser M. Ottanelli, eds, *Italian Workers of the World: Labor Migration and the Formation of Multiethnic States* (Urbana, IL: University of Illinois Press, 2005).

14. Sucheng Chan, *Asian Americans*, pp. 30–1.

15. William H. Sewell, Jr, 'Social Mobility in a Nineteenth-Century European City: Some Findings and Implications', *Journal of Interdisciplinary History*, 7 (Autumn 1976), 232–3.

16. James Henretta, 'The Study of Social Mobility: Ideological Assumptions and Conceptual Bias', *Labor History*, 18 (Spring, 1977), 165–77.

17. Edward Pessen, *Riches, Class, and Power in America before the Civil War* (Lexington, MA: D. C. Heath, 1973); Stephan Thernstrom, *Poverty and Progress: Social Mobility in a Nineteenth Century City* (Cambridge, MA: Harvard University Press, 1964).

18. Jo Blanden, Paul Gregg and Stephen Machin, 'Intergenerational Mobility in Europe and North America: A Report Supported by the Sutton Trust', Centre for Economic Performance, April 2005 http://www.suttontrust.com/reports/IntergenerationalMobility.pdf (1 July 2006), pp. 5–6, 19.

19. Thernstrom and Knights, 'Men in Motion', pp. 7–35; Knights, *Plain People of Boston*.

20. Hans Norman, 'Swedes in America', in Harald Runblom and Hans Norman, eds, *From Sweden to America: A History of the Migration* (Minneapolis, MN: University of Minnesota Press, 1976), p. 271.

21. Mark Wyman, *Round Trip to America: The Immigrants Return to Europe, 1880–1930* (Ithaca, NY: Cornell University Press, 1993), p. 65.

22. Victor Greene, *Faith and Fatherland: The Rise of Polish and Lithuanian Ethnic Consciousness in America* (Madison, WI: State Historical Society of Wisconsin, 1975); Maldwyn Jones, *American Immigration*

(Chicago, IL: University of Chicago Press, 1960), pp. 226–7; Anthony Kuzniewski, *Faith and Fatherland: The Polish Church War in Wisconsin, 1896–1918* (Notre Dame, IN: Notre Dame University Press, 1980); John Bodnar, *The Transplanted: A History of Immigrants in Urban America* (Bloomington, IN: Indiana University Press, 1985), pp. 161–2; Jay P. Dolan, *The Immigrant Church: New York's Irish and German Catholics, 1815–1865* (Baltimore, MD: Johns Hopkins University Press, 1975).

23. For the fascinating story of this trans-Atlantic community in Russia, Canada and the American Great Plains, see Royden Loewen, *Family, Church, and Market: A Mennonite Community in the Old and New Worlds, 1850–1930* (Urbana, IL: University of Illinois Press, 1993). See also Perry Bush, *Two Kingdoms, Two Loyalties: Mennonite Pacifism in Modern America* (Baltimore, MD: Johns Hopkins University Press, 1998), pp. 19–25, 27–9.

24. Wyman, *Round Trip to America*, p. 5.

25. Lars-Goran Tedebrand, 'Remigration from America to Sweden', in Runblom and Norman, eds, *From Sweden to America*, p. 209.

26. Theodore Saloutos, *They Remember America: The Story of the Repatriated Greek-Americans* (Berkeley, CA: University of California Press, 1956); Ioanna Laliotou, *Transatlantic Subjects: Acts of Migration and Cultures of Transnationalism between Greece and America* (Chicago, IL: University of Chicago Press, 2004), pp. 73–80.

27. Barry R. Chiswick and Timothy J. Hatton, 'International Migration and the Integration of Labor Markets', IZA Bonn Discussion Paper No. 559 August 2002.

28. Wyman, *Round Trip to America*, p. 10.

29. Tedebrand, 'Remigration from America to Sweden', p. 225.

30. Ray Allen Billington, *The Protestant Crusade* (New York: Macmillan, 1938).

31. David Roediger, *The Wages of Whiteness: Race and the Making of the American Working Class* (London: Verso, 1991), Chap. 7; Noel Ignatiev, *How the Irish Became White* (New York: Routledge, 1996); Alexander Saxton, *The Rise and Fall of the White Republic: Class Politics and Mass Culture in Nineteenth-Century America* (London: Verso, 1990). For the draft riots, Adrian Cook, *The Armies of the Street: The New York City Draft Riots of 1863* (Lexington, KY: University Press of Kentucky, 1974).

32. Alexander Saxton, *The Indispensable Enemy: Labor and the Anti-Chinese Movement in California* (Berkeley, CA: University of California Press, 1971).

33. See, for example, 'The Races that Go into the American Melting Pot', *New York Times* (Sunday Magazine) (21 May 1911), p. 2; Madison Grant, *The Passing of the Great Race; or, The Racial Basis of European History* (New York: C. Scribner, 1916).

34. Mark Wyman, *Round Trip to America*, p. 6.

35. Ibid.

36. Maureen E. Montgomery, *'Gilded Prostitution': Status, Money, and Transatlantic Marriages, 1870–1914* (London: Routledge, 1989), pp. 2, 21–2, and passim for other examples, such as Lady Nancy Astor.

37. Robin Winks, *The Blacks in Canada: A History*, 2nd edn (Montreal: McGill-Queens University Press, 1997), pp. 232–47.

38. Paul F. Sharp, 'When Our West Moved North', *American Historical Review*, 55 (January 1950), 286–91.

5 Unwilling Immigrants and Diaspora Dreams

1. The original estimates by Philip Curtin have been revised upward. Curtin, *The African Slave Trade: A Census* (Madison, WI: University of Wisconsin Press, 1969); Stanley L. Engerman and Eugene Genovese, eds, *Race and Slavery in the Western Hemisphere: Quantitative Studies* (Princeton, NJ: Princeton University Press, 1975); Paul Lovejoy, 'The Volume of the Atlantic Slave Trade: A Synthesis', *Journal of African History*, 23 (No. 2, 1982), 473–501. For global aspects, see Janet J. Ewald, 'Slavery in Africa and the Slave Trades from Africa', *American Historical Review*, 97 (April 1992), 465–85.

2. Cited in James A. McMillin, *The Final Victims: Foreign Slave Trade to North America, 1783–1810: A Reassessment of the Post-revolutionary Slave Trade* (Columbia, SC: University of South Carolina Press, 2004), pp. 16–17, 30–2.

3. Ira Berlin, *Many Thousands Gone: The First Two Centuries of Slavery in North America* (Cambridge, MA: Belknap Press of Harvard University Press, 1998), pp. 314–15, 344–5.

4. Michael Tadman, 'The Demographic Cost of Sugar: Debates on Slave Societies and Natural Increase in the Americas', *American Historical Review*, 105 (December 2000), 1534–75.

5. P. J. Staudenraus, *The African Colonization Movement, 1816–1865* (New York: Columbia University Press, 1961), pp. 9–11, 34.

6. An earlier settlement in 1820 had failed due to the impact of tropical diseases. Staudenraus, *African Colonization Movement*, pp. 65–6. Robin W. Winks, *The Blacks in Canada: A History*, 2nd edn (Montreal: McGill-Queens University Press, 1997), pp. 72–3; Lamin Sanneh, *Abolitionists Abroad: American Blacks and the Making of Modern West Africa* (Cambridge, MA: Harvard University Press, 1999), pp. 51–2; Christopher Fyfe, *A Short History of Sierra Leone*, new edn (London: Longman, 1979), pp. 22–8. On Liberia, see also Hollis R. Lynch, 'Sierra Leone and Liberia in the Nineteenth Century', in J. F. Ade Ajayi and Ian Espie, eds, *A Thousand Years of West African History* (1965; Ibadan, Nigeria: Ibadan University Press, 1967), pp. 329–33; Andrew H. Foote, *Africa and the American Flag* (1854; Folkestone: Dawsons of Pall Mall, 1970), pp. 113–40. See, more generally, Cassandra Pybus, *Epic Journeys of Freedom: Runaway Slaves of the American Revolution and Their Global Quest For Liberty* (Boston, MA: Beacon Press, 2006).

7. M. R. Delany and Robert Campbell, *Search for a Place: Black Separatism and Africa, 1860*, Introduction by Howard H. Bell (Ann Arbor, MI: University of Michigan Press, 1969), p. 36. On Bowen and Stanley, see Peter Duignan and L. H. Gann, *The United States and Africa: A History* (New York: Cambridge University Press, 1984), pp. 98–9, 126–7. On Bowen, see Lysle E. Meyer, 'Thomas Jefferson Bowen and Central Africa: A Nineteenth-Century Missionary Delusion', in Meyer, *The Farther Frontier: Six Case Studies of Americans and Africa, 1848–1936* (Selinsgrove, PA: Susquehanna University Press, 1992), pp. 15–32. See also J. E. Flint, 'The Growth of

European Influence in West Africa in the Nineteenth Century', in Ade Ajayi and Espie, *West African History*, pp. 359–79.

8. Cyril E. Griffith, *The African Dream: Martin R. Delany and the Emergence of Pan-African Thought* (University Park, PA: Pennsylvania State University Press, 1975), p. 16.

9. Victor Ullman, *Martin R. Delany: The Beginnings of Black Nationalism* (Boston, MA: Beacon Press, 1971), pp. 224–5.

10. Alexander Keyssar, *The Right to Vote: The Contested History of Democracy in the United States* (New York: Basic Books, 2000), p. 55.

11. See Robert S. Levine, *Martin Delany, Frederick Douglass, and the Politics of Representative Identity* (Chapel Hill, NC: University of North Carolina Press, 1997).

12. Carl N. Degler, *Neither Black nor White: Slavery and Race Relations in Brazil and the United States* (New York: Macmillan, 1971), p. 60.

13. David W. Blight, 'Martin R. Delany', http://college.hmco.com/history/readerscomp/rcah/html/ah_024000_delanymartin.htm (1 June 2005).

14. Herbert Gutman, *The Black Family in Slavery and Freedom, 1750–1925* (New York: Pantheon, 1976); Peter Kolchin, *American Slavery, 1619–1877* (New York: Penguin, 1995), p. 158.

15. Chris Dixon, *African America and Haiti: Emigration and Black Nationalism in the Nineteenth Century* (Westport, CT: Greenwood, 2000), p. 69.

16. Paul Gilroy, *The Black Atlantic: Modernity and Double Consciousness* (Cambridge, MA: Harvard University Press, 1993).

17. Dixon, *African America and Haiti*.

18. Don E. Fehrenbacher, 'Only His Stepchildren: Lincoln and the Negro', *Civil War History*, 20 (December 1974), 293–310; George M. Fredrickson, 'A Man but not a Brother: Abraham Lincoln and Racial Equality', *Journal of Southern History*, 41 (February 1975), 39–58; Michael Vorenberg, 'Abraham Lincoln and the Politics of Black Colonization', *Journal of the Abraham Lincoln Association*, Summer 1993, http://www.historycooperative.org/journals/jala/14.2/vorenberg.html (28 September 2005).

19. For ambivalence towards Africa, see James T. Campbell, *Songs of Zion: The African Methodist Episcopal Church in the United States and South Africa* (New York: Oxford University Press, 1995), pp. 77–89.

20. Nell Irvin Painter, *Exodusters: Black Migration to Kansas after Reconstruction* (1976; New York: Knopf, 1977).

21. Ibid., p. 145.

22. Campbell, *Songs of Zion*, pp. 77–89; Edwin S. Redkey, *Black Exodus: Black Nationalism and Back to Africa Movements, 1890–1910* (New Haven, CT: Yale University Press, 1969), pp. 170–1; J. R. Oldfield, *Alexander Crummell (1819–1898) and the Creation of an African-American Church in Liberia* (Lewiston, Pa.: The Edwin Mellen Press, 1990), pp. 110–11; Delany and Campbell, *Search for a Place*, p. 61.

23. Judith Stein, *The World of Marcus Garvey: Race and Class in Modern Society* (Baton Rouge, LA: Louisiana State University Press, 1986), pp. 10–11.

6 Racial and Ethnic Frontiers

1. Frances Roe Kestler, compl., *The Indian Captivity Narrative: A Woman's View* (New York: Garland, 1990), p. 229.
2. Charles Sellers, *The Market Revolution: Jacksonian America, 1815–1846* (New York: Oxford University Press, 1991), p. 8.
3. Robert Remini, *Andrew Jackson and the Course of American Empire, 1767–1821* (New York: Harper & Row, 1977), p. 194.
4. Michael Rogin, *Fathers and Children: Andrew Jackson and the Subjugation of the American Indian* (New York: Pantheon, 1975), pp. 189, 199.
5. Ann Laura Stoler, 'Tense and Tender Ties: The Politics of Comparison in North American History and (Post) Colonial Studies', *Journal of American History*, 88 (December 2001), 829–65.
6. George M. Fredrickson, 'Mulattoes and Métis: Attitudes toward Miscegenation in the United States and France since the Seventeenth Century', *International Social Science Journal*, 57 (March 2005), 103–57; Gary Nash, *Red, White, and Black: The Peoples of Early America* (Englewood Cliffs, NJ: Prentice-Hall, 1974), p. 279; Carl N. Degler, *Neither Black nor White: Slavery and Race Relations in Brazil and the United States* (New York: Macmillan, 1971), pp. 228–9; Jack D. Forbes, 'The Historian and the Indian: Racial Bias in American History', *The Americas*, 19 (April 1963), 358.
7. Ira Berlin, *Slaves Without Masters: The Free Negro in the Antebellum South* (New York: Pantheon Books, 1974).
8. Richard White, *The Middle Ground: Indians, Empires, and Republics in the Great Lakes Region, 1650–1815* (New York: Cambridge University Press, 1991), pp. 66–75, 324, 342, 455; Patrick J. Jung, 'French–Indian Intermarriage and the Creation of Métis Society', http://www.uwgb.edu/wisfrench/library/index.htm (30 June 2005) (quote); Patrick J. Jung, 'Forge, Destroy, and Preserve the Bonds of Empire: Native Americans, Euro-Americans, and Métis on the Wisconsin Frontier, 1634–1856', PhD dissertation, Marquette University, 1997, p. 5.
9. William G. McLoughlin, *Cherokee Renaissance in the New Republic* (Princeton, NJ: Princeton University Press, 1986), p. 352. On Cherokee intermarriage, see especially pp. 31–2, 331–3.
10. Patrick Wolfe, 'Land, Labor, and Difference: Elementary Structures of Race', *American Historical Review*, 106 (June 2001), 866–905.
11. 'Forum: Thomas Jefferson and Sally Hemmings Redux', *William and Mary Quarterly*, 3rd series, 57 (January 2000), 121–98ff.
12. *Thomas Jefferson: Writings* (New York: Library of America, 1984), p. 266.
13. Bernard W. Sheehan argued that humanitarian motives of assimilation lay behind this policy but so too did practical considerations, particularly the thirst for land. Sheehan, *Seeds of Extinction: Jeffersonian Philanthropy and the American Indian* (Chapel Hill, NC: University of North Carolina Press, 1973); Reginald Horsman, *Expansion and American Indian Policy, 1783–1812* (East Lansing, MI: Michigan State University Press, 1967), especially pp. 109–10.
14. Wolfe, 'Land, Labor, and Difference', p. 868 n9.
15. Ronald N. Satz, *American Indian Policy in the Jacksonian Era* (1974; Norman, OK: University of Oklahoma Press, 2002).

16. Anthony F. C. Wallace, *Jefferson and the Indians: The Tragic Fate of the First Americans* (Cambridge, MA: Belknap Press of Harvard University Press, 1999), p. 18.

17. Quoted Walter Williams, 'US Indian Policy and the Debate over Philippine Annexation: Implications for the Origins of American Imperialism', *Journal of American History*, 66 (March 1980), 811.

18. McLoughlin, *Cherokee Renaissance*, pp. 367–8. See also Ralph Henry Gabriel, *Elias Boudinot, Cherokee, and His America* (Norman, OK: University of Oklahoma Press, 1941); Theda Perdue, ed., *Cherokee Editor: The Writings of Elias Boudinot* (Athens, GA: University of Georgia Press, 1996).

19. Jung, 'French–Indian Intermarriage and the Creation of Métis Society' (quote); Jung, 'Forge, Destroy, and Preserve the Bonds of Empire', pp. 489–90.

20. Brian W. Dippie, *The Vanishing American: White Attitudes and U.S. Indian Policy* (1982; Lawrence, KA: University Press of Kansas, 1991); R. David Edmunds, 'Native Americans, New Voices: American Indian History, 1895–1995', *American Historical Review*, 100 (June 1995), 718.

21. David J. Weber, *The Mexican Frontier, 1821–1846: The American Southwest under Mexico* (Albuquerque, NM: University of New Mexico Press, 1982), pp. 170–8.

22. Albert K. Weinberg, *Manifest Destiny: A Study of Nationalist Expansionism in American History* (Baltimore, MD: Johns Hopkins University Press, 1935; Quadrangle, 1963), p. 112; David Pletcher, *The Diplomacy of Annexation: Texas, Oregon and the Mexican War* (Columbia, MO: University of Missouri Press, 1973).

23. Ronald Robinson and John Gallagher with Alice Denny, *Africa and the Victorians: The Official Mind of Imperialism* (London: Macmillan, 1961); John Gallagher and Ronald Robinson, 'The Imperialism of Free Trade', *Economic History Review*, 2nd series, 6 (No. 1, 1953), 1–15.

24. Weinberg, *Manifest Destiny*, p. 112.

25. Pekka Hämäläinen, 'Reversed Colonialism: Indian–European Encounters on the Southern Plains, in the Southwest, and in Northern Mexico, 1700–1850', unpublished paper, CISH 20th Congress, Sydney, July 2005.

26. Thomas R. Hietala, *Manifest Design: Anxious Aggrandizement in Late Jacksonian America* (Ithaca, NY: Cornell University Press, 1985), p. 153.

7 America's Civil War and Its World Historical Implications

1. Jonathan D. Spence, *The Search for Modern China* (New York: Norton, 1999), pp. 170–8.

2. In Britain, those who distrusted democracy found their opinions confirmed by the war. R. J. M. Blackett, *Divided Hearts: Britain and the American Civil War* (Baton Rouge, LA: Louisiana State University Press, 2001), pp. 7, 12, 35; Hugh Dubrulle, 'A Military Legacy of the Civil War: The British Inheritance', *Civil War History*, 49 (No. 2, 2003), 154.

3.   Sven Beckert, 'Emancipation and Empire: Reconstructing the Worldwide Web of Cotton Production in the Age of the American Civil War', *American Historical Review*, 109 (December 2004), 1416.

4.   For a standard if dated survey of diplomatic and political history, see D. P. Crook, *The North, the South, and the Powers, 1861–1865* (New York: Wiley, 1974).

5.   Frances Clarke, ' "Let All Nations See": Civil War Nationalism and the Memorialization of Wartime Voluntarism', *Civil War History*, 52 (No. 1, 2006), 76.

6.   Robin W. Winks, *Canada and the United States: The Civil War Years* (Baltimore, MD: Johns Hopkins University Press, 1960), pp. 13, 19, 69–103, 208–9.

7.   Blackett, *Divided Hearts*, pp. 119, 230–1.

8.   Ernest Scott, *The Shenandoah Incident, 1865* (Melbourne: Government Printer, 1925).

9.   Lance Janda, 'Shutting the Gates of Mercy: The American Origins of Total War, 1860–1880', *Journal of Military History*, 59 (January 1995), 7–8.

10. Earl J. Hess, 'Tactics, Trenches, and Men in the Civil War', in Stig Forster and Jörg Nagler, eds, *On the Road to Total War: The American Civil War and the German Wars of Unification, 1861–1871* (Cambridge: Cambridge University Press, 1997), p. 486.

11. Dubrulle, 'Military Legacy', p. 154.

12. Jay Luvass, *The Military Legacy of the Civil War: The European Inheritance* (Chicago, IL: University of Chicago Press, 1959).

13. Carl Degler, 'The American Civil War and the German Wars of Unification: The Problem of Comparison', in Forster and Nagler, eds, *On the Road to Total War*, pp. 65–6.

14. Wallace D. Farnham, 'The Weakened Spring of Government: A Study in Nineteenth-Century American History', *American Historical Review*, 68 (April 1963), 662–80.

15. Beckert, 'Emancipation and Empire', p. 1422.

16. Jay Sexton, *Debtor Diplomacy: Finance and American Foreign Relations in the Civil War Era, 1837–1873* (Oxford: Clarendon Press, 2005), pp. 130–3, 240–1.

17. Degler, 'American Civil War', p. 71.

18. Peter Kolchin, *American Slavery, 1619–1877* (New York: Hill & Wang, 1993), p. 215.

19. Eric Foner, *Nothing but Freedom: Emancipation and its Legacy* (Baton Rouge, LA: Louisiana State University Press, 1983), pp. 42, 72.

20. Steven Hahn, 'Class and State in Postemancipation Societies', *American Historical Review*, 95 (February 1990), 81–98.

21. Leon F. Litwack, *Been in the Storm So Long: The Aftermath of Slavery* (New York: Knopf, 1979), pp. 539, 540.

22. Michael Fellman, 'Robert E. Lee: Postwar Southern Nationalist', *Civil War History*, 46 (September 2000), 195.

23. George D. Harmon, 'Confederate Migration to Mexico', *Hispanic American Historical Review*, 17 (November 1937), 458–87.

24. Daniel E. Sutherland, 'Exiles, Emigrants, and Sojourners: The Post-Civil War Confederate Exodus in Perspective', *Civil War History*, 31 (No. 3, 1985), 237–56.

25. William C. Davis, 'Confederate Exiles', *American History Illustrated*, 5 (No. 3, 1970), 30–43; William Clark Griggs, *The Elusive Eden: Frank McMullan's Confederate Colony in Brazil* (Austin, TX: University of Texas Press, 1987), p. 146.

26. Rebecca J. Scott, *Slave Emancipation in Cuba: The Transition to Free Labor, 1860–1899* (Pittsburgh: University of Pittsburgh Press, 1985), p. 10.

27. Ibid., p. 38.

28. C. A. Bayly, *The Birth of the Modern World, 1780–1914: Global Connections and Comparisons* (Oxford: Blackwell, 2004), p. 166.

29. Ibid., p. 164.

30. C. Vann Woodward, *Origins of the New South: 1877–1913* (Baton Rouge, LA: Louisiana State University Press, 1951), pp. 342–3.

31. R. A. Huttenback, 'The British Empire as a "White Man's Country": Racial Attitudes and Immigration Legislation in the Colonies of White Settlement', *Journal of British Studies*, 13 (November 1973), 108–37, does not deal with the US case. But see Marilyn Lake, 'The White Man under Siege: New Histories of Race in the Nineteenth Century and the Advent of White Australia', *History Workshop Journal*, 58 (No. 1, 2004), 41–62.

32. '[I]t would be running the slavery argument into the ground to make it apply to every act of discrimination which a person may see fit to make as to guests he will entertain, or as to the people he will take into his coach or cab or car; or admit to his concert or theatre, or deal with in other matters of intercourse or business'. (Justice Bradley), http://www.tourolaw.edu/patch/Civil/ (30 December 2005).

33. Charles Price, *The Great White Walls are Built: Restrictive Immigration to North America and Australasia, 1836–1888* (Canberra: Australian Institute of International Affairs in association with Australian National University Press, 1974).

34. Charles H. Pearson, *National Life and Character: A Forecast* (London: McMillan, 1893); Lake, 'The White Man under Siege', pp. 41–62.

35. August Meier, *Negro Thought in America, 1880–1915* (Ann Arbor, MI: University of Michigan Press, 1963), p. 22; Benno C. Schmidt, Jr, 'Principle and Prejudice: The Supreme Court and Race in the Progressive Era, Part 3: Black Disfranchisement from the KKK to the Grandfather Clause', *Columbia Law Review*, 82 (June 1982), 844; William E. Leuchtenburg, 'Progressivism and Imperialism: The Progressive Movement and American Foreign Policy, 1898–1916', *Mississippi Valley Historical Review*, 39 (December 1952), 498; Kelly Miller, 'The Effect of Imperialism Upon the Negro Race', *Anti-Imperialist Broadside*, No. 11 (Boston, MA: New England Anti-Imperialist League, n.d. [1900]); http://www.boondocksnet.com/ai/ailtexts/miller00.html (20 September 2005).

8 How Culture Travelled: Going Abroad, c. 1865–1914

1.   F. E. Clark, *Our Journey Around the World: An Illustrated Record of a Year's Travel of Forty Thousand Miles through India, China, Japan,*

Australia, New Zealand, Egypt, Palestine...Spain with Glimpses of Life in Far Off Lands As Seen through a Woman's Eyes by Mrs. H. E. Clark (Hartford, CT: Worthington, 1897), p. 311.

2. Edward L. Widmer, *Young America: The Flowering of Democracy in New York City* (New York: Oxford University Press, 1999), p. 203; George Francis Train, *Young America Abroad* (London: Seth Low, 1857), p. 58.

3. Herbert Hoover, *The Memoirs of Herbert Hoover*. Vol. 1. *Years of Adventure, 1874–1920* (New York: Macmillan, 1952), pp. 66, 75; Geoffrey Blainey, 'Herbert Hoover's Forgotten Years', *Business Archives and History*, 3 (No. 1, 1963), 53–70.

4. Christopher Endy, 'Travel and World Power: Americans in Europe, 1890–1917', *Diplomatic History*, 22 (Fall 1998), 565, 567.

5. Howard Murraro, 'American Travellers in Rome, 1848–1850', *Catholic Historical Review*, 29 (January 1944), 470–2.

6. William R. Moody, *D. L. Moody* (1931; New York: Garland Publishing, 1988), p. 396; Ruth Bordin, *Frances Willard: A Biography* (Chapel Hill, NC: University of North Carolina Press, 1986), p. 51.

7. Charles Denby, Jr, 'America's Opportunity in Asia', *North American Review*, 166 (January 1898), 32–3.

8. E. D. and A. Potts, eds, *A Yankee Merchant in Goldrush Australia: The Letters of George Francis Train, 1853–55* (London: Heineman, 1970), pp. xviii–xix.

9. [Elizabeth Cochrane Seaman], *Nellie Bly's Book: Around the World in Seventy-Two Days* (New York: Pictorial Weeklies, 1890).

10. Bernard A. Weisberger, 'Elizabeth Cochrane Seaman', *Notable American Women*, 3 vols (Cambridge, MA: Belknap Press of Harvard University Press, 1971), hereafter *NAW*, III: 253–5.

11. Ian Tyrrell, *Woman's World/Woman's Empire: The Woman's Christian Temperance Union in International Perspective, 1880–1930* (Chapel Hill, NC: University of North Carolina Press, 1991).

12. Quoted Bordin, *Willard*, p. 51.

13. Roderick Nash, 'The Exporting and Importing of Nature: Nature-Appreciation as a Commodity, 1850–1980', *Perspectives in American History*, 12 (1979), 527.

14. Joan Jacobs Brumberg, 'Zenanas and Girlless Villages: The Ethnology of American Evangelical Women, 1870–1910', *Journal of American History*, 69 (September 1982), 347–71.

15. Walter Colton, *Ship and Shore, in Madeira, Lisbon, and the Mediterranean* (New York: A. S. Barnes & Co., 1851).

16. Harriet Martineau, *Society in America* (New York: Saunders & Otley, 1837).

17. *Pandita Ramabai's American Encounter: The Peoples of the United States (1889)*; translated and edited by Meera Kosambi (Bloomington, IN: Indiana University Press, 2003), pp. 16, 243; Padmini Sengupta, *Pandita Ramabai Saraswati: Her Life and Work* (London: Asia Publishing House, 1970), pp. 154, 155, 162–63; Uma Chakravarti, *Rewriting History: The Life and Times of Pandita Ramabai* (New Delhi: Kahli for Women, 1998), pp. 333–4; Ramabai Sarasvati, *The High-Caste Hindu Woman*, New edn (New York: F. H. Revell, 1901); Antoinette Burton, *At the Heart of the Empire: Indians*

and the Colonial Encounter in Late-Victorian Britain, 1st Indian edn (New Delhi: University of California Press, 1998), pp. 89, 93, 105.

18.   Ben J. Wattenberg, *The Statistical History of the United States from Colonial Times to the Present* (New York: Basic Books, 1976), pp. 404–6.

19.   Daniel Kilbride, 'Travel, Ritual, and National Identity: Planters on the European Tour, 1820–1860', *Journal of Southern History*, 69 (No. 3, 2003), 549–584.

20.   Mary Pratt, *Imperial Eyes: Travel Writing and Transculturation* (New York: Routledge, 1992).

21.   Mary Schriber, *Writing Home: American Women Abroad, 1830–1920* (Charlottesville, VA: University Press of Virginia, 1997), p. 9.

22.   Ibid., pp. 9, 2. On travel see Foster Rhea Dulles, *Americans Abroad: Two Centuries of European Travel* (Ann Arbor, MI: University of Michigan Press, 1964).

23.   Ian Tyrrell, *Woman's World*, p. 104; for an example see Josiah Strong, *Our Country, Its Possible Future and Its Present Crisis*, rev. edn (New York: Baker & Taylor, 1891), pp. 209, 220, 225.

24.   'American Travel Writers', http://erc.lib.umn.edu:80/dynaweb/travel/blyaroun/@Generic__BookView (15 February 2005).

25.   Brigitte Bailey, 'There's No Place Like Home: Gender, Nation, and the Tourist Gaze in the European "Year of Revolutions": Kirkland's *Holidays Abroad*', *American Literary History*, 14 (No. 1, 2002), 60–82.

26.   Schriber, *Writing Home*, p. 141.

27.   Philip Pauly, 'The World and All That Is in It: The National Geographic Society, 1888–1918', *American Quarterly*, 31 (No. 4, 1979), 528, 532.

28.   Clark, *Our Journey*, pp. 593, 603, 624, 350, 349, 604.

29.   Eyal Naveh, 'A Spellbound Civilization: The Mediterranean Basin and the Holy Land According to Mark Twain's Travel Book *Innocents Abroad*', *Mediterranean Historical Review*, 5 (No. 1, 1990), 44–61; Bennett Kravitz, 'Geographies of the (American) Mind in *The Innocents Abroad*', *American Studies International*, 35 (No. 2, 1997), 52–76.

30.   Mark Twain, *The Innocents Abroad*, ed. DeLancey Ferguson (1868; London: Collins, 1954), p. 120.

31.   Ibid., p. 73. Twain's ambiguities in his treatment of European culture are analysed in Peter Messent, *Mark Twain* (Basingstoke: Macmillan, 1997), Chap. 2.

32.   Twain, *Innocents Abroad*, p. 149.

33.   Schriber, *Writing Home*, p. 4.

34.   Francis E. Clark, *Memories of Many Men in Many Lands: An Autobiography* (Boston, MA: United Society of Christian Endeavor, 1922), pp. 675, 702.

35.   Peter Duignan and L. H. Gann, *The United States and Africa: A History* (New York: Cambridge University Press, 1984), pp. 126–7; Frank McLynn, *Stanley: Sorcerer's Apprentice* (Oxford: Oxford University Press, 1992); Harold E. Hammond, 'American Interest in the Exploration of the Dark Continent', *Historian*, 18 (Spring 1956), 202–29.

36.   Howard Mumford Jones, *The Age of Energy: Varieties of American Experience, 1865–1915* (New York: Viking Press, 1971), pp. 280, 281, 263, 264, 265, 291, 292.

37.   Stephen L. Baldwin, *Foreign Missions of the Protestant Churches*...(New York: Eaton & Mains, 1900), p. 260; Ussama Makdisi, 'Anti-Americanism

in the Arab World: An Interpretation of a Brief History', *Journal of American History*, 89 (September 2002), 540–1; James A. Field, *America and the Mediterranean World, 1776–1882* (Princeton, NJ: Princeton University Press, 1969), 199–206, 350, 357.

38. Michael Parker, *The Kingdom of Character: The Student Volunteer Movement for Foreign Missions, 1886–1926* (Lanham, MD: University Press of America and American Society of Missiology, 1998).

39. David Fahey, *Temperance and Racism: John Bull, Johnny Reb, and the Good Templars* (Lexington, KY: University Press of Kentucky, 1996).

40. Tyrrell, *Woman's World*, Chap. 10.

41. Frank Thistlethwaite, *America and the Atlantic Community: Anglo-American Aspects, 1790–1850* (1959; New York: Harper Torchbooks, 1963), p. 85.

42. Nancy Boyd, *Emissaries: The Overseas Work of the American YWCA, 1895–1970* (New York: The Woman's Press, 1986), pp. 3–6.

43. C. Howard Hopkins, *History of the Y.M.C.A. in North America* (New York: Association Press, 1951), pp. 340–1, 342.

44. Shirley S. Garrett, *Social Reformers in Urban China: The Chinese Y.M.C.A., 1895–1926* (Cambridge, MA, Harvard University Press, 1970), pp. 77, 78.

45. W. T. McCutcheon, 'Phoebe Worrall Palmer', *NAW*, III: 13; Richard Carwardine, *Transatlantic Revivalism: Popular Evangelicalism in Britain and America, 1790–1865* (Westport, CT: Greenwood, 1978).

46. Bordin, *Willard*, p. 87.

47. William G. McLoughlin, Jr, *Modern Revivalism: Charles Grandison Finney to Billy Graham* (New York: Ronald Press, 1959), pp. 177–265.

48. But see Eric Hobsbawm, *The Age of Revolutions, 1789–1848* (1962; London: Abacus, 1994), pp. 272–3; C. A. Bayly, *The Birth of the Modern World, 1780–1914: Global Connections and Comparisons* (Oxford: Blackwell, 2004), pp. 344–5.

49. Bayly, *Birth of the Modern World*, pp. 345, 347ff; Eric Hobsbawm, *The Age of Capital, 1848–1875* (1975; London: Abacus, 1977), pp. 321–32.

50. Timothy Marr, 'Imagining Ishmael: Studies of Islamic Orientalism in America from the Puritans to Melville', PhD dissertation, Yale University, 1998, pp. 2, 7–8.

51. Ibid., Chap. 3, 'Domestic Orients'.

52. Hobsbawm, *Age of Capital*, p. 321.

53. Bayly, *Birth of the Modern World*, p. 331.

54. Ronald Numbers, *Prophetess of Health: Ellen G. White and the Origins of Seventh-Day Adventist Health Reform*, rev. edn (Knoxville, TN: University of Tennessee Press, 1992), pp. 172–3, 182–3; C. C. Goen, 'Ellen Gould Harmon White', *NAW*, III: 585–8.

55. Daniel Walker Howe, 'Victorian Culture in America', in Howe, ed., *Victorian America* (Philadelphia, PA: University of Pennsylvania Press, 1976), p. 6; Robert Kelley, *The Transatlantic Persuasion: The Liberal–Democratic Mind in the Age of Gladstone* (New York: Knopf, 1969).

56. Tyrrell, *Woman's World*, pp. 69, 188, 277.

57. Richard Pells, 'From Modernism to the Movies: The Globalization of American Culture in the Twentieth Century', *European Journal of American Culture*, 23 (September 2004), 144.

58. Lawrence W. Levine, *Highbrow/Lowbrow: The Emergence of Cultural Hierarchy in America* (Cambridge, MA: Harvard University Press, 1988), pp. 17–52.

59. Grant Wacker, 'Marching to Zion: Religion in a Modern Utopian Community', *Church History*, 54 (No. 4, 1985), 497; Clark, *Memories*, p. 294; Alden R. Heath, 'Apostle in Zion', *Journal of the Illinois State Historical Society*, 70 (No. 2, 1977), 98–113.

60. Joy S. Kasson, *Buffalo Bill's Wild West: Celebrity, Memory, and Popular History* (New York: Hill & Wang, 2000), pp. 67–8.

61. A. G. Spalding, *America's National Game: Historic Facts concerning the Beginning, Evolution, Development and Popularity of Base Ball....* (New York: American Sports Publishing Company, 1911), pp. 251–65; see also Mark Lamster, *Spalding's World Tour: The Epic Adventure That Took Baseball Around The Globe—And Made it America's Game* (New York: Public Affairs, 2006).

62. Kasson, *Buffalo Bill's Wild West*, pp. 66, 65.

63. See Ian Tyrrell, 'American Exceptionalism and Anti-Americanism' in Brendon O'Connor and Andrei S. Markovits, eds, *Anti-Americanism: A History*, Vol. 2 (Oxford, Eng.: Greenwood Press, forthcoming, 2007). In Australia, attitudes towards the United States had a long history of ambivalence. Russel Ward, *Australia*, rev. edn (Sydney: Ure Smith, 1967), p. 176. For anti-Americanism in a key case, see Philippe Roger, *The American Enemy: The History of French Anti-Americanism*, transl. Sharon Bowman (Chicago, IL: University of Chicago Press, 2005), especially p. 260.

64. Paul Reddin, *Wild West Shows* (Urbana, IL: University of Illinois Press, 1999), pp. 94, 110, 111–12.

65. A. G. Spalding, *America's National Game: Historic Facts concerning the Beginning, Evolution, Development and Popularity of Base Ball....*, abridged version (San Francisco, CA: Halo Books, 1991), p. 155; Bruce Mitchell, 'Baseball in Australia: Two Tours and the Beginnings of Baseball in Australia', *Sporting Traditions*, 7 (November 1990), 2–24.

66. Spalding, 1991 edn, p. 237; Sayuri Guthrie-Shimizu, 'For Love of the Game: Baseball in Early U.S.–Japanese Encounters and the Rise of a Transnational Sporting Fraternity', *Diplomatic History*, 28 (No. 5, 2004), 637–62.

67. See the description at http://www.thisisbradford.co.uk/bradford__district/100_years/1903.html (15 June 2005); Thomas M. Barrett, 'All the World's a Frontier: How Cossacks Became Cowboys', *Humanities*, 22 (September/October 2000) at http://www.neh.gov/news/humanities/2001-05/wildwest.html, (11 October 2005).

68. Spalding, 1991 edn, pp. 252, 254, 244.

69. Rob Kroes, 'American Empire and Cultural Imperialism: A View from the Receiving End', p. 7, in 'The American Impact on Western Europe: Americanization and Westernization in Transatlantic Perspective', Conference at German Historical Institute, Washington, March 25–27, 1999.

70. Kroes, 'American Empire and Cultural Imperialism', p. 8.

71. Colleen Cook, 'Germany's Wild West: A Researcher's Guide to Karl May', *German Studies Review*, 5 (February 1982), 68; Christopher Frayling, *Spaghetti Westerns: Cowboys and Europeans from Karl May to Sergio Leone* (London: I. B. Tauris, 1998), pp. 103–17.

72.   John F. Sears, 'Bierstadt, Buffalo Bill, and the Wild West in Europe', in Rob
       Kroes, R. W. Rydell and D. F. J. Bosscher, eds, *Cultural Transmissions and
       Receptions: American Mass Culture in Europe* (Amsterdam: VU University
       Press, 1993), p. 11.
73.   Sarah Meer, 'Competing Representations: Douglass, the Ethiopian Seren-
       aders, and Ethnic Exhibition in London', in Alan J. Rice and Martin Craw-
       ford, eds, *Liberating Sojourn: Frederick Douglass & Transatlantic Reform*
       (Athens, GA: University of Georgia Press, 1999), p. 146. The minstrels were
       fitted into an ethnological discourse with the 'Other', including Southern
       African tribesmen and New Zealand Maori.
74.   Richard Waterhouse, *From Minstrel Show to Vaudeville: The Australian
       Popular Stage, 1788–1914* (Kensington: UNSW Press, 1990), pp. 43–4.
75.   Meer, 'Competing Representations', pp. 161–2.
76.   Mira Wilkins, *The Emergence of Multinational Enterprise: American Busi-
       ness Abroad from the Colonial Era to 1914* (Cambridge, MA: Harvard
       University Press, 1970), p. 20.
77.   'Biographical Sketches of Brewster, Massachusetts', at history.rays-
       place.com/bios/brewster-ma.htm (1 October 2005).
78.   Potts and Potts, 'George Francis Train: An Introductory Sketch', in Potts
       and Potts, *A Yankee Merchant in Goldrush Australia: The Letters of George
       Francis Train, 1853–55*, p. xxii.
79.   Quoted Watt Stewart, *Henry Meiggs: Yankee Pizarro* (1946; Honolulu, HI:
       University Press of the Pacific, 2000), p. 329.
80.   Jessica Teisch, ' "Home Is Not So Very Far Away": Californian Engineers in
       South Africa, 1868–1915', *Australian Economic History Review*, 45 (July
       2005), 139–55.
81.   Geoffrey Blainey, 'Hoover's Forgotten Years', pp. 53–70.
82.   Teisch, ' "Home Is Not So Very Far Away" ', p. 141. See also Wilkins,
       Emergence of Multinational Enterprise, p. 215.
83.   Teisch, ' "Home Is Not So Very Far Away"', p. 141; Blainey, 'Hoover's
       Forgotten Years', pp. 53–70.
84.   Hoover, *Memoirs*, p. 131.
85.   Ibid., pp. 47–58.
86.   Ibid., p. 67.
87.   Teisch, ' "Home Is Not So Very Far Away" ', pp. 139, 159.
88.   Wilkins, *Emergence of Multinational Enterprise*, pp. 36–7.
89.   Ian Tyrrell, *Deadly Enemies: Tobacco and its Opponents in Australia* (Kens-
       ington: University of New South Wales Press, 1999), pp. 13–16.
90.   William C. Davis, 'Confederate Exiles', *American History Illustrated*, 5
       (No. 3, 1970), 30–43; William Clark Griggs, *The Elusive Eden: Frank
       McMullan's Confederate Colony in Brazil* (Austin, TX: University of Texas
       Press, 1987), pp. 145–6.
91.   Eileen P. Scully, *Bargaining with the State from Afar: American Citizen-
       ship in Treaty Port China, 1844–1942* (New York: Columbia University
       Press, 2001), especially p. 6. See also David M. Pletcher, *The Diplomacy of
       Involvement: American Economic Expansion across the Pacific, 1784–1900*
       (Columbia, MO: University of Missouri Press, 2001).
92.   Pletcher, *Diplomacy of Involvement*, pp. 117–19.
93.   Brent to Mrs Whitelaw Reid, 21 July 1905, Charles Henry Brent Papers,
       Library of Congress; Charles S. Kennedy, *The American Consul: A History*

of the United States Consular Service, 1776–1914 (Westport, CT: Greenwood Press, 1990), pp. 147, 170–1; Scully, *Bargaining with the State from Afar*, pp. 69–71.

94. Lloyd G. Churchward, *America & Australia: An Alternative History* (Sydney: APCOL, 1979), pp. 58–9.

9 Building the Nation-State in the Progressive Era: The Transnational Context

1. Benedict Anderson, *Imagined Communities: Reflections on the Origin and Spread of Nationalism*, rev. edn (London: Verso, 1991).

2. Theda Skocpol, *Protecting Soldiers and Mothers: The Political Origins of Social Policy in the United States* (Cambridge, MA: Harvard University Press, 1992); Richard Bensel, *Yankee Leviathan: The Origins of Central State Authority in America, 1859–1877* (New York: Cambridge University Press, 1990).

3. On the fusion of nation and state, see Wilbur Zelinsky, *Nation into State: The Shifting Symbolic Foundations of American Nationalism* (Chapel Hill, NC: University of North Carolina Press, 1988); on state structures, Stephen Skowronek, *Building a New American State: The Expansion of National Administrative Capacities, 1877–1920* (New York: Cambridge UP, 1982). For a guide to recent scholarship, see Brian Balogh, 'The State of the State among Historians', *Social Science History*, 27 (No. 3, 2003), 455–63.

4. Phillip S. Paludan, 'The Civil War as a Crisis of Law and Order', *American Historical Review*, 77 (October 1972), 1016–17, 1021, 1026; Rush Welter, *The Mind of America, 1820–1860* (New York: Columbia University Press, 1975), p. 396, for the ubiquity of Fourth of July orations and their cultural and political significance. See also David Waldstreicher, *In the Midst of Perpetual Fetes: The Making of American Nationalism, 1776–1820* (Chapel Hill, NC: University of North Carolina Press, 1997).

5. This symbolism was compromised by confusion over the national anthem, with the composition of a rival, *America (My Country 'tis of Thee)* in 1832, based on the music of the British national anthem. Not until 1931 did the US adopt the Star Spangled Banner as the official anthem.

6. John C. Torpey, *The Invention of the Passport: Surveillance, Citizenship and the State* (New York: Cambridge University Press, 1999), p. 95.

7. John Higham, 'America in Person: The Evolution of National Symbols', *Amerikastudien*, 36 (Spring 1991), 474.

8. D. W. Meinig, *The Shaping of America: A Geographical Perspective on 500 Years of History*. Vol. 3. *Transcontinental America, 1850–1915* (New Haven, CT: Yale University Press, 1998), pp. 189–93.

9. Richard Gowers, 'Contested Celebrations: The Fourth of July and Changing National Identity in the United States, 1865–1918', PhD thesis, University of New South Wales, 2004.

10. Robert Wiebe, *The Search for Order, 1877–1920* (New York: Hill & Wang, 1967).

11. Richard W. Stewart, General Editor, *American Military History*, Vol. 1: *The United States Army and the Forging of a Nation, 1775–1917* (Washington, DC: United States Army, 2005), pp. 369–70.

12. Gaines M. Foster, *Moral Reconstruction: Christian Lobbyists and the Federal Legislation of Morality, 1865–1920* (Chapel Hill, NC: University of North Carolina Press, 2002); Richard Hamm, *Shaping the Eighteenth Amendment: Temperance Reform, Legal Culture, and the Polity, 1880–1920* (Chapel Hill, NC: University of North Carolina Press, 1995).

13. Richard Schneirov, Shelton Stromquist and Nick Salvatore, eds, *The Pullman Strike and the Crisis of the 1890s: Essays on Labor and Politics* (Urbana, IL: University of Illinois Press, 1999).

14. Quoted Daniel T. Rodgers, *Atlantic Crossings: Social Politics in a Progressive Age* (Cambridge, MA: Belknap Press of Harvard University Press, 1998), p. 247.

15. Ibid., pp. 240–1; Seth Koven and Sonya Michel, 'Womanly Duties: Maternalist Politics and the Origins of Welfare States in France, Germany, Great Britain, and the United States, 1880–1920', *American Historical Review*, 95 (October 1990), 1076–108.

16. Rodgers, *Atlantic Crossings*, p. 250.

17. Victor S. Clark, *The Labour Movement in Australasia: A Study in Social Democracy* (New York: H. Holt & Co., 1906); Henry Demarest Lloyd, 'New Zealand: Newest England', *Atlantic Monthly*, 84 (No. 506, December 1899), 789–94.

18. Peter J. Coleman, *Progressivism and the World of Reform: New Zealand and the Origins of the American Welfare State* (Lawrence, KA: University Press of Kansas, 1987); Coleman, 'New Zealand Liberalism and the Origins of the American Welfare State', *Journal of American History*, 69 (September 1982), 379, 384–5, 390 (quote).

19. L. E. Fredman, *The Australian Ballot: The Story of an American Reform* (East Lansing, MI: Michigan State University Press, 1969).

20. Rodgers, *Atlantic Crossings*, p. 345.

21. Ian Tyrrell, *True Gardens of the Gods: Californian–Australian Environmental Reform, 1860–1930* (Berkeley, CA: University of California Press, 1999), Chap. 8.

22. From this financial base, World War I produced the greatest increase in expenditure to that time in American history. The 1918 budget was larger than all the budgets from 1791 to 1916 put together. As a result, the national debt, in steady decline per capita after the Civil War, grew exponentially once more.

23. Maldwyn Jones, *American Immigration* (Chicago, IL: University of Chicago Press, 1960), p. 253.

24. Rudolph J. Vecoli, 'Primo Maggio: May Day Observances Among Italian Immigrant Workers, 1890–1920', *Labor's Heritage*, 7 (Spring 1996), 28–41; David Goldway, 'A Neglected Page of History: The Story of May Day. A Talk Sponsored by The Friends Of The Wellfleet Public Library, Wellfleet, Massachusetts, May, 1989', *Science & Society*, 69 (No. 2, 2005), 218–24.

25. Vecoli, 'Primo Maggio', p. 30 (quote); Michael Kazin and Steven J. Ross, 'America's Labor Day: The Dilemma of a Worker's Celebration', *Journal of American History*, 78 (December 1992), 1294–323.

26. Stuart McConnell, 'Reading the Flag: A Reconsideration of the Patriotic Cults of the 1890s', in John Bodnar, ed., *Bonds of Affection: Americans Define their Patriotism* (Princeton, NJ: Princeton University Press, 1996), p. 118.

27. Jones, *American Immigration*, p. 262.

28. For a full list of the Dillingham Commission reports, see 61st Congress, 3rd session, Sen. Doc No. 761, *Reports of the Immigration Commission: The Immigration Situation in Other Countries* (Washington, DC: Government Printing Office, 1911), p. iii. For a modern analysis, see Robert F. Zeidel, *Immigrants, Progressives, and Exclusion Politics: The Dillingham Commission, 1900–1927* (De Kalb, IL: Northern Illinois University Press, 2004), Chaps 2–6.

29. Aristides Zolberg, *A Nation by Design: Immigration Policy in the Fashioning of America* (Cambridge, MA: Harvard University Press, 2006), Chap. 7.

30. Torpey, *Invention of the Passport*, p. 117.

31. National Center For Infectious Diseases, Division of Global Migration and Quarantine, 'History of Quarantine', http://www.cdc.gov/ncidod/dq/history.htm (1 February 2005); Victor Heiser, *An American Doctor's Odyssey: Adventures in Forty-five Countries* (New York: W. W. Norton, 1936), pp. 16–17.

32. Jones, *American Immigration*, pp. 262–3; Heiser, *Odyssey*, pp. 16–17.

33. E. O. Essig, *A History of Entomology* (1931; New York: Hafner Pub Co., 1965), pp. 527, 529–36; Tyrrell, *True Gardens*, Chap. 9.

34. Henry David Thoreau, *Walden and Other Writings*, ed. Brooks Atkinson (New York: Modern Library, 1992).

35. Steven J. Holmes, *The Young John Muir: An Environmental Biography* (Madison, WI: University of Wisconsin Press, 1999), especially Chap. 1; Henry Nash Smith, *Virgin Land: The American West as Symbol and Myth* (Cambridge, MA: Harvard University Press, 1950).

36. Roderick Nash, *Wilderness and the American Mind* (New Haven, CT: Yale University Press, 1967).

37. William T. Hornaday, *Our Vanishing Wild Life: Its Extermination and Preservation* (New York: Charles Scribner's Sons, 1913), pp. 100, 102.

38. John M. MacKenzie, *The Empire of Nature: Hunting, Conservation, and British Imperialism* (Manchester: Manchester University Press, 1988).

39. John F. Reiger, *American Sportsmen and the Origins of Conservation* (New York: Winchester Press, 1975), p. 51. For American anxieties over conservation, see Donald Pisani, 'Forests and Conservation, 1865–1890', *Journal of American History*, 72 (September 1985), 340–59.

40. Reiger, *American Sportsmen*, p. 76. For the European impact, see especially Michel F. Girard, 'Conservation and the Gospel of Efficiency: Un modèle de gestion de l'environnement venu d'Europe?' *Histoire Sociale/ Social History*, 23 (May 1990), 63–80.

41. *Report of the National Conservation Commission, February 1909*, 3 vols (Washington, DC: Government Printing Office, 1909).

42. Wiebe, *The Search for Order*.

43. On the pledge, see Marilyn H. Paul, 'I Pledge Allegiance...', *Prologue*, 24 (No. 4, 1992), 390–3; John W. Baer, 'The Pledge of Allegiance: A Short History', in http://history.vineyard.net/pledge.htm (23 March 2004); Robert

W. Rydell, 'The Pledge of Allegiance and the Construction of the Modern American Nation', *Rendezvous*, 30 (No. 2, 1996), 13–26, especially 22; Cecilia O'Leary, *To Die For: The Paradox of American Patriotism* (Princeton, NJ: Princeton University Press, 1999), pp. 161–71.

44. Kurt Piehler, 'The War Dead and the Gold Star: American Commemoration of the First World War', in John R. Gillis, ed., *Commemorations: The Politics of National Identity* (Princeton, NJ: Princeton University Press, 1994), pp. 174–5; and Albert Boime, *The Unveiling of the National Icons: A Plea for Patriotic Iconoclasm in a Nationalist Era* (New York: Cambridge University Press, 1998).

45. Michelle A Krowl,' "In the Spirit of Fraternity": The United States Government and the Burial of Confederate Dead at Arlington National Cemetery, 1864–1914', *Virginia Magazine of History and Biography*, 111 (No. 2, 2003), 175.

46. *New York Times* (12 November 1921), p. 4; S. Thomas, 'Known But to God', *Naval History*, 10 (No. 6, 1996), 45–8; http://www.arlingtoncemetery.org/visitor_information/amphitheater.html (18 October 2005). For examples of how nationalist patriotic activity solidified around the commemoration of World War I in cities, see John Bodnar, *Remaking America: Public Memory, Commemoration, and Patriotism in the Twentieth Century* (Princeton, NJ: Princeton University Press, 1992), pp. 86, 97.

47. Roy L. Garis, *Immigration Restriction: A Study of the Opposition to and Regulation of Immigration into the United States* (New York: Macmillan, 1927), p. 131.

10   The Empire That did not Know Its Name

1. W. A. Williams, *The Tragedy of American Diplomacy*, rev. edn (1959; New York: Delta Books, 1961); Williams, *Empire as a Way of Life* (New York: Oxford University Press, 1980).

2. Robert W. Larson, *New Mexico's Quest for Statehood, 1846–1912* (Albuquerque, NM: University of New Mexico Press, 1968), p. 304; Earl S. Pomeroy, 'The American Colonial Office', *Mississippi Valley Historical Review*, 30 (March 1944), 521–32; Pomeroy, *The Territories and the United States, 1861–1890: Studies in Colonial Administration* (Philadelphia, PA: University of Pennsylvania Press, 1947).

3. Walter Williams, 'US Indian Policy and the Debate over Philippine Annexation: Implications for the Origins of American Imperialism', *Journal of American History*, 66 (March 1980), 810, 813, 814; Brian M. Linn, 'The Long Twilight of the Frontier Army', *Western Historical Quarterly*, 27 (Summer 1996), 141–67.

4. Frank Schumacher, 'The American Way of Empire: National Tradition and TransAtlantic Adaptation in America's Search for Imperial Identity, 1898–1910', *German Historical Institute Bulletin*, no. 31 (Fall 2002), 37, 45 n15, 49 n49.

5. Josiah Strong, *Our Country, Its Possible Future and its Present Crisis*, rev. edn (New York: Baker & Taylor, 1891), p. 220; R. N. Leslie, Jr, 'Christianity and the Evangelist for Sea Power: The Religion of A.T. Mahan', in

John B. Hattendorf, ed., *The Influence of History on Mahan: The Proceedings of a Conference Marking the Centenary of Alfred Thayer Mahan's "The Influence of Sea Power Upon History, 1660–1783"* (Newport, RI: Naval War College Press, 1991), pp. 136–7.

6.   Strong, *Our Country*, p. 226; Strong, *Expansion under New World-Conditions* (1900; New York: Garland, 1971), p. 278 (final quote); Mahan, 'Hawaii and Our Future Sea Power', (1893), in Mahan, *The Interest of America in Sea Power, Present and Future* (London: Sampson, Low, Marston and Co., 1898), pp. 48, 52–3.

7.   Richard Collin, *Theodore Roosevelt: Culture, Diplomacy, and Expansion: A New View of American Imperialism* (Baton Rouge, LA: Louisiana State University Press, 1985).

8.   David Reynolds, 'American Globalism: Mass, Motion, and the Multiplier Effect', in A. G. Hopkins, ed., *Globalization in World History* (London: Pimlico, 2002), p. 245.

9.   Frederick Jackson Turner, 'The Middle West', *International Monthly*, 4 (December 1901), 794.

10.   Stuart C. Miller, *'Benevolent Assimilation': The American Conquest of the Philippines, 1899–1903* (New Haven, CT: Yale University Press, 1982); Paul Kramer, 'Empires and Exceptions: Race and Rule between the British and United States Empires, 1880–1910', *Journal of American History*, 88 (March 2002), 1314–53; Glenn May, *Social Engineering in the Philippines: The Aims, Execution, and Impact of American Colonial Policy, 1900–1913* (Westport, CT: Greenwood, 1980), pp. 179–81.

11.   Christina Duffy Burnett and Burke Marshall, 'Between the Foreign and the Domestic: The Doctrine of Territorial Incorporation, Invented and Reinvented', in Christina Duffy Burnett and Burke Marshall, eds, *Foreign in a Domestic Sense: Puerto Rico, American Expansion, and the Constitution* (Durham, NC: Duke University Press, 2001), pp. 1–3.

12.   Laura Briggs, *Reproducing Empire: Race, Sex, Science, and U.S. Imperialism in Puerto Rico* (Berkeley, CA: University of California Press, 2002), p. 33.

13.   J. A. C. Gray, *Amerika Samoa: A History of American Samoa and its United States Naval Administration* (Annapolis, MD: United States Naval Institute, 1960), p. 158.

14.   'William Crawford Gorgas', American National Biography Online, 15 May 2005.

15.   Michael Adas, 'Improving on the Civilizing Mission? Assumptions of United States Exceptionalism in the Colonization of the Philippines', in Lloyd Gardner and Marilyn B. Young, eds, *The New American Empire: A 21st Century Teach-in on U.S. Foreign Policy* (New York: New Press, 2005), pp. 153–81.

16.   Anne L. Foster, 'Models for Governing: Opium and Colonial Policies in Southeast Asia, 1898–1910', in Julian Go and Anne L. Foster, eds, *The American Colonial State in the Philippines: Global Perspectives* (Durham, NC: Duke University Press, 2003), p. 111.

17.   John M. Gibson, *Physician to the World: The Life of General William C. Gorgas* (Durham, NC: Duke University Press, 1950), p. 102; Marie D. Gorgas and Burton J. Hendrick, *William Crawford Gorgas: His Life and Work* (Garden City, NY: Doubleday, Page and Co., 1924), pp. 138–9.

18. Victor Heiser, *An American Doctor's Odyssey: Adventures in Forty-Five Countries* (New York: W. W. Norton, 1936), p. 34; *New York Times* (12 September 1912), p. 7.

19. Gorgas and Hendrick, *Gorgas*, p. 222.

20. Reynaldo C. Ileto, 'Cholera and the Origins of the American Sanitary Order in the Philippines', in David Arnold, ed., *Imperial Medicine and Indigenous Societies* (Manchester: Manchester University Press, 1988), pp. 125–44.

21. Arnold H. Taylor, *American Diplomacy and the Narcotics Traffic, 1900–1939* (Durham, NC: Duke University Press, 1969), p. 31.

22. Foster, 'Models for Governing', pp. 111–12.

23. For the standard summary, see Robert Rydell, *All the World's a Fair: Visions of Empire at American International Expositions, 1876–1916* (Chicago, IL: University of Chicago Press, 1984).

24. Paul Kramer, 'Making Concessions: Race and Empire Revisited at the Philippines Exposition, St Louis, 1901–1905', *Radical History Review*, 73 (1999), pp. 73–114.

25. Jessica Beth Teisch, 'Engineering Progress: Californians and the Making of a Global Economy (India, South Africa, Palestine, Australia)', PhD dissertation, University of California, Berkeley, 2001, pp. 1–19.

26. *Greater America: The Latest Acquired Insular Possessions* (Boston, MA: Perry Mason Co., 1909), pp. 67–84.

27. Susan Schulten, 'The Making of the *National Geographic*: Science, Culture, and Expansionism', *American Studies*, 41 (Spring 2000), 5, 15, 23.

28. National WCTU, *Annual Report*, 1900, p. 94.

29. *Union Signal*, 7 March 1901, p. 9; 12 December 1901, p. 8 (quote).

30. Brian M. Linn, 'Long Twilight', p. 143; Brian M. Linn, *The Philippine War, 1899–1902* (Lawrence, KA: University Press of Kansas, 2000).

31. *Union Signal*, 7 October 1909, p. 3.

32. For anti-imperialist arguments by Democrats in the 1900 campaign, see Rebecca J. Taylor, *Philippine Facts from American Pens* (Washington, DC: Jeffersonian Democrat Pub. Co., 1900). On anti-imperialism, see Robert L. Beisner, *Twelve against Empire: The Anti-Imperialists, 1898–1900*, rev. edn (Chicago, IL: University of Chicago Press, 1985); E. Berkeley Tompkins, *Anti-Imperialism in the United States: The Great Debate, 1890–1920* (Philadelphia, PA: University of Pennsylvania Press, 1970); Philip S. Foner and Richard C. Winchester, eds, *The Anti-Imperialist Reader: A Documentary History of Anti-imperialism in the United States*, Vol. 1 (New York: Holmes & Meier, 1984).

33. On variants of American empire, see Gray, *Amerika Samoa*; William H. Haas et al., *The American Empire: A Study of the Outlying Territories of the United States* (Chicago, IL: University of Chicago Press, 1940); Raymond Carr, *Puerto Rico: A Colonial Experiment* (New York: New York University Press, 1984); Briggs, *Reproducing Empire*; Burnett and Marshall, eds, *Foreign in a Domestic Sense*.

34. Roger Bell, *Last Among Equals: Hawaiian Statehood and American Politics* (Honolulu, HI: University of Hawaii Press, 1984), pp. 48–9, 68–71.

35. José-Manuel Navarro, *Creating Tropical Yankees: Social Science Textbooks and U.S. Ideological Control in Puerto Rico, 1898–1908* (New York: Routledge, 2002).

36. A. T. Mahan, *The Influence of Sea Power upon History 1660–1783* (London: Sampson Low, Marston, Searle & Rivington, 1890); Jon Sumida, 'Alfred Thayer Mahan, Geopolitician', *Journal of Strategic Studies* (G.B.) 22 (Nos 2–3, 1999), 51, 57.

37. Emily S. Rosenberg, *Financial Missionaries to the World: The Politics and Culture of Dollar Diplomacy, 1900–1930* (Durham, NC: Duke University Press, 2003), especially pp. 1–3.

38. For a modern version of this idea, see Joseph S. Nye, *Soft Power: The Means to Success in World Politics* (New York: Public Affairs, 2004).

39. Leslie, 'Christianity and the Evangelist for Sea Power', p. 138 (quote); Brian Stanley, 'Church, State and the Hierarchy of "Civilization": The Making of the "Missions and Government" Conference, Edinburgh, 1910', in Andrew Porter, ed., *The Imperial Horizons of British Protestant Missions, 1880–1914* (Grand Rapids, MI: William B. Eerdmans, 2003), p. 61.

40. Brian Stanley, 'Church, State and the Hierarchy of "Civilization" ', p. 62.

41. See A. T. Mahan, *The Harvest Within: Thoughts on the Life of the Christian*, cited in Leslie, 'Christianity and the Evangelist for Sea Power', pp. 127–39.

42. A. T. Mahan, 'Effects of Asiatic Conditions upon International Policies', *North American Review*, 528 (November 1900), 616.

43. Stanley, 'Church, State and the Hierarchy of "Civilization" ', p. 61.

44. For land/labour ratios and economic development, see H. J. Habakkuk, *American and British Technology in the Nineteenth Century: The Search for Labour-saving Inventions* (Cambridge: Cambridge University Press, 1962). For a different view, see Carville Earle and Ronald Hoffman, 'The Foundation of the Modern Economy: Agriculture and the Costs of Labor in the United States and England, 1800–1860', *American Historical Review*, 85 (December 1980), 1055–94. On the United States' greater resource-intensive and capital-intensive industrialization from 1880 to 1940, see Gavin Wright, 'The Origins of American Industrial Success', *American Economic Review*, 80 (September 1990), 651–68.

45. *Report of the National Conservation Commission, February 1909*, 3 vols (Washington, DC: Government Printing Office, 1909), II: 282–3.

46. Ibid., p. 266.

47. Howard Zinn, *A People's History of the United States* (New York: Harper & Row, 1980), p. 294.

48. William Cronon, *Nature's Metropolis: Chicago and the Great West* (New York: W. W. Norton, 1991).

49. David A. Hounshell, *From the American System to Mass Production, 1800–1932: The Development of Manufacturing Technology in the United States* (Baltimore, MD: Johns Hopkins University Press, 1984), pp. 217–61.

50. Taylorism, too, was exported. See Lucy Taksa, 'All a Matter of Timing: The Diffusion of Scientific Management in New South Wales, Prior to 1921', PhD thesis, University of New South Wales, 1993; J.-C. Spender and Hugo J. Kijne, *Scientific Management: Frederick Winslow Taylor's Gift to the World?* (Boston, MA: Kluwer Academic Publishers, 1996).

51. Charles S. Maier, 'Between Taylorism and Technocracy: European Ideologies and the Vision of Industrial Productivity', *Journal of Contemporary History*, 5 (No. 2, 1970), 27–61.

52. Mark Pendergrast, *Uncommon Grounds: The History of Coffee and How It Transformed Our World* (New York: Basic Books, 1999), p. 62. Imports

more than quadrupled from 1865 to 1900. Ben J. Wattenberg, *The Statistical History of the United States from Colonial Times to the Present* (New York: Basic Books, 1976), pp. 900–2.

53. Richard P. Tucker, *Insatiable Appetite: The United States and the Ecological Degradation of the Tropical World* (Berkeley, CA: University of California Press, 2000).

54. Grover Cleveland, 'Fourth Annual Message' (second term) at http://www.presidency.ucsb.edu/ws/index.php?pid=29537 (9 October 2005).

55. Louis A. Pérez, Jr, *Cuba: Between Reform and Revolution* (New York: Oxford University Press, 1988), pp. 149–52.

56. Cleveland, 'Fourth Annual Message'.

57. Samuel Hays, *Conservation and the Gospel of Efficiency: The Progressive Conservation Movement, 1890–1920* (Cambridge: Harvard University Press, 1959); Donald Pisani, 'Forests and Conservation, 1865–1890', *Journal of American History*, 72 (September 1985), 340–59.

58. John Mason Hart, *Empire and Revolution: The Americans in Mexico since the Civil War* (Berkeley, CA: University of California Press, 2002), p. 307.

59. Frederick A. McKenzie, *The American Invaders* (1902; New York: Arno Press, 1976), pp. 6, 96, 181, 1.

11   The New World Order in the Era of Woodrow Wilson

1. Woodrow Wilson, *Message to Congress*, 63rd Cong., 2d Sess., Senate Doc. No. 566 (Washington, DC: Government Printing Office, 1914), pp. 3–4.

2. On the war and its impact see, e.g. David Kennedy, *Over Here: The First World War and American Society* (New York: Oxford University Press, 1980); Richard L. Watson, Jr, *The Development of National Power: The United States, 1900–1919* (Boston: Houghton Mifflin, 1976).

3. Arthur S. Link, *Woodrow Wilson and the Progressive Era, 1910–1917* (New York: Harper & Row, 1954), pp. 271–3.

4. Kurt Piehler, 'The War Dead and the Gold Star: American Commemoration of the First World War', in John R. Gillis, ed., *Commemorations: The Politics of National Identity* (Princeton, NJ: Princeton University Press, 1994), pp. 171–80.

5. *How You Gonna Keep 'em Down on the Farm*. 1919. W. Donaldson, S. Lewis, J. Young Arr., Kit Johnson.

6. N. Gordon Levin, Jr, *Woodrow Wilson and World Politics: America's Response to War and Revolution* (New York: Oxford University Press, 1968), pp. 236–51; Arno J. Mayer, *Politics and Diplomacy of Peacemaking: Containment and Counterrevolution at Versailles, 1918–1919* (New York: Knopf, 1967).

7. John W. Coogan, 'Wilsonian Diplomacy in War and Peace', in Gordon Martel, ed., *American Foreign Relations Reconsidered, 1890–1993* (London: Routledge, 1993), pp. 74–5; Lloyd Ambrosius, *Woodrow Wilson and the American Diplomatic Tradition* (New York: Cambridge University Press, 1987), pp. 68–9; William Roger Louis, 'African Origins of the

Mandates Idea', *International Organization*, 19 (Winter 1965), 20–36; David Levering Lewis, *W. E. B. Du Bois: Biography of a Race, 1868–1919* (New York: Henry Holt, 1993), pp. 576–8.

8. Joan Hoff-Wilson, *American Business & Foreign Policy, 1920–1933* (Lexington, KY: University Press of Kentucky, 1971); Alan Dawley, *Changing the World: American Progressives in War and Revolution* (Princeton, NJ: Princeton University Press, 2002), p. 312, argues that the stand is better characterized as unilateralist. For a definition, see Michael Hogan, 'Introduction', in Hogan, ed., *The Ambiguous Legacy: U.S. Foreign Relations in the 'American Century'* (New York: Cambridge University Press, 1999), p. 6.

9. Hoff-Wilson, *American Business & Foreign Policy*; William Appleman Williams, 'The Legend of Isolationism in the 1920's', *Science and Society*, 18 (Winter 1954), 1–20; Akira Iriye, *The Globalizing of America, 1913–1945*. The Cambridge History of American Foreign Relations, Vol. 5 (Cambridge: Cambridge University Press, 1993), pp. 103–15.

10. Jens Ulff-Møller, *Hollywood's Film Wars with France: Film Trade Diplomacy and the Emergence of the French Film Quota Policy* (Rochester, NY: University of Rochester Press, 2001), pp. 51–3.

11. See Frank Costigliola, *Awkward Dominion: American Political, Economic, and Cultural Relations with Europe, 1919–1933* (Ithaca, NY: Cornell University Press, 1984).

12. Ian Tyrrell, 'Prohibition, American Cultural Expansion, and the New Hegemony in the 1920s: An Interpretation', *Histoire Sociale/Social History*, 27 (November 1994), pp. 439–40.

13. Victoria de Grazia, *Irresistible Empire: America's Advance through 20th-Century Europe* (Cambridge, MA: Harvard University Press, 2005), p. 231.

14. Ibid., p. 165.

15. Emily Rosenberg, *Spreading the American Dream: American Economic and Cultural Expansion, 1890–1945* (New York: Hill & Wang, 1982), p. 111.

16. Richard Taylor, *The Politics of the Soviet Cinema 1917–1929* (Cambridge: Cambridge University Press, 1979), pp. 95–6, 98; Denise Youngblood, *Movies for the Masses: Popular Cinema and Soviet Society in the 1920s* (New York: Cambridge University Press, 1992).

17. Petrine Archer-Straw, *Negrophillia: Avant-Garde Paris and Black Culture in the 1920s* (London: Thames & Hudson, 2000).

18. de Grazia, *Irresistible Empire*, pp. 65–73.

19. Ibid., p. 170.

20. Dawley, *Changing the World*, Chap. 2 and passim.

21. Jane Addams, *Newer Ideals of Peace* (New York: Macmillan, 1907), p. 18.

22. William Preston, Jr, *Aliens and Dissenters: Federal Suppression of Radicals, 1903–1933* (Cambridge, MA: Harvard University Press, 1963), especially Chap. 8; Kennedy, *Over Here*, pp. 290–91; Robert K. Murray, *Red Scare: A Study in National Hysteria, 1919–1920* (Minneapolis, MN: University of Minnesota Press, 1955).

23. *Pershing's Crusaders*, March Militaire composed by E. T. Paull (1918), at Digital Music Collections, National Library of Australia, http://nla.gov.au/nla.mus-an5299978.

24. Robert D. Cuff, *The War Industries Board: Business–Government Relations during World War I* (Baltimore, MD: Johns Hopkins University Press,

1973); Paul A. C. Koistenen, 'The Industrial–Military Complex in Historical Perspective: World War I', *Business History Review*, 41 (Winter 1967), 378–403.

25. Ellen Carol DuBois, *Harriot Stanton Blatch and the Winning of Woman Suffrage* (New Haven, CT.: Yale University Press, 1997), pp. 64, 70; Leila J. Rupp, *Worlds of Women: The Making of an International Women's Movement* (Princeton: Princeton University Press, 1997).

26. Frank Farrell, *International Socialism and Australian Labour: The Left in Australia, 1919–1939* (Sydney: Hale & Iremonger, 1981), pp. 115–16, 121–4.

27. Allen F. Davis, *American Heroine: The Life and Legend of Jane Addams* (New York: Oxford University Press, 1973), pp. 260–7.

28. Judith Stein, *The World of Marcus Garvey: Race and Class in Modern Society* (Baton Rouge, LA: Louisiana State University Press, 1986), pp. 2, 30, 109–10, 124.

29. Mae M. Ngai, *Impossible Subjects: Illegal Aliens and the Making of Modern America* (Princeton, NJ: Princeton University Press, 2004), pp. 9–10.

12 Forces of Integration: War and the Coming of the American Century, 1925–70

1. Wendell L. Willkie, *One World* (New York: Simon and Schuster, 1943), p. 2; Henry R. Luce, 'The American Century', *Life*, February 1941, reprinted in *Diplomatic History*, 23 (Spring 1999), especially 'America's Vision of our World', 168–71; Michael J. Hogan, ed., *The Ambiguous Legacy: U.S. Foreign Relations in the 'American Century'* (New York: Cambridge University Press, 1999).

2. Barry and Judith Colp Rubin, *Hating America: A History* (New York: Oxford University Press, 2004), p. 126; Philippe Roger, *The American Enemy: The History of French Anti-Americanism*, transl. Sharon Bowman (Chicago, IL: University of Chicago Press, 2005), pp. 14, 324; Alvin Z. Rubenstein and Donald E. Smith, 'Anti-Americanism in the Third World', in Thomas Thornton, ed., *Anti-Americanism: Origins and Context*, Special Issue, *The Annals of the American Academy of Political and Social Science* (Beverly Hills, CA: Sage Publications, 1988), p. 36.

3. For these debates, see Raimund Lammersdorf, ed., *The American Impact on Western Europe: Americanization and Westernization in Transatlantic Perspective* (German Historical Institute, Washington, DC, March 25–27, 1999), http://www.ghi-dc.org/conpotweb/westernpapers/index.html (30 July 2006).

4. Mae M. Ngai notes this interpretation in *Impossible Subjects: Illegal Aliens and the Making of Modern America* (Princeton, NJ: Princeton University Press, 2004), p. 10.

5. Daniel T. Rodgers, *Atlantic Crossings: Social Politics in a Progressive Age* (Cambridge, MA: Belknap Press of Harvard University Press, 1998), p. 412.

6. Ibid., p. 410.

7. Ibid., pp. 445, 437.

8. Peter J. Sehlinger, rev. of *African Americans in the Spanish Civil War: 'This Ain't Ethiopia, But It'll Do,'* in *Journal of Military History*, 57 (January 1993), 163.

9. David Kennedy, *Freedom from Fear: The American People in Depression and War, 1929–1945* (New York: Oxford University Press, 1999), pp. 398–9.

10. Akira Iriye, *The Globalizing of America, 1913–1945*. The Cambridge History of American Foreign Relations, Vol. 5 (Cambridge: Cambridge University Press, 1993), p. 155.

11. Kennedy, *Freedom from Fear*, pp. 505–11; Walter LaFeber, *The Clash: A History of U.S.–Japan Relations* (New York: W. W. Norton, 1996), Chap. 6, especially p. 184.

12. Neil Smith, *American Empire: Roosevelt's Geographer and the Prelude to Globalization* (Berkeley, CA: University of California Press, 2003), p. 275.

13. See the International Monetary Fund figures at www.imf.org/external/np/exr/center/mm/eng/mm_dr_01.htm (29 July 2006).

14. Mark Stoler, 'The Second World War in US History and Memory', *Diplomatic History*, 25 (Summer 2001), 384.

15. Geir Lundestad, 'Empire by Invitation? The United States and Western Europe, 1945–1952', *Journal of Peace Research*, 23 (September 1986), 263–77.

16. Frank Ninkovich, *The Diplomacy of Ideas: U.S. Foreign Policy and Cultural Relations, 1938–1950* (New York: Cambridge University Press, 1981); Reinhold Wagnleitner, *Coca-Colonization and the Cold War: The Cultural Mission of the United States in Austria after the Second World War*, transl. Diana M. Wolf (Chapel Hill, NC: University of North Carolina Press, 1994); Reinhold Wagnleitner, 'The Irony of American Culture Abroad: Austria and the Cold War', in Lary May, ed., *Recasting America: Culture and Politics in the Age of Cold War* (Chicago, IL: University of Chicago Press, 1989), pp. 285–301.

17. Frank Ninkovich, *U.S. Information Policy and Cultural Diplomacy* (New York: Foreign Policy Association, 1995).

18. Giles Scott-Smith, 'The Congress for Cultural Freedom, the End of Ideology and the 1955 Milan Conference: "Defining the Parameters of Discourse" ', *Journal of Contemporary History*, 37 (No. 3, 2002), 437–55.

19. James Burnham, *The Struggle for the World* (London: Jonathan Cape, 1947).

20. Elizabeth Vihlen, 'Jammin' on the Champs-Elysées: Jazz, France and the 1950s', in Reinhold Wagnleitner and Elaine Tyler May, eds, *'Here, There and Everywhere', The Foreign Politics of American Culture* (Hanover, NH: University Press of New England, 2000), pp. 157–8; Penny Von Eschen, ' "Satchmo Blows up the World": Jazz, Race and Empire during the Cold War', ibid., pp. 163, 167; Michael May, 'Swingin' under Stalin: Russian Jazz during the Cold War and Beyond', ibid., p. 189; Alan L. Heil, Jr, *Voice of America: A History* (New York: Columbia University Press, 2003), pp. 288–301; Laurien Alexandre, *The Voice of America: From Détente to the Reagan Doctrine* (Norwood, NJ: Ablex Publishing Corp., 1988), pp. 3, 9.

21. Luce, 'American Century', pp. 168–71.

22. Richard P. Tucker, *Insatiable Appetite: The United States and the Ecological Degradation of the Tropical World* (Berkeley, CA: University of California Press, 2000), pp. 190–1; Gabriel Kolko, *Main Currents in Modern American History* (New York: Harper & Row, 1976), pp. 197–8, 384–90; Alfred Eckes, Jr, and Thomas W. Zeiler, *Globalization and the American Century* (New York: Cambridge University Press, 2003), pp. 111–12.

23. Eckes and Zeiler, *Globalization*, pp. 111–12.

24. See, for example, D. Goodman and M. Redclift, eds, *The International Farm Crisis* (New York: St Martin's Press, 1989).

25. D. A. Irwin, 'The GATT's Contribution to Economic Recovery in Post-War Europe', in B. Eichengreen, ed., *Europe's Postwar Recovery* (New York: Cambridge University Press, 1995), cited in http://grove.ship.edu/econ/trade/Irwin_on_us_trade.html (14 August 2004).

26. Kenneth Scott Latourette, 'Missionaries Abroad', *Annals of the American Academy of Political and Social Science, 368,* Americans Abroad (November 1966), 21–30, at 23.

27. Ibid., p. 27.

28. Robert A. McCaughey, 'In the Land of the Blind: American International Studies in the 1930s', *Annals of the American Academy of Political and Social Science*, New Directions in International Education, 449 (May 1980), 6.

29. Sandra C. Taylor, *Advocate of Understanding: Sidney Gulick and the Search for Peace with Japan* (Kent, OH: Kent State University Press, 1984); Jennifer C. Snow, 'A Border Made of Righteousness: Protestant Missionaries, Asian Immigration, and Ideologies of Race, 1850–1924', PhD dissertation, Columbia University, 2003; LaFeber, *The Clash*, p. 145.

30. McCaughey, 'In the Land of the Blind', pp. 2, 5.

31. Ibid., p. 6.

32. Latourette, 'Missionaries Abroad', pp. 28–9.

33. Ibid., p. 28.

34. Tomoko Akami, *Internationalizing the Pacific: The United States, Japan, and the Institute of Pacific Relations in War and Peace, 1919–45* (New York: Routledge, 2003); Akira Iriye, *Global Community: The Role of International Organizations in the Making of the Contemporary World* (Berkeley, CA: University of California Press, 2002), p. 27; Jon Thares Davidann, ' "Colossal Illusions": US–Japanese Relations in the Institute of Pacific Relations, 1925–1938', *Journal of World History*, 12 (No. 1, 2001), 155–82.

35. Emily S. Rosenberg, *Spreading the American Dream: American Economic and Cultural Expansion, 1890–1945* (New York: Hill & Wang, 1982), p. 120.

36. Peter J. Bell, 'The Ford Foundation as a Transnational Actor', *International Organization*, 25 (Summer 1971), 465–78; Francis X. Sutton, 'The Ford Foundation: The Early Years', *Daedalus*, 16 (1987), 59, 63, 69, 70.

37. Iriye, *Global Community*, p. 19.

38. Sutton, 'Ford Foundation', pp. 49, 59, 63.

39. McCaughey, 'In the Land of the Blind', pp. 1–16.

13 Insular Impulses: Limits on International Integration, 1925–70

1. As Maldwyn Jones, *American Immigration* (Chicago, IL: University of Chicago Press, 1959), states, the McCarran–Walter Act of 1952 did not truly liberalize the quota system (p. 286).

2. Mae M. Ngai, *Impossible Subjects: Illegal Aliens and the Making of Modern America* (Princeton, NJ: Princeton University Press, 2004), p. 7.

3. Ibid., p. 8.

4. Ibid., p. 7; Aristides Zolberg, *A Nation by Design: Immigration Policy in the Fashioning of America* (Cambridge, MA: Harvard University Press, 2006), pp. 255–6, 269–70.

5. Cecilia O'Leary, *To Die For: The Paradox of American Patriotism* (Princeton, NJ: Princeton University Press, 1999), p. 231. John W. Baer put it thus: 'The Pledge was now both a patriotic oath and a public prayer'. See his 'The Pledge of Allegiance: A Short History', in http://history.vineyard.net/pledge.htm (23 March 2004); Lee Canipe, 'Under God and Anti-Communist: How the Pledge of Allegiance Got Religion in Cold War America', *Journal of Church and State*, 45 (Spring 2003), 310, 314.

6. Albert Boime, *The Unveiling of the National Icons: A Plea for Patriotic Iconoclasm in a Nationalist Era* (New York: Cambridge University Press, 1998), pp. 136–7.

7. Karal Ann Marling and John Wetenhall, *Iwo Jima: Monuments, Memories, and the American Hero* (Cambridge, MA: Harvard University Press, 1991), pp. 17–19, 92–4, 104–5, 115, 117.

8. Peter Schrijvers, *The GI War against Japan: American Soldiers in Asia and the Pacific during World War II* (New York: New York University Press, 2002), p. 157.

9. Susan Schulten, *The Geographical Imagination in America, 1880–1950* (Chicago, IL: University of Chicago Press, 2001), p. 238.

10. Neil Smith, *American Empire: Roosevelt's Geographer and the Prelude to Globalization* (Berkeley, CA: University of California Press, 2003).

11. Paul Simon, 'The U. S. Crisis in Foreign Language', *Annals of the American Academy of Political and Social Science*, New Directions in Higher Education, 449 (May 1980), 31, 32, 33.

12. Ben J. Wattenberg, *The Statistical History of the United States from Colonial Times to the Present* (New York: Basic Books, 1976), p. 404.

13. Schrijvers, *GI War against Japan*.

14. By one (amateur history) estimate, 'one million American soldiers married women from over fifty different countries'. Some 750,000 were said to have returned to the United States. 'Digger History: An Unofficial History of the Australian & New Zealand Armed Services', at http://www.diggerhistory.info/pages-conflicts-periods/ww2/war_brides.htm (30 May 2005); Elfrieda Berthiaume Shukert and Barbara Smith Scibetta, *The War Brides of World War II* (Novato, CA: Presidio, 1988), p. 1. Jones, *American Immigration*, p. 284 has the figure of 150,000 for the first 5 years after the war.

15. Jones, *American Immigration*, p. 284.

16. While the story is based on personal observation, the generalization is confirmed by Rosemary Campbell, *Heroes and Lovers: A Question of National Identity* (Sydney: Allen & Unwin, 1989), p. 188; E. Daniel Potts and Annette Potts, *Yanks Down Under, 1941–45: The American Impact on Australia* (Melbourne: Oxford University Press, 1985), p. 398.

17. Shukert and Scibetta, *War Brides*, pp. 97, 248. For another case, superficially treated, see Juliet Gardiner, *Over Here: The GIs in Wartime Britain* (London: Collins & Brown, 1992), pp. 202–13.

18. John Willoughby, 'The Sexual Behavior of American GIs During the Early Years of the Occupation of Germany', *Journal of Military History*, 62 (No. 1, 1998), 160–3.

19. Maria Höhn, *GIs and Fräuleins: The German–American Encounter in 1950s West Germany* (Chapel Hill, NC: University of North Carolina Press, 2002), pp. 126–7, 137–8, 264, 272; John Willoughby, *Remaking the Conquering Heroes: The Postwar American Occupation of Germany* (New York: Palgrave, 2000).

20. Hohn, *GIs and Fräuleins*, p. 132.

21. Somerset R. Waters, 'The American Tourist', *Annals of the American Academy of Political and Social Science*, 368, Americans Abroad (November 1966), 115; Christopher Endy, *Cold War Holidays: American Tourism in France* (Chapel Hill, NC: University of North Carolina Press, 2004), Chap. 4.

22. Rosalie Schwartz, *Pleasure Island: Tourism and Temptation in Cuba* (Lincoln, NE: University of Nebraska Press, 1997).

23. Wattenberg, *Statistical History*, p. 404.

24. Marguerite S. Shaffer, *See America First: Tourism and National Identity, 1880–1940* (Washington, DC: Smithsonian Institution Press, 2001), p. 4. The Great Northern Railway adopted the 'See America First' slogan in 1906 to promote resort facilities in Montana.

25. Christine M. Skwiot, 'Itineraries of Empire: The Uses of U.S. Tourism in Cuba and Hawai'i, 1898–1959', PhD dissertation, Rutgers State University, New Brunswick, 2002, pp. 13, 235ff.

26. Ruth Vasey, *The World According to Hollywood, 1918–1939* (Madison, WI: University of Wisconsin Press, 1997), pp. 227–8.

27. Richard Pells, 'From Modernism to the Movies: The Globalization of American Culture in the Twentieth Century', *European Journal of American Culture*, 23 (September 2004), 149.

28. Charles Beard and Mary Beard, *America in Midpassage* (1939; New York: Macmillan, 1959), pp. 592, 593, 596.

29. Reinhold Wagnleitner, 'American Cultural Diplomacy, the Cinema, and the Cold War in Central Europe', Department of History, University of Salzburg, Working Paper 92-4, www.history-journals.de/articles/hjg-eartic-j00133.html (12 August 2005).

30. David Halberstam, *War in a Time of Peace: Bush, Clinton, and the Generals* (New York: Scribner, 2001), p. 160; Lawrence K. Grossman, 'The Pathfinder', http://archives.cjr.org/year/96/6/books-murrow.asp (12 August 2005).

31. Frank Ninkovich, *U.S. Information Policy and Cultural Diplomacy* (New York: Foreign Policy Association, 1995), p. 10.

32. Wattenberg, *Statistical History*, p. 113; no author, *Open Doors, 1955–56* (New York: The Institute, 1956). In 1994, foreign students in the US numbered more than seven times the American students studying abroad. 'Opportunities for U.S. College Students to Study at African Universities', *Journal of Blacks in Higher Education*, 8 (Summer 1995), 26.

33. Elizabeth Cobbs Hoffman, *All You Need Is Love: The Peace Corps and the Spirit of the 1960s* (Cambridge, MA: Harvard University Press, 1998), p. 91.

34. Mary L. Dudziak, *Cold War Civil Rights: Race and the Image of American Democracy* (Princeton, NJ: Princeton University Press, 2000), pp. 87–8, 130–1.

35. Ibid., p. 86; 'Executive Order 9981' http://www.trumanlibrary.org/9981a. htm (30 September 2006); Morris J. MacGregor, Jr, *Integration of the Armed Forces, 1940–1965*, Defense Studies Series, Washington, DC, Center of Military History United States Army, 1985, http://www.army.mil/cmh-pg/books/integration/IAF-12.htm (14 July 2006).

36. Dudziak, *Cold War Civil Rights*, pp. 33, 27.

37. Penny M. Von Eschen, *Race Against Empire: Black Americans and Anticolonialism, 1937–1957* (Ithaca, NY: Cornell University Press, 1997), p. 3.

38. Paul Robeson, quoted ibid., p. 171.

39. Judith Stein, *The World of Marcus Garvey: Race and Class in Modern Society* (Baton Rouge, LA: Louisiana State University Press, 1986).

40. Robin D. G. Kelley, ' "But a Local Phase of a World Problem": Black History's Global Vision, 1883–1950', *Journal of American History*, 86 (December 1999), 1054.

41. Von Enschen, *Race Against Empire*, p. 186.

42. For this section, see Clarence Lang, 'African Americans, Culture and Communism (Part 1): When Anti-Imperialism and Civil Rights Were In Vogue', *Against the Current*, 2000, http://www.solidarity-us.org/atc/84Lang.html (1 August 2005).

43. Ibid.; Von Eschen, *Race Against Empire*, especially pp. 156, 159–62.

44. Von Enschen, *Race Against Empire*, p. 174.

45. James T. Campbell, *Middle Passages: African American Journeys to Africa, 1787–2005* (New York: Penguin, 2006); Kevin K. Gaines, *American Africans in Ghana: Black Expatriates and the Civil Rights Era* (Chapel Hill, NC: University of North Carolina Press, 2006).

46. For surveys and a literature review, see Micheline R. Ishay, *The History of Human Rights: From Ancient Times to the Globalization Era* (Berkeley, CA: University of California Press, 2004), pp. 65–116, 126–7, 176–8; Kenneth Cmiel, 'The Recent History of Human Rights', *American Historical Review*, 109 (February 2004), 117–35.

47. Arthur M. Schlesinger, Jr, 'Human Rights and the American Tradition', in William P. Bundy, ed., *Foreign Affairs: America and the World, 1978* (New York: Pergamon Press, 1979), p. 505.

48. 'The Speech by Hubert Humphrey that Helped Trigger Strom Thurmond's Candidacy for President in 1948', History News Network, http://hnn.us/articles/1165.html (8 August 2005).

14   From the 1970s to New Globalization: American Transnational Power and Its Limits, 1971–2001

1. Jeremy Suri, *Power and Protest: Global Revolution and the Rise of Detente* (Cambridge, MA: Harvard University Press, 2003), 88–96, 166–72, 237; David Caute, *Sixty-Eight: The Year of the Barricades* (London: Hamish Hamilton, 1988), p. 185.

2. Elizabeth Grieco, 'The Foreign Born from Vietnam in the United States', Migration Policy Institute, http://www.migrationinformation.org/ USfocus/print.cfm?ID=197 (25 March 2006).

3. Stuart I. Rochester and Frederick Kiley, *Honor Bound: American Prisoners of War in Southeast Asia, 1961–1973* (Annapolis, MD: Naval Institute Press, 1999), pp. 204–5, 278–81, 478, 597.

4. Keith Beattie, *The Scar that Binds: American Culture and the Vietnam War* (New York: New York University Press, 1998), pp. 7, 13–15, 18–19, 70–1.

5. Stan Luger, 'Market Ideology and Administrative Fiat: The Rollback of Automobile Fuel Economy Standards', *Environmental History Review*, 19 (Spring 1995), 77–93.

6. Ibid.; Edmund P. Russell, III, 'Lost among the Parts per Billion: Ecological Protection at the United States Environmental Agency, 1970–1993', *Environmental History*, 2 (January 1997), 29–51.

7. Alfred E. Eckes, Jr and Thomas Zeiler, *Globalization and the American Century* (New York: Cambridge University Press, 2003), p. 209.

8. Steven High, *Industrial Sunset: The Making of North America's Rust Belt, 1969–1984* (Toronto: University of Toronto Press, 2003).

9. For IT transfers, see William Lazonick, 'Globalization of the ICT Labor Force', http://www.schumpeter2006.org/conftool/uploads/255/2-Lazonick_ Globalization_of_the_ICT_Labor_Force_20060503.pdf. On the South, see Timothy Minchin, *Hiring the Black Worker: The Racial Integration of the Southern Textile Industry, 1960–1980* (Chapel Hill, NC: University of North Carolina Press, 1999), epilogue; David L. Carlton and Peter A. Coclanis, *The South, the Nation, and the World: Perspectives on Southern Economic Development* (Charlottesville, VA: University of Virginia Press, 2003).

10. Gray Brechin, *Imperial San Francisco: Urban Power, Earthly Ruin* (Berkeley, CA: University of California Press, 1999); Martin Shefter, *Capital of the American Century: The National and International Influence of New York City* (New York: Russell Sage Foundation, 1993).

11. Toby Miller, Nitin Govil, John McMurria and Richard Maxwell, *Global Hollywood* (London: BFI Publishing, 2001), p. 48.

12. Victoria de Grazia, *Irresistible Empire: America's Advance through 20th-Century Europe* (Cambridge, MA: Harvard University Press, 2005), p. 469.

13. Somerset R. Waters, 'The American Tourist', *Annals of the American Academy of Political and Social Science*, 368, Americans Abroad (November 1966), p. 112; World Tourism Organization figures at 'Global tourism: growing fast', [3 September 2004], at http://www.peopleandplanet.net/doc. php?id=1110 (1 September 2006).

14. Miller, Govil, McMurria and Maxwell, *Global Hollywood*, p. 48.

15. Christopher J. Jordan, *Movies and the Reagan Presidency: Success and Ethics* (Westport, CT: Praeger, 2003), especially pp. 68, 73, 146. Rather than simply remaining a projection of American values these films may have been shaped by the attractions of foreign markets. Hollywood producers often had an eye to the elemental tastes not just of the youths who made up a growing proportion of American audiences but to the limited command of American cultural complexities among overseas audiences. Simplistic messages about American culture fed foreign stereotypes as much as they did domestic cultural imperatives. The variability of Hollywood's impact and possibilities for reinterpretation of its values is a refrain in David W. Ellwood and Rob Kroes, eds, *Hollywood in Europe: Experiences of a Cultural Hegemony* (Amsterdam: VU University Press, 1994).

16. David Harvey, *A Brief History of Neoliberalism* (New York: Oxford University Press, 2005), pp. 8–9.

17. William B. McAllister, *Drug Diplomacy in the Twentieth Century: An International History* (London: Routledge, 2000), pp. 196–8, 200–1.

18. Alfred W. McCoy, *The Politics of Heroin in South East Asia* (New York: Harper & Row, 1972), pp. 220–1, 246–7 and Chap. 7 generally.

19. 'On the Campaign Against Drug Abuse: The President and Mrs. Reagan, from the White House, September 14, 1986', http://www.presidentreagan.info/speeches/drugs.cfm (27 March 2006).

20. Marc Cooper, 'Plan Colombia', *The Nation* (19 March 2001).

21. On alcohol, see Lawrence Spinelli, *Dry Diplomacy: The United States, Great Britain, and Prohibition* (Wilmington, DE: Scholarly Resources, 1989).

22. See Walter LaFeber, *Michael Jordan and the New Global Capitalism* (New York: W. W. Norton, 1999).

23. Alan Brinkley, *American History: A Survey*, 11th edn (New York: McGraw-Hill, 2003), pp. 934–5.

24. www.census.gov/Press-Release/www/releases/archives/population/000419.html (21 August 2005).

25. 'English Should Be Our Official Language', *The Phyllis Schlafly Report*, 29, No. 5 (December 1995) at http://www.eagleforum.org/psr/1995/psrdec95.html (29 March 2006).

26. Energy Information Agency, 'Energy in the United States: 1635–2000', September 2003, http://www.mnforsustain.org/energy_in_the_united_states_1635-2000.htm#Figure%203 (8 July 2005).

27. Stephanie J. Battles and Eugene M. Burns, 'United States Energy Usage and Efficiency: Measuring Changes Over Time', http://www.eia.doe.gov/emeu/efficiency/wec98.htm (1 August 2005).

28. UNCED Collection, United Nations Conference on Environment and Development Collection at www.ciesin.org/datasets/unced/unced.html (30 March 2006).

29. James Charleton, 'The United States and the World Heritage Convention', http://www.icomos.org/usicomos/Symposium/SYMP00/charleton.htm (10 August 2005).

30. Michael H. Glantz et al., *Drought Follows the Plow: Cultivating Marginal Areas* (New York: Cambridge University Press, 1994).

31. John Sharpless, 'World Population Growth, Family Planning, and American Foreign Policy', in Donald T. Critchlow, ed., *The Politics of Abortion and*

Birth Control in Historical Perspective (University Park, PA: Pennsylvania State University Press, 1996), p. 93; Terri Bartlett, 'How the Global Gag Rule Undermines U.S. Foreign Policy and Harms Women's Health', http://www.populationaction.org/resources/factsheets/factsheet_5.htm (28 March 2006).

32. Helen Caldicott, *A Desperate Passion: An Autobiography* (New York: W. W. Norton, 1996); Lawrence S. Wittner, *Toward Nuclear Abolition: A History of the World Nuclear Disarmament Movement, 1971 to the Present* (Stanford, CA: Stanford University Press, 2003), pp. 29, 30, 32, 172.

33. Wittner, *Toward Nuclear Abolition*, p. 176.

34. Quotes from Lawrence S. Wittner, 'What Activists Can Learn from the Nuclear Freeze Movement', *History Network News*, 18 August 2003; see also Wittner, *Toward Nuclear Abolition*, p. 315.

35. Lawrence S. Wittner, 'The Power of Protest: The Campaign against Nuclear Weapons Was Not Simply an Ideological Movement: It Was a Potent Political Force', *Bulletin of Atomic Scientists*, 60 (July–August 2004), 20–6; Wittner, *Toward Nuclear Abolition*, pp. x, 370–7, 383–401, especially 396.

36. Walter LaFeber, *The American Age: U.S. Foreign Policy at Home and Abroad*, Vol. 2, *Since 1896* (New York: W. W. Norton, 1994), pp. 775–6.

37. Arthur M. Schlesinger, Jr, 'Human Rights and the American Tradition', in William P. Bundy, ed., *Foreign Affairs: America and the World, 1978* (New York: Pergamon Press, 1979), p. 521; David F. Schmitz and Vanessa Walker, 'Jimmy Carter and the Foreign Policy of Human Rights: The Development of a Post-Cold War Foreign Policy', *Diplomatic History*, 28 (January 2004), 113–43.

38. David Carleton and Michael Stohl, 'The Foreign Policy of Human Rights: Rhetoric and Reality from Jimmy Carter to Ronald Reagan', *Human Rights Quarterly*, 7 (May 1985), 216–17.

39. An American-based group, Human Rights Watch, followed in 1978, and soon spread across Asia, Europe and Africa.

40. Harry M. Scoble and Laurie S. Wiseberg, 'Human Rights and Amnesty International', *Annals of the American Academy of Political and Social Science*, 413 (May 1974), 23, 25, 26.

41. Roger Hood, *The Death Penalty: A World-wide Perspective* (1989; Oxford: Oxford University Press, 1996); Amnesty International, *United States of America: The Death Penalty* (London: Amnesty International Publications, 1987); Richard C. Dieter, 'International Perspectives on the Death Penalty: A Costly Isolation for the U.S.', http://www.deathpenaltyinfo.org/article.php?scid=45&did=536 (5 September 2005).

42. Bill Clinton, reported in 'Wallach's Road to Activism: Trade Agreements and Consumer Protection', http://www.pbs.org/wgbh/commandingheights/shared/minitext/int_loriwallach.html# (29 March 2006).

43. Defenders of Wildlife, 'Keeping America's Tuna Dolphin-safe', http://www.defenders.org/wildlife/new/dolphins.html (20 March 2006).

44. 'Canada–U.S. Lumber Trade Disputes', http://www.for.gov.bc.ca/het/softwood/disputes.htm (4 April 2006).

45. 'OECD Multilateral Agreement on Investment Fact Sheet', Friends of The Earth–US, February 19, 1997 at http://www.globalpolicy.org/socecon/bwi-wto/oecd-mai.htm (28 March 2006).

46. 'Wallach's Road to Activism'.

47. Martha Kruger, 'Israel: Balancing Demographics in the Jewish State', http://www.migrationinformation.org/Feature/display.cfm?ID=321 (2 April 2006).

48. Raphael Danziger and Bradley Gordon, 'End American Aid to Israel?: No, It Remains Vital', http://www.meforum.org/article/259, *Middle East Quarterly* (September 1995).

49. Peter L. Hahn, *Caught in the Middle East: U.S. Policy toward the Arab-Israeli Conflict, 1945–1961* (Chapel Hill, NC: University of North Carolina Press, 2004).

Epilogue: 'Nothing will Ever be the Same': 9/11 and the Return of History

1. Mary L. Dudziak, ed., *September 11 in History: A Watershed Moment?* (Durham, NC: Duke University Press, 2003), p. 2.

2. Niall Ferguson, *Colossus: The Rise and Fall of the American Empire* (2004; London: Penguin, 2005), pp. 3–7; Max Boot, *The Savage Wars of Peace: Small Wars and the Rise of American Power* (New York: Basic Books, 2002), p. 352.

3. http://www.whitehouse.gov/news/releases/2004/07/20040702-8.html; http://www.whitehouse.gov/news/releases/2004/01/20040120-7.html (12 August 2004).

4. Martin Shaw, 'Risk-Transfer Militarism: The New Western Way of War', 13 November 2001, http://www.theglobalsite.ac.uk/justpeace/201shaw.htm (9 July 2005).

5. David Frum and Richard Perle, *An End to Evil: How to Win the War on Terror* (New York: Random House, 2003).

6. Cited in Nicholas Guyatt, *Another American Century: The United States and the World after 2000* (London: Zed Books, 2000), p. 182.

Further Reading

Anderson, Bonnie. *Joyous Greetings: The First International Women's Movement, 1830–1860* (Oxford: Oxford University Press, 2000).

Beckert, Sven. 'Emancipation and Empire: Reconstructing the Worldwide Web of Cotton Production in the Age of the American Civil War', *American Historical Review*, 109 (December 2004), 1405–38.

Bender, Thomas, ed. *Rethinking American History in a Global Age* (Berkeley, CA: University of California Press, 2002).

Bender, Thomas. *Nation Among Nations: America's Place in the World* (New York: Hill & Wang, 2006).

Berlin, Ira. *Many Thousands Gone: The First Two Centuries of Slavery in North America* (Cambridge, MA: Belknap Press of Harvard University Press, 1998).

Bodnar, John. *The Transplanted: A History of Immigrants in Urban America* (Bloomington, IN: Indiana University Press, 1985).

Campbell, James T. *Middle Passages: African American Journeys to Africa, 1787–2005* (New York: Penguin Press, 2006).

Carwardine, R. *Transatlantic Revivalism: Popular Evangelicalism in Britain and America, 1790–1865* (Westport, CT: Greenwood, 1978).

Crook, D. P. *The North, the South, and the Powers, 1861–1865* (New York: Wiley, 1974).

Davies, Edward. *The United States in World History* (New York: Routledge, 2006).

Davis, David Brion. *The Problem of Slavery in the Age of Revolution, 1770–1823* (Ithaca, NY: Cornell University Press, 1975).

Dawley, Alan. *Changing the World: American Progressives in War and Revolution* (Princeton, NJ: Princeton University Press, 2002).

de Grazia, Victoria. *Irresistible Empire: America's Advance through 20th-Century Europe* (Cambridge, MA: Harvard University Press, 2005).

DuBois, Ellen. 'Woman Suffrage: The View from the Pacific', *Pacific Historical Review*, 69 (November 2000), 539–51.

Dudziak, Mary L. *Cold War Civil Rights: Race and the Image of American Democracy* (Princeton, NJ: Princeton University Press, 2000).

Dudziak, Mary L., ed. *September 11 in History: A Watershed Moment?* (Durham, NC: Duke University Press, 2003).

Eckes, Alfred E., Jr and Zeiler, Thomas. *Globalization and the American Century* (New York: Cambridge University Press, 2003).

Field, James A. *America and the Mediterranean World, 1776–1882* (Princeton, NJ: Princeton University Press, 1969).

Forster, Stig and Nagler, J., eds. *On the Road to Total War: The American Civil War and the German Wars of Unification, 1861–1871* (Cambridge: Cambridge University Press, 1997).

Gilroy, Paul. *The Black Atlantic: Modernity and Double Consciousness* (Cambridge, MA: Harvard University Press, 1993).

Go, Julian and Foster, Anne L., eds. *The American Colonial State in the Philippines: Global Perspectives* (Durham, NC: Duke University Press, 2003).

Greene, Jack P. *The Intellectual Construction of America: Exceptionalism and Identity* (Chapel Hill, NC: University of North Carolina Press, 1993).

Guarneri, Carl J. 'Abolitionism and American Reform in Transatlantic Perspective', *Mid-America*, 82 (Winter–Summer 2000), 21–49.

Hietala, Thomas. *Manifest Design: Anxious Aggrandizement in Late Jacksonian America* (Ithaca, NY: Cornell University Press, 1985).

Hunter, Jane. *The Gospel of Gentility: American Women Missionaries in Turn-of-the-Century China* (New Haven, CT: Yale University Press, 1984).

Iriye, Akira. *Global Community: The Role of International Organizations in the Making of the Contemporary World* (Berkeley, CA: University of California Press, 2002).

Kramer, Paul. 'Empires and Exceptions: Race and Rule between the British and United States Empires, 1880–1910', *Journal of American History*, 88 (March 2002), 1314–53.

Kroes, Rob and Rydell, Robert. *Buffalo Bill in Bologna* (Chicago, IL: University of Chicago Press, 2005).

LaFeber, Walter. *The American Age: U.S. Foreign Policy at Home and Abroad*, 2 vols (New York: W. W. Norton, 1994).

LaFeber, Walter. *The Clash: A History of U.S.–Japan Relations* (New York: W. W. Norton, 1996).

Levin, N. Gordon, Jr. *Woodrow Wilson and World Politics: America's Response to War and Revolution* (New York: Oxford University Press, 1968).

Miller, Toby, Govil, N., McMurria, J. and Maxwell, R. *Global Hollywood* (London: BFI Publishing, 2001).

Ngai, Mae M. *Impossible Subjects: Illegal Aliens and the Making of Modern America* (Princeton, NJ: Princeton University Press, 2004).

O'Leary, Cecilia. *To Die For: The Paradox of American Patriotism* (Princeton, NJ: Princeton University Press, 1999).

Rauchway, Eric. *Blessed Among Nations: How the World Made America* (New York: Hill & Wang, 2006).

Reynolds, David. 'American Globalism: Mass, Motion and the Multiplier Effect', in A. G. Hopkins, ed., *Globalization in World History* (London: Pimlico, 2002), pp. 220–42.

Rodgers, Daniel T. *Atlantic Crossings: Social Politics in a Progressive Age* (Cambridge, MA: Belknap Press of Harvard University Press, 1998).

Rosenberg, Emily. *Spreading the American Dream: American Cultural and Economic Expansion* (New York: Hill & Wang, 1983).

Rupp, Leila J. *Worlds of Women: The Making of an International Women's Movement* (Princeton, NJ: Princeton University Press, 1997).

Tucker, Richard P. *Insatiable Appetite: The United States and the Ecological Degradation of the Tropical World* (Berkeley, CA: University of California Press, 2000).

Tyrrell, Ian. *Woman's World/Woman's Empire: The Woman's Christian Temperance Union in International Perspective* (Chapel Hill, NC: University of North Carolina Press, 1991).

Tyrrell, Ian. *True Gardens of the Gods: Californian–Australian Environmental Reform, 1860–1930* (Berkeley, CA: University of California Press, 1999).

Wilkins, Mira. *The History of Foreign Investment in the United States to 1914* (Cambridge, MA: Harvard University Press, 1989).

Wilkins, Mira. *The Emergence of Multinational Enterprise: American Business Abroad from the Colonial Era to 1914* (Cambridge, MA: Harvard University Press, 1970).

Wittner, Lawrence S. *The Struggle Against the Bomb*, 3 vols (Stanford, CA: Stanford University Press, 1993–2003).

Wolfe, Patrick. 'Land, Labor, and Difference: Elementary Structures of Race', *American Historical Review*, 106 (June 2001), 866–905.

Wyman, Mark. *Round Trip to America: The Immigrants Return to Europe, 1880–1930* (Ithaca, NY: Cornell University Press 1993).

Zolberg, Aristides. *A Nation by Design: Immigration Policy in the Fashioning of America* (Cambridge, MA: Harvard University Press, 2006).

Index

Lusitania (ship), 157
Lyncoya, 74–5, 77

Maconochie, Alexander, 45
Madison, James, 13, 16, 19
Mahan, Alfred Thayer, 136, 147–9
Malthus, Thomas, 16
Malthusian implications, of population
    growth, 22
Man and Nature (1864), 131
Manifest Destiny, ideas of,
    81, 130
Mann Act (1910), 122
Marr, Timothy, 106
Marsh, George Perkins, 131
Marshall Plan, 178, 193
Martineau, Harriet, 99
Marx, Karl, 6, 43, 91
Mathew, Theobald, Father, 47
Maury, Matthew, 90
May, Karl, 110–11
McCarthyism, 179, 184, 199
McKinley, William, 138, 148
Mead, Elwood, 124
Médecins sans Frontières, 5, 217
media industries, 160, 162, 194–5,
    209–11, 213
Meiggs, Henry, 112–13
Meiji Revolution, 87
Melville, Herman, 4–5
Mennonites, in America, 59
Mexican history, 2, 14
Mexican War (1846–48), 82, 157
Mikado, The, 103
Millerite Movement, 107
missing in action (MIA) syndrome,
    204
missionaries, 103, 106–7, 141, 181–3
*Missionary Travels and Researches in
    South Africa*, 68
Moby Dick, 4
Monroe Doctrine (1823), 19, 88,
    137–8, 148, 157
Moody, Dwight, 96, 105–6
Mormons, 107
Morrill Tariff (1862), 50
Mott, John, 105
Muir, John, 98

Multilateral Agreement on Investment,
    220
My Lai Massacre (1968), 202

Napoleonic Wars, 12, 14–15, 24, 86
National Banking Act (1864), 34
National Defense Education Act
    (1958), 190
national exceptionalism, 8, 48, 58,
    129–30, 179–80, 189, 231n16
National Flag Convention, 189
National Geographic, 100–1, 142
national identities, 3, 12, 52, 87, 188
National Reclamation Act (1902), 124
nationalism, United States, 9, 12, 87,
    118–20, 165, 189
Native Americans, 75, 76,
    79, 81, 108–9
*Nellie Bly's Book: Around the World
    in Seventy-Two Days*, 97
Neutrality Acts (1935–37), 173
New Deal programmes, 172–3
New York Stock Exchange, 88
Nixon, Richard, 202, 204, 212
non-governmental organizations
    (NGOs), 3, 183–5, 216–19
North American Free Trade
    Agreement (NAFTA), 208, 220
North American Review, 62
North Atlantic Treaty Organization
    (NATO), 178
Notes on Virginia, 77
Nullification Controversy (1828–33),
    120

O'Neill, Robert Lincoln, 191
OPEC oil cartel energy crisis, 205
Open Door policy, 141, 147–8, 176
Operation Enduring Freedom, 228
opium trade, 22–3
    policies, 141–2
Oppenheimer, J. Robert, 184
Organization for Economic
    Cooperation and Development
    (OECD), 220–1
Our Journey around the World, 95
Owen, Robert, 46
Owen, Robert Dale, 46
Oxfam, 217